IN THE SHADOW OF SHARI'AH

MATTHEW J. NELSON

In the Shadow of Shari'ah

Islam, Islamic Law, and Democracy in Pakistan

Columbia University Press
New York

Columbia University Press
Publishers Since 1893
New York Chichester, West Sussex

Library of Congress Cataloging-in-Publication Data

Nelson, Matthew J.
In the shadow of shari'ah : Islam, Islamic law, and democracy in Pakistan / Matthew J. Nelson.
p. cm.
Includes bibliographical references and index.
ISBN 978-0-231-70072-6 (alk. paper)
1. Land tenure (Islamic law)—Pakistan. 2. Inheritance and succession (Islamic law)—Pakistan. 3. Islamic law—Pakistan. 4. Land tenure—Law and legislation—Pakistan—History. 5. Inheritance and succession—Pakistan—History. 6. Land reform—Pakistan. 7. Democracy—Pakistan. I. Title.

KPL659.N45 2010
346.549104'32—dc22

2010020087

∞

Columbia University Press books are printed on permanent and durable acid-free paper. This book is printed on paper with recycled content.
Printed in India

c 10 9 8 7 6 5 4 3 2 1

PUBLISHER'S NOTE

The italicization in this book reflects the choices of the author and not those of the publisher.

CONTENTS

For My Family

PREFACE

In recent years scholarly interest in the relationship between Islam and democracy has expanded enormously. The literature has grown in several different directions, focusing on the democratic predilections of Islamic civil society organizations, Islamic social movements, Islamic (or 'Islamist') political parties, and several different forms of Islamic intellectual engagement, including the engagement of elite Muslim scholars with the terms of Islamic jurisprudence or *fiqh*. Very few, however, have chosen to examine the ways in which the terms of Islamic law are debated and negotiated by ordinary (lay) Muslims in the context of local elections. Indeed, very few have sought to examine the ways in which ordinary Muslims combine their ideas about Islamic law with the terms of competitive electoral 'accountability'.

Targeting those with an interest in the relationship between Islam and democracy around the world, this book draws attention to the value of a more thoroughly 'political' approach to Islamic law. Stressing the challenges confronted by a significant cross-section of landowning lay Muslims *in Pakistan*, this book aims to show how a deeper understanding of the interaction between Islam, Islamic law, and the terms of electoral accountability can improve our understanding of the relationship between Islam and democracy *in general*.

Typically, when I am asked about the focus of this book, I note that this is a book about the political economy of landed property relations in Pakistan and, more specifically, the political economy of landed property disputes involving Islamic laws of inheritance in which female heirs are entitled to a specific share of every Muslim estate. I then go on to explain that, notwithstanding their identity as faithful Muslims, many of the families I describe in this book are inclined to *resist*

Islamic laws of inheritance because they wish to secure the integrity of specific agnatic (all-male) estates. In fact the focus of this book lies, primarily, in its assessment of the political implications that flow from a basic tension between (a) the application of Islamic *law* and (b) agnatic or 'tribal' *customs* that seek to disinherit Muslim women.

Focusing on Pakistan's largest and most influential province, the Punjab, this book explains that under British colonial rule (1849–1947) the disinheritance of Muslim women was formally permitted by law. In fact Muslim families throughout the Punjab were routinely confronted with a choice of laws: some chose *shari'ah*; others, custom. After the independence of India and the formation of Pakistan in 1947, however, this formally demarcated 'choice' was removed; in fact the terms of tribal custom were slowly replaced with a postcolonial alternative—one alternative—known as Muslim Personal Law.

Coming straight to the heart of the matter, however, the second half of this book goes on to note that the parameters of local politics and, more specifically, local notions of electoral accountability, were dramatically transformed as a result of this shift: this shift from custom to *shari'ah*. In particular, those with disputes regarding inheritance and, more specifically, the inheritance rights of Muslim women, found themselves embroiled in an entirely new pattern of postcolonial political engagement—one in which, striving to prevent the fragmentation of their 'agnatic' estates, many men (and some women) lent rhetorical support to the terms of *shari'ah* while, at the same time, seeking to avoid its effective or consistent enforcement. Indeed, many voters began to evaluate the merits of their elected representatives in terms of their ability to circumvent the strict enforcement of what had come to be regarded as a 'fixed' or 'immutable' *shari'ah*.

'So you see', I often say in summing up, 'this is a book about the link between Islam, Islamic law, and democracy—one that focuses, primarily, on the ways in which specific efforts to introduce Islamic laws of inheritance came to shape and, in many ways, transform prevailing expressions of postcolonial electoral accountability'.

The basic narrative of this book clearly points to an account of Islam, Islamic law, and democracy. But it also points to an empirical environment in which the leading actors—lay Muslim landowners in colonial and postcolonial Punjab—appear to have (a) very little interest in any regimented application of Islamic law and, yet, at the same time, (b) very little interest in changing the law in their favour. In fact, precisely insofar as this is the case, the basic terms of this book appear to challenge several rather conventional assumptions regarding the relationship between Muslims and their engagement with the terms of Islamic law, the terms of Islamic law itself (vis-à-vis the rights of individual women), and, perhaps most importantly, the 'democratic' practice of negotiating, and potentially revising, the content of *de jure* laws.

Most of the existing literature regarding Islam, Islamic law, and democracy in South Asia (and around the world) touches upon three basic assumptions. And, in this book, all three of these assumptions are directly challenged.

The first assumption is closely related to the notion that Islamic law as a whole tends to run contrary to the interests of Muslim women. The second involves the notion that, with the exception of those who identify themselves as 'non-practicing' Muslims, Muslim voters tend to value the introduction and, in due course, the consistent enforcement (sometimes informally) of *shari'ah*. The third, moving away from the terms of Islam and Islamic law towards those of democracy, begins with the notion that voters tend to cast their votes for those who promise to introduce (and enforce) more appealing laws, believing that, in due course, these voters will seek to hold their elected officials accountable for their promises; in fact, those who manage to introduce 'new' and 'better' laws are expected to be elected and then re-elected, whereas those who fail to accomplish this task are expected to be dismissed in favour of their opponents. In effect, this third and final assumption holds that the logic of democracy itself is closely tied to active patterns of engagement (and adjustment) vis-à-vis the content of local laws.

In the context of this book, however, each and every one of these three basic assumptions will be carefully scrutinized. The notion that Islamic law runs contrary to the interests of Muslim women, for instance, will be examined in the context an empirically grounded case in which Islamic laws of inheritance are compared with the terms of 'tribal' custom and shown to proceed 'in favour of Muslim women'. The notion that practicing Muslims mobilize politically to press for the introduction and enforcement of Islamic law is, similarly, revisited in the context of an empirically grounded case in which, practically speaking, many Muslims remain rather ambivalent—indeed, a case in which many Muslims appear to vote *for* the introduction of Islamic law but *against* its consistent enforcement. And, finally, the notion that voters seek to hold their elected officials accountable for the production of new and better laws becomes a case in which the law itself is considered to be religiously or historically 'fixed', such that the terms of electoral 'accountability' become almost totally disconnected from the production of 'better' laws. Indeed the notion that voters will hold their elected representatives accountable for the production of 'better' laws becomes a case in which the notion of electoral accountability is reduced to 'irregular patterns of enforcement' (full stop).

Clearly, this shift from simple *a priori* assumptions to hard empirical evidence has important implications for those with an interest in the relationship between Islam, Islamic law, and democracy. Focusing on lay Muslim strategies vis-à-vis the terms of both Islamic law and electoral accountability, for instance, we may conclude that Islam and democracy are largely compatible. (After all, Muslim voters clearly use competitive elections to hold their elected officials 'accountable' for the 'representation' of their legal interests.) We may decide that Islam and democracy are largely incompatible. (Insofar as the law in question tends to be regarded as religiously or historically 'fixed', local notions of democratic accountability tend to remain completely set apart from the negotiation of 'new' and 'better' laws.) In fact this rather dramatic shift in favour of hard empirical evidence tends to cast a number of the most important questions—for example, questions regarding compatibility—in a very different light. This evidence does not resolve the question of compatibility, as it were, once and for all; it merely allows us to assess the issue of compatibility more definitively in a particular time and place.

Throughout this book, the challenge for those with an interest in exploring the relationship between Islam, Islamic law, and democracy does not lie in resolving the question of compatibility at the level of any *a priori* assumptions. On the contrary, the challenge lies in developing an entirely new approach to the question of compatibility itself—in many ways a more thoroughly grounded approach that allows us to determine exactly why local Muslims 'think what they think', 'want what they want' and 'do what they do' (with respect to the terms of both Islamic law and electoral accountability) in a particular time and place.

Are the terms of Islamic law religiously or historically 'fixed'? Maybe they are, maybe the aren't. Do the terms of Islamic law 'favour' the rights of Muslim women? Maybe, maybe not. These are not the questions that I will answer in the context of this book. In fact, turning to the case of colonial and postcolonial Punjab, the question is really this: How should we account for the 'political' and, more specifically, the 'electoral accountability' implications that flow from a widely-held belief that the 'favourable' treatment of Muslim women *is* legally 'fixed'? How should we account for the theoretical implications associated with *this* understanding of *shari'ah* in a particular time and place?

The challenge does not lie in explaining whether Islam and democracy are 'compatible' or 'incompatible' in any ontologically enduring sense. No, the challenge lies in explaining how Islam and democracy might *become* more or less compatible owing to the historically embedded forms of agency associated with empirically observable Muslims. What do individual Muslims want and, historically speaking, why do they want it? What do they do, and why do they do it? Why do lay Muslims engage the specific terms of Islamic law in the particular way that they do? And, in the end, what do their specific patterns of legal engagement mean for the underlying terms of Islam, Islamic law, and democracy? These are the questions that I will take up and address in the context of this book.

The historical context of this book is specific—even unique. But, as I will explain, the theoretical implications of an historically embedded approach to the relationship between Islam, Islamic law, and democracy extend much further. In fact, although this book begins with a rather detailed account of landed property relations, legal change (from 'custom' to *shari'ah*), and the logic of local politics in colonial and postcolonial Punjab (1849–1999) (Chapters 1–5), it ends with an assessment of what it actually means to construct an empirically grounded account of the relationship between 'Islam' and 'democracy' in general (Chapter 6). The history is unique, but the implications of this history—the theoretical implications of an historically embedded approach to political and religious understanding—these are not unique at all.

ACKNOWLEDGEMENTS

I must begin with a note of thanks to my extraordinary advisers at Columbia: Ayesha Jalal, for teaching me that an investigation of Muslim politics often begins with an investigation of individual Muslims; Ira Katznelson, for teaching me that history and political science do not exist at opposite ends of the academic spectrum; and, of course, Anthony Marx, for teaching me that a deeper understanding of the present often begins with a thorough understanding of the past. The support and encouragement of these three scholars made this book what it is.

Thanks, also, to the many scholars and colleagues who provided me with detailed comments on various aspects of the manuscript along the way, including Rochana Bajpai, Paul Brass, Partha Chatterjee, Nicholas Dirks, Thrainn Eggertsson, David Gilmartin, Erik Jensen, Sudipta Kaviraj, Laleh Khalili, David Laitin, Sunita Parikh, Philip Oldenburg, Pakistan Supreme Court Justice Shafi-ur-Rahman, Francis Robinson, Lloyd I. Rudolph, Ashutosh Varshney, and the members of a special workshop on 'South Asian Muslims and the State' at the University of Edinburgh in March 2005.

For research and fellowship support, I would like to thank the Graduate School of Arts and Sciences and the Center for Historical Social Science at Columbia, the Law and Social Science Division of the National Science Foundation, and the American Institute of Pakistan Studies. In addition, I would like to thank the Foreign Language Area Studies (FLAS) programmes at Columbia, the University of Washington (Seattle), and the University of California (Berkeley). And, of course, I would like to thank Yale University for a postdoctoral fellowship in conjunction with the Department of Political Science and the

Yale Center for International and Area Studies (2002–3) as well as the Institute for Advanced Study in Princeton, where The Wolfensohn Family Membership (2009–10) allowed me to complete the final draft.

For additional support in Lahore, I would like to thank the Berkeley Urdu Language Program in Pakistan, as well as the many friends and colleagues who shared their experiences and enthusiasm with me along the way, including Chaudhry Fawad Ahmad, Cassandra Balchin, Ijaz Ahmed Chaudhry, Huma Chughtai, Grace Clark, Cabeiri de Bergh Robinson, Mohammad Maqbool Ellahi, Kathy Hansen, Humayoun Ihsan, Maulvi Muhammad Iqbal, Waseem Amjad Jaral, Ashraf Ali Khan, Naveeda Khan, Raja Amir Khan, Lisa Laumann, Farina Mir, Carla Petievich, Richard Ponzio, Sean Pue, Ziaullah Ranjah, Jeff Redding, Mohammad Riaz, Sohail Akbar Warraich, and Andrew Wilder, as well as the incomparable Jalal family and the extraordinarily generous Tahir family.

In addition, I must extend a special note of gratitude to the former Additional Registrar of the Lahore High Court, Mr Syed Ijaz Qutb, without whom none of the research for this book would have been possible, as well as Professor Sajjad Naseer, in the Department of Political Science at Punjab University, who kindly agreed to provide me with an institutional affiliation during my first years in Pakistan. I would also like to thank the enormously helpful staff members I encountered in various libraries and archives throughout Pakistan, including the Lahore Public Library, the Punjab University Library, the National Institute of Public Administration (NIPA), the Civil Services Academy, the Shirkat Gah Women's Resource Centre, and the Punjab University Law College Library, under the watchful eye of Professor Dil Mohammad Malik. In Islamabad, special thanks go to the staff of the National Documentation Centre, the National Library, the National Archives, under Mr Atique Zafar Sheikh (DG), and the National Assembly Library, under the indefatigable Mr Naeem Siddiqui. And, finally, in London, a very special note of gratitude is required for the remarkably helpful and efficient staff of the Oriental and India Office Collection (OIOC) at The British Library.

For my time 'in the field', thanks go to the unusually hospitable family of Civil Judge Kamran Basharat Mufti, who hosted me, at various points, in Gujrat, Lahore, Sheikhupura, and Sialkot, as well as Senior Civil Judge Zafar Iqbal Khan (Sargodha) and Senior Civil Judge Salah-ud-Din (Lahore). Perhaps most importantly, however, I would like to express my deepest thanks to the extraordinary staff members who maintain the district-level record rooms in Lahore, Sialkot and Sargodha. Their patience, their assiduity, and their delightful sense of humour carried me through the most difficult and important parts of this project. Without them, and many others I have unfortunately failed to mention, I would have nothing to show for my efforts.

In Berkeley, where this journey began with a Hindi language programme several years ago, thanks go to the remarkable Parsley family, and in London, to their close friends (and mine) the amazing Howard family. And of course, more than anything else, I would like to thank my own wonderful family: my mother Ann, my father Keith, my twin brother Adam, and George. This book is for them. Without their constant support, their endless encouragement, and their willingness to tolerate my desire to spend extended periods of time in South Asia even when they wanted me to spend more time with them 'up at the lake' or in London, this book would not exist.

LIST OF FIGURES, MAPS, AND TABLES

Figures

Maps

Tables

TERMINOLOGY AND TRANSLITERATION

In studies regarding Islamic law it is conventional to draw a distinction between the terms of *shari'ah* (the 'path'), defined as a righteous path of moral conduct outlined by Allah and his Prophet Mohammad both in the Qur'an and in the prophetic *sunnah* (that is, the prophetic example), and those of *fiqh*, or 'jurisprudence', which refers to the interpretive interventions of faithful Muslims and their ongoing efforts to understand the terms of *shari'ah* with the help of things like *ijma* or 'consensus', *qiyas* or 'analogical reasoning', and the shifting terms of *maslaha* or 'social welfare'. It is also conventional to describe *siyasa shari'ah* or *qanun* (that is, state-based laws or 'statutes') as a third domain of law—a domain including what has come to be known, particularly in South Asia, as 'Muslim Personal Law'.

This book, focusing on just one area of law, namely inheritance, does not lend itself to such a straightforward set of distinctions. In fact the realm of *fiqh* and *qanun* in this area tend to remain quite closely related to an account of the fractional shares outlined in the text of the Qur'an itself, such that, with respect to *fiqh*, the terms of *'ilm al-fara'id* or 'the science of [heritable] shares' typically amount to an exercise in mathematics and, with respect to *qanun*, most state based statutes simply reference specific Qur'anic *suras*, or 'verses', without any elaboration (apart from occasional comments regarding unusual or exceptional cases like the case of 'children with predeceased parents'). In other words, the terms *shari'ah*, *fiqh*, and *qanun* do not lend themselves to any easy pattern of terminological differentiation when it comes to the domain of inheritance.

In light of this situation I have chosen to adhere to local forms of expression regarding inheritance in colonial and postcolonial Punjab, relying on the term *shari'ah* to describe *all* forms of Islamic and Muslim personal law. I should stress, however, that this choice should not be allowed to obscure the ways in which the terms of *'ilm al-fara'id* are related to the practice of *fiqh*. Nor should it be allowed to diminish the extent to which the terms of Muslim personal law are in fact embedded within the realm of *siyasa shari'ah* or *qanun*.

The same Arabic word is transcribed in enormously varied ways in the literature: *sharia*, *shari'a*, *shariah*, *sharî'a*, and so on. I have opted for a single spelling throughout: *shari'ah*. Arabic, Urdu, and Punjabi words, including Arabic, Urdu, and Punjabi names and places, have been spelt phonetically and without diacritics to make the text more accessible. These terms are defined, throughout the book, within the text itself. (A glossary is also provided for easy reference.)

GLOSSARY

abadi-deh	the residential portion of a village
abadkar	a settler; here, a settler with land allocated in a canal colony
abwab	a charge for the use of water ('water rent')
ala malik	a 'superior' proprietor; here, a proprietor with additional responsibilities for village administration and revenue collection
alim (sing.); *ulema* (pl.)	a religious scholar (typically trained in a *madrasa*)
bachh	a term used by the state to describe the method of distributing land revenue obligations among individual shareholders
bhaiachara	a term used to designate the allocation of (colonial) revenue responsibilities on the basis of cultivating 'possession'
begar	unpaid (forced) labour
bighas	a term used to outline a quantity of land defined by cultivating 'possession' (usually, a quantity of land measured in terms of ploughs or the amount of land that could be cultivated by a single pair of bullocks)
biraderi	a kinship group claiming (real or imagined) common agnatic descent
biswas	a term used to outline a quantity of land defined by ancestral 'shares'
dacoity	banditry

darkhwast malguzari	a revenue contract between shareholders and the (colonial) revenue administration
dastbardar	a term used to describe the 'withdrawal' of a legal case from the courts
dera	a term used to describe the sitting area (or private salon) of a prominent community member
dharma shastras	sacred Hindu texts
dhaul	a strip of raised dirt used to define the boundary of a field
fard bachh khatawar	the register of land revenue distribution among individual shareholders (a preliminary document used to construct the village *jamabandi*)
fiqh	Islamic jurisprudence
ghair maurusi	a tenant-at-will
goonda	a thug
got	a term used to denote 'caste' (without any explicit Hindu connotation)
haboob	miscellaneous rural taxes paid by cultivators to proprietors
haq-e-shufa	a term used by Muslims to describe the right of preemption
hiba	an Islamic 'gift'
hissadar	a village shareholder (of land)
ijtehad	a term used to describe the process of independent human reasoning in matters of Islamic law and jurisprudence
'ilm al-fara'id	the Islamic law of inheritance (lit. knowledge of shares)
intiqal	a term used to describe the mutation or modification of revenue records owing to landed property transfers involving sale, gift, mortgage, exchange, or inheritance
izzat	honour (closely tied to the practice of *riwaj* or custom)
jagirdar	the holder of an estate in which a large portion of the land revenue is retained by the proprietor rather than the (colonial) state (see also *taluqdar*)

jamabandi	a village-level account of land-based revenue obligations held by individual shareholders (see *fard bachh khatawar*)
kachehri	the district headquarters (containing district-level courts and offices related to revenue administration and the police)
kammi	a landless labourer
kanal	a unit of measurement for land
khata	a family estate
khewat	a 'holding' (referring to a piece of land)
lambardar	a leading member of the village proprietary body (usually but not always associated with a particular kinship group—for example, the members of a particular *patti*)
madrasa	a Qur'anic school
malik (*mullick*)	proprietor
malikan-deh	the hereditary body of (revenue-paying) village proprietors
manqasim	'divided' (for example, an estate that has been divided or partitioned) (see also *taqsim*)
maurusi	an 'occupancy' tenant enjoying a heritable right of cultivation (without any corresponding right of ownership or alienation)
mauza	an estate or a village (see also *mehal* or *deh*)
mehalwari	a system of land revenue allocation in which the responsibility for revenue payments is held jointly by the village as a whole or jointly by a particular subsection of that village (for example, by those belonging to a particular *patti*)
mufaad	benefit or advantage
mufti	a private (non-state-based) Muslim jurist
munshi	a personal assistant or aide
mushtarka	a system of land revenue allocation in which property is held jointly by those with particular ancestral 'shares'
nazim	a local mayor

pagvand	a term used to describe the division of an estate by inheritance in which all sons inherit equally (regardless of the number of wives)
panchayat	an adjudicative council of elders, usually a village-based council of elders (often associated with the elders of a particular kinship group or *biraderi*)
pardah	a term used to describe the seclusion of women, usually with reference to seclusion in private family spaces (for example at home)
patti	a term used to describe specific subsections of a village—usually referring to subsections containing members of a common kinship group (see also *taraf*)
pattidari	a term used to designate the allocation of (colonial) revenue responsibilities on the basis of ancestral 'shares' in which each share is held separately
patwari	a local record keeper; a village-level member of the district land revenue administration
pergunah	a term used to describe the subsections of a district (see also *tehsil*)
qabza (*kubza*)	possession (as in 'possession of a piece of land')
qanun	a term used to describe state-based laws or statutes
qazi	a state-based Muslim jurist
razeenama	a compromise agreement (usually a written agreement)
riwaj	'custom' (closely tied to notions of *izzat* or honour)
riwaj-i-am	a village, *tehsil*, or district-level digest of customary law containing a summary of 'tribal' customs
rubakar-i-akhir	the executive summary of a settlement paper
ryot	a cultivator with proprietary rights

ryotwari	a system of land revenue allocation in which revenue responsibilities are held by individual cultivators or *ryots*
sadr malguzar	a term used to describe someone responsible for paying a portion of the government revenue demand
safarish	a term used to describe the use of connections to gain privileged access (for example privileged access to bureaucratic favours, employment opportunities, and so on)
shajra kishtwar	a village field map
shajra nasb	a genealogical tree (lit. a map of fate)
shamilat	the village commons
shari'ah	the moral or religious 'path' followed by Muslims; a term used to describe Islamic 'law'
siyasa shari'ah	state-based 'religious' (or *shari'ah*-based) statutes
sura	a Qur'anic verse
taluqdar	the holder of an estate in which a large portion of the land revenue is held by the proprietor rather than the (colonial) state (see also *jagirdar*)
taqlid	a pattern of adherence to previously established forms of authority (for example the views of earlier scholars and *imams*) in matters of Islamic law or jurisprudence
taqsim	partition (a term used to describe the partition of a joint family estate into separate holdings)
taraf	a term used to describe the subsections of a village—usually referring to subsections containing members of a common kinship group (see also *patti*)
tehsil	a term used to describe the subsections of a district
thana	a police station
ushr	an Islamic tax on agricultural production

wajib-ul-arz	a village administration paper created during periodic settlement operations to provide an account of 'village' custom
zail	an administrative unit used to designate a group of (usually contiguous) villages led by ostensibly related *lambardars*
zamindar	a landed proprietor
zamindari	a system of land revenue allocation associated with individual proprietors (often holding large estates)
zan, zar and zamin	women, wealth, and land (a common phrase closely tied to key elements of *izzat*)
zat	a kinship-based 'clan'

INTRODUCTION

LAW AND THE LOGIC OF LOCAL POLITICS IN PAKISTAN

In his book *The Unplanned Revolution: Observations on the Process of Socio-economic Change in Pakistan* (2002), Pakistan-based economist, anthropologist, and activist Arif Hasan draws our attention to an important point, one familiar to students of Partha Chatterjee (*The Politics of the Governed* 2004), the Subaltern Studies Collective, and modern South Asian politics in general. Hasan notes that, since the independence and partition of British India and the formation of Pakistan in 1947, the process of social, economic, and political change in Pakistan has been uneven. On the one hand, he notes that demographic and economic changes, particularly in the context of urbanization, have produced a wholesale transformation of the postcolonial social order. And, yet, at the same time, he argues that the state itself has changed more slowly and, in many cases, not at all. In fact, Hasan argues, the formal institutions of the postcolonial state remain closely tied to the legacy of an intransigent colonial past. Whereas the interests of the people have changed, in other words, the institutions of the state have not.

Like Chatterjee, Hasan is interested in the prospects for democracy in South Asia and, more specifically, what might be called 'the microfoundations of postcolonial democratization'. He is particularly interested in the creative strategies that individuals in Pakistan use to confront the hurdles erected by what he regards as an isolated, intransigent, and largely authoritarian postcolonial regime—focusing, specifically, on the relatively *ad hoc* processes whereby a set of dynamic informal institutions emerging from below come to challenge and, ultimately, overwhelm the rigid institutions of both the colonial and, in due course, the modern postcolonial state. These informal institutions, constructed in the context of what Chatterjee refers to as 'political society', reflect the terms of an incipient (albeit unruly) form of modern postcolonial 'democracy'.

The material that Hasan and Chatterjee use to develop their arguments, ostensibly from the bottom up, is precisely the sort of material that you will encounter in the context of this book. By and large it concerns local efforts to undermine, avoid, or at the very least circumvent existing laws—in effect, local efforts to circumvent specific features of the state. Yet the conclusions that Chatterjee and Hasan reach, as regards the question of democracy, are almost exactly the *opposite* of the conclusions that I will reach in the context of this book. In fact, when it comes to an assessment of postcolonial politics in South Asia and, more specifically, the prospects for democracy in western (postcolonial) Punjab, where the majority of this book unfolds, the conclusions reached by Hasan and Chatterjee are, in many ways, the mirror image of my own.

In the context of this book ordinary citizens routinely seek to circumvent existing laws. But they do not appear to do so because they regard the law (or the state) as 'unchanging' or reminiscent of some distant colonial 'past'. On the contrary, most of those seeking new ways to circumvent existing postcolonial laws are well aware that, within the postcolonial context that surrounds them, many of the most important laws—indeed, many of the most important features of the postcolonial state—have *changed*. In fact the source of local frustration with the substance of existing laws does not appear to lie in any detailed assessment of the 'past'. Instead it lies in a rather specific set of challenges posed by an evolving postcolonial 'present'.

This is particularly true, I contend, when it comes to the postcolonial legal framework concerning land—the most important economic and political resource in South Asia by far. In fact the best example of this pattern—this pattern of dramatic institutional change followed by diverse expressions of postcolonial political transformation—appears to involve a rather familiar set of laws affecting the ownership and inheritance of land. This set of laws, traditionally known as *'ilm al-fara'id*, or the science of ancestral shares, is often referred to as the Islamic Law of Inheritance.

Based on several years of detailed field research in the Muslim-majority districts of western Punjab, the central theme of this book emerges from an assessment of the ways in which local laws of inheritance—and, thus, regulations pertaining to the ownership of ancestral (agricultural) land—were changed (from 'custom' to *shari'ah*) and, in turn, how these changes led to the emergence of an entirely new logic of local (electoral) politics, one that, over time, became inextricably bound up with local efforts to circumvent, or avoid, the formal laws of Pakistan's 'Islamic' state.

The promise of 'democracy', 'democratization' and/or 'democratic consolidation' remains rather dramatically unfulfilled in Pakistan, but, in the context of this book, I do not explain this failure in terms of any lack of change on the part of the state itself. On the contrary, I argue that the failure of Pakistan's postcolonial democratization is related to the terms of an emerging and increasingly complex disjuncture between the substance of postcolonial reforms ('custom' → *shari'ah*) and the enduring focus of local economic and political demands.

This gap is best explained in terms of a persistent tension between (a) kinship-based notions of *riwaj*, or 'custom', tied to specific expressions of kinship-based economic and political solidarity, and (b) the specific substance of a very different (and more thoroughly individualized) set of affiliations bound up with a particular understanding of Islam and, more specifically, a rather consistently 'ahistorical' approach to the terms of Islamic law (see Fig. 1 below).

This tension, between the terms of custom and local notions of Islamic law, boils down to one rather simple but extremely important point: whereas the former (custom) seeks to deny the inheritance rights of women, the latter (Islam) seeks to define and defend them. The problem, of course, lies in the fact that individual Muslims and their families have found themselves deeply divided between the competing terms of these—in many ways, their own—ostensibly conflicting desires.

Fig. 1. The gap: custom v. Islam

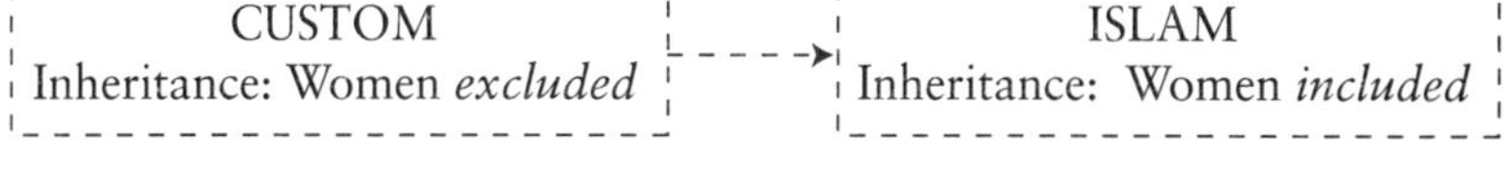

My argument regarding the logic of local politics and the failure of democracy in Pakistan is not limited to a simple description of postcolonial efforts to shift from one set of laws to another (see Fig. 1). Nor is it circumscribed by an historically embedded account of what led to, or caused, this initial alteration in the law. On the contrary, the focus of my argument *begins* with an effort to place this institutional shift 'from custom to *shari'ah*' on one side of the explanatory equation—treating it, primarily, as a rather complex independent variable (IV)—and then, having done so, seeking to examine the *consequences* of this shift within an historically embedded account of postcolonial Muslim 'agency' (focusing, primarily, on the ways in which this rather dramatic change affected prevailing conceptions of political 'representation', electoral 'accountability', and the emerging shape of 'democracy') (DV) (see Fig. 2, below). How did local efforts to introduce the terms of Islam and/or Islamic law affect, shape, or define a particular relationship with 'democracy'?

Fig. 2. Independent, intervening, and dependent variables

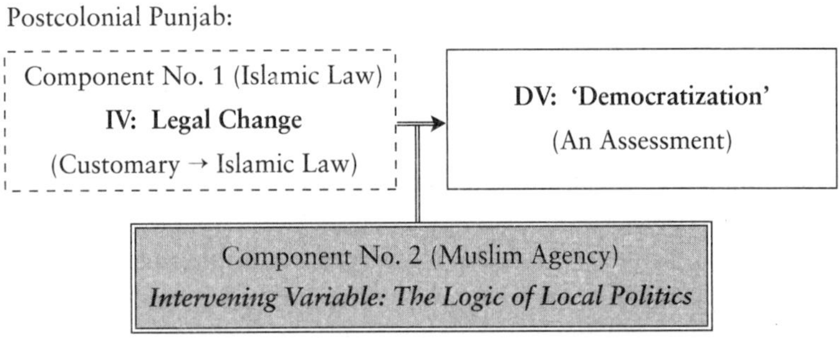

As 'the laws of custom' gave way to 'the laws of Islam' between 1947 and 1999 throughout the Muslim-majority districts of western Punjab, many families went to considerable lengths—and, in many cases, great expense—to undercut the process of effective legal enforcement. In fact, as the twentieth century progressed, following the formation of Pakistan in 1947, the expanding scope of *shari'ah* appeared to inaugurate a rather frantic search for extralegal ways to preserve the custom of female disinheritance—and, thus, the integrity of existing ancestral estates.

This much was not entirely unexpected. The surprise, I argue, lay in the specific strategies that small, large, and especially medium-sized landowners adopted to protect their landed interests—strategies that, I maintain, shed a great deal of light on the emerging relationship between Islam, Islamic law, and democracy. Indeed, as time passed, a growing number of landowners did not choose their political representatives on the basis of any effort to amend, improve, extend, or restrict the reach of existing (Islamic) laws—laws they had a tendency to regard as religiously or historically 'fixed'. Instead, they simply began to select their representatives (for example, in the context of local body or union council elections) on the basis of a proven ability to undermine, circumvent, or avoid the specific Islamic laws that concerned them.

The introduction of Islamic laws of inheritance favouring the rights of individual Muslim women, in other words, produced an entirely new logic of political and, at least ostensibly, 'democratic' accountability. Elections produced a rotation of elites, and these elected elites functioned as 'accountable intermediaries' linking individual citizens to a wide range of locally embedded state institutions (including local courts). But the expectations attached to these elected representatives, as 'accountable intermediaries', did not appear to reinforce conventional notions of 'democracy'. In particular, the role of elected representatives did not appear to support any effort to transform local economic and political demands into new or more appealing laws. Instead, the role of elected elites seemed to lie in treating existing laws as politically inaccessible, untouchable, or 'fixed', and, then, having done so, holding these ostensibly immutable laws in abeyance—not unlike a crossing guard who might be called upon to stop traffic in an effort to protect the movement of local pedestrians.

The laws themselves (as noted above) were regarded as inflexible, unchanging, and immune to any sort of political intervention. But, as I will explain, the practical *effect* of this view lay in a radical transformation of local ideas regarding electoral accountability and, I will argue, a radical denigration of conventional 'democratic' norms.

Islam, Islamic Law, and Democracy 'in Theory'

Scholars like Arif Hasan and Partha Chatterjee maintain that, since independence and partition in 1947, the formal institutional environment of the postcolonial state has remained relatively isolated and unchanging. But a closer look reveals that this is simply not the case. The state has changed a great deal and local patterns of decision-making have changed right along with it. But, again, these changes have not proceeded in tandem; in fact, more often than not, they have proceeded at cross-purposes. In postcolonial Punjab the state adopted the language of *shari'ah*. But, on the ground, even a cursory glance would reveal that most of the population simply refused to follow along. More often than not, they continued to insist on a critical distinction between their 'rhetorical' commitment to female-friendly expressions of *shari'ah*, on the one hand, and their 'practical' attachment to patrilineal notions of *riwaj*, or custom, on the other.

Throughout the latter half of the twentieth century, their rhetorical commitment to *shari'ah* was of course rather easy to identify. In the language of Erving Goffman (1959) this commitment appeared 'on stage'. But their practical attachment to *riwaj* was often more difficult to apprehend. This attachment remained carefully hidden 'behind the scenes'. In fact, building on this 'practical' attachment to *riwaj*, most citizens slowly came to rely on a rather complex pattern of 'private' political exchange, one in which locally elected leaders were called upon to engage and, in many ways, unsettle the institutions of the postcolonial state (including the postcolonial district courts) in return for the *political* support of those who wished to preserve the integrity of their ancestral (agnatic) estates—notwithstanding the substance of existing postcolonial laws. Locally elected leaders, in other words, were called upon to manage and manipulate the state in ways that might succeed in leaving the law intact ... but never fully (or consistently) enforced.

Many have argued that, throughout the nineteenth century, an uncompromising colonial state struggled relentlessly to impose an alien property regime in South Asia, achieving a certain measure of what Ranajit Guha (1998) has called 'dominance without hegemony'. Others, recalling the work of scholars like Arif Hasan and Partha Chatterjee, have taken this argument one step further, insisting that even after independence and partition the most important features of the colonial regime were aggressively sustained by formal incentive structures, lingering legal constraints, and the raw coercive power of an isolated authoritarian regime.

A closer look at the history of colonial and postcolonial Punjab, however, reveals something else. In fact the most important features of the colonial landed property regime endured (informally) long after a number of important changes within the formal apparatus of the modern postcolonial state ('custom' → *shari'ah*). In other words, what sustained the colonial regime—particularly in the context of what many refer to as *zan*, *zar*, and *zamin*, or women, wealth, and land—was neither the law nor the bureaucracy (nor the military) considered in isolation. On the contrary, what sustained this regime even after the moment of independence was an active, deliberate, and consistent logic of countervailing (participatory and accountable) local politics—in effect, a deeply conservative logic embedded within competitive landowning efforts to preserve the terms of 'tribal' custom even *within* a set of ostensibly 'religious' institutions.

As noted above, most people did not choose to abandon the formal institutions of the postcolonial state. When it came to 'family matters' and, more specifically, family *property* matters, they simply used these institutions of the state to accomplish alternative (and, more precisely, conservative) economic and political ends.

If the conservative microfoundational mechanism lying at the very centre of this study, however, involves a special configuration of local strategies related to a specific understanding of local customs—indeed, if it is really true, as I will argue in Chapters 1 and 2, that the specific shape of these customary interests, preferences, and strategies emerged in the context of a particular sequence of events in the late-nineteenth-century colonial administration of just one district (District Sialkot)—how will this microfoundational mechanism survive in the context of a much larger effort to delineate the relationship between 'Islam' and 'democracy' in general? Indeed, if the logic of local politics that lies at the very centre of this book is linked to a unique historical sequence and a particular combination of strategies focused on the pursuit of specific substantive goals, how will the basic features of this argument hold up in the context of prevailing disciplinary concerns regarding rigorous out-of-sample testing (or controlled cross-national comparison)? The answer, I think it may be fairly safe to say, is 'not terribly well'.

In the past, when political scientists set out to explain something like 'the rigidity of landed property relations in the context of significant institutional change' or 'the relationship between institutional change (custom → *shari'ah*) and the consolidation of democracy', they were generally inclined to limit their efforts to the search for a plausible correlation between a specific set of independent variables (IV) and a specific, isolated outcome (DV). But, in recent years, the frontiers of the discipline have shifted, moving away from isolated IV's and DV's toward a more compelling account of the 'intervening' variables that lie, as it were, 'in between'. In fact a growing number of social scientists have taken a specific interest in producing empirically justifiable accounts of the microfoundational processes that produce and, in many cases, reproduce a given outcome—for instance, democratization (or the lack of it)—over time.

In other words, reflecting some of the work undertaken by Peter Hall (2000), those with an interest in the problem of social scientific explanation increasingly shy away from cases in which there is supposed to be 'a one-to-one correspondence between distant factor X and ultimate outcome Y' in favour of an account of processes marked by 'extensive interaction effects, in which X [for instance, the introduction of Islamic law] *conduces* towards Y [for example, the success or failure of democracy] ... via a series of intermediary stages in which the interaction of other variables [for example, the transformation of Muslim 'agency'] is also important'.[1]

Indeed, as Hall explains, the frontiers of the discipline now have a tendency to focus on the specification of precise causal 'mechanisms', moving beyond (statistical) probabilities, if you will, toward a detailed account of specific explanatory 'processes'.

Previously, when social scientists limited themselves to the study of isolated independent and dependent variables (X and Y) set apart from detailed process-based mechanisms, they were generally forced to rely, at some level, on a standard set of intervening assumptions regarding the specific terms of individual motivation or 'agency'. Individuals in situation X, for instance, were said to proceed towards outcome Y because, for the most part, the individuals in question were believed to conform to some *a priori* motivational logic grounded in, say, ideas about 'efficiency', concerns about 'class', or the specific 'injunctions' of Islam. In fact mainstream social scientists rarely found it necessary to concern themselves with a study of the historical record at the level of individual choices (or agency), because, when it came to an evaluation of their work, they were almost never judged by the extent to which their arguments conformed to the ideas actually expressed by individual actors during the intervening parts of their story—for example, at the level of specific (or substantive) 'debates'.

In recent years, however, social scientists have begun to take a greater interest in the middle of the story, moving beyond Time T (origins) and Time T + 1 (outcomes) to, say, Time T + 1/4 or, perhaps, T + 5/8. In taking this step, however, many social scientists have begun to notice that their *a priori* assumptions regarding the nature of individual motivation no longer seem to suffice. At the very least, they have begun to find that these assumptions tend to maintain a rather poor fit with the substance of historically embedded debates. Precisely insofar as this is the case, however, those with an interest in the explanatory mechanisms located in the 'middle' of the story have found themselves looking for a way to pry open the black box of individual preferences, recording what individuals actually say and do on the ground. In other words, social scientists have begun to appreciate the merits of what John R. Bowen (1999) has called 'theoretically informed microhistorical accounts of complex social processes'.[2]

This is, of course, exactly the sort of thing that I came to appreciate in the context of my own attempt to explain the surprising rigidity of landed property relations, the logic of local politics that sustained those relations, and (within this logic) the rather awkward relationship between Islam, Islamic law, and democracy in the context of postcolonial Punjab. Indeed, the closer I came to an appreciation for the terms of individual Muslim *agency*—for instance, the closer I came to an empirically accurate account of the link between local notions of 'honour' (*izzat*), local expressions of Islamic law (*shari'ah*), and local approaches to dispute resolution, litigation, or voting—the more I found that I would have to abandon broad out-of-sample comparisons in favour of a truly *explanatory* framework grounded in the demands of one (and only one) case.[3]

In 1946, during the earliest days of the behavioralist revolution, the historian R.G. Collingwood pointed out that social scientists 'may begin by discovering the outside of an event'.[4] But in the end, he argued, this was never enough. In fact he maintained that the social scientist 'must always remember that the event was an action, and that his main task is to think himself into this action, to discern the thought of its agent'. The problem of explanation was, therefore, at least for those who opted to embrace Collingwood's approach, merely 'the further business of making this reenactment explicit, in the form of a narrative account, so that the investigator's understanding [could] be communicated to others'[5] There was, in fact, 'no such thing as [a] supposed further stage of ... [so-called] scientific history, ... because an historical fact, once genuinely ascertained [and] grasped by ... [a] reenactment of the agent's thought in his mind, is already explained'.[6]

The challenge, Collingwood maintained, was not a challenge of 'understanding' via conceptual or analytical 'generalization'. It was, rather, a challenge of 'understanding' via specific empirical 'explanation'. In fact, once a social scientist was finally ready to generalize, there was, from the point of view of *understanding*, Collingwood argued, 'nothing of value ... left for the generalization to do'.[7]

CONCLUSION

This book does not attempt to 'discern the thought of local agents' in an attempt to understand or explain the relationship between Islam and democracy in every part of Pakistan. Its focus is limited to colonial and postcolonial Punjab—the most densely populated and, for that matter, the most powerful province in the country. Indeed, with more than half of the total population in Pakistan, the Punjab alone is sufficiently crowded to make it the fifteenth largest 'country' in the world—larger than Britain, France and Italy, not to mention Turkey, Egypt and Iran.

For present purposes, however, these statistics are neither here nor there. It is far more important to note that, contrary to a number of commonly held assumptions, the laws governing landed property relations in colonial Punjab (1849–1947)—and, especially, colonial laws of inheritance—were not defined in terms of what has generally gone by the name of 'religious' personal law. Instead, as I will explain in Chapters 1 and 2, these laws were defined in terms of specific 'tribal' customs.

The details of these customs, and the manner in which they were delineated by colonial administrators and judges, will be addressed below. For the time being, however, it is necessary to mention—by way of introduction—two things about the specific terms of 'tribal' custom, both of which relate to the critical question of inheritance. The first concerns exogamous marriage patterns, or the fact that, customarily, marriages were arranged in ways that led each newly married woman to travel, with a dowry provided by her parents, to the village and, more specifically, to the household of her new husband. Typically, these marriages were arranged with distant relatives, such that, in local terms, marriages were arranged 'within the extended family, caste, or tribe' but 'outside of the local village'.

The second issue concerns the status of married women in the context of specific ancestral estates. By and large, dowries were regarded as a form of early inheritance and, as a result, women were completely excluded from the inheritance of agricultural land. In fact it was widely acknowledged that, given the nature of existing (exogamous) marriage patterns, any effort to *include* married women would lead to the *fragmentation* of local estates and, ultimately, a sharp decline in the productive capacity of the land.

After the independence of British India and the formation of Pakistan in 1947, however, the laws of inheritance were changed. In particular, owing to the rhetorical and, to a certain extent, the ideological thrust of the Pakistan Movement led by Mohammad Ali Jinnah and his party, the All-India Muslim League, the terms of 'tribal' custom were rejected and, eventually, replaced by a specific understanding of Islam. Local customs favouring the disinheritance of married women, in other words, were replaced by formal written laws in which the rights of all women (married and unmarried) were clearly and carefully defined.

Precisely insofar as this was the case, however, smallholding peasants (representing a significant portion of the population) found themselves in a rather awkward situation, one in which they were confronted with a host of incentives to 'say one thing' according to conventional interpretations of Islam while, at the same time, proceeding to 'do another' according to the particular constraints of custom. In fact, as my research unfolded, first in District Lahore, then in Sialkot, and, finally, in Sargodha, I discovered that a thorough understanding of this approach to 'two-tiered' decision making, in which individuals attempted to reconcile the terms of custom with prevailing interpretations of Islam, was absolutely indispensable for anyone with an interest in explaining the rigidity of landed property relations, the logic of local politics that sustained those relations, and, ultimately, the relationship between 'Islam' and 'democracy' over time.

The challenge, in other words, lay in coming to grips with the fact that existing laws were unambiguously stacked against the preservation of 'agnatic' (all-male) estates. And yet, for the most part, these estates endured. In fact, as the remainder of this book will explain, the challenge lay in showing exactly how and why the logic of local politics in the context of postcolonial Punjab came to reflect an entirely new logic of local electoral accountability, one in which local politicians were routinely called upon to circumvent existing postcolonial laws in an effort to shepherd their constituents through the overlapping layers of their own (apparently conflicting) desires—*izzat* and the terms of 'tribal' custom, on the one hand; Islam, on the other. The latter (Islam) almost always prevailed in principle. But the former prevailed in practice.

Neither the people nor their politicians chose to abandon the formal institutions of the postcolonial state. They simply used these institutions to accomplish alternative (in fact countervailing) economic and political ends. In doing so, however, they proceeded to redefine the logic of postcolonial political accountability—with enormous implications for the rule of law and, ultimately, the fate of democracy itself.

PART ONE

CONSTRUCTING THE 'LAW OF THE LAND' (1849–1947)

Part One: Summary

As an account of Islam and democracy, the central theme of this book grows out of a pattern in which ordinary Muslims call upon their elected representatives in a persistent effort to avoid the implementation of Islamic laws of inheritance—in effect, a persistent effort to 'circumvent *shari'ah*' (*'ilm al-fara'id*). That very process, however, raises an important question, namely, why do they do this? What do they want *instead*?

Chapters 1 and 2 provide a detailed response to this question—one with notable historical significance and, as I will explain in Chapter 6, considerable theoretical significance as well. Drawing special attention to the shifting terms of landed property relations in three Muslim-majority districts of western Punjab, namely Lahore, Sialkot, and Sargodha, Chapter 1 begins with an historically embedded effort to explain exactly 'what people wanted' and 'why they wanted it' following the annexation of the Punjab by the British in 1849. At the heart of this effort lies a detailed account of the ways in which individual villagers, responding to the work of the colonial state, came to redirect and, ultimately, reshape the policies of the state itself.

This is, in effect, an account of the ways in which (a) individual villagers brought a specific sense of local 'customs' regarding female disinheritance to bear on late-nineteenth-century colonial efforts to preserve the integrity of agnatic (all-male) estates (1849–1900) and, following on from this, an account of the ways in which (b) colonial administrators went out of their way to reinforce specific features of this historically embedded response (1900–47).

During the first half of the twentieth century, the underlying tension between the terms of 'tribal' custom, on the one hand, and those of Islam, on the other, produced considerable strain within the context of anti-colonial (Muslim) political mobilization, as the Muslims of colonial Punjab, firmly attached to the ecumenical terms of 'tribal' custom, held out against expressions of anti-colonial nationalism constructed along religious or communal lines in other parts of North India. Chapter 2 (1900–47) traces the specific terms of this early-twentieth-century political tension in the context of a series of rather specific questions regarding the inheritance of agricultural land.

CUSTOM (women excluded) Punjab Unionist Party	v.	**ISLAM** (women included) All-India Muslim League

1

WHO OWNS THE LAND? (1849–1900)

REVENUE ADMINISTRATION, LEGAL ADMINISTRATION, AND RURAL INDEBTEDNESS

British administrators in late-nineteenth-century Punjab often congratulated themselves, not for the overwhelming strength of their army, but rather for the meticulous standards of their land revenue administration and the strict impartiality of their courts. With an attitude born out of self-aggrandizement more than anything else, they maintained that, under their 'marauding' predecessors, the Sikhs, landed property had been completely insecure and therefore utterly worthless. British rule brought security and, hence, value. Indeed, as Lieutenant-Colonel C.H. Buck pointed out in 1937, quoting a rather famous revenue manual prepared by James Thomason in 1844, 'the first step ... towards the creation of a private 'right' in land ... was to place such a limit on the demand of the government as would leave to the proprietors a profit which would [in turn, by virtue of its stability,] constitute a valuable [right]'.[1]

Unfortunately, colonial administrators throughout the Punjab quickly discovered that most of the loans secured by this increasingly stable 'right' were not used to finance valuable agricultural improvements. Instead, they discovered, these loans were used to pay for lavish weddings, petty gambling, and protracted litigation in the district and appellate courts. In fact within the space of just twenty years after the British conquest of the Punjab in 1849 the problem of rural indebtedness had reached epidemic proportions. Land was being transferred from defaulting hereditary landowners to 'alien' moneylenders at an ever-increasing rate, and 'village communities' (generally regarded as the soul of British India) were said to be falling apart.

British administrators, torn between their economic principles and their political premonitions, were up in arms. But at the very centre of this emerging crisis lay a series of misgivings regarding the consequences of British rule itself and, in particular, colonial efforts to introduce (and enforce) *individual* landed property rights.

Much to their surprise, British administrators discovered that the effect of clearly defined landed property rights and free market exchange was not increased prosperity—at least not in the Punjab. Instead, they discovered, the result was widespread indebtedness.[2] To be sure, exclusive rights gave the land added value, but when commodity prices dropped, as they did during the late 1860s, loans secured on agricultural land could not be repaid, and the colonial courts enforced a number of sales to satisfy the terms of existing debtor contracts.

Initially, of course, British administrators were not alarmed by this trend. Instead they hailed the role of private property in facilitating the consolidation of modern market forces, and, following Sir Henry Sumner Maine, they welcomed what they perceived to be another important step in the natural progression from 'status' to 'contract'. Gradually, however, their naïve economic confidence turned into grave political concern. What the revenue administration gave to hereditary 'agriculturalists', namely, landed property rights, the legal administration increasingly took away in the form of enforced transfers to 'alien' moneylenders, dividing ancestral village communities and provoking violent rural unrest. Indeed, the introduction and enforcement of clearly defined landed property rights—easily the most important objective of the colonial administration throughout the latter half of the nineteenth century—was increasingly said to *undermine* the stability of the state itself.

In what follows, I will use a rather detailed account of this rural indebtedness crisis to accomplish two things. First, I will use this account to introduce a number of important terms—terms drawn from the colonial revenue administration that will resurface, again and again, throughout the remainder of this book. (In fact in many ways the next fifteen pages or so could be said to provide an annotated glossary of sorts, without which the remainder of this book would remain, almost literally, incomprehensible.)

Second, I will use this account of specific terminology to describe the broader economic and historical context behind what emerged as an official policy of support, not for the regulatory capacity of English Common Law or, for that matter, religious personal law—Hindu law, Muslim law, and so on—but, rather, for the preservation and, in due course, the official reinforcement of local 'tribal' customs. In fact this account of late-nineteenth-century efforts to reinforce the terms of 'tribal' custom will serve as a basic point of departure for the remainder of my argument regarding the halting construction of an historically specific relationship between Islam, Islamic law, and democracy.

Throughout the latter half of the nineteenth century, the British colonial state sought to promote, as a matter of economic principle, the value of individual landed property rights. In fact such an approach was consistent with the terms of both English and Muslim personal law. As time passed, however, a closer look at the historical record reveals that, notwithstanding specific colonial *intentions*, this respect for 'individual' rights slowly gave way to a widespread appreciation for 'collective' economic (and political) responsibilities—not only amongst the British, but also, and more importantly, amongst their landowning subjects.[3] The question for both parties was exceedingly simple: who owns the land? But the answer was astonishingly complex. British administrators may have *intended* to promote the value of individual rights. But, in the end, their actions did *not* support their intentions.

This chapter aims to explain exactly why the colonial state embraced the approach it did—showing, in effect, how the underpinnings of the colonial state prompted a series of unanticipated adjustments in favour of 'tribal' custom over time.

REVENUE ADMINISTRATION, LEGAL ADMINISTRATION

Shortly, after the Battle of Chillianwala, the Battle of Gujrat, and the subsequent annexation of the Punjab during the spring of 1849, the Governor-General of India, Lord Dalhousie, announced that British administrators in the Punjab would strive to 'uphold native institutions and practices as far as they are consistent with the distribution of justice to all classes'. More specifically, he declared that 'with the knowledge now generally prevalent respecting [co-ownership in the context of] village coparcenaries, there is no apprehension that our officers will not exert themselves to maintain these important bodies in all their integrity'.[4]

This reference to the term 'coparcenary' is extremely important, and most of the next fifteen pages or so will be devoted to an illumination of its place in the late-nineteenth-century lexicon of rural administrators throughout colonial Punjab. Indeed, it is worth pointing out that the language of the colonial land revenue administration would be virtually impossible to understand apart from contemporary ideas about the composition of the 'village community' and, within this, the membership of the village 'coparcenary'. It is in fact particularly important to keep in mind that colonial ideas about what came to be known as 'the hereditary body of village proprietors' (that is, the *malikan-deh*)

Map 1. British India map highlighting the Punjab (in black)

and, subsequently, the payment of the government land revenue, were closely tied to the notion of 'coparcenary' community cohesion throughout colonial North India.

These ideas boiled down to the notion that each member of the (so-called) 'village proprietary body' could be (and should be) held both 'jointly' and 'severally' responsible for the payment of the government revenue demand.[5] In other words, according to the colonial revenue administration, each *hissadar* or 'shareholder' within a village community or 'coparcenary' was expected to pay some portion of the local revenue demand. But, in the event of any default—for example, within a particular estate—each member of that estate was expected to be held 'jointly' responsible for the debts, obligations, and arrears of his related 'co-sharers'.[6]

In fact, for several years after Lord Dalhousie's declaration in 1849 regarding the importance of preserving village coparcenary communities 'in all their integrity', the most important question facing the colonial revenue administration was, almost invariably, 'who belongs to the village coparcenary'? Who counts as an official 'co-sharer'? What are the boundaries of the village 'community'? And, perhaps most importantly, who actually 'owns' the land? Is it the individual or the group? And if it is, in fact, the 'group', how is that group defined?

Revenue Administration

Initially, settlement officers in the Punjab were guided in their response to these questions by manuals prepared for their colleagues in other parts of British India.[7] In particular, they were guided by the work of James Thomason, who wrote a manual entitled *Directions for Revenue Officers in the Northwestern Provinces* (1844), and, later, by the work of G.C. Barnes, the Commissioner of Lahore, who wrote a manual designed to introduce the administrative structures of India's Northwestern Provinces to officials throughout the Punjab.[8]

In order to understand these *Directions*, some attention to the framework within which they were written—indeed, the very language within which they were composed—is essential. In fact the following list of terms should be read with this purpose in mind. Together, these terms (and the maps they were used to illuminate) provide an historically embedded introduction to the remainder of this chapter and, ultimately, the remainder of this book as a whole.

Map 2. British Punjab map highlighting four districts: Lahore (lower centre), Sialkot (upper centre), Sargodha (left) and Ludhiana (right in black)

Map 3. District Ludhiana map highlighting three *tehsils* and one village (in black)

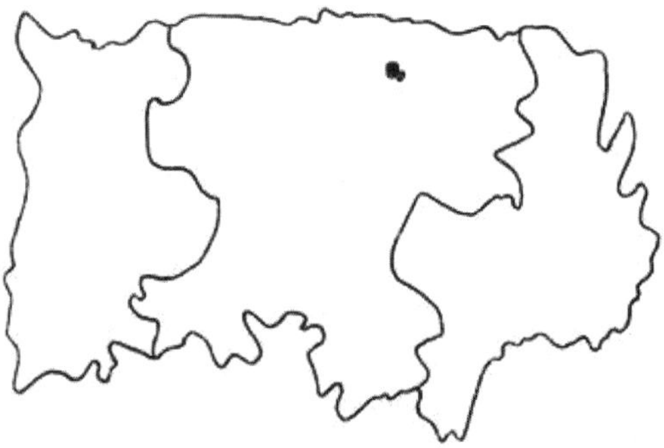

Map 4. Village map highlighting two *tarafs*: *taraf* A (left-hand all white); *taraf* B (right-hand stripes)

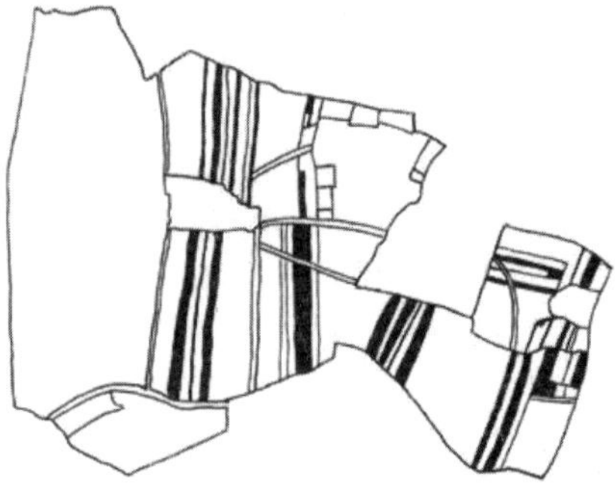

N.b. Adapted from Richard Saumerez Smith (1996), pp. 144–5.

Within each presidency or province (see Map 1, above) there were often several different 'districts' (Map 2). And, within each district, there were generally three or four *tehsils* or 'subdistricts' (Map 3), each containing several hundred *mauzas* or *mehals*—that is, 'estates' or 'villages' (Map 4). And of course, each village contained a small cluster of mud and brick houses that defined its residential area. This area was known as the *abadi-deh*.

The land surrounding this *abadi-deh* was, in turn, usually divided into two or more *tarafs* or *thokas*, that is, 'village subdivisions' (see Map 4: *taraf* A; *taraf* B). And, more often than not, these smaller subdivisions overlapped with an equal number of *pattis* or *tholas*, that is, land held (and often further subdivided) by specific ancestral 'tribes'. Thus, Barnes explained, the entire structure of the Punjab could be imagined in the form of a single telescopic map, beginning with each 'district' and ending with the territory connected to a specific (agricultural) 'tribe'.

Within each 'tribal' *patti*, however, Barnes explained that there were usually several different *khewats*, or 'holdings', each divided among a number of dispersed but distinguishable fields. And, more often than not, each and every one of these 'fields' contained a number of different 'plots'. In fact, Barnes explained, each estate or village typically contained several hundred different plots, with the *khewat* or 'holding' of each owner coming together in the form of five or more 'plots' scattered across several different 'fields' within a particular ('tribal') *patti*.

For the most part, however, Barnes was not concerned with the demarcation of specific 'fields' or 'plots'. Instead he was concerned with the production of a routine document known as the *shajra kishtwar*, that is, the 'village field map'. (Many of these maps, drawn onto brittle white sheets and stored in the offices of the district *kachehri*, or headquarters, survive even today.) In fact, when push came to shove, Barnes noted that the key to each village 'settlement' did not lie in the production of the village 'field map', but rather in the production of the revenue *documents* this map was designed to consolidate and represent.

Among these documents, which (taken together) included a detailed list of each village owner, cultivator, field and seasonal crop, the most important was, basically, a type of 'running account' listing the parameters of each fractional share within the larger revenue landscape of the village. These shares were defined in terms of (a) the land itself (for example, 3/235ths of the village) as well as (b) the amount of money paid for its use—that is, its 'rent' (from the perspective of the proprietor who 'owned' the land) or its 'revenue' (from the perspective of the state) (for example, 3/235ths of the 'revenue'). This running account was known as the *jamabandi* and, in late-nineteenth and early-twentieth-century colonial Punjab, this was the most important document of all.

In addition to the *jamabandi*, however, each settlement included a number of 'supplementary' documents, each of which was closely related to the text of the *jamabandi* itself. The first was the *shajra nasb*, or 'map of fate', which was, for all intents and purposes, a genealogical tree tracing the lineage of each male owner to the founding father of the village—in effect, a detailed record of (all-male) inheritance. The second was the *darkhwast malguzari*, which amounted to an official contract with the revenue payers themselves. The third was the *wajib-ul-arz* or the 'village administration paper'. And, finally, the fourth was the *riwaj-i-am* or the 'digest of tribal custom'.[9]

Each of these many documents, in addition to the executive summary lodged with each local settlement (known as the *rubakar-i-akhir*), will be taken up in greater detail below. Their significance, however, lay in the fact that, strictly speaking, they defined the formal legal connection between the colonial state and its subjects for nearly a hundred years (1849–1947). In effect they defined who owned what and, legally speaking, who controlled whom (and how) throughout colonial Punjab.

Distributing the Land Revenue: 'Individual' Obligations, 'Village' Tenures

The specific purpose for which these documents were created—namely, the distribution of the government revenue demand and the division of that demand among individual owners and taxpayers—differed enormously throughout British India. The primary difference surfaced in the use of the term *sadr malguzar*, or 'official revenue payer', and more specifically, the divergent uses of this term to describe a group of villagers known as 'hereditary cultivators with possession' (that is, the official 'co-sharers' of each village).

In the Northwestern Provinces, which lie beyond the scope of this book, a small number of cultivators were classified as 'hereditary' proprietors. But, as it happens, most of those with an attachment to the land as cultivators were classified as *maurusi*, or 'occupancy' tenants, and *ghair marusi*, or 'tenants-at-will'.

Those classified as hereditary proprietors were considered co-sharing members of 'the village proprietary body' and, as such, they were endowed with certain rights and privileges—for example, the right to a share in the *shamilat*, or village 'commons', the right to participate in the management of village affairs, and (above all) the right to alienate their land. Those classified as tenants, on the other hand, were excluded from these rights. In fact at the level of cultivation the only way to distinguish the rights of an official 'owner', an official 'co-sharer', or a village 'coparcener' from those of a simple 'cultivator' lay in the ability of the former—that is, the coparcener—to alienate, or dispose of, his land.

In the Punjab, a similar pattern of classification was introduced. But, in this case, the distribution of the government demand *within* the village varied from village to village depending upon its designation as a *pattidari* village or a *bhaiachara* village—a distinction that will resurface numerous times throughout the remainder of this book.

Briefly stated, *pattidari* tenures described the division of a particular village—that is, the division of the cultivated land, the *shamilat* or commons, and the payment of any government revenue demand—in terms of *biswas* or 'ancestral shares', that is, according to prevailing laws of inheritance: for instance, Hindu laws of inheritance for Hindus and Sikhs, Muslim laws of inheritance for Muslims, and customary laws of inheritance for those who customarily departed from the terms of their own 'religious' personal law. Even when all of the land in the village was managed in common, then, each member of the village proprietary body in a so-called *pattidari* village was associated with a specific legal right—and, thus, a specific obligation vis-à-vis the colonial revenue adminisration—equal to the extent of his own ancestral 'share' (as recorded on the 'map of fate', that is, the genealogical tree known as the *shajra nasb*).

Bhaiachara tenures, on the other hand, described the division of the village in terms of 'possession', that is, in terms of the amount of land actually cultivated by an individual or his tenants (for example, in terms of ploughs or *bighas*). In *bhaiachara* villages, therefore, 'possession' was the measure of a person's rights and responsibilities even when the extent of that possession extended beyond (or below) the limits of his precise ancestral 'share'.[10]

Initially, in their efforts to make sense of the village proprietary body, colonial administrators throughout the Punjab regarded *pattidari* and *bhaiachara* tenures as static departures from a single 'artistocratic' ideal. In effect, they believed that *pattidari* and *bhaiachara* tenures amounted to something like an 'adulterated' form of individualized 'aristocratic' control.

Fig. 3. Land tenure systems in historical (theoretical) perspective: from 'ancestry' to 'usufruct'

Ancestral Rights → Usufructuary Rights

zamindari	*mushtarka*	*pattidari*	*bhaiachara*	*ryotwari*
aristocratic single owner	ancestral shares	**ancestral shares**	**cultivating possession**	cultivating possession
[Bengal]	[Northwestern Provinces / Punjab]			[Madras]

As individual settlement operations grew more and more elaborate throughout the latter half of the nineteenth century, however, colonial administrators began to adjust this view. In particular, they began to see these tenures as discrete steps in a universal evolutionary progression—moving away from specific ancestral rights associated with the tribe or the family as a whole (*mushtarka* tenures) towards a greater appreciation for 'usufructuary' rights and a pattern of more thoroughly 'individualized' cultivation (see Fig. 3).

In order to explain how the colonial revenue administration came to embrace this extremely important (evolutionary) view, it may help to describe the administrative terminology surrounding a purely illustrative 'sample' village founded by a (Hindu) 'aristocrat' or *zamindar* (see Fig. 4, below). In particular, it may help to describe, in colonial terms, exactly what happened to the ownership of this village, defined in terms of specific ancestral 'shares' (as opposed to cultivating 'possession'), over time.[11]

When the 'founding father' of this purely illustrative village died, colonial administrators assumed that Hindu laws of inheritance would intervene to ensure that the landed coparcenary would be divided (equally) among this founding father's sons. If these sons—say, these four sons—opted to manage their land 'in common', then, according to the language of the colonial revenue administration, the prevailing pattern of 'ownership' in the village would be a *zamindari mushtarka* pattern.

If, however, each son decided to cultivate his land *separately* (within the terms of his own ancestral 'share'), this pattern would not be known as a *zamindari 'mushtarka'* pattern. Instead it would be described as a *pattidari* pattern: A v. B v. C, and so on.

Eventually, however, even this pattern might change. Say, for example, two of the brothers found themselves with two sons apiece, while the remaining two brothers had only one son each. At this point, the village would be left with (a) four grandchildren cultivating one half of the village and (b) two grandchildren cultivating the remaining half (perhaps with the help of tenants from a neighbouring village). The land revenue, in turn, would be paid in six different portions, each according to a specific 'ancestral' share (4 x 1/8) + (2 x 1/4). But, at this point, the pattern of ownership would still be described as—technically speaking—a *pattidari* pattern.

Fig. 4. Land tenure: *zamindari*, *zamindari mushtarka*, *pattidari*

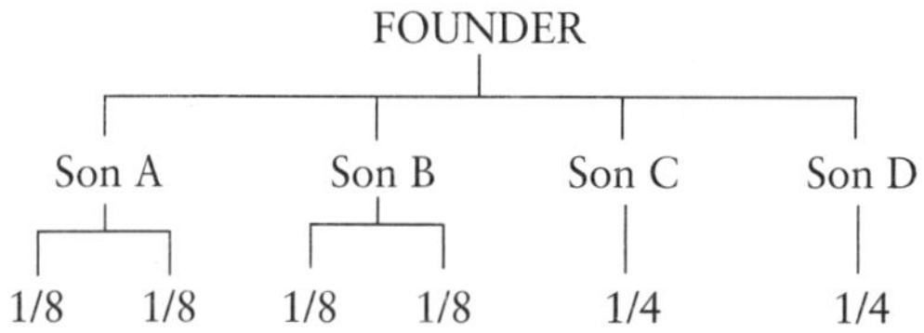

Within a few generations, however, even this pattern could begin to unravel. Say, for instance, two heirs converted to Islam, creating a schism within the village: one heir died childless after dedicating some of his land to the village mosque in a *waqf*, or religious endowment, while the other continued to adhere to Islamic laws of inheritance. A third heir might gift a portion of his land to his sister (who, following custom, would be expected to marry outside the village). And, in due course, another relatively wayward heir might opt to mortgage his land to pay off some of his debts. Soon the ancestral 'shares' of the original co-sharers and their six children might be encroached upon (or simply forgotten), and, eventually, cultivating 'possession' would become the only discernable measure of right.

At this point, as far as the colonial land revenue administration was concerned, the village could no longer be categorized as a 'share-based' *pattidari* village. Instead it was (finally) a 'possession-based' *bhaiachara* village.[12]

Of course the significance of this illustration lay in the extent to which it illuminated the relationship between (a) the specific terminology of the colonial state, (b) local notions of 'ownership', and (c) the structure of the colonial land revenue administration as a whole. Indeed, as soon as the form of land tenure *(zamindari, zamindari mushtarka, pattidari, bhaiachara)* was decided, each *hissadar* or 'shareholder' could be linked with a specific portion of the existing revenue demand—say, a portion equal to (a) his ancestral 'share' *(pattidari)* or (b) the amount of land in his 'possession' *(bhaiachara)*. These portions were then recorded in an extremely important document known as the *fard bachh khatawar*, or 'the register of distribution among shareholders'.[13] (Shareholder A, for instance, might be recorded as the 'owner' of 3/235ths of the 'revenue' as it was assessed, on the basis of detailed productivity estimates, in the context of Village X.)

Without the *fard bachh khatawar*, and, indeed, without all of the documents used to produce the *jamabandi* from which the *fard bachh khatawar* was derived, the question of 'ownership' would have been, quite literally, impossible to address throughout colonial Punjab. In fact the land revenue administration as a whole would have been, for all intents and purposes, inconceivable. As James Douie pointed out in his rather famous book entitled, simply, *A Settlement Manual* (1899): 'a settlement which merely determined the revenue to be paid, without at the same time recording who should be responsible for its payment, would obviously be a futile operation'.[14]

Collecting the Land Revenue: 'Village' Settlements, 'Ancestral' Elites

Those responsible for the satisfaction of the government demand—in effect, the 'owners' of local agricultural land—represented two very different types of coparcenary shareholders, namely (a) the 'hereditary cultivators' themselves, against whom the government demand was actually assessed, and (b) the local coparcenary agents from whom this demand was collected.

Even as the colonial state declared itself to be 'the supreme owner' of all land in the Punjab, in other words, district-level administrators laboured intensively to construct an elaborate system of what they called 'intermediate' owners. Working from the bottom up, for instance, most cultivators were reduced to the status of mere 'tenants'. But, owing to the policies of the colonial state, some cultivators were elevated to the status of 'hereditary' proprietors—for example, *zamindars* in Bengal, *ryots* in Madras and Bombay, and, in the specific context that concerns us here, all of the different types of *hissadars* in the *pattidari* and *bhaiachara* estates of the Northwestern Provinces, Oudh and the Punjab. Even beyond this, however, some *hissaders* were further reclassified as a special class of *jagirdars, taluqdars, or lambardars*, that is, *ala maliks*, or 'superior' proprietors. And, in due course, these 'superior' proprietors were charged with the collection of the revenue itself.[15]

In Bengal, Madras, and Bombay, individual *zamindars* and *ryots* paid their shares directly to the government. But, in the Northwestern Provinces, Oudh and the Punjab, 'joint' family (or village) ownership was far more common. And, in this context, superior proprietors (for example, *lambardars*) became extremely important as local tax collectors. In fact, throughout the latter half of the nineteenth century, leading *lambardars* emerged as, perhaps, the key link between the colonial state, on the one hand, and its expanding menagerie of revenue-paying subjects, on the other.[16]

Legal Administration

Officially, village *lambardars* simply collected the sums demanded by the government from individual members of the village proprietary body (keeping a small portion for themselves as a form of remuneration for their service to the state). But, in practice, their position was always a bit more complex, particularly insofar as they became embroiled, as intermediaries, in the adjudication of local disputes—disputes involving, for instance, (a) the construction of the revenue records themselves, (b) the revision of these records between each occasional resettlement, and (c) the contestation of specific records in court. In fact the role of the village *lambardar*, or headman, typically 'representing' a particular local *patti* (such that a village with four separate *pattis* was often associated with four separate *lambardars*), was absolutely central in every single case.

As the colonial land revenue settlement continued throughout the latter half of the nineteenth century, for instance, the number of problematic entries in the revenue records slowly began to increase. And, in due course, the rate of litigation rose dramatically. This pattern continued even after 1877, when the original settlement operations were discontinued following the promulgation of a new Land Revenue Act. In fact, after 1877, local settlement officers were simply refashioned as a permanent revenue staff focused on the careful entry of *intiqal*, or 'mutations', in the revenue records themselves—that is, changes in the local *jamabandi* owing to the emergence of voluntary transfers in the form of sale, mortgage, gift or exchange, and, especially, 'involuntary' transfers emerging as a result of inheritance.[17]

Unfortunately, as Settlement Officer C. Minchin pointed out in his summary of the settlement operations undertaken in District Dera Ghazi Khan as early as 1863, this process of recording voluntary and involuntary mutations was not always the most reliable process. As a matter of fact, Minchin wrote, 'the time of [the local] *patwaris* [that is, the village record keepers] is now almost wholly taken up in preparing their annual papers', but, in the preparation of these papers, he noted, 'the details ... are nearly all fictitious and untrustworthy, so that really these *patwaris* are employed for years in adding up imaginary sums, for which they are paid by the *zamindars* [with a percentage of the government demand]'.[18]

With this rather haphazard process in mind, what follows is simply an attempt to describe the disputes that emerged in somewhat greater detail, drawing special attention to the relationship between two very different types of disputes, namely (a) cases involving voluntary transfers (for example, sales and gifts) and (b) cases involving involuntary episodes of complex or contested inheritance.

Significantly, both types of cases refer back to specific debates within the colonial revenue administration regarding the relative importance of individual 'possession' and collective (that is, ancestral or tribal) 'shares'. The colonial state almost invariably preferred the former (that is, individual rights of possession). But, in practice, owing to the evolving interests of local agriculturalists themselves, the latter almost invariably prevailed.

Voluntary Transfers and the Revenue Courts: Partition, Preemption

A certain number of *mal* or 'revenue' cases threw up detailed questions regarding the specific terms of cultivating possession and, especially, detailed allegations involving hereditary proprietors and the competing claims of local occupancy tenants.[19] As important as these cases regarding the claims of local tenants may have been, however, these were not the cases that tended to clog the daily docket of most judges. In fact, the most common disputes did not involve the lives of tenants at all. Instead they tended to involve two or more members of the village coparcenary body (often related members) fighting about the extent of their respective ancestral 'shares'.

In the Punjab, as in the Northwestern Provinces, individual plots could not be permanently alienated—for example, by sale, gift, or exchange—until they had been completely 'separated' or, legally speaking, 'partitioned' from the joint family estate of which they were (originally) considered to be a part. In effect, whole ancestral estates could be exchanged. But, in an effort to preserve the underlying (share-based) parameters of the village 'coparcenary', unpartitioned plots could not.

Even *after* the formal 'partition' of a joint family *khata*—in effect, a joint family estate—into separate 'holdings' or *khewats*, however, neighbouring shareholders reserved what was known as the right of preemption, that is, the right of first refusal with respect to each and every sale within their own ancestral estate.[20] In fact, more often than not, cases regarding so-called 'voluntary' transfers took the form of (a) suits for *taqsim* or 'partition' followed, almost immediately, by (b) suits for *haq-e-shufa* or 'preemption'.

Indeed, as Daya Krishna Kapur pointed out in his study of late-nineteenth and early-twentieth-century litigation patterns, this sequence was extremely common—so common, in fact, that, by the time he completed his study in 1926, the total number of suits for pre-emption in the context of colonial Punjab had risen to 'more than half the total' in the rest of British India combined![21]

The strength of kinship-based collectivities as defined by the terms of the co-sharing village coparcenary, in other words, was almost never unilaterally 'imposed' by the colonial administration. On the contrary, as these cases for preemption clearly reveal, the boundaries of the coparcenary were often tenaciously reinforced even *within* specific suits for 'partition'.[22]

'Possession', if you will, may have emerged as an explicit evolutionary principle. But, in practice, even a cursory glance would reveal that ancestral 'shares' were carefully and deliberately preserved.

Involuntary Transfers and the Civil Courts: Female Disinheritance

In Bengal, Madras, and Bombay, 'involuntary' inheritance cases—that is, cases involving the adjudication of specific ancestral shares—were governed by Hindu law (for Hindus) and Muslim law (for Muslims).

But, in non-regulation territories like the Punjab, these ‘involuntary’ cases were often governed by the terms of local ‘custom’ as recorded in a document known as the *iqrar-nama* or, more commonly, the *wajib-ul-arz* (that is, the ‘village administration paper’ mentioned above). Douie (1899), for his part, referred to the *wajib-ul-arz* as the centrepiece of the settlement report as a whole, mostly because, through its compendium of local habits, norms, and regulations, ‘it intended to show the whole of the constitution of the village’.[23]

After more than forty years of unrivalled preeminence (1822–65), however, the *wajib-ul-arz* was joined and, eventually, superseded by another, even more important (but slightly different) compendium of customs. This compendium was known as the *riwaj-i-am* or the digest of ‘tribal’ custom. And, like the *wajib-ul-arz*, the *riwaj-i-am* intended to capture the whole of the ‘constitution’ of each village through a detailed enumeration of the rules, regulations, and ‘customs’ pertaining to the ownership and inheritance of land.

Like the *wajib-ul-arz*, the *riwaj-i-am* itself amounted to little more than a thin volume containing a series of questions posed to a large gathering of ‘tribal’ elders in each village or *tehsil*.[24] These questions concerned tribal genealogy, marriage, divorce, guardianship, adoption, inheritance, wills, and, oddly enough, the special property of women. In fact ‘the special property of women’ was just one small part of the questionnaire—included, almost as an afterthought, near the very end. But, as an exceptional case, it also illuminated the most important aspect of local custom (by far), namely, the preservation of the village proprietary body through the systematic *exclusion* of women from the ownership (and inheritance) of land.

It is almost impossible to overstate the centrality of this issue, not only with respect to the land revenue administration itself, but also, and perhaps more importantly, with respect to the legal administration and the terms of customary law. Briefly stated, questions regarding the inheritance of agricultural land were decided in the civil courts according to either (a) religious personal law or (b) ‘village’ and (eventually) ‘tribal’ custom. And, throughout the latter half of the nineteenth century, the most important features of ‘tribal’ custom were related to ‘the special property of women’ and, as a closely related issue, the practice of female disinheritance.

In the Punjab, several administrators noted that, as a matter of custom, women were married within their *got* or *biraderi* (that is, within their caste or tribe) but outside of their village-based *zat* or clan. In other words, women were married 'within their caste' but, at the same time, outside of that caste as it existed within the territorial confines of their village.[25] Insofar as they married outside of these territorial confines, however, many administrators went on to note that sisters, daughters, and their children were routinely excluded from the inheritance of agricultural land—and, for that matter, any immovable property—by their brothers, or (when they had no brothers) by their fathers, their uncles, and their grandfathers. In other words, by 'custom', daughters received no immovable property at all if there were also sons, and girls were maintained by their fathers only until the moment of their marriage (outside of their natal village).[26]

Widows, similarly, were maintained by their sons unless a decision was taken to divide or 'partition' the family estate—in which case widows were often provided with a small plot of land in the form of a 'limited' lifetime interest.[27] (Eventually, however, upon the death of such widows, any small plot they may have received was simply returned to the nearest male relatives of 'the last full male owner'. In other words, the widow herself did not 'own' the property that was included in her limited lifetime interest. She was simply 'maintained' by it.)

Certainly, this pattern of female disinheritance was not universal, and initially, settlement officers paid a great deal of attention to specific exceptions.[28] In particular, they noted that female disinheritance was more common in the eastern districts of the Punjab, where the Brahmanical influences of Hindu law prevailed, and less common in the western frontier area, where Muslims tended to enjoy a sizeable majority.[29] Similarly, they noted that, as a deviation from 'religious' personal law, the terms of 'tribal' custom were far more common in rural areas among agricultural tribes (for example, among local Jats and Rajputs) than they were in urban areas among prominent commercial, professional, and religious tribes (for example, among the Arains, the Kashmiris, and the Sheikhs).[30]

If at all the terms of female disinheritance were ignored, however, most administrators went on to point out that the practice of exogamy was typically ignored as well, particularly among local Muslims, who seemed to favour close-cousin 'endogamous' marriages (especially among first cousins) in an effort to keep their land 'in the family'. (See Chapter 2.)

As a general rule, however, most administrators noted that, even in the western districts of colonial Punjab, among 'practicing Muslims', the custom of female disinheritance rarely faltered.[31]

Occasionally, scholars writing about colonial Punjab have noted that, because the colonial revenue administration placed the burden of taxation on the village as a whole, female disinheritance simply emerged, within the colonial state, as a matter of financial necessity.[32] In particular, they argue that married daughters settled away from the village of their birth could not be expected to meet the revenue demands imposed by the colonial state on their home villages. And, *as a result*, they contend, these daughters were simply disinherited in an effort to ensure that their fathers, their brothers, and their uncles were able to meet the colonial revenue demand—disinheritance as a 'consequence' of colonial revenue policy, so to speak, rather than a deliberate defence of enduring (agnatic) norms.

Others insist that, insofar as the colonial state sought to reinforce 'agnatic' forms of (all-male) tribal kinship, families were simply compelled to disinherit their daughters, their sisters, and their mothers (for example, by the colonial courts) despite their own better judgment. In effect, they argue, the disinheritance of local women was merely a legal fiction invented (or exaggerated) by an array of inflexible imperial jurists.

Unfortunately, both of these two views tend to place their theoretical cart before their empirical horse, ignoring the fact that, wherever land was regarded as a valuable commodity, families tended to adhere to the practice of female disinheritance even *before* the British arrived. In addition, they seem to forget that elsewhere in British India—even in places like the Northwestern Provinces, where the *mehalwari* (village-wise) pattern of revenue administration was in force—the colonial courts had a tendency to downplay the terms of 'tribal' custom in an effort to retain (and reinforce) religious personal laws.[33]

Efforts to enforce the custom of female disinheritance in the context of colonial Punjab, in other words, were not a simple extension of colonial policy as it already existed elsewhere in British India. On the contrary, these efforts emerged, throughout the Punjab, as a rather dramatic *revision* of existing colonial policy.

Certainly, the data gathered during the course of late-nineteenth-century settlement operations throughout *both* eastern *and* western Punjab were tied to a series of intense administrative debates—debates that, eventually, elevated the notion of agnatic (all-male) inheritance to the status of a new administrative orthodoxy. Initially, this new orthodoxy was linked to the collection of the colonial land revenue. But eventually, as I will explain, it seemed to acquire a life of its own, becoming the most important feature of (a) late-nineteenth-century colonial efforts to *preserve* the wellbeing of the 'village proprietary body' as well as (b) early-twentieth-century Muslim efforts to *resist* the enforcement of (female-friendly) 'Muslim personal laws'.

On the one hand, of course, the colonial revenue administration remained firmly committed to the introduction and enforcement of 'individual peasant proprietorship' throughout the latter half of the nineteenth century. But, as I will now proceed to explain, both in the remainder of this chapter and in the next, the colonial courts developed a special attachment to the preservation of specific (agricultural) 'tribes', with enormous consequences for the adjudication of local disputes and, more importantly, the inheritance of 'ancestral' agricultural land.

THE CRISIS OF RURAL INDEBTEDNESS

Many insist that the construction of the *jamabandi* in each *mehal* (estate), like the production of the *riwaj-i-am* in each *tehsil* or district, was exceedingly formulaic, at least insofar as it relied on a small number of callow settlement officers armed with nothing more than a regimented set of carefully standardized forms. Others, however, are more reluctant to dismiss the output of these young officers. They claim that the *jamabandi* and the *riwaj-i-am* provide an unprecedented level of insight into the economic and social relations of countless rural villages—an invaluable resource, in a way, for those with an interest in late-nineteenth-century debates and decisions as they actually unfolded 'on the ground'.

In what follows, a number of land revenue settlement operations will be discussed in some detail, first in District Lahore (1860, 1873, 1894), then in Sialkot (1865, 1895), and finally in Shahpur (Sargodha) (1866, 1894).

This review is designed to (a) introduce each of the districts that I will discuss, at various points, throughout the remainder of this book and, then, to (b) shed just a bit more light on the basic allocation, revenue, and legal issues outlined above. It is also designed to illuminate a certain amount of district-wise variation within these issues while, at the same time, beginning to illuminate some of the shifting interests associated with individual landowners within what came to be known, during the latter half of the nineteenth century, as 'the crisis of rural indebtedness'.

The question for local settlement officers in each district was deceptively simple: 'who owns the land'? Along the way, however, this question became increasingly complex. In fact, local efforts to answer this question changed, quite dramatically, over time—from Lahore, in 1860, for instance, to Sialkot just five years later.

The case of Sialkot (1865) is particularly important, and my treatment of it will be somewhat more detailed as a result. Indeed, it would hardly be an exaggeration to say that a certain rather peculiar series of events in District Sialkot (1851–65) changed the course of history throughout colonial Punjab, shifting the focus of the colonial revenue administration away from the rights of individual cultivators with 'possession' towards those of individual owners firmly embedded within particular agricultural 'tribes'. Initially, the impact of this shift was confined to Sialkot. But eventually it extended much further, embracing every family throughout colonial Punjab.

Three Districts

District Lahore: 1860, 1873, 1894

District Lahore lies on the famous Grand Trunk Road halfway between Kabul and Delhi. In the nineteenth century it was dominated by a single urban centre with a strong mix of Hindus, Muslims and Sikhs. Initially, the district itself was composed of three *tehsils*, namely Lahore, Kasur, and Chunian, and within these *tehsils*, the land was evenly divided among *pattidari* and *bhaiachara* estates.

Lahore 1860. The first regular settlement was submitted in 1860 by R.E. Egerton on behalf of his colleagues, Sir Richard Temple, R.H. Davies, and J.H. Morris. Surprisingly, Egerton noted that most of the occupancy tenants in Lahore paid little or no rent to the village *hissadars*. 'It is extraordinary', he remarked, 'to see how the proprietors decline to assert their claims'. 'Even in villages where the assessment has been much reduced', he noted, tenants were allowed 'to retain their holdings [independently] on the payment of the government demand'.[34]

Naturally, many proprietors were well aware of the link between productivity, rent, and the colonial revenue assessment. And, with this in mind, it is entirely possible that many of them simply refused to collect their own private 'rent' in order to avoid (or reduce) the local government 'demand'. Even if this was the case, however, Egerton was deeply perplexed. More often than not, he noted, the *hissadars* of Lahore seemed to misunderstand the value of their proprietary rights altogether. In fact they often seemed to regard these rights as a revenue liability—and nothing else.

Initially, the newly conquered districts of the Punjab had been granted a 10 per cent reduction on the existing government demand.[35] But, as Egerton pointed out, even this did not appear to be enough. On the contrary, he noted that several proprietors simply deserted their villages in order to avoid paying any share of the government demand at all. In other words, as Egerton was quick to point out, the government found itself in a rather awkward position, offering a *further* reduction of 11 per cent in order to draw 'reluctant proprietors' back to their very own land.[36]

Lahore 1873. When L.S. Saunders submitted the second regular settlement of District Lahore thirteen years later, in 1873, little had changed.[37] In fact, Saunders explained, a closer look at the district-level data revealed almost no change at all. If anything, he noted, an increasing number of proprietors had simply begun to use the settlement operations as an opportunity not to *expand* their share of the village land, but rather to *consolidate* (or 'de-fragment') what little land they had. What mattered, in other words, was not the problem of alienation from 'ancestral' rural landowners to 'alien' (mostly urban) moneylenders—at least not yet—but rather a shifting pattern of voluntary exchange among neighbouring 'ancestral' co-sharers.

Turning to the question of local custom, however, Saunders drew special attention to what he regarded as a general shift away from the terms of 'village' custom, as documented in the *wajib-ul-arz*, toward those of 'tribal' custom, as revealed in the *riwaj-i-am*: 'Local laws and customs', he wrote, 'differ with each tribe, caste, or religion, and *not* ... with the village [as a whole]' (emphasis added).[38]

Focusing on local customs concerning marriage, for example, Saunders appeared to be particularly interested in the importance of 'exogamy' and the problems associated with lavish wedding ceremonies. 'Marriages and the expenses attending them', he explained, 'are the most fruitful source of debt' in the district. And, yet, departing from convention, Saunders did not proceed to blame the local *hissadars* for their own extravagance. Instead, he blamed the government. 'Thanks to our light revenue', he wrote, recalling the additional adjustments made by R.E. Egerton in 1860, 'the credit of [the local] *zamindars* is particularly good, and the more money a banker can lend to [him], the more prosperous he becomes'.[39]

In other words, Saunders explained, reflecting a highly unorthodox attitude that would become increasingly prominent over time, the land revenue assessment as a whole had a tendency to threaten precisely those it was ostensibly designed to help—namely, hereditary proprietors. Initially, for instance, the revenue administration seemed to ensure that each proprietor would have enough credit to pay for, say, a lavish wedding. But later on, when that proprietor could not repay his loans, the same administration ensured that the source of his credit—namely, his land—would be summarily transferred to his creditors. In other words, Saunders argued, ongoing efforts to combine local agricultural *interests* with newfangled colonial *institutions* did not appear to construct the terms of economic (or financial) success. Instead, Saunders noted, these efforts appeared to create a recipe for severe and growing unrest.

Lahore 1894. Finally, in 1894, George Casson (G.C.) Walker completed the third regular settlement of Lahore.[40] And, between 1873 and 1894, Walker noted that three important changes had begun to emerge, all of which, for better or worse, pointed to the increasing 'individualization' of colonial landed property rights.

First, Walker drew attention to a noticeable shift away from *pattidari* tenures (defined in terms of ancestral 'shares') to *bhaiachara* tenures (defined in terms of 'possession'). Second, he noted that there had been an increasing number of suits for *taqsim* (that is, the 'partition' of joint family estates). And, finally, he pointed to a growing number of usufructuary mortgages—something he regarded as a sure sign of debt and, eventually, the (permanent) transfer of land from hereditary agriculturalists to ostenensibly 'alien' moneylenders.[41]

Initially, Walker described this move away from *pattidari* toward *bhaiachara* forms of land tenure in terms of local 'cultivation' patterns. But eventually he took his argument one step further, describing this trend in terms of a more general shift away from 'collective' to 'individualized' forms of landownership. Unfortunately, as Walker himself pointed out, this shift in the direction of individualization only seemed to exacerbate the problem of rural indebtedness and the transfer of land from agriculturists to moneylenders. In particular, he noted that, after a joint family *khata* was partitioned (for example, in favour of existing ancestral shares) many small owners found themselves holding quite a bit more land—in fact, more land than they could handle. And, owing to the limited productivity of the land in their possession, they often found that they were unable to pay their share of the local government demand.

As a result, Walker noted, many local proprietors were forced to mortgage their land to larger owners (and, increasingly, to moneylenders as well), becoming, for all intents and purposes, occupancy 'tenants' on their own 'ancestral' land.

Others, however, eager to enjoy a higher standard of living as quickly as possible, offered up their newly partitioned shares as collateral for short-term loans, driving themselves further and further into debt. In fact, Walker explained, the first owner may have had 'more land than he [could] manage', but the second was simply careless. 'Flushed with his sudden prosperity', he noted, the second simply 'rushed into extravagant and disorderly living, which, [more often than not], ended in his total ruin and the transfer of ... his land'.[42] In other words, Walker explained, what began with a simple loan (or mortgage) concluded with a massive disruption in the strength of the (ancestral) community, and, in many cases, the stability of the state as a whole.

District Sialkot: 1865, 1895

District Sialkot lies approximately one hundred miles outside of Lahore in the submontane region of northern Punjab. On a clear day the snowy peaks of Kashmir are visible from its rooftops. The land surrounding the main *qasbah*, or town, was divided, throughout the latter half of the nineteenth century, into four *tehsils*, namely Sialkot, Daska, Pasrur, and Zafarwal. And, when Edward Augustus (E.A.) Prinsep finally completed his first regular settlement report in 1865, the district itself was divided into 1,976 (mostly *pattidari*) estates, each of which had been surveyed by two *patwaris*, a *chaudhary purtal*, or village headman, and a supervisor, who 'checked the entries and attested the work as it proceeded on the spot'. In fact, according to Mr Prinsep, renowned for his meticulousness, the notion of a 'speedy settlement' had been 'positively prohibited'.[43]

Sialkot 1865. In 1865, Prinsep devoted most of his attention to a number of rather important changes in the *bachh* (that is, the method of distributing the government demand among all of the 'shareholding' *hissadars*). In fact, referring to his work near the hamlet of Shikargarh, and more specifically his 'rediscovery' of local ancestral 'shares', he wrote: 'The experience of one *pergunah*, [namely, Shikargarh, suggested that], ... if precautionary steps were not taken ... villages [may be] registered as belonging to one class of tenure, and that possession was the measure of a man's right, when [in fact] ... shares *did* exist, and were not only recognized, but actually followed'.[44]

Indeed the practical steps that Prinsep used to ensure an accurate settlement in Shikargarh played an important part in the formulation of his own rather specific ideas—in particular, his attempt to construct a detailed *shajra nasb*, or genealogical tree, *before* proceeding with the construction of the settlement as a whole. 'Seeing how property is held almost universally by *tribes*, how [much] more readily understood is a *share* as the expression of a man's liability', he remarked, 'I am not surprised that there should be this adherence to the *putteedaree* type of tenure' (emphasis added).[45]

By far the most important consequence of the first regular settlement in Sialkot, however, was the bitter debate it produced in the context of emerging ideas about the substance of local customs ('village' v. 'tribal' custom) throughout colonial Punjab—a debate that culminated, three years later, in the promulgation of the Punjab Tenancy Act of 1868.

At the heart of this debate lay considerable uncertainty about the rights of 'hereditary cultivators with possession'. These cultivators had been given clearly defined proprietary-cum-ownership rights during the Preliminary Settlement of Sialkot overseen by a senior revenue official named Sir Richard Temple. But, in several cases, these rights were set aside, and eventually cancelled, by Mr Temple's subordinate—in fact his understudy—Mr Prinsep.[46]

The consequences of this rather bold manoeuvre, however, were not confined to Sialkot. In fact, before long, they echoed all the way from Lahore to London, engaging many of the most influential administrators in the (by now enormous) British Empire. The specific disagreements that Prinsep unleashed will be discussed in greater detail in Chapter 2. But a brief summary is necessary here as well, particularly insofar as these debates affected the work of the colonial land revenue administration after 1865.

Sir Richard Temple, for his part, represented the venerable tradition of The Punjab School, a tradition deeply committed to the preservation of the village proprietary body. And, for the most part, Temple's first (preliminary) settlement acknowledged cultivating 'possession', measured in terms of ploughs, or the amount of land that could be cultivated by a single pair of bullocks, as the measure of a specific proprietary 'right'. In other words, following Thomas Munro in Madras and the Benthamite ideas espoused by James Mill in his well-known *History of British India* (1817), Temple placed his emphasis not on the identification of individual 'landlords', but rather on the identification of individual 'cultivators' living within each village community. He simply redefined these cultivators (by executive fiat) as village 'proprietors' with specific 'ownership' rights.

In fact, as Temple was quick to point out during the first (preliminary) settlement, most villages throughout Sialkot were only too willing to include as many 'cultivator-owners' as possible. Under the Sikhs, he noted, proprietorship had been seen as a burden more than a benefit. And, as a result, there was little reason to object when the British proposed a wider distribution of the existing government demand. 'In those days', Temple argued, 'the competition was for tenants rather than for land, [so] proprietors were only too happy to see us record [those tenants] as occupancy *ryots*' (that is, cultivating proprietors).[47]

Within the space of just a few years, however, Temple was compelled to add that, increasingly, as the stability of the colonial regime and the limited nature of its settlement demands became more widely known, 'the competition was coming to be for land rather than for tenants'. And, indeed, he noted, *'the landlords might probably have changed their opinions'* (emphasis added).[48]

Certainly, when E.A. Prinsep arrived to complete the work originally undertaken by Mr Temple, the situation 'on the ground' had changed dramatically. Above all, Prinsep found that the stability of the colonial administration had increased the value of the land and, as a result, many 'long-lost proprietors' had begun to reassert their rights, not in terms of ploughs or cultivating 'possession', but rather in terms of specific ancestral 'shares'. Needless to say, this led to the *de facto* exclusion of many occupancy tenants, including those with 'proprietary' or 'ownership' rights granted, just a few years before, by Temple.

As noted above, however, Prinsep simply cancelled the work of his mentor, returning the benefits of individual proprietorship, at least as he understood them, to those with a claim to specific *ancestral* 'shares'.[49]

At the time, appealing to the increasingly famous work of Sir Henry Sumner Maine, Prinsep attributed his approach to an intimate acquaintance with the history of 'the village community'. In fact, as G.R.G. Hambly (1964) explains, 'Prinsep believed that his predecessors had constructed the record of rights without [any] reference to the past history of the province and, by ignoring existing relationships within the village community, had committed [a] very real injustice'.[50]

Unfortunately, despite this appeal to the historical sensibility of Sir Henry Sumner Maine, Maine himself embraced the 'evolutionary' terms of the official revenue doctrine, and, in due course, sided with Temple—somewhat further along the evolutionary continuum—arguing that, wherever possible, and for the sake of 'progress', 'possession' should be used as the measure of proprietary right, not ancestral 'shares'.

Sir John Lawrence, the Governor of the Punjab, simply changed his mind in the middle of the debate. Initially, he praised Prinsep for his energy, his assiduity and his enthusiasm. But eventually he adopted a more critical view, asking why the members of the village proprietary body in places like Shikargarh had refused to claim exclusive ownership rights 'in the first place', that is, when Temple was in Sialkot several years before. 'The Punjabee is not backward to complain', Lawrence wrote to Prinsep in the summer of 1866. 'How came he to be silent for so many years'?[51]

Clearly, Lawrence noted, the landowners themselves seemed rather fickle, if not altogether conflicted. And yet, I would argue, they *were* conflicted. In fact, just a few years earlier, the proprietors of District Sialkot had been extremely eager to distribute the rights of ownership as widely as possible. Temple, therefore, was not 'wrong' in his assessment; he simply offered his assessment 'before' the situation had changed. Indeed, by 1865, the proprietors of Sialkot were no longer interested in distributing their rights as widely as possible. Instead they were interested in *limiting* the distribution of these rights to those with ancestral 'shares'.

What changed, of course, was the situation 'on the ground'. Indeed the increasing value of land had conditioned the replies offered by the same landowners living in the same villages at different points in time, leading Temple and Prinsep to draw completely different conclusions about the relative importance of 'cultivating' and 'ancestral' ('individual' and 'collective') landed property relations. In fact, every indication seems to suggest that their sources were the same (namely, the hereditary cultivators of District Sialkot), but times had changed, and, as a result, their data (grounded in the opinions expressed by a common pool of local elites) were almost entirely different.

Needless to say, the controversy surrounding this dilemma was profound. In fact, it was probably the most important controversy in late-nineteenth-century colonial Punjab. Who was right? Who had his finger on the pulse of 'the village community'? Who was in touch with the 'preferences' of the local proprietors themselves?

Some insisted that Temple was pro-tenant (that is, pro-cultivator), whereas Prinsep was pro-landlord (pro-proprietor). Others, seeking to expand upon this point, claimed that Temple was committed to the advancement of 'individual' rights (possession), whereas Prinsep was devoted to the preservation of specific 'family' shares. Some maintain that Temple was more 'progressive', defending the rights of tenants, but others simply turn this equation upside down, arguing that Prinsep was more 'progressive' insofar as he sought to reinforce the 'ancestral' rights of widows (that is, women with 'limited' lifetime estates) and minors.

The fact of the matter, however, is fairly clear. Both men drew their inspiration from Maine, and both drew a certain amount of strength from enduring contradictions within the colonial state. Indeed, as Hambly himself points out, 'there is no reason to suppose that [Prinsep] derived his ideas solely from the ... English or Bengali enthusiasm for landlords'. On the contrary, Hambly notes, 'his training and experience had been almost wholly within the Punjab [itself]'. In other words, Prinsep merely 'diagnosed a malaise which even his opponents recognized to be there, and [he based] his proceedings ... not upon any theoretical assumptions, but [rather] upon empirical investigation'.[52] In fact scholars are generally inclined to admit that, when it came to the first (preliminary) and second (regular) settlement of Sialkot, Temple was relatively hasty and ideological, whereas Prinsep was empirically sensitive and meticulous.

Sialkot 1895. Thirty years later, in 1895, J.R. Dunlop-Smith submitted the second (revised) settlement of District Sialkot.[53] Already the population of the district had grown to more than a million, of whom nearly 920,000 lived in rural areas. Within these areas, however, each proprietor was associated with an average *khata* amounting to just three acres, suggesting that the fragmentation of agricultural land was already well under way. In fact, with this in mind, Dunlop-Smith went out of his way to highlight two recent trends, namely (a) the shift from *pattidari* to *bhaiachara* forms of land tenure and (b) the growing number of 'permanent' (as opposed to 'temporary' or 'mortgage-based') alienations.[54]

Cutting straight to the heart of the matter, Dunlop-Smith noted that, throughout Sialkot, tribal subdivisions (that is, *pattis*) were generally eager to maintain their commitment to specific ancestral shares, according to 'the general thrust of popular opinion', even when the individual members living *within* a particular *patti* 'abandoned' those shares and opted to record their liabilities in terms of (individualized) cultivating possession.[55]

Fig. 5. Shifting land tenures: *pattidari*, *bhaiachara*

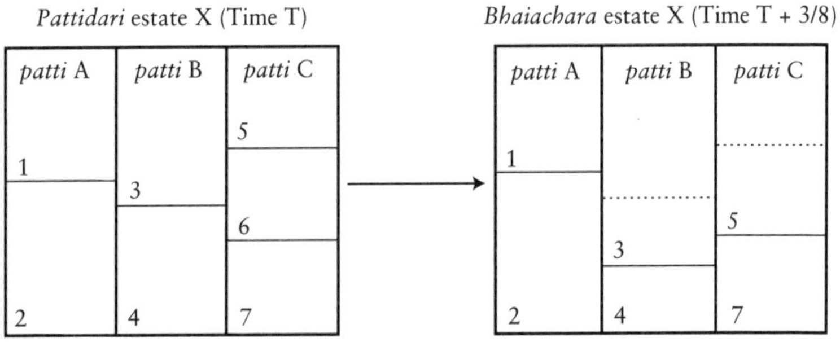

N.b. Discrete *pattis* remain intact even as specific 'shares' begin to shift.

When considered at the level of local *pattis*, in other words, Dunlop-Smith explained that the 'individualization' of landed property rights was not at all incompatible with the consolidation, or at least the preservation, of local 'tribal' solidarities (see Fig. 5 above: *pattis* A, B, and C). As a matter of fact, he argued, the structure of the colonial administration made it possible to achieve both goals—that is, both individualization and enduring forms of 'tribal' or *patti*-based solidarity—simultaneously.

Throughout his assessment, however, the prevailing form of land tenure (*pattidari* v. *bhaiachara*) struck Dunlop-Smith as far less important than the increasing number of legally 'permanent' alienations. In fact, he argued, the land revenue administration would carry on regardless of the form of land tenure, but the increasing number of alienations threatened to remove existing landowners altogether (with profound implications for the stability of the state itself). 'In 1865', he wrote, recalling the work of E.A. Prinsep, '*zamindars* and ... moneylenders had hardly begun to realize the stability of tenure assured to the former by ... British rule and the consequent large increase in the value of the security they could offer'. But 'since then', he added (in 1895), '[the] expropriation of the old landowning class[es] has gone on briskly'.[56]

District Sargodha: 1866, 1894

District Sargodha is located approximately one hundred fifty miles from Lahore in the dry, dusty region of western Punjab. In 1866, Gore Ouseley and W.G. Davies submitted the first regular settlement of what, at the time, was known as District Shahpur. Drawing attention to the most striking feature of the district—namely its desolation—they noted that 'of this vast tract no less than 89 percent is in a state of nature'. 'But', they added, foreshadowing some of the most important economic changes in the history of colonial Punjab, 'it may confidently be stated that the want of the means of irrigation is the sole obstacle in the way of its gradual reclamation'.[57]

Sargodha 1866. According to Ouseley and Davies, three issues lay at the heart of District Shahpur and its (colonial) administration. These three issues concerned: (a) village boundary disputes, (b) village tenures, and (c) local customs regarding the inheritance rights of women. In Shahpur, unlike Sialkot, they explained, the primary shift was not from 'ancestral' rights to cultivating 'possession'. Instead it was a gradual shift from 'no clearly defined rights at all' to rights based loosely on 'the possession of tribal kinship factions'.

According to Ouseley and Davies, this shift began with a series of rather acrimonious boundary disputes. 'When regular settlement operations commenced' five years after the annexation of the Punjab, in 1854, Ouseley remarked, the local *zamindars*, 'knowing our respect for prescriptive rights, determined to divide the ... jungle among themselves'. 'They accordingly established little outposts with a few men and a few head of cattle ... at distances of several miles round the parent village'. And, having done so, they proposed 'to encircle [these cattle] all in one ring fence, which was [supposed] to represent their village boundary—[in effect, the extent of their ownership]'.[58]

As Ouseley pointed out, however, this practice threatened to allow 'a few thousand cattle grazers' to appropriate the entire desert as their own valuable property.[59] Departing from the methods adopted in the fertile districts of Lahore and Sialkot, therefore, the demarcation of the villages in District Shahpur did not follow the possession of 'land' *per se*. Instead, it followed the possession of 'cattle'. 'The villages were called [upon] to state how many head of cattle they possessed', Ouseley explained, 'and they were allowed a certain area of wasteland calculated upon the number of their cattle at four acres per head'.[60]

Nevertheless, Ouseley discovered, disputes were frequent and lively. Above all, Ouseley found that it was exceedingly difficult to count the number of cattle in each village. In fact, more often than not, villagers would acquire cattle on a temporary basis in order to increase their allocation of the surrounding land. '[The] villages are almost all connected with each other by relationship or marriage', he explained, 'and they used to shift their cattle, not only into each other's villages, but even into the neighbouring districts'.[61]

Furthermore, Ouseley and Davies found that the boundaries between villages were unclear, if not altogether invisible. At one point, for instance, Ouseley was called upon to adjudicate a boundary dispute between the *zamindars* of Mitha Tiwana and Ookleymohlan. 'I found that the disputed boundary was nearly ten miles from one village and seven miles from the other', Ouseley wrote, and 'the dispute itself extended over five or six miles of desert'.[62] 'During my ride', he explained, he was taken, 'by one party or the other, to see the marks of their *kubza* [that is, their possession], which were little patches of ground of the size of a quarter of an acre or so, scattered over distances of a mile or more from each other, in which somebody had sown a few seeds of *bajra*, which had never ripened owing to want of rain'. 'The existence of these spots', he wrote, 'appeared to be known [only] to a few men on either side, and from the recriminations which used to follow on their being brought to notice, I believe [that] they were ploughed up and the seeds cast secretly at night, and then neglected altogether, as the object was not to attract the attention of the opposite party to the progress that was being made in securing ground until the settlement *ahilkars* [officials] should commence [their] operations'.[63]

Obviously, Davies concluded, 'the lands in dispute belong to no one in particular, and owing to the contending parties being the *mullicks* [that is, the 'proprietors'] of Mitha Tiwana and the neighbouring *zamindars*, the process of taking evidence would lead to a great deal of false swearing and [a pattern of] endless delay'.[64] (For a related pattern, see Chapter 5.)

Even if the existing village boundaries were not entirely clear, and the division of the government demand among the members of the village proprietary body was equally problematic, however, the form of land tenure in the village was (quite unexpectedly) almost never in dispute. 'Pedigree tables had been drawn out in the first instance', Davies reported, following the lead established by E.A. Prinsep in Sialkot just a few years before, 'but it was found that, although the genealogies of the village communities were well known, and there *were* often *turufs* and *puttees*, or as they are called here *vurhees*, ... these had not been acted on for several generations'.[65] In fact, Davies reported, 'possession prevailed according to [village] custom or usage and *not* ... ancestral shares' (emphasis added).[66]

The prevalance of *bhaiachara* villages, however, raised a number of rather familiar questions regarding the status of 'hereditary cultivators with possession'. Indeed, Davies remarked, 'the term "hereditary cultivator" [that is, occupancy tenant] was not understood in the district of Shahpoor for several years after the annexation of the Punjab'. In particular, he noted that 'there were parties who, though they had no claim to proprietary title, asserted a claim to cultivate the land in their possession'.[67] '[I] first enquired whether the cultivator asserted any proprietary claims', Davies explained, but 'as a rule, [I found] such a claim ... rarely raised'. In particular, he noted that, 'among Mahomedans, the idea of hereditary property is very strong, and a man whose family has been one hundred years out of possession is still popularly recognized as the owner of what once belonged to his ancestors'. As a result, he noted, 'the cultivator at once answered that he was not the owner, but that such a person was'.[68]

If nothing else, then, Ouseley and Davies drew considerable attention to a number of enduring *contradictions* within the colonial regime, contradictions that grew out of the uncertain status of 'hereditary cultivators with possession'. On the one hand, of course, Davies himself claimed to follow the rule of possession, designating most villages as *bhaiachara* villages. But, on the other, he readily admitted that, in most cases, those with cultivating 'possession' explicitly *denied* any 'proprietary' claims. In fact he noted that, despite the existence of a *bhaiachara bachh*, only cultivators with 'ancestral' claims were recognized (locally) as 'proprietors'.[69]

In any event, Ouseley and Davies noted that the number of disputes concerning landed property rights in the district courts of Shahpur equalled, if it did not actually exceed, the total number of cases in any other district. The most common types of dispute, moreover, were those in which 'parties out of possession sued those in possession for whole villages or for particular plots of land'.[70] (Needless to say, these remain the most common types of dispute even today.)

But there was a second type of dispute, involving inheritance, which was also exceedingly common. In fact these two rather different categories of disputes, one regarding possession and the other regarding inheritance, were not entirely unrelated. As Davies was quick to point out, most disputes boiled down to cases in which 'parties in possession of a certain portion of land sued a descendent of [their] common ancestor, [one who was] in possession of a larger share, [in order] to obtain [a] reallotment in accordance with [their alleged] ancestral shares'.[71]

Disagreeing with Prinsep, however, Davies noted that most of these claims for partition in favour of (agnatic) ancestral shares were rejected. 'Enquiry everywhere showed [us] that, as far as the memory of living men carried them back, possession had been unequal'.[72] And, in keeping with the designation of most villages as *bhaiachara* villages, in which the terms of 'possession' prevailed (albeit *within* existing *pattis*), Davies added that possession was regarded as 'the sole criterion for regulating each man's rights and liabilities', the only exception being the partition of lands formerly held in common—that is, the formal reclassification of *zamindari mushtarka* lands as newfangled *pattidari* estates.[73]

Indeed, this was consistent with the policy of the colonial government as a whole—a policy summed up, with stunning conviction and remarkable simplicity, by Lieutenant-Governor D.F. McLeod in 1867. 'It is remarkable', he wrote, 'with what tenacity ancestral claims have been urged, and how freely they have been conceded in most parts of the Punjab [for example, in District Sialkot], notwithstanding vicissitudes which have vastly altered the state of actual holdings from that of ancestral title'. And yet, McLeod added, driving a wedge between the work of E.A. Prinsep in Sialkot and that of Ouseley and Davies in Shahpur, 'the tendency in all village systems must be more or less to lead to the formation of coparcenaries in which ... *possession alone* determines the [individual's revenue] share' (emphasis added).[74]

Sargodha 1894. More than twenty-five years later, in 1894, however, J. Wilson submitted the second regular settlement of District Shahpur.[75] And, as Wilson pointed out, much had changed. In particular, he noted that the number of agriculturists in Shahpur had risen by more than 60 per cent, from 33,641 to 54,023, even as the size of the average holding had *also* increased, by more than 40 per cent, from 9 to 13 acres. What accounted for this rather unusual development was of course the extension of canal irrigation and, thus, an increasing amount of fertile agricultural land. In fact, Wilson explained, Shahpur had had only 2,192 acres of canals in 1866, but by 1894 this number had jumped to 87,654. Indeed, with the introduction of canals—in this case, the introduction of 'private' canals supported by specific 'tribal' elites seeking to reinforce prevailing patterns of local 'tribal' dominance—the amount of cultivable land had more than trebled.[76]

In order to account for the social, ecological, and political impact, and indeed the sheer magnitude of this change, a brief description of canal colony irrigation (and, more specifically, the pattern of agricultural resettlement that accompanied the establishment of canal colonies within the colonial state) is essential.[77]

In his brief monograph entitled 'Colonization in the Rechna Doab' (1929), for instance, Deva Singh described the colonization process in District Lyallpur (now known as Faisalabad)—a prototypical canal colony established after 1882 between the Ravi and the Chenab Rivers. Between 1892 and 1909, he noted, nearly 19 million acres had been opened up for colonization and systematically allotted to peasants from the more densely populated districts of eastern Punjab (including, for example, Lahore and Sialkot). The canal colonies, he explained, were a remarkable economic and engineering achievement. But, even more than this, he noted that their most important features concerned demographics. In fact, he argued, 'the new canal colonies were intended ... to colonize the area', in demographic terms, with 'well-to-do yeomen of the best class who would constitute healthy agricultural communities of the best Punjab type'.[78]

The most important feature of the canal colonies, in other words, concerned their approach to the resettlement of specific agricultural 'tribes'. 'Generally speaking', Singh noted, 'the peasant grantees (*abadkars*) in each village belong to the same tribe, profess the same religion, and originate from the same home district'. In fact, he explained, even army pensioners were settled 'with due reference to regiments, as well as tribes, religions, and districts'.[79]

Thus, Singh argued, the larger part of each resettlement effort was devoted to a meticulous characterization of various tribes in terms of their (allegedly inherent) 'cultivating potential'. The Jat Sikhs from Amritsar, for example, were described in terms of 'their fine physique, their thrifty habits, and their capacity for patient toil'; the Arains of Hoshiarpur, Jullundur, and Lodhiana were 'good' agriculturists, 'submissive, hardworking, and frugal'; and so on.[80]

In countless ways, the canal colonies of western Punjab were carefully 'contrived' communities. In fact it could be said that, in the pattern of their development and the nature of their subsequent colonization, these colonies exhibited late-nineteenth-century ideas about the village community, the village proprietary body, land revenue administration, and 'tribal' custom more clearly than any other setting. For the purposes of this book, in fact, what is interesting is not the extent to which these colonies departed from the norm. Instead, the really interesting dimension lies in the extent to which they extended—and, in many ways, even exaggerated—that norm, for example, turning areas that were previously *bhaiachara* areas in which 'possession' was regarded as the measure of individual rights into areas in which (agnatic) 'ancestral' claims mattered at least as much (if not more).

Indeed, the case of Shahpur is illuminating precisely insofar as well-known 'tribal' leaders, including the Tiwanas and the Noons, anticipated, assimilated and extended the ideas of the colonial state, using the construction of 'private' canals to cement the idiom of 'tribal' solidarity (and 'tribal' control) even beyond the limits of existing 'village' communities.

When J. Wilson returned to complete the second regular settlement of District Shahpur in 1894, therefore, he devoted special attention to two issues, both of which involved the special significance, the stability, and the security of local agricultural 'tribes'. The first concerned an apparent increase in the number of cases for *taqsim* or 'partition' within existing ancestral estates. The second concerned specific trends in the 'alienation' of (ancestral) agricultural land.

On the one hand, of course, Wilson regarded the increasing number of cases for 'partition' as a positive trend, at least insofar as it furthered the individualization of landed property rights (or so he believed). At the same time, however, Wilson noted that individual cases for partition were not encouraged, but rather resisted, by the courts, which tended to insist on the preservation of local 'customs' as recorded in the *riwaj-i-am*. Wilson was obviously peeved at this. In fact he continued to insist that '[the] rapid separation of rights in the land is a marked feature in the progress of [any] district'. 'It is', he wrote referring to 'the principles of political economy', 'a great advantage, as an owner put in separate possession ... is likely to develop [his land] much faster and cultivate it much better than he did when other shareholders might claim a portion of the joint holding in his possession'. Nevertheless, and despite his own deeply held convictions regarding the natural course of 'progress', Wilson was prepared to concede that, when all was said and done, partition also had its 'drawbacks', mostly involving the conflict between *pattidari* and *bhaiachara* forms of land tenure.[81]

'In a considerable number of estates', Wilson wrote, drawing attention to some of the contradictions lying at the very centre of the colonial regime, 'a clause was entered in the administration paper [at the time of the] regular settlement saying that the whole or a defined portion of the common land [that is, the *shamilat*] should *not* be considered liable to partition, but should always be kept common property, for the grazing of the cattle of the whole community'. And, yet, Wilson noted, 'in some cases, circumstances have so altered—more specifically where canal irrigation has been made available—as to make it highly desirable, in the interests of ... the landowners, that a portion of this reserved land *should* be divided and brought under cultivation' (emphasis added). Unfortunately, he wrote, in an effort to vent some of his own accumulating frustration, 'both the revenue and the civil courts have so far practically held that the clause referred to [above] *forbids* the owners to divide the land until all interested [parties within the village or the *patti*] agree' to the partition—something that Wilson himself regarded as 'an almost impossible condition'.

Nevertheless, Wilson argued, the letter of the law mattered very little in practice. 'It is', he noted, cutting straight to the heart of the matter, quite common for 'energetic and unscrupulous sharers in the common land to take possession of a portion of it and exclude from it their weaker neighbours' despite the strict terms of the law. In other words, he explained, the number of 'formally registered partitions' had not increased, but—in Shahpur at least—the *de facto* partition of the commons was already well under way.[82]

It is, however, important to keep in mind that those who interpreted this trend as a sweeping push for 'the individualization of landed property rights' may have jumped the gun. First of all, it is important to note that full-fledged legal 'partitions' were always extremely rare. And, secondly, among those that actually occurred (even illegally), it is important to recognise that most merely shifted the focus of local tenures away from *zamindari mushtarka* to *pattidari* tenures. In other words, the primary importance attached to 'ancestral shares' was only rarely disturbed, and, I would argue, it was almost never destroyed. (See Fig. 5, above.) In fact, even illegal partitions had a tendency to extend (or consolidate) the holdings of specific 'tribal' leaders *within* a particular local *patti*, implying 'factional' consolidation more than explicit 'individual' control.

Even as the total number of individuals controlling access to the village commons grew smaller and smaller, then, collective obligations and agnatic kinship, as the organizing principles of the community, were scarcely abandoned. In fact if anything they were simply redefined in favour of 'tribal' elites.

Turning, finally, to the (increasingly familiar) question of alienation, however, Wilson noted that the amount of land sold in District Shahpur each year had climbed to 3 per cent of the total land in the district (excluding state land). And, drawing attention to the primary source of anxiety among his contemporaries, Wilson noted that 'about half of this fraction annually passes into the hands of [alien] non-agriculturalists'.[83]

'The chief cause' of this disturbing trend, Wilson explained, referring to the problem of alienation to non-agriculturalists, was '[the] great rise in the money value of land, which [has] made the [mostly Hindu] moneylending classes anxious to get a hold upon it by advancing money on every opportunity to improvident Musalman landowners'. This, 'combined with [the colonial] legal system, which [made] it possible to obtain and execute decrees containing more interest than capital', had produced a number of rather unsettling trends, most of which concerned (a) the rapid fragmentation of the village proprietary body (in favour of 'non-agriculturalists'), (b) the destabilization of the colonial budget, and, ultimately, (c) the growing possibility of widespread rural unrest.[84]

The Rural Indebtedness Crisis

Rural indebtedness and the alienation of land to satisfy existing moneylender contracts flew in the face of everything prominent British administrators believed about the village proprietary body, the village community, and the terms of customary law. On the one hand, of course, the sale of land to satisfy existing contracts was merely the logical extension of existing proprietary rights. And, yet, at the same time, the sale of land from 'agriculturalists' to 'moneylenders' pointed to the fragmentation of joint family ownership and, in a growing number of cases, the disintegration of the village proprietary body. In short, the sale of land to local moneylenders pointed to the triumph of 'possession' over ancestral shares, 'alienation' over inheritance, and 'individual' over collective landed property relations.

Once upon a time, these trends might have been welcomed as a sign of economic and social 'progress'. But, as the nineteenth century drew to a close, these trends were increasingly regarded as economically troublesome, socially disruptive, even subversive. More often than not, Douie noted in his famous *Settlement Manual* (1899), 'a large amount of land transfer, especially when the purchasers and mortgagees are moneylenders, is a sign of embarrassment among the landowning classes, and the rapid growth of [such] alienations in any tract is an unhealthy symptom'.[85]

Broadly speaking, the origins of this late-nineteenth-century rural indebtedness crisis lay in the economic dislocations of the late 1860s, when international prices for products like cotton collapsed following the end of the American Civil War. Naturally, the fall in prices associated with this collapse led an increasing number of agriculturists to take out significant loans. But, as the colonial administration was quick to point out, these loans were not taken to cover the cost of agricultural improvements or land revenue payments. Instead they were used to cover the cost of lavish weddings, gambling debts, and the high cost of civil litigation. And, when these loans could not be repaid, moneylenders visited the district courts, arguing that the sale of land must be authorized to recover lingering debts.

The sale of land, however, typically involved the partition and hence the fragmentation of joint family holdings, and thus the infiltration of 'hereditary' *pattis* by 'alien' moneylenders with no ancestral links to the land—all in all, a source of considerable economic and political concern for innumerable colonial administrators.[86]

In 1897, Sir Denzil Ibbetson, the Lieutenant-Governor of the Punjab, was appointed Secretary to the Government of India. Almost immediately, the number of mutations involving the alienation of agricultural land to moneylenders (not to mention the crush of civil litigation surrounding these mutations) became his central concern. This was a rather complex source of concern, however, because, according to Ibbetson, the colonial revenue administration deserved a certain amount of *praise* for the introduction of individual landed property rights—widely regarded as a source of considerable satisfaction throughout rural Punjab. And, yet, at the same time, Ibbetson was also keen to note that the revenue administration deserved a certain amount of *blame* for the reckless extension of rural credit, and hence, recalling the work of L.S. Saunders (1873 Lahore), the reckless extravagance of so many individual proprietors.

The legal administration, similarly, was duly acknowledged for its role in clarifying and preserving the institutional bond between individual tenants, landowners, *lambardars*, and the colonial state. But it was also blamed for compromising this bond whenever it enforced the sale of 'ancestral' agricultural land.

'It is no answer to say that in the vast majority of cases [these] transfers are voluntary', noted Ibbetson, because 'in the first place it is our system that has, for the first time, made such transfers possible'.

'But that is not all', he added. 'At every step of the process, from the beginning to the end, our system makes it easier for the landowner to plunge into debt, and assists the moneylender in dragging him down'. 'We may not make the contracts', he argued, 'but it is we [who] enforce them'.[87] And of course, as one officer pointed out, 'tropical storms break suddenly'. 'The Indian peasant', he argued, 'endures till endurance is no longer possible; then follow riot, arson, and murder, as in the Deccan in 1875 or, still more dangerous, rebellion in times of stress, as in the Northwestern Provinces in 1857'.[88]

Occasionally, in their efforts to garner support for the cause of rural 'stability', the advocates of reform drew attention to macro-level concerns like the strength of the colonial budget or 'the security of the western frontier'. But, more often than not, colonial administrators turned to the minutiae of the revenue records and, more specifically, the terms of an enduring clash between and among two rather hostile administrative traditions: utilitarian theories of individual peasant proprietorship, on the one hand, and historically embedded ideas about the tenacity of 'tribal' custom, on the other.

Sir John Strachey, for his part, represented the utilitarian tradition of James Mill, Thomas Munro, James Thomason, and Sir Richard

Temple. 'Whatever sentimental regret might be caused by the break-up of the old village communities and the transfer of ownership to the moneylending classes', Strachey wrote, 'these things were part of the unalterable march of progress'.[89] And, yet, even as Strachey articulated this rather familiar 'neoliberal' refrain, those committed to the preservation of the village proprietary body vehemently and consistently disagreed. In fact, as one officer from the Central Provinces by the name of J.A. Temple pointed out, Strachey's notion of progress frequently amounted to little more than a reprehensible racket in practice. 'When proprietary rights were first bestowed', Temple explained, recalling the experience of R.E. Egerton in Lahore (1860), these rights 'were so little understood and appreciated that in many instances ... persons had to be brought in and ordered to lay claim to the villages'.[90]

Nevertheless, Temple added, drawing special attention to the underlying terms of his own rather paternalistic critique, it quickly became known to local moneylenders 'what [this] gift [of proprietorship] really meant', particularly when local shareholders discovered that 'by signing papers, the meaning of which was quite unintelligible to them, they could have sums [of credit] which seemed illimitable to them to squander'. And, yet, he argued, 'when the day of reckoning arrived', and the debts of these common shareholders were finally called in, 'they came to know what they had done, but [by then] it was too late'. 'In this way', he recalled, 'enormous areas (and many hundreds of estates) have been acquired for merely nominal sums by some of the local moneylenders'.[91]

The question, Temple argued, did not concern the fact of rural indebtedness as it related to the extension of specific rights in land. Instead it concerned the political implications of this relationship. And on this point J.A. Temple acknowledged that the debate was alive and well. According to Sir Richard Temple, writing in Lahore, in 1865, these events were just another sign of economic and social 'progress'. But according to J.A. Temple, writing just a few years later, in Chhattisgarh (Central Provinces), they were a sign of impending political 'disaster'.

Initially, few of those sitting in Lahore agreed with J.A. Temple, located nearly a thousand miles away. But, when the Central Provinces exploded in a rage of rural unrest (1875), many of those sitting in Lahore began to change their minds.

The Problem: Economic Choices, Political Consequences

As events began to shift in the Central Provinces after 1875, Justice C.S. Lindsay of the Lahore High Court continued to insist that there was no immediate cause for alarm. The alienation of land from agriculturalists to moneylenders, he argued, merely demonstrated the successful introduction of landed property rights and the transfer of these rights from 'inefficient' to 'productive' owners—in other words, the successful introduction of a lively market economy.[92]

To illustrate this point, Lindsay turned to the revenue records, arguing that fears about the widespread and increasing alienation of land from 'agriculturalists' to 'moneylenders' were simply unfounded. Reviewing mutations made between 1869 and 1874, for instance, he pointed out that the sale of agricultural land throughout the Punjab was actually extremely rare.

According to Lindsay, for instance, court-sanctioned sales were almost entirely unknown (only one in five years) and, even beyond this, voluntary sales were exceedingly uncommon (6,000 per year, involving 0.3 per cent of the proprietors). The average area of revenue-paying land involved in these sales, moreover, was in fact astonishingly small (less than one acre per square mile). And, in any case, he noted, 'there appears to be no valid reason for supposing that all these transfers, whether by sale or usufructuary mortgage, are made to the moneylending class, or are in consequence of [the] pressures [exerted by] debts'. On the contrary, he found that *most* land transfers were made, '*not* to ... bankers, but [rather] to brother-agriculturalists', a pattern explained, at least in part, by existing laws of preemption.[93]

'I am no advocate for the sale of land indiscriminately by the courts', he declared, 'but there are cases where there is no remedy and the sale of the debtor's land must take place'. Loan agreements, in other words, must be enforced. 'What is the use of supporting a thoroughly careless, extravagant landlord'? he asked. The policy of the British should be 'to maintain those who strive to maintain themselves'.[94]

Justice P.S. Melvill, however, strongly disagreed. He believed that the ruthless enforcement of existing contracts was inappropriate in the Punjab. In fact, he noted, the severe economic distortions and the dire political consequences described by Justice Lindsay would almost certainly become far worse if the government failed to interfere with the strict enforcement of local contracts. 'I know it to be a fact', he wrote, 'that in parts of the Jullundur and Hoshiarpur Districts, ... land has been, and is now being daily transferred, by sale or mortgage, to moneylenders in payment of old and new claims, and chiefly because of the impossibility of meeting the demand for interest, past and current'.[95] In fact, Melvill argued, the plight of the 'hereditary agriculturalist' was truly grim. 'They found themselves a few years after the introduction of British rule in the possession of landed property, which heretofore had been of no appreciable market value, but which now enabled them to raise money at pleasure'. Unfortunately, he explained, 'they have too commonly used their newborn credit without reflection, borrowing more money than was fairly needed ... and squandering the excess in superfluities of living'.[96]

Yet, Melvill argued, even more reprehensible than the carelessness of local landowners was the cunning behaviour of local moneylenders. 'They are, as a general rule, rapacious and unscrupulous', he declared. 'Payments by the debtor are either not credited at all, or are credited at less than their value, and exorbitant interest is piled on interest'. Indeed, responding to his critics, Melvill noted that, while moneylenders might be *expected* to invest their capital in the improvement of their estates, they had not done so thus far. Instead, he argued, 'the hereditary banker, the *bania*, the *sahukar*, evicts the cultivating proprietor from his land, and the latter, driven from house to home, becomes a disaffected and disloyal subject'. Within fifty years, Melvill warned, 'the government may find itself face to face with a serious *political* danger' (emphasis added).[97]

Departing from accepted notions of rural finance, and for that matter basic ideas about rural credit and debt, then, the late-ninenteenth-century rural indebtedness crisis was slowly reconceptualized, not in terms of an indebtedness crisis affecting 'individual' spendthrifts, but rather with specific reference to the experience of locally indebted 'groups'. And, even then, *economic* groups (for example, 'agriculturalists' and 'moneylenders') were thought to be considerably less important than specific *religious* groups (for example 'Hindu' bankers and 'Muslim' cultivators). 'The alienation of the old and new proprietors was accentuated by a difference in religion', many argued, as 'the lender is almost invariably a Hindu and the borrower a more or less bigoted [*sic*] Muhammadan'.[98]

The crisis of rural indebtedness, in other words, was not merely an economic crisis. In due course it was re-interpreted as a political crisis grounded in the shifting status of specific religious groups. (For details, see Chapter 2.) Indeed, for many administrators, the question was not *whether* to interfere with the enjoyment of individual landed property rights, but rather *how* to interfere for the sake of (a) the village proprietary body, (b) the strength of the colonial revenue administration, and, ultimately, (c) the survival of the state as a whole.

The Solution: The Punjab Alienation of Land Act (1900)

The most controversial approach to the problem of late-nineteenth-century rural indebtedness involved restrictions on the alienation of land from agriculturalists to moneylenders. In fact, initially, revenue administrators shied away from this approach. After all, it promised to harm those it was ostensibly designed to help, for example by reducing the value of land and, hence, rural credit. In fact, a few moneylenders even went so far as to suggest that, with a reduction in the number of potential buyers and a resulting decrease in demand, the price of land would fall by as much as 95 per cent, leading farmers to *dacoity*, or banditry, in a desperate effort to meet their daily expenses.

By 1900, however, most administrators agreed that a reduction in the price of land, and hence rural credit, was a small price to pay for the liberation of the village proprietary body from the clutches of ostensibly 'alien' moneylenders. The enjoyment of 'individual landed property rights', in other words, was far less important than the integrity of 'the village proprietary body' as a body of hereditary—indeed, agnatic—ancestral agricultural 'tribes'.

In October 1900 the Punjab Alienation of Land Act (1900) was signed by Lord Curzon, the Viceroy of India. Above all, it (a) prohibited the permanent alienation of land from agriculturists to moneylenders and (b) limited usufructuary mortgages to twenty years or the lifetime of the mortgagor. In short, it subordinated 'individual' landed property rights to the preservation of collective 'tribal' attachments in no uncertain terms.

What is interesting about the Punjab Alienation of Land Act (1900), however, is not only the extent to which it subordinated individualized forms of ownership to collective obligations and 'kinship-based' affinities by limiting the right of free exchange to officially designated agricultural 'tribes', but also, and perhaps more importantly, the extent to which it relied on late-nineteenth-century ideas about the nature of 'the village proprietary body', the village 'coparcenary', and 'tribal' custom to justify its far-reaching aims.

These late-nineteenth-century ideas regarding the nature of the village proprietary body reflected not only the work of Locke, Ricardo, Bentham, Mill, Munro, Maine and Temple (in favour of 'individual' peasant proprietorship), but also—and, I would argue, more importantly—the work of those who first apprehended and then reconfigured the terms of the *shajra kishtwar* (the village field map), the *shajra nasb* (the genealogical 'map of fate'), and of course the *riwaj-i-am* (the digest of tribal custom). In fact without these colonial records, constructed by men like E.A. Prinsep, it is entirely possible that the growing number of late-nineteenth-century landed property alienations (from agriculturists to moneylenders) would have been interpreted, not as a 'political' crisis involving the disintegration of so-called agricultural 'tribes', but rather as an 'economic' catharsis (of sorts), transferring individual rights from 'anæmic' to 'efficient' local landowners.

'It is, indeed, still argued by a few', noted Sir Denzil Ibbetson in 1895, 'that free trade in land is necessarily good, and that the replacement of an owner who has shown himself to be thriftless and incompetent by one with superior intelligence and greater command of capital cannot be other than beneficial'. And, yet, Ibbetson explained, the government itself increasingly rejected this view. 'Even from the economical point of view', he argued, 'there is little truth in this contention'.[99] In fact, as J.A. Temple pointed out, capturing the experience of many administrators in his rather telling description of the Central Provinces, credit was not always constructive.

Economic self-interest, however, was only the first half of the story, and the less important half at that. The other half of the story concerned legal matters. In fact, as the government was quick to point out, the demise of the village proprietary body was 'immensely aided and accelerated by the mechanical nature of our judicial system, and by our views on the subject of contract'. 'We have construed literally and enforced *au pied de lettre*', they noted, 'contracts which were framed in the spirit of oriental hyperbole, which neither party ever intended or expected to be carried out in full, which followed the traditions of a people for whom the ideal of justice is *compromise*' (emphasis added). (See also Chapter 5.) 'We have', in effect, 'replaced the justice of the ruler with the machinery of the law, and [in doing so, we] have imported into an eastern country a judicial system, the rigidity and technicality of which are alien to the eastern mind and unsuited to the moral circumstances of the people, and which, chicanery apart, offers enormous advantages to that education, astuteness, and length of purse in which the moneylender is so far superior to the landowner'.[100]

In fact, as time passed, British colonial administrators blamed neither the 'reckless' agriculturists nor the 'rapacious' moneylenders for the late-nineteenth-century crisis of rural indebtedness. Instead they blamed themselves. The source of the crisis, it seemed, did not lie in the land, the people, or the structure of indigenous institutions; instead it lay in the manner of apprehending, recording, and transforming these institutions into a distinctively colonial notion of 'progress'.

Throughout the latter half of the nineteenth century, British administrators used their records as well as their laws to strike the proper balance between 'individual' rights and 'collective' obligations. Some believe that they favoured one or the other of these two objectives. But, as I have tried to explain, this was not necessarily the case. In fact they had a tendency to pursue both objectives at the same time, introducing a host of administrative contradictions and, eventually, a flood of local disputes.

Even as the financial benefits of a regime devoted to the introduction and enforcement of individual landed property rights began to accumulate, then, the political costs associated with the legal enforcement of these rights began to accumulate as well (at an even faster rate). And, by the turn of the century, the administrative tide had finally begun to turn. In fact by 1895 a prominent group of colonial administrators had submitted a brief-but-urgent memorandum to endorse the possibility of sweeping restrictions on the power to alienate specific interests in land for the sake of existing landowners and the survival of the colonial state. 'We are not concerned with the individual', they wrote. 'Our sole object is to save the land of the family'.[101]

CONCLUSION

The Punjab Alienation of Land Act (1900) was of course the most important piece of legislation in colonial Punjab by far. In fact, in many ways it defined the shape of landed property relations for the next hundred years (1900–99), even after its own rather abrupt but significant demise (1948).

This Act accomplished many things, several of which will be examined in Chapter 2. But above all it infused local forms of 'tribal' solidarity and colonial constructions of 'tribal' custom with an entirely new significance. In fact it would hardly be an exaggeration to say that, in the wake of the late-nineteenth-century rural indebtedness crisis, the Punjab Alienation of Land Act (1900) set the stage for an entirely new set of local conflicts, decisions, and debates—debates regarding divergent constructions of community throughout colonial Punjab: 'village' v. 'kinship', 'kinship' v. 'creed' and so on.

The Punjab Alienation of Land Act (1900) did not emerge as an established illustration of entrenched colonial interests. On the contrary, it represented the culmination of more than fifty years of bitter administrative experience, the most important feature of which involved a complex (and occasionally combative) revenue-based debate. When the British conquered the Punjab in 1849, the dominant features of the colonial revenue administration were already in place. In Bengal, Madras and Bombay, the revenue was attached to *individuals*—*zamindars* in Bengal, *ryots* in Madras and Bombay. But in the Northwestern Provinces, and eventually in the Punjab as well, the administrative bias of the colonial state shifted to an account of 'individuals' located *within* larger 'groups'.

Some, following the work of Sir Richard Temple, stressed the importance of 'village' groups, whereas others, following E.A. Prinsep, drew attention to the importance of local agricultural 'tribes'. And yet, as I will explain in the remainder of this book, the process whereby the latter (tribes) came to prevail over the former (villages) must be regarded as one of the most important changes in the history of colonial—and postcolonial—Punjab. It was, primarily, a history of changing local preferences: *who wanted what and why?*

In the autumn of 1849, shortly after the defeat of Maharaja Ranjit Singh, Lord Dalhousie announced that the colonial state would strive to 'uphold native institutions and practices as far as they are consistent with the distribution of justice to all classes'. Needless to say, his comments raised a number of questions regarding the substance of local, or 'native', institutions. For several years, the colonial administration sought to follow in the footsteps of prominent administrators in the Northwestern Provinces, assigning landed property rights within one of two rather different types of *manqasim* or 'divided' estates: in *pattidari* estates the revenue was distributed according to ancestral 'shares' whereas, in *bhaiachara* estates, it reflected the terms of 'possession'. Most administrators regarded the former (ancestral shares) with a palpable sense of concern, whereas the latter (possession) evoked the specific terms of 'progress'.

When Sir Richard Temple arrived in Sialkot in the summer of 1851 to begin his 'preliminary settlement' of the district, his biases were perfectly clear: 'possession' whenever possible; 'ancestry' if absolutely necessary. After all, Temple was well aware that, administratively, 'individualization' was the name of the game. And, indeed, the first assessment of District Sialkot contained few surprises.

The second settlement submitted by E.A. Prinsep (1865) was, however, considerably more controversial. In fact, as I have already begun to explain, it altered the course of history. When Prinsep submitted his files, few were prepared to dispute his notes. But, having said this, even fewer were prepared to deny the underlying implications of his work. In fact it was easy to see that Prinsep was playing with fire, calling into question the biases and the assumptions of the colonial state itself—assumptions about the primacy of cultivating possession, the importance of peasant proprietorship, the value of individual rights, and, indeed, the inevitable march of 'progress'.

Suddenly, assumptions became questions, and questions became dilemmas. What should the colonial state promote? What did local conditions demand? Dilemmas became options, and options became the source of an enormous administrative debate. In fact, what began with a simple exercise in empirical observation quickly degenerated into a *bona fide* 'critical juncture'. Theoretically speaking, this was the beginning of an entirely new story—the product of a particular sequence of events and the inauguration of a new set of preferences, indeed, an entirely new logic focused on the preservation of specific 'tribal' norms.

Many scholars, drawing attention to the influence of Jeremy Bentham, Thomas Munro, Holt Mackenzie, and (somewhat surprisingly) even Sir Henry Sumner Maine, argue that colonial administrators were inspired by a crusading utilitarian ideology throughout the nineteenth century, one that compelled them, following Munro, 'to confirm private property in the soil where [they] found it, and to create it, where it [did] not yet exist'.[102] Others, however, focusing on a more conventional reading of Maine, as well as the experience of Lord Lugard, Lord Hailey, and their colleagues in British Africa some years later, maintain that colonial administrators were driven by a racist ideology that compelled them to reinforce the strength of locally dominant 'tribes'. And, yet, I would argue, both views are correct. In their rush to generalize, however, both views tend to overlook the historical specificity of the contexts that concern them, and therein, the importance (indeed, the theoretical importance) of historical context itself.

Before 1865, colonial administrators stressed the rights of individuals, drawing attention to the importance of alienation and the value of free market exchange. But, after 1865, they shifted their attention to the preservation of larger groups, restricting the right of alienation in order to prevent the disintegration of ancestral estates. Indeed, even if colonial administrators *arrived* in the Punjab with an explicit interest in the promotion of 'individual' peasant proprietorship, they left with an interest in the preservation of specific agricultural 'tribes'.[103]

But of course this is not a book about the shifting preferences of the colonial state. It is, for the most part, a book about the preferences, the values, and the strategies embraced by individual Muslim landowners. When it comes to landed property relations, in other words, the challenge lies in providing an empirically grounded account of what these landowners actually 'wanted' and 'why they wanted it' in the context of colonial Punjab. *How* were local preferences defined and, more importantly, *why* were they defined as they were?

Again, the experience of those living in Lahore, Sialkot, and Sargodha is instructive. In fact, like the colonial state itself, those living in these three districts appeared to change their minds. When the colonial revenue administration arrived in Lahore, for instance, many cultivators simply disappeared, denying any claim to any portion of the land whatsoever—at least for a while. But, later on, as the revenue demands of the government were reduced (and the value of their land increased), they returned to their villages, turning away from the terms of 'possession' in favour of specific ancestral 'shares'.

Of course the challenge lies in understanding (or explaining) these patterns and the preferences they illuminated, not *apart* from the debates that preoccupied the colonial state, but *within* them, combining an account of formal and informal institutions with a more nuanced effort to explain 'what really happened' on the ground.

Before 1865, colonial administrators were committed to the introduction and enforcement of individualized landed property rights. But, after 1865, they were confused. When the Punjab Alienation of Land Act was finally promulgated, in 1900, some were convinced that the colonial state was taking a giant step 'backwards'. But, of course, most were convinced that, as far as the security of the colonial state was concerned, 'backwards' was 'forwards'.[104] In other words, the security of the state itself depended upon a deliberate effort to preserve (a) the integrity of existing ancestral 'shares' and (b) the strength of specific agricultural 'tribes'. And of course the private interests embedded within countless rural estates were remarkably similar. The terms of 'possession' were not entirely unknown, but, as a general rule, local efforts to move in the direction of 'possession' were articulated *within* an enduring attachment to specific (agnatic) 'tribes'.

2

WHO INHERITS THE LAND? (1900–1947)

HINDU LAW, MUSLIM LAW, CUSTOMARY LAW AND NATIONALISM

Increasingly, and especially after 1900, debates about the proper way to demarcate and distribute landed property rights—for instance, disagreements about the relative importance of *pattidari* and *bhaiachara* forms of land tenure—gave way to a series of disagreements regarding the proper legal context within which to regulate the transfer of these rights between and among eligible owners. In fact, over time, as these debates evolved, bitter and protracted disagreements regarding the relative importance of (a) 'tribal' custom and (b) religious personal law (for example, Muslim Personal Law)—particularly in the context of disputes concerning the inheritance rights of women—became increasingly important.

As Cyril P.K. Fazal, one of the most prolific members of a special board convened to examine the effects of the Punjab Alienation of Land Act (1900)—namely, the Punjab Board of Economic Inquiry—pointed out, different customary and religious personal laws had profoundly different implications for the shape of local *politics*. In fact, Fazl noted, the 1900 Act, with its preference for specific agricultural 'tribes', had come, 'by one of those curious chances which play such [an] unexpected part ... in politics', to be regarded as 'a *communal* measure': rural Muslim agriculturalists, on the one hand; urban Hindu professionals, on the other.[1]

According to Cyril P.K. Fazal, urban professionals had a tendency to support the terms of 'religious' personal law, whereas rural agriculturists had a tendency to support enduring 'tribal' norms. In fact, by 1937, the differences between these two groups had grown to such an extent that Raja Narendra Nath, a conservative Hindu activist from Lahore, felt compelled to describe the conflict between them in no uncertain terms: 'The Unionists', he explained, cutting straight to the heart of the matter with a sardonic reference to the (predominantly rural) Punjab Unionist Party, 'believe that the Land Alienation Act [1900] is to them what the [religious] Vedas and the Holy Qur'an are to the [urban] Hindus and [Muslims]'.[2] (See Fig. 6 below.)

Fig. 6. R.N. Nath: early twentieth-century party politics in the Punjab

Punjab Unionist Party	**All-India Muslim League**	**Hindu Mahasabha, etc.**
The Punjab Alienation of Land Act	The Holy Qur'an	The Vedas
('tribal' custom)	(*shari'ah*)	(*sastras*)
RURAL	URBAN	URBAN

Of course the implications of this remark and, more specifically, its 'legal' and 'political' references, are difficult to digest without a detailed understanding of (a) the Vedas (Hindu scripture), (b) the Holy Qur'an (Muslim scripture), and, most importantly of all, (c) the 'custom-friendly' principles that many agriculturalists had come to identify with the specific terms of the Punjab Alienation of Land Act (1900).

The remainder of this chapter is, however, explicitly devoted to the cultivation of just such an understanding, drawing special attention to the link between the terms of religious personal law, on the one hand, and the party-based politics of early-twentieth-century colonial landed property relations, on the other—beginning in the autumn of 1900, when the Punjab Alienation of Land Act came into force, and concluding in the autumn of 1947, when colonial Punjab gave way to Pakistan amidst both the triumph and the trauma of partition.

Suffice it to say, at least for the time being, that the political landscape of early-twentieth-century colonial Punjab was composed of three main groups, each of which was defined, following the comments of Raja Narendra Nath, in terms of its ideas about the proper relationship between (a) landed property relations and (b) particular laws of inheritance. The first of these three groups was composed of urban Hindus and the terms of Hindu personal law; the second was composed of urban Muslims and the content of the Holy Qur'an; and of course the third, representing the overwhelming *majority*, including *both* Hindus *and* Muslims (as well as Sikhs), was defined by the terms of its attachment to the agnatic 'customs' associated with particular agricultural 'tribes'.

This chapter addresses the laws governing inheritance associated with each of these three groups, explaining, first, how the colonial state sought to understand their respective laws and second, why the differences between those laws mattered so much, politically, in the years between 1900 and 1947. Throughout, I will use an historically specific account of the contested relationship between religious personal law, on the one hand, and 'tribal' custom, on the other (particularly in the context of private disputes regarding the inheritance rights of women) to introduce and explain the emergence of a politically significant gap between two key parties, namely, the All-India Muslim League, led by Mohammad Ali Jinnah, and the Punjab Unionist Party, representing diverse 'tribal' factions.

The nature of the gap between these two parties can be stated quite succinctly: whereas the former, the All-India Muslim League, tended to support the inheritance rights of Muslim women; the latter, quite emphatically, did not.

LEGAL CODIFICATION AND FEMALE DISINHERITANCE

Legal Codification

Before I turn to the implications of Hindu and Muslim personal law in the context of early-twentieth-century provincial politics, however, it may help to examine the legal tradition against which *both* Hindu *and* Muslim personal law were asserted. This is, of course, the tradition of 'tribal' custom.

In fact throughout this chapter it is extremely important to keep in mind that, from Kangra, north of Delhi, to Kohat, south of Peshawar, *most* families—that is, most Hindu families, most Sikh families, and most Muslim families—had a well-documented tendency to shy away from the terms of 'religious' personal law.[3] Indeed, as countless administrators, judges, and historians went to considerable lengths to point out, *most* families adhered to specific 'tribal' norms.[4]

'It had long been felt by those best acquainted with the habits and customs of the rural population', noted W.H. Rattigan in his well-known *Digest of Civil Law for the Punjab* (1881), 'that neither the Shara [that is, the *shari'ah*] nor the Shastras really exercised any direct influence' in the Punjab. '[T]he Hindu and the Muhammadan, though differing in religion, were often united together in the village community', Rattigan explained, and, in this context, they were brought together 'by the same common rules regulating the devolution and disposal of [landed] property, which, [both] in theory and ... in practice, was recognized as involving *a community of interests*' tied to the survival of specific *agnatic* 'tribes' (emphasis added).[5]

What distinguished the Punjab from the rest of British India, in other words, was not the importance of religion (or religious faith) *per se*. What distinguished the Punjab was the prevailing significance of 'agnatic' kinship, and more specifically, the formal legal recognition of a special relationship between vertically segmented landed property relations, enduring tribal kinship networks, and the ecumenical enforcement of specific 'tribal' norms. In fact as the nineteenth century drew to a close it became increasingly clear that, although unfettered individual ownership rights were regarded as 'an ideal type', segmented (kinship-based) restrictions affecting those rights had come to be regarded as a clearly established—indeed, a legally sanctioned—fact.

Disagreements about the transformation of the rural economy, in other words, did not begin with simple assumptions regarding the existence of 'individual' rights or, for that matter, the finer points of 'religious' personal law. On the contrary, these disagreements began with a series of disagreements regarding different *types* of 'customary' collectivities: villages v. tribes. What follows is merely an attempt to account for the specific terms of these disagreements, focusing, rather narrowly, on the shifting terms of three rather important debates.

The first of these three debates, pitting Sir Henry Sumner Maine against Sir Charles Lewis Tupper, concerned the relative importance of 'village' and 'tribal' custom—a debate that was resolved not once, not twice, but three times in favour of specific (agricultural) 'tribes'.[6] The second debate, pitting Lahore High Court Justice William Henry (W.H.) Rattigan against Mr James Thorburn, concerned the underlying administrative value of legal 'codification'.[7] This debate was resolved, in keeping with the outcome of the first debate, in favour of an explicit push for the codification of 'tribal' custom—not at a provincial level (following Rattigan) but rather at a district level (following Thorburn).

The third debate emerged in the context of a special meeting known as the Codification of Customary Law Conference in Simla.[8] This debate did not address the question of codification itself. In fact, by the time this debate emerged, in 1915, the value of codification was already taken for granted. As the chair of the conference, Lieutenant-Governor Sir Michael O'Dwyer, was quick to point out, however, the specific *parameters* of this codification process remained uncertain. And, in due course, this is what the conference aimed to decide: what exactly should be taken to represent the *boundaries* of an agricultural 'tribe' for the purposes of 'codification' (and who, specifically, should decide)?

Defining Custom: Village (Maine) v. Tribe (Tupper)

The first and, perhaps, the most significant of these three debates pitted Sir Henry Sumner Maine, Legal Member of the Viceregal Council in Delhi, against Sir Charles Lewis Tupper, Under-Secretary to the Government of India in the Home, Revenue, and Agriculture Department. In fact in many ways this debate unfolded as an extension of the settlement controversy that had emerged, several years before, in District Sialkot, when Sir Richard Temple battled his understudy, Mr Prinsep, for the authority to define the customary rights of 'hereditary cultivators with possession'.

Temple, it will be recalled, following Regulation VII (1822), used twelve years of uninterrupted occupancy as a common standard for converting local forms of cultivating 'possession' into full 'proprietorship'. And, remaining deeply loyal to the anti-aristocratic tradition of James Mill, in London, and Sir Thomas Munro, in Madras, he proceeded to classify most of the villages in Sialkot as *bhaiachara* villages, distributing the revenue according to 'possession' and recording the rights of each villager in the local *wajib-ul-arz*. As noted above, however, his understudy, Mr. Prinsep, adopted a very different approach. In fact Prinsep completely reversed almost everything Temple had done.

It is, of course, impossible to deny that Edward Augustus (E.A.) Prinsep harboured a certain bias in favour of hereditary landowners. But, at the same time, it is equally clear that this bias enjoyed a certain amount of documented empirical support—not in any 'absolute' or 'ahistorical' sense, but rather, in a specific 'historical' sense grounded in the administrative events of late-nineteenth-century Punjab. Indeed, what changed between the first (preliminary) settlement and the second (regular) settlement of Sialkot was not the ideological orientation of the colonial state. (That came later.) What changed was the economic and political orientation of several thousand individuals—individual *cultivators*—as they defined their interests on the ground.

As noted above, many members of the village proprietary body were reluctant to assert the full extent of their (potential) rights during the first (preliminary) settlement. But later on—and owing for the most part to a moderate and predictable rate of assessment—the value of agricultural land increased, and, in due course, many of those who had (initially) sought to diminish their claims rushed forward to correct what they considered to be the 'errors' of the first (preliminary) settlement. In fact they did not merely rush forward to claim their ancestral rights through litigation. They simply evicted hundreds, even thousands, of occupancy tenants. And, of course they did so without a second thought. Just as the second (regular) settlement was getting under way, then, Prinsep found himself confronted with a crisis of social dislocation and profound confusion on the part of the district courts.

At issue was not merely the ownership rights of 'hereditary proprietors' or 'individual cultivators with possession'. As it happens, this was a secondary issue. The primary issue concerned the customary rights that 'hereditary proprietors' enjoyed when it came to dismissing those—in fact, evicting those—with claims based solely on their status as 'individual cultivators with possession'. According to Temple, they had no such rights. In other words, the rights of 'inferior proprietors with cultivating possession' were secure. But according to Prinsep, Temple was simply out of touch with the substantive features of local 'customs' as these were defined 'on the ground'. In fact, Prinsep argued, Temple had simply fallen prey to a common ailment within the senior ranks of the colonial bureaucracy, namely 'wishful thinking'.

Turning away from the *wajib-ul-arz* to the *riwaj-i-am*, then, Prinsep maintained that hereditary proprietors did in fact enjoy a 'customary' right of eviction. And of course he argued that this right could not, and should not, be infringed. In short, he pointed to information collected in 'the digest of tribal custom' (that is, the *riwaj-i-am*) to support his claim that superior proprietorship based on heredity was 'more secure'

Fig. 7. Land tenure and customary law in the Punjab: Temple v. Prinsep

I. *Temple* (*village*)	II. *Prinsep* (*tribe*)
Customary Law	
village administration paper	digest of tribal custom
wajib-ul-arz	*riwaj-i–am*
rights of cultivators	rights of 'hereditary proprietars'
prohibition regarding eviction	no prohibition regarding eviction
'Cultivators with Possession'	
first settlement: 'proprietors'	second settlement: 'tenants'

than inferior proprietorship based on possession, not only in Sialkot, but throughout colonial Punjab.

To prove his point, Prinsep personally examined the rights and customs associated with more than 10,000 plots in *tehsil* Shikargarh. And then, after five years, when he was completely satisfied that the first settlement (supported by Temple) had been incorrect, he proceeded to adjust the rights associated with a considerable number of these plots, converting village after village from *bhaiachara* into *pattidari* tenures.

In the process, however, he completely reinterpreted the terms of local custom, turning away from cultivating rights and 'village' custom as recorded in the *wajib-ul-arz* to ancestral rights and 'tribal' custom as recorded in the *riwaj-i-am*.[9] In other words, his target was not confined to the finer points of the first (preliminary) settlement at the level of specific ownership rights. His target was the underlying terms of colonial 'customary' law.

Fig. 8. Land tenure and customary law in the Punjab: Maine v. Tupper

I. Maine (*village*)	*II. Tupper* (*tribe*)
Land Tenure	
cultivating possession	ancestral shares
occupancy; twelve years	heredity; no limitation
maurusi = *malguzar*	*zamindar* = *hissadar*
bhaiachara villages	*pattidari* villages
Customary Law	
wajib-ul-arz	*riwaj-i–am*

When the ensuing controversy was revisited, some twenty years later, by Maine and Tupper, it no longer stressed the relationship between land tenure, revenue, and the stability of the colonial exchequer. Instead it revolved around opposing views of local 'customary' law. (See Figs. 7 and 8.)

According to Sir Henry Sumner Maine, *hereditary* rights and 'tribal' custom were being replaced by *usufructuary* rights and 'village' custom throughout the Punjab at an ever-increasing rate. In fact, Maine even went so far as to suggest that 'real' kinship linkages (within the village proprietary body) were simply a thing of the past. And, for precisely this reason, he claimed that the regulation of the village community should proceed according to 'village' custom as recorded in the *wajib-ul-arz*.

Tupper, however, based in the Home, Revenue, and Agriculture Department, disagreed, noting that 'local kinship linkages', whether real or imagined, were alive and well, not only in District Sialkot, but throughout colonial Punjab—and, for that matter, throughout North India. Moreover, he explained that agnatic kinship continued to guide the devolution of landed property relations among ordinary villagers, and, as a result, the regulation of landed property (especially in the context of 'voluntary' or 'involuntary' alienations) should not proceed according to 'village' custom as recorded in the *wajib-ul-arz* (or, for that matter, according to 'religious' personal law). Instead it should follow 'tribal' custom as recorded in the *riwaj-i-am*.

In the end, of course, the terms of this debate were never fully resolved. In fact the Punjab Tenancy Act (1868) was passed, just three years after Prinsep completed his work in Sialkot, to protect the rights of 'cultivators with possession', even as the Punjab Laws Act (1872) was passed, just a few years later, to preserve the integrity of specific tribal shares. As noted above, in Chapter 1, however, the Punjab Alienation of Land Act tipped the balance just that much further—after 1900—in favour of 'tribal' shares.

Codifying Custom: Predictability (Rattigan) v. Flexibility (Thorburn)

If Sir Henry Sumner Maine and Sir Charles Lewis Tupper disagreed about *which* 'custom' to codify (village v. tribal custom), however, Justice William Henry Rattigan and Mr James Thorburn disagreed about *whether* (and *how*) to codify 'custom' at all. Indeed, as the nineteenth century came crashing to an end, the emergence of an expanding crisis of rural indebtedness led many administrators to worry that, even if they *wanted* to codify the terms of custom, any effort to *do* so would merely produce a suffocating pattern of increasingly inflexible reforms—in many ways, a pattern of reform naïvely devoted to the promulgation of a judicial system 'the rigidity and technicality of which' were 'alien to the eastern mind'.[10]

In fact, as the nineteenth century drew to an end, a growing number of administrators seemed to believe that, although the terms of codification were 'valuable' insofar as they implied a certain level of 'consistency', consistency itself would almost certainly amount to an assault on the 'organic integrity' of the village community and its ostensibly 'evolving' norms.

As a judge on the Lahore High Court, W.H. Rattigan was very well acquainted with the tremendous variety of customary law in the context of colonial Punjab. But, for the most part, his appreciation for this variety led him to support a rather centralized approach to the task of codification focused, primarily, on the expertise of jurists based in Lahore.[11] As the nineteenth century came to an end, however, Rattigan found that his focus on the value of a more thoroughly *centralized* approach to reform was *not* taken for granted. In fact, James Thorburn and many others appeared to believe that the key to stability lay in a deeper appreciation for administrative *adaptability*—an appreciation for district-level decision-making and, above all, shifting *local* norms.[12]

Rattigan's position, stressing the expertise of prominent officials based in Lahore, typified the views of many senior officials throughout North India. In fact, as a reflection of late-nineteenth-century ideas regarding the value of ongoing (centralized) reform—a view typically associated with the administrative legacy of Sir Henry Sumner Maine—Rattigan's approach to the question of legal codification is worth reviewing at some length.

'It may be true', Rattigan argued, 'that there are internal, silently operating powers which ... make for ... the transmutation of a set of ideas, based upon tribal or family ownership, into another and a totally different conception of the rights of property based upon [unfettered] individualism'. But, 'unless I am egregiously mistaken', he added, '*it is not the policy of our administration to further or hasten this change*' (emphasis added). 'We may not be able to prevent the eventual splitting up of the village communities as they still exist in the Punjab', he noted. 'They, like other social institutions, may be subject to an inexorable law of decay'. But, 'although we may not be able to stop altogether this current of individualistic thought from slowly undermining the foundations on which village property is based, *it is within our power to retard and weaken this ... process*'.

'One method of doing so', Rattigan explained, 'would seem to be by fostering in the minds of the people an abiding reverence for all that is wholesome and profitable in that great principle of association, for which the land itself furnishes a real, permanent, and all-sufficient basis'. 'We should', he continued, drawing attention to the administrative preference for *bhaiachara* village tenures, 'not be asphyxiating progress, but [rather] ensuring the prosperity of the agricultural classes by preserving for them the *possession* of their lands and the constitution of their communities' in all their integrity. 'We should', he argued, 'not be introducing any novel or distasteful legislation, but doing our best to maintain all that was healthy and good in a system which was suited to the people'.[13] And of course, in an effort to achieve this end, he wrote, returning to the question of codification, the state 'should ... have certainty for uncertainty—*a written and stable law instead of a wilderness of judicial precedents*'.[14]

In fact, Rattigan argued, the colonial state shouldered a special responsibility for the codification of local customs, not for purely economic reasons, but, rather, for specifically political reasons—namely, the preservation of local property relations, the integrity of the village proprietary body, and (ultimately) the wellbeing of the state as a whole.

Even as the underlying merits of legal codification came to be embraced within the colonial administration, however, the underlying framework for this task (particularly when it came to the codification of 'village' or 'tribal' customs) remained a matter of considerable, even vociferous, disagreement. James Thorburn, for instance, refused to accept the notion that 'village' or 'tribal' customs should be codified on a 'general' (that is, a provincial) basis; in fact, Thorburn insisted that *district-level* administrators should be empowered to define the terms of 'custom' as these terms became 'ripe for declaration' ... one *tehsil* at a time.[15]

According to Mr Thorburn, the terms of economic and social 'progress' should not be restrained by sclerotic patterns tied to the notoriously cumbersome process of 'provincial' legal reform. Instead, the terms of economic and social 'progress' should be encouraged and, wherever possible, accelerated on a community basis tied to shifting 'local' norms. 'Whatever disadvantages attach to a system of *unwritten* [local] law, and of these we are fully sensible', noted one member of the Lahore High Court, quoting Lord Chief Justice Cockburn in a rather forceful statement supporting the views articulated by Mr Thorburn, 'it has at least this advantage, that its elasticity enables those who administer it to adapt it to the varying conditions of society, and to the requirements and habits of the age in which we live'.[16]

Unfortunately, nearly twenty years after this debate regarding the relative merits of 'provincial' and 'district-level' efforts first emerged in Lahore, the question of codification itself remained unresolved. In fact the positions articulated by *both* Rattigan *and* Thorburn during the 1890s remained an important subject of debate (without interruption) until the summer of 1915, when the Lieutenant Governor of the Punjab, Sir Michael O'Dwyer, inaugurated the Codification of Customary Law Conference in Simla, a prominent hill-country retreat located high above the capital of the Raj in Delhi.

The Codification of Customary Law Conference (1915)

Stressing the importance of stable landed property relations for the wellbeing of the colonial state as a whole, O'Dwyer indicated that an underlying appreciation for the terms of legal and administrative certainty was desirable in and of itself. Even beyond this appreciation for the intrinsic value of legal certainty, however, O'Dwyer noted that greater predictability was particularly desirable as a special check on the scourge of speculative litigation that customary law, with its apparently infinite range of 'interpretive flexibility', so often seemed to encourage. 'The present state of affairs fosters ruinous litigation and produces all the evils invariably caused by uncertainty in the law', O'Dwyer complained, adding that a concerted effort to place some matters 'beyond the reach of controversy in court' would almost certainly have the effect of making 'titles' and, by extension, the colonial budget, more 'secure'.[17]

Above all, O'Dwyer explained that the challenge facing the conference delegates lay in producing greater certainty in the law without, at the same time, producing 'too much' certainty. In fact the challenge lay in proceeding with the task of codification without, at the same time, 'rushing in to stereotype the obsolete'. '[Although an] Arain village on the outskirts of Lahore [may] outgrow its tribal customs much more rapidly than a community of the same caste [living] in the wilds of ... Mianwali [bordering Shahpur]', noted one delegate, drawing special attention to O'Dwyer's familiar concerns, the chief task lay in working with an equal degree of sensitivity in both contexts. 'What we want to ensure is liberty to the former to advance and to the latter to stand still ... the one untrammelled by customs ... it has outgrown and the other unbewildered by innovations which are [somehow] premature'.[18]

Not surprisingly, most of those who attended the Codification of Customary Law Conference agreed with O'Dwyer about the desirability of legal codification. But, contrary to some of the recent literature regarding a colonial push for 'state simplification' (Scott 1998), most of the conference delegates did *not* oppose the mind-boggling 'diversity' of existing local norms. Instead, they merely opposed the *ad hoc* definition of those norms and, therein, their ongoing legal 'abuse'.

Moving away from any specific interest in obscuring or eliminating existing forms of 'diversity', then, the conference delegates quickly settled on four key issues, each of which appeared to *embrace* the notion of 'diversity' while, at the same time, seeking new ways to *manage* that diversity within the provincial courts.

First, cutting straight to the chase, the conference delegates asked whether the terms of local 'custom' could be codified at all, and assuming they could, whether the process of codification itself would actually succeed in addressing the scourge of speculative (mostly civil) litigation. Second, they asked how the terms of custom might be codified—by legislative fiat or majority vote—and, if by majority vote, then, what the local voting constituency should be (the 'village' or the 'tribe').

Finally, coming straight to the most contentious issue of all, they asked whether further legislation should, following Rattigan, specify the terms of customary law as expressed by the majority within *the province as a whole* or, following Thorburn, delegate that task to senior administrative officers within each and every *tehsil*.

Surprisingly, those who attended the conference reached an agreement, almost immediately, regarding the possibility of codification and the value of clear and simple rules for those with an interest in securing existing titles and reducing the spread of speculative litigation. Less surprising, however, was the fact that they appeared to disagree about almost everything else. 'The real difficulty', noted the final conference report, was 'to find an equitable definition of the terms "community" and "large majority," or in other words, to determine the communal unit for the purpose of codification'.[19] The real difficulty, in other words, concerned the relative value of 'villages' versus 'tribes'.

In the end, however, following Prinsep, the final report declared that local customs should be codified by 'majority vote' among 'the tribes of each *tehsil*', and, following Thorburn, that the specific terms of customary law should be left to official notification within the 'local' (*tehsil*-level) government.

The reasoning behind this attachment to the views previously expressed by a junior administrative officer (namely, E.A. Prinsep) was, however, almost entirely pragmatic. In fact, as the final report went on to explain, referring specifically to the *riwaj-i-am*, 'codes of custom have been framed or revised for all the leading tribes in each *tehsil* after detailed enquiry from the tribal representatives' in 'all [of the] settlements carried out since 1871'. Moreover, the report explained, these codes were known to deal with 'practically all the subjects in regard to which codification is desired', and, indeed, 'they possess considerable evidential value and afford substantial assistance to the courts in deciding disputes as to custom' (even though, as 'rebuttable presumptions', they carried 'no legal presumption of truth').[20]

In other words, as the final report of the conference went on to explain, the process of legal codification vis-à-vis the terms of 'tribal' custom at the level of each *tehsil* came to be regarded as an administrative possibility—indeed, an administrative priority—primarily because, following the work of E.A. Prinsep in Sialkot (fifty years before), the process of codification itself was already well under way.

Female Disinheritance

Reinforcing the underlying biases of the colonial state, the final report of the Codification of Customary Law Conference (1915) clarified a number of issues regarding the special administrative status of 'tribal' (as opposed to 'village') customs. But, even before the ink was dry, this report was said to foreshadow many of the sentiments expressed later on by Cyril P.K. Fazal and Raja Narendra Nath. In particular, this report was believed to express a certain bias 'against religion' and, more specifically, a specific bias against 'religious personal law' on the part of the provincial government.

'It appears', noted Sir Michael O'Dwyer at the start of the conference, 'that a section of the urban population of the province, which as a rule is governed either by Hindu or Muhammadan law, is under the delusion that it is the intention of the [provincial] government to substitute the rules of agricultural custom for personal laws founded on the *dharma shastras* [that is, Hindu law] or the *shariyat* [Muslim law]'.[21] But, as the Lieutenant-Governor went on to point out, the government had no such intention. In fact, he insisted, nothing could be further from the truth, as the distinction between 'rural agriculturalists who followed custom' and 'urban professionals who followed the terms of religious personal law' was never in question. On the contrary, he argued, this distinction remained firmly embedded within the full range of legal choices consistently entertained by the courts.

O'Dwyer's attention to this emerging allegation regarding the 'anti-religious' orientation of the colonial state, however, illuminated a critical and enduring link between (a) specific forms of customary and religious personal law, (b) landed property relations, and (c) the logic of local politics in late-nineteenth and, especially, early-twentieth-century Punjab—a link that many had come to associate with the emergence of an increasingly worrisome gap between the (mostly urban) Hindu population, on the one hand, and (mostly rural) Muslims, on the other.

Urban Hindus, for their part, were often believed to support a specific commitment to the terms of religious personal law (in this case, Hindu personal law). And, throughout the early part of the twentieth century, this commitment had become increasingly explicit with the emergence of several religious-cum-political reform movements like the Punjab Hindu Swaraksha, the Hindu Mahasabha, and, to some extent, even the Indian National Congress under 'Mahatma' M.K. Gandhi.[22] Local Muslims, on the other hand, were seen as comparatively divided, with a small urban minority holding fast to the terms of religious personal law (*shari'ah*) even as the overwhelming majority continued to embrace specific 'tribal' norms (*riwaj*).

Within this divided Muslim community, urban Muslims tended to throw their weight (politically) behind the All-India Muslim League, which was established, in 1906, just one year after the 'communal' bifurcation of Bengal.[23] But, as I will now proceed to explain, rural Muslims remained considerably less parochial (at least in a religious sense). Joining forces with rural Hindus and rural Sikhs to form the

Punjab Unionist Party, in 1923, they persisted in their defence of enduring 'tribal' norms. And, of course, in doing so, they expressed a rather persistent tendency to provoke the ire of urban 'religious' critics like Raja Narendra Nath—critics who accused the Unionists of equating the terms of 'tribal' custom with the (Hindu) Vedas and the text of the Holy Qur'an.

Inheritance: Hindu Law, Muslim Law

In order to understand this emerging legal-cum-political confrontation—urban v. rural—concerns about the task of legal *codification* must be combined with a deeper understanding of core legal *substance*. In particular, it is necessary to examine the divergent terms of Hindu, Muslim, and 'tribal' customary law, particularly when it came to the inheritance of agricultural land and, especially, the inheritance rights of women.

Hindu law. Within Hindu law, there are two main schools of thought, known as the Dayabhaga School and the Mitakshara School. And, within these two schools of thought, there are two main points of distinction, both of which help to illuminate the differences between Hindu law, on the one hand, and Muslim law, on the other.[24] The first point of distinction concerns 'joint family' property, 'partition', and the 'alienation' of ancestral land. The second point concerns the critical issue of inheritance.

(The following discussion is somewhat technical, but, when I return to the question of customary law below, the linkages between Hindu law, on the one hand, and 'tribal' custom, on the other—and, more specifically, the ways in which *both* traditions cut against the specific terms of Islam—will become perfectly clear.)

According to the Dayabhaga School of Hindu law prevailing among the Hindus of Bengal, fathers are the exclusive owners of (ancestral) 'joint family' property until the very moment of their death. This means that sons are not co-owners, and, as a result, they cannot apply for the 'partition' of any 'joint family' estate. According to the Mitakshara School of Hindu law prevailing in Benares, Madras, and Bombay, however, sons *are* co-owners. In other words, as I will discuss when I return to the question of 'tribal' custom (below), sons are entitled to apply for the 'partition' of joint family property, even though their individual 'shares' cannot be fully 'alienated' without filing for 'partition' first.[25]

When it comes to inheritance, however, the rights of individual sons are not the most thoroughly contested issue in the context of Hindu law. In fact the inheritance rights of women are far more complex (and controversial). According to Jimutavahana, the compiler of a comprehensive legal digest regarding Hindu law in the twelfth century CE, Dayabhaga rules of inheritance stress the importance of 'spiritual efficacy', or the ability of specific heirs to bestow particular 'blessings' on the deceased. In particular, Jimutavahana noted that male heirs are able to bestow *more* 'merit' than female heirs.[26] And, as a result, women are invited to participate in the funeral rites of their relatives only insofar as they are able to stand in for future generations of men (for example, as mothers who may, in due course, bear further sons).

However, according to the Mitakshara rules of inheritance, following Vijnaneshwara, special emphasis is placed on 'agnatic' kinship pure and simple.[27] Here, men exclude women (full stop) and more remote men who qualify as agnates, or relations through other men, exclude nearer men who are cognates, or relations through women. In other words, according to the Mitakshara rules—and, as I will explain in just a moment, according to the terms of 'tribal' custom as well—distant agnatic nephews exclude the sons of a sister. In fact, insofar as women are entitled to inherit any ancestral property at all, they do not do so as 'full' owners. Instead, they inherit in the form of a 'limited' lifetime estate—in effect, a usufructuary estate held for the purposes of their 'maintenance' (but never alienated) until the moment of their death.[28] Thus, women may *take* as 'temporary legatees', but they may never *give* as 'full-fledged legators'.

All of these details regarding Dayabhaga and Mitakshara laws of inheritance may seem exceedingly technical. But, when I return to a discussion of 'tribal' custom in a moment, their political relevance in the context of colonial Punjab will become more apparent; indeed the similarities between Mitakshara laws of inheritance and the rules of 'tribal' custom in the context of colonial Punjab are striking—all the more so because the latter were followed by rural Hindus, Sikhs, *and* Muslims, even *after* the nationalist movement began to pull these communities apart.

Muslim law. It is of course extremely important to understand that, when compared to Hindu law, Muslim laws of inheritance provide considerable relief to women. In fact, even though Muslim men, following the distribution of every ancestral estate, tend to receive twice as much as Muslim women, the Muslim laws of inheritance (known as *'ilm al-fara'id*, or 'the science of [ancestral] shares') are widely regarded as the most important and progressive laws in the whole corpus of Islamic jurisprudence—so much so that the Prophet himself is reported to have said, in a rather well-known *hadith*, that the laws of inheritance constitute 'half the sum of *'ilm*' (that is, religious 'knowledge').[29] (Indeed, unlike most of the laws that scholars commonly treat as 'Islamic' laws, Muslim laws of inheritance draw their authority and, in particular, their special focus on the inheritance rights of women, directly from the Holy Qur'an.[30])

Within the context of Muslim personal law, moreover, both Sunnis and Shi'as acknowledge a common group of what are typically known as 'Qur'anic heirs', each of whom is mentioned in the text of the Qur'an itself (along with a specific fractional 'share').[31] This list includes mothers, grandmothers, spouses, daughters, sisters, son's daughters, uterine brothers, and fathers. And of course, with the exception of fathers, all of these heirs are women, or related through women, meaning that, as a carefully demarcated group, this group is distinguished precisely insofar as it departs from the patrilineal model of agnatic (all-male) kinship prevailing in colonial Punjab .[32]

As Lucy Carroll (1983, 1985) points out, almost every interpretation of Islamic law, no matter how strained, departs from the terms of (classical) Hindu law and the terms of (agnatic) 'customary' law to the extent that it brings the rights of individual Muslim women to bear on the collective rights of a more traditional 'all-male' community. In fact, as Carroll explains, it is for precisely this reason that Sunnis and Shi'as alike 'regard the law of succession as the central core of their jurisprudential and social heritage'.[33] Or, as N.J. Coulson (1971) declares, taking this argument regarding the special status of *'ilm al-fara'id* one step further, 'nowhere is the fundamental Islamic ideology of law as the manifestation of the divine will more clearly demonstrated than [it is] in the [Islamic] law of inheritance'.[34]

In view of this, however, it is simply impossible to ignore the central dilemma for the rural Muslim majority of colonial Punjab, where conventional interpretations of religious personal law were regularly (even 'customarily') *ignored*. Of course Coulson goes on to explain that this pattern of explicit legal circumvention is not altogether surprising in the context of an agricultural economy dominated by small and deeply fragmented plots. In fact, he writes, the terms of *'ilm al-fara'id* 'must inevitably produce, particularly in regard to land, either an extensive incidence of joint ownership or an excessive fragmentation of property, according to whether [or not] the heirs insist upon division'.[35] But, insofar as this is (following Coulson) *inevitably* the case, there is simply no way to ignore the fact that rural Muslim agriculturalists throughout the Punjab found themselves in a rather profound legal bind.

In fact, neither joint ownership nor fragmentation presented itself as an attractive option for these Muslims, particularly in the midst of an early-twentieth-century context defined by vivid memories of late-nineteenth-century indebtedness. Formally defined 'joint ownership', for instance, bore an unmistakable resemblance to the prevailing pattern of ownership under the specific terms of Hindu law. (In fact, there was an entirely separate legal category specifically designed to deal with the property of 'Hindu' Joint Families.) And, of course, 'fragmentation' was already associated with a bitter economic and political scourge of epidemic proportions. Yet, for the rural Muslim majority, the only alternatives seemed to lie in (a) the partition of the land itself—hardly a desirable option, given the tiny size of most holdings—or (b) outright circumvention of their own 'religious' personal laws.

Those with immovable property (for example, land) favoured legal 'circumvention' (in effect, 'a defence of tribal custom'). Those with movable property (for example, cash and other goods) turned away from 'tribal' custom toward the specific terms of *shari'ah*. The former, representing the overwhelming rural majority, joined the Punjab Unionist Party. But the latter, representing a powerful urban minority, supported the expanding presence of Mohammad Ali Jinnah and his party, the All-India Muslim League.

Inheritance: Customary Law

In the Punjab, the terms of 'customary law' reminded some colonial administrators of Hindu law, and more specifically, the Mitakshara School of Hindu law prevailing in Benares.[36] A second group of administrators, however, noted that, even if customary law followed certain 'normative' principles, the specific nature of these principles was extremely difficult to ascertain. 'The tribal law of the Punjab has little or no connection with either Hindu or Muhammadan Law', noted Badr-ud-Din Qureshi (1932), a prominent advocate in Lahore. In fact, he noted, the 'tribal' law of the Punjab followed its own principles—principles often described as 'autonomous' and 'enduring'.[37]

Indeed, many administrators appeared to take this rather sweeping view one step further, refusing to accept the notion that the terms of 'tribal' custom resembled any 'law' at all. For the most part, they argued, the terms of 'tribal' custom were little more than a menagerie of variations and exceptions—a dynamic congeries of constantly shifting norms.[38] In fact what colonial administrators, judges, and advocates throughout the Punjab actually experienced within the terms of 'tribal' custom was often little more than an elaborate set of 'rebuttable' presumptions—a set of assumptions, axioms, and corollaries based on a general pattern of attachment to the principle of 'agnatic' solidarity.

Core assumption. The first and most important of these (ostensibly 'rebuttable') presumptions concerned the practice of matrimonial exogamy, or the notion that women married within their 'tribe' but outside of their natal 'village'.[39]

It is, however, important to point out that, throughout the Punjab, this practice of marital exogamy was always less important than the terms of practical control. In fact the 'presumption' of exogamous marriage patterns was often 'rebutted' in cases where endogamous marriages—for example, marriages between first cousins—allowed local families to accomplish the same objective, namely, 'agnatic' control, in slightly different ways.[40] (See Fig. 9, below.)

Axioms. Even beyond this core assumption regarding the prevalence of exogamous marriage patterns, however, colonial ideas about the underlying terms of 'tribal' custom drew attention to three important axioms. All three concerned intestate succession, and all three stressed the terms of agnatic (all-male) kinship.

Fig. 9. Illustration: first cousin marriage

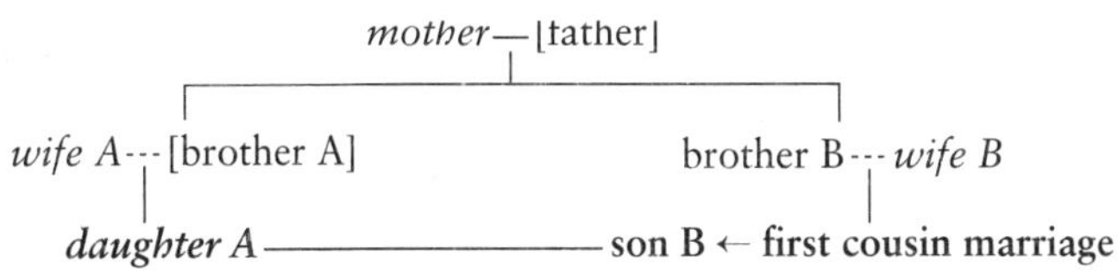

N.b. According to Muslim personal law, daughter A 'inherits' from brother A. But, in practice, the land is controlled by her husband, the son of brother B. This outcome is identical to that of an exogamous marriage combined with 'female disinheritance'.

First and foremost, male descendents (for example, sons and son's sons) were taken to exclude all other descendants.[41] In other words, the principle of succession in cases of 'ancestral' property was strictly defined by gender. In addition, however, the right of 'representation' was rigorously maintained, meaning that, if a man died before his father, the deceased son's sons would inherit in place of the man himself—they would 'represent' their father in a position equal to the father's brothers.[42] And, finally—building on the first axiom—women were entirely excluded from the inheritance of 'ancestral' land.[43]

Corollaries. Beyond these three basic axioms, however, at least three corollaries obtained as well, each of which reinforced the underlying logic of (agnatic) 'tribal' kinship. First, in a rule recalling the Dayabhaga School of Hindu law, sons were not allowed to apply for the partition of a joint family estate until after the death of their father. Second, the rule of succession was typically—but not always—*pagvand* or *per capita*, meaning that all sons shared equally (whether or not they had the same mother).[44] And, third, a clear distinction was made between 'ancestral' property (that is, property that was itself inherited), from which daughters were excluded, and 'acquired' property, from which they were not excluded (although, in practice, even the 'acquired' property ostensibly inherited by a woman was not regarded as her own special property—it was generally regarded as the unrestricted property of her husband).[45] In any case, sisters were excluded altogether, except in preference to complete strangers.[46]

Needless to say, most of these corollaries merely extended the principle of agnatic kinship to various aspects of intestate succession. But, in due course, a further set of corollaries extended this principle even beyond the question of inheritance—for example, to the rules governing wills, gifts, and the right of alienation enjoyed by those with 'limited' lifetime estates (that is, widows, mothers, and unmarried daughters).

Following Hindu law but departing from Muslim law, for instance, 'tribal' custom prohibited the preparation of a will outright.[47] Gifts were, for the most part, allowed, but, in direct opposition to both Hindu law and Muslim law (not to mention English Common Law), 'voluntary' donations were almost always predicated on the explicit approval of the larger co-sharing community. In fact in many cases each gift was subject to the specific approval of a local *lambardar*.[48]

Alienation was always circumscribed by the law of preemption, but even beyond this, widows and mothers holding 'limited' lifetime interests were systematically prevented from alienating any portion of the family's 'ancestral' property (except in cases of obvious financial necessity—for example, marriage expenses or outstanding land revenue payments).[49] In some cases, women were given permission to alienate their 'limited' lifetime interests to specific 'reversioners', that is, to surviving male heirs. But, in these cases, the process of alienation itself merely 'accelerated the inheritance'.[50]

What mattered, in every case, was not the simple fact of 'alienation' but rather the problem of access to and control over 'ancestral' agricultural land. For instance, wills and gifts, like unrestricted alienations merely provided individuals with an opportunity to avoid existing rules of succession. (In other words, they provided individuals with an opportunity to exercise their ownership rights independently.) And, of course, as a general rule, the terms of 'tribal' custom were specifically designed to prevent this.

As 'rebuttable' presumptions, however, this list of core assumptions, axioms, and corollaries was never endowed with the full force of law. In fact, for all intents and purposes, the terms of customary law in the context of colonial Punjab were never more than a dense thicket of shifting legal conjecture—so much so that, as many administrators and judges were quick to point out, legal exceptions were commonly seen as the norm. Indeed, for all their efforts to appreciate (and enforce) the terms of local 'custom', most administrators were prepared to concede that the terms of 'tribal' custom articulated by specific 'tribal' elders were always rather unavoidably vague.

'I am decidedly of the opinion', wrote J.B. Lyall, one of the most prominent colonial administrators in the history of late-nineteenth-century Punjab, 'that as a general rule, these statements of tribal custom will not deserve the presumption of truth'. 'If it is grotesque to propound these questions to a select assembly of [tribal] headmen', he noted, 'it is much more so to propound them to the men of one village, most of whom, after listening to a few questions [regarding, say, inheritance, wills, or adoption], will be so bored and stupified that they will agree to almost anything [in order] to get away'.[51]

Indeed, even under ideal administrative conditions, the terms of customary law were notoriously unreliable. Sometimes they hinted at general principles. But, more often than not, they amounted to unsubstantiated claims about local or family 'exceptionalism' and sweeping flights of fancy regarding the notion of 'agnatic' (all-male) solidarity.[52]

Of course no one doubts that colonial administrators throughout the Punjab sought to understand and enforce the terms of 'tribal' custom—not necessarily at the expense of religious personal law, but rather, in tandem with it. The problem lay in their ability to discern what the terms of custom actually were. Indeed, as everyone knew, the real problem lay in the fact that, whatever was unclear about the prevailing terms of 'tribal' custom (or the relative importance of 'tribal' custom and 'religious' personal law) was also unclear about colonial efforts to regulate, revise, and reform the ownership and inheritance of land—the very foundation of their own rather tenuous economic and political regime.

THE NATIONALIST MOVEMENT, 1900–1947

Despite the ambiguity surrounding customary law, or perhaps precisely because of it, cases concerning the relative importance of 'tribal' custom and 'religious' personal law dominated the judicial docket in almost every district of the Punjab, from Gurgaon in the east to Dera Ghazi Khan in the west. In fact, throughout the late-nineteenth and early-twentieth centuries, preemption, gift, adoption, and inheritance cases were filed by thousands of Hindu, Sikh, and Muslim litigants every year.

It would probably be an exaggeration to say that every litigant sought an exemption from the terms of his or her 'religious personal law' (Hindu or Muslim law). But it would not be an exaggeration to say that most did. In fact, in comparative terms, the number of appeals involving 'religious' personal law lagged behind the number of appeals involving 'tribal' custom by a margin of (at least) three to one.

What is interesting about the case law record, however, is not only the efforts of colonial administrators to make sense of individual disputes in the context of competing legal traditions. In fact what really stands out is the creativity of individual *litigants* as they sought to make sense of the *courts*, using the flexible terms of the prevailing legal landscape to their own (strategic) advantage, and ultimately resisting (quite successfully) any asphyxiating move in the direction of greater 'codification'.[53]

Landed Property Litigation

During the first part of the twentieth century, a judge by the name of T.P. Ellis compiled a new legal digest entitled, simply, *A Judge's Notebook* (1912). This *Notebook* covered every aspect of customary law, from 'adoption' to '*zat*', but it began with a rather telling section entitled 'Matters to be Considered in Determining if Agricultural Custom or [Personal] Law is Followed'. This section included a list of questions, some of which are mentioned in the following figure (Fig. 10), together with the answers that would have led a colonial judge to decide a case according to the specific terms of custom as opposed to religious personal law.[54]

Fig. 10. Custom or law: five matters to be considered

1. 'Is the district one [in which] customary law generally prevails'?
   Answer in favour of custom: Yes.
2. 'How did [the litigants] originally acquire land'?
   Answer in favour of custom: Founders of the village; inheritance.
3. 'What proportion of the village area do [the litigants] hold'?
   Answer in favour of custom: A large proportion; a *taraf* or a *patti*.
4. 'Have they a share in the *shamilat*'?
   Answer in favour of custom: Yes.
5. 'Do they furnish *lambardars*'?
   Answer in favour of custom: Yes.

Together, these questions specified some of the criteria used to classify each litigant as an 'agriculturalist' governed by custom (for example, a *zamindar* or a *maurusi*) or a 'non-agriculturalist' governed by the terms of religious personal law: for example, a moneylender, a government servant, a trader, or a *kammi* (landless labourer). At the same time, however, these rather basic questions illuminated some of the enduring tensions described above, for example, between agriculture as 'an occupational feature of village life' and agriculture as 'an hereditary feature of tribal kinship'. Indeed, as Ellis himself pointed out, drawing attention to the terms of the Punjab Alienation of Land Act (1900), 'members of non-agricultural tribes are not held to follow custom [just] because they own land and live with agriculturalists'. Instead, he explained, what mattered was neither 'occupation' nor 'heredity' (considered in isolation) but 'hereditary occupation'.[55] Quite simply, Ellis explained, some individuals were born into agricultural tribes. Others were not.

For Ellis, the questions posed above were not merely rhetorical. On the contrary, they were useful in the context of his daily experience as a judge. Above all, they helped him to determine which body of law to apply in a particular case.

The first chapter of *A Judge's Notebook* (1912), for instance, was devoted to a list of precedents identifying 'tribes that follow [religious personal] law' and 'tribes that follow custom'. Each list was divided into two sections. The first dealt with Hindu tribes (law v. custom); the second, with Muhammadan tribes (law v. custom).

Among the 'Muhammadan tribes', the relationship between religious law and tribal custom was always rather complicated—a fact that Ellis himself illustrated with a careful study of the Kashmiri Sheikhs living in District Sialkot and the Syeds living in and around Multan.[56] According to Ellis, both groups represented 'upper-caste' Muslims, particularly insofar as they sought to trace their lineage to the tribes of the Arabian peninsula and, hence, the birthplace of Islam. (In fact, in the case of Qureshis, Ellis pointed to a further connection with the tribe of the Prophet himself.) Yet, although a certain number of these tribes were alleged to follow Muslim personal law, Ellis noted that *most did not*. In fact he explained that, amongst the Syeds of Multan, as among the Brahmans of Gujranwala or Rawalpindi, widows were provided with nothing more than a 'limited' lifetime estate.[57]

For all intents and purposes, Ellis concluded that most of the families included in his study did not adhere to the norms of 'religious' personal law. Instead they followed 'custom'. But this generalization did not end with the 'upper-caste' Sheikhs of Sialkot, the 'upper-caste' Syeds of Multan, or the Qureshis. On the contrary, it included the Awans, the Arains, the Gujjars, the Jats, and several Rajputs as well. Indeed the larger point, for Ellis, lay in drawing attention to the fact that, in late-nineteenth and early-twentieth-century colonial Punjab, religious personal law (that is, Anglo-Mohammadan Law) was always the 'exception', not the 'rule', among local Muslims.[58]

Landed Property Disputes (1860–1900): Hindus, Muslims

In order to appreciate the implications of this point—and, more specifically, its political implications for the emerging conflict between the 'loyalist' Punjab Unionist Party and the anti-colonial or 'nationalist' All-India Muslim League—it may help to understand, more directly, how the terms of 'tribal' custom and 'religious' personal law actually unfolded on the ground in the context of local (family) disputes. Fortunately, this aspect of late-nineteenth-century community affairs was discussed, in considerable detail, by Lahore-based Justice W.H. Rattigan and his colleague, Justice Charles Boulnois, in a rather famous book entitled *Notes on Customary Law* (1878).

As prominent judges affiliated with the Chief Court of the Punjab, Rattigan and Boulnois were very well equipped to document the relationship between land, law, and the logic of local custom in the context of colonial Punjab. In fact their *Notes on Customary Law* quickly emerged as a standard text for those with an interest in learning more about the circumstances under which 'tribal' custom might be expected to prevail over 'religious' personal law (and *vice versa*)—not in any explicitly *political* sense, but rather in an everyday *legal* sense—throughout the Punjab.

Like the work undertaken by T.P. Ellis in 1912, the work of Rattigan and Boulnois was divided into two parts—one concerning Hindus and Sikhs 'who followed custom' and one concerning Muslims 'who followed custom'. The former focused on cases concerning alienation, preemption and, above all, inheritance. The latter focused on the experience of individual widows and their right to a specific 'Qur'anic share' (*shari'ah*) as opposed to a 'limited' lifetime estate (custom).

Turning, first, to the distribution of ancestral property among Hindus and Sikhs, Rattigan and Boulnois cut straight to the heart of the matter, noting that, as a rule, 'daughters and their sons, as well as sisters and their sons, are excluded by near male collaterals'. To illustrate this point, they took up the relatively famous case of *Atma Singh vs. Massamat Attar Kaur* (PR1870:47)—a case involving a family of Sikhs in which the Deputy Commissioner of Lahore found that 'by the custom of the Sikh Jats, as by Hindu law, sisters are not recognized as heirs'.[59]

The case itself opened with the death of 'the famous Sardar Jaola Singh' and, subsequently, the death of his only male descendent, Ladho Singh (Padhania), who died without any sons. But, upon the death of Ladho Singh, his sister, *Massamat Attar Kaur*, claimed his property and took possession of it.

After a brief inquiry, the Deputy Commissioner produced the following summary: 'The plaintiffs', he pointed out (referring to Atma Singh), 'have asserted that, by the custom of the Sikh Jats, the sister is incompetent to inherit', whereas 'the defendants [*Attar Kaur*] have asserted that, by the custom of the country, she both can and does'.

Fig. 11. *Atma Singh vs. Massamat Attar Kaur* (1870)

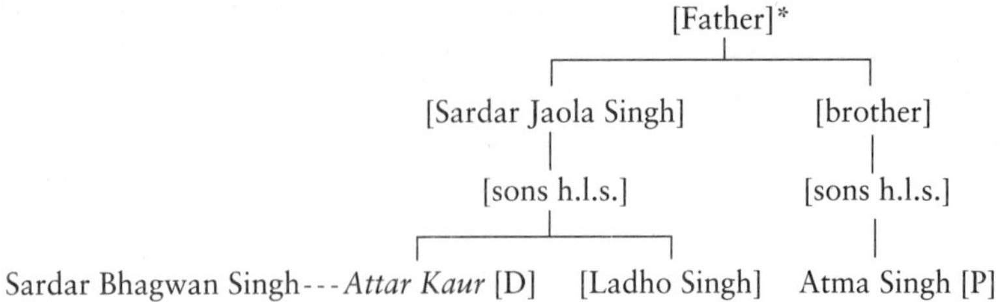

*N.b. [brackets] = deceased; *italics* = female; [D] = defendant; [P] = plaintiff

The evidence, explained the Deputy Commissioner, was 'very much inferential', focused almost exclusively on the inheritance rights of daughters. As the Commissioner noted, however, 'if the daughter is excluded by the custom of the country, if the feeling against succession in the female line is so strong among the Sikhs that daughters' claims [even in the form of a 'limited' lifetime estate] are refused, ... then it may be fairly presumed that the sister, who is unknown to Hindu law, is excluded also'. 'Any other supposition', he wrote, 'would be extravagant, and the sister's right, if existing, must be capable of easy and direct proof'.[60]

In sum, the Commissioner found that the existence of a custom excluding sisters had, in fact, been proved: 'By documentary evidence of the highest value, by evidence which, although rebuttable, is still good till rebutted', he wrote, referring to the customs recorded in the *riwaj-i-am*, 'the plaintiffs have established the custom of the Sikh Jats of [the] Lahore [District] ... to be the entire exclusion of the female line'.[61]

Turning away from local Hindus and Sikhs to local Muslims, however, the court recognized few differences. 'The resemblance between the customs of Hindu and Muhammadan village proprietors', argued Rattigan and Boulnois, 'is mainly caused by the retention of the latter of the custom of giving an interest for life to the widow, and excluding females, in certain cases, from inheritance'. 'The village system common to both', they added, drawing attention to larger themes within the colonial administration, 'results in a certain similarity, whether we regard the village in its earliest, or *zamindari* form, or in the development to which it tends, [namely] the imperfect and perfect *pattidari* [forms], and whether the village is one in which inheritance gives the measure of right [*pattidari*] or one in which that right is given by possession [*bhaiachara*]'.[62]

In other words, they noted, the custom of female disinheritance prevailed among *both* Hindus and Sikhs *and* local Muslims, even apart from specific questions regarding land tenure. Indeed, individualization may have been an important feature of some 'inexorable law of decay' within the village community. But, as a general rule, the individualization of inheritance rights for Hindu, Sikh, and Muslim women lagged quite some distance behind.

In their examination of Muslim agriculturalists following custom, then, Rattigan and Boulnois paid less attention to the shifting terms of land tenure and more attention to the specific principle of female disinheritance. 'The question of the daughter's right to inherit in preference to brothers and nephews was much contested', they wrote.[63] And, indeed, as the Deputy Commissioner of District Jullundur—and, later, an appellate bench of the Chief Court in Lahore—hastened to point out, the evidence on this point was mixed.[64] On the one hand, Rattigan and Boulnois explained, 'the Muhammadan *maulvis* [religious elites] gave very decided opinions *in favour of the daughter*' (emphasis added).[65] But, on the other hand, many families continued to favour 'custom'.

To illustrate this point, Rattigan and Boulnois took up the case of *Miran Buksh vs. Piru* (PR1868:29), which began with the death of a sonless proprietor by the name of Karam Buksh living in *tehsil* Naroda. Apparently, Karam gifted all of his land to one of his daughters (*Piru*) shortly before his death, excluding all of his brothers as well as his remaining daughters. This, in turn, prompted the Chief Court to note, with reference to some of the dilemmas posed by exogamous marriage patterns among (landowning) rural Muslims, that 'the succession of a married daughter ... is a matter of frequent contest'.[66]

On the one hand, Rattigan and Boulnois noted that, 'by the Muhammadan law as laid down by Macnaghten [*Principles of Moohummudan Law* (1825)], the daughter ... [was] entitled to a proportionate [Qur'anic] share along with the other heirs'.[67] On the other hand, however, they noted that three witnesses had come forward to testify that, contrary to his own religious personal law, which permitted testamentary succession only to the extent of one-third of any single estate, Karam Buksh had gifted *all* of his property to just one daughter, namely *Piru*.

Fig. 12. *Miran Buksh* vs. *Piru* (1868)

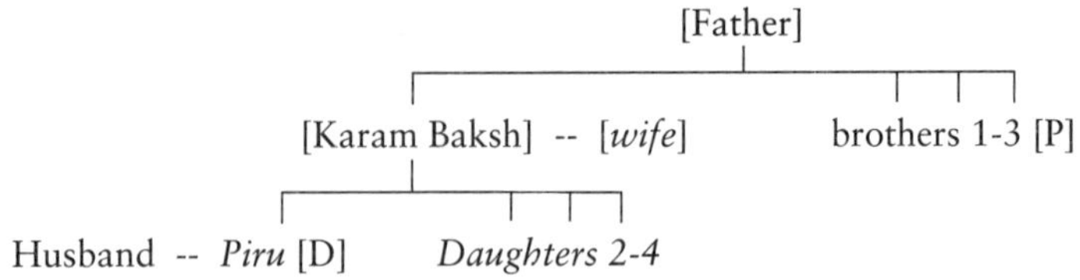

In the end, however, the court concluded that the testimony of these three witnesses was unconvincing, or, as they wrote, 'of little weight', mostly because the local *lambardar*, a man by the name of Kader Buksh, had personally visited the court and decisively rebutted their testimony.[68] In fact the judges noted that Kader Buksh had come forward and explained that, according to the revenue records—that is, according to the local *haqdaran-e-zamin* (the record of rights in land)—*Piru* was not recorded as the owner of the full estate after all. Instead she was the owner of just one-fourth.

In other words, focusing on the family tree (and the lack of any written will), *Piru* was recorded as the owner of her precise 'Qur'anic' share. And, when the court demanded an inquiry into the existence of any local custom *departing* from the specific terms of Muslim law, the brothers of Karam Baksh had nothing to show for their case. In fact their case was subsequently dismissed.

Needless to say, the relationship between Muslim personal law and 'tribal' custom was not always so clearly defined, particularly when it came to the inheritance rights of local women. In fact, more often than not, the enforcement of *shari'ah* fell short. To illustrate this point, Rattigan and Boulnois turned to the case of *Shadi vs. Massamat Bhai* (PR1874:257), which began with a man by the name of Alfu and one of his grandsons, Dulu, who was a Jat *biswadar*, or shareholder, in the village of Kotla (Jullundur).[69] When Dulu died, he was survived by his one and only daughter, *Shadi*. (See Fig. 13, below.)

Massamat Bhai was a descendent of Alfu as well, albeit a great-grandson related not through Dulu but rather through his brother. Yet, as Rattigan and Boulnois explained, Massamat Bhai 'claimed the land on the ground that, *by custom, the inheritance did not descend to a daughter*' (emphasis added).[70]

Initially, the evidence presented by Massamat Bhai in favour of a custom supporting female disinheritance was deemed insufficient, and

Fig. 13. *Shadi* vs. *Massamat Bhai* (1874)

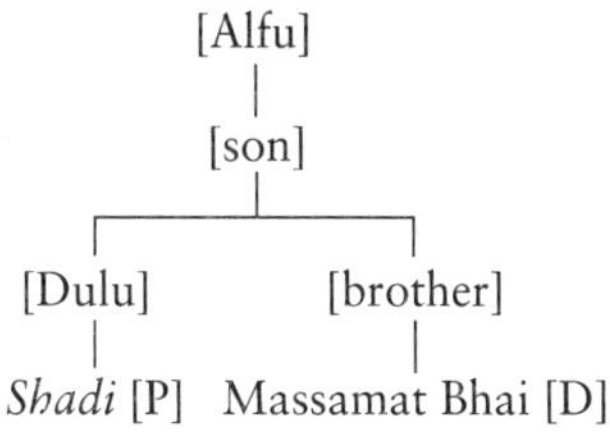

his case was decided according to Muslim personal law. But, on appeal, this decision of the lower court was overturned, and (notwithstanding his status as a 'confessing Muslim') Massamat Bhai succeeded in proving his ties to 'custom'.

Laying the matter, finally, to rest, the decision handed down by the Chief Court in Lahore focused on the competing strength of Muslim personal law and the testimony offered by several 'tribal' leaders in the neighbouring village of Dhurial. 'Subah, the *lambardar* of Dhurial, together with [all] the *zaildars* of a neighboring *zail*', wrote the Chief Court in its final judgment, referring to the terms of an administrative unit (*zail*) led by the leading *lambardars* of several (usually contiguous) villages, 'have given strong evidence that inheritance is regulated by custom, and not by Muhammadan law'. 'In questions of inheritance', the judges went on to say, 'a "*fatwa*" is never taken to decide doubtful points'. In particular, they noted, 'if Muhammadan law were ordinarily followed in cases of inheritance, [then] it would be natural to refer to it where daughters were concerned'. Yet, as the court pointed out, 'in no case have daughters been shown to have shared with sons'.[71]

The proof of this critical point, however, did not rely on the opinions issued by any local *maulvi*. Instead it relied on the oral testimony presented by Subah (the neighbouring *lambardar*). 'This witness, in this court', wrote the leading judge, spelling out the relative importance of *shari'ah* and 'tribal' custom in the context of colonial Punjab, 'denies that Muhammadan law has ever been followed in matters of inheritance'.[72] In fact, he wrote, binding the oral testimony of the *lambardar* to the strength of the colonial revenue record—and, more specifically, to the contents of a *wajib-ul-arz* drawn up for five neighbouring villages (all owned by the same group of Kanjah Jats)—widows and sisters are always excluded from the inheritance of agricultural land. 'Among the Kanjah Jats of Kottah [*sic*] and the [surrounding] neighbourhood', he concluded, 'inheritance is governed by custom [and] not by Muhammadan law'.[73]

And so, like hundreds of thousands (even millions) of women in the context of colonial Punjab, *Shadi* was disinherited not because the terms of her religious personal law were acknowledged and enforced, but rather because they were acknowledged and then avoided by Subah, the neighbouring *lambardar*.

Landed Property Disputes (1900–1920): Lahore, Sialkot, Sargodha

A significant portion of the most revealing information regarding the application of customary law, however, was not found in the litigation files maintained by the Chief Court of Lahore. Instead it was buried in the records maintained by the Punjab Board of Revenue, and, more specifically, in the settlement literature produced by this Board, for example, in the 'revised' settlement reports of Lahore (1916), Sialkot (1917), and Shahpur (1918).

In 1916, for instance, the *riwaj-i-am* prepared by Settlement Officer R.C. Bolster in Lahore focused on 'the transmutation of communal into individualistic theories of ownership' and, more specifically, on the extent to which this transmutation was reflected in 'the expanding liberties of daughters'.[74]

The standard by which this process of change was measured, however, is quite revealing. Regarding the expanding scope of individual liberties, for instance, Bolster pointed to the inheritance rights of women, noting that, in 1856, even before the first regular settlement of Lahore was completed (in 1860), most of the women living in the district were 'absolutely excluded by collaterals'.[75] By 1868, however, Bolster went on to stress the fact that a few tribes—the Arains, the Awans, and the Rajputs—had begun to provide their daughters with small parcels of land as 'gifts'. And, within just twenty-five years (1868–92), he noted with a certain sense of satisfaction that the transition from 'collective' to 'individual' expressions of 'right' was more or less complete. In fact, Bolster declared, some Muslim women were *included* in the inheritance of agricultural land almost as a matter of course.[76]

Unfortunately, Bolster failed to note that many of the tribes included in his assessment (for example, the Arains of Lahore) were widely known for their attachment to the practice of marital endogamy—a practice that, according to later officials, did much to explain the 'anomalous' pattern of ownership embedded within their apparently 'shifting' customs of inheritance.[77] What Bolster took to be a robust body of empirical evidence regarding the emergence of a dramatic transition from 'collective' to 'individual' landed property rights, in other words, was really nothing of the sort. In fact a careful look at some of Bolster's 'evidence' clearly reveals the extent of his misunderstanding.

After compiling a representative list of cases concerning sale, gift, mortgage, and inheritance, for instance, Bolster set out to document '[the] increasing tendency for women to alienate ... [their ancestral rights in] land'.[78] His list included more than 250 cases involving the alienation of agricultural land by widows, daughters, sisters, and sisters' sons. But, upon closer inspection, it is clear that more than half of these cases (59 per cent) involved just two tribes, namely the Arain Muslims of Lahore and the Jat Sindhu Sikhs of *tehsil* Chunian. What Bolster took to be a bold new trend regarding the inheritance rights of local women (and the relaxation of local attachments to the preservation of 'agnatic coparcenaries'), in other words, was actually rather limited. In fact, within the Punjab as a whole, even a cursory glance revealed that the 'trend' he sought to identify was, for all intents and purposes, more or less invisible.

In Sialkot, the issue was viewed through similar lenses. As a matter of fact, a revision of the local *riwaj-i-am* was commissioned in the autumn of 1917 precisely because, as an indicator pointing towards the 'individualization' of landed property rights, 'there was reason to suspect a change in the matter of alienations to daughters and the [*de facto*] succession of females'.[79]

As Settlement Officer D.J. Boyd was quick to point out, however, this trend in favour of 'individualization' was rather difficult to substantiate empirically. In fact, after a series of carefully constructed inquiries, Boyd wasted no time in saying that he was 'considerably impressed by the hold that the agnatic theory [of inheritance still] had upon the mass of the people'. 'The right of alienation outside the family and the succession of married daughters', he reported, 'were as a rule ... denied'.[80]

In Shahpur, however, the prevailing state of affairs was alleged to be completely different. 'Even twenty years ago', wrote Settlement Officer M.S. Leigh in 1918, drawing attention to the fact that, in a demographic sense, the proportion of Muslims in Shahpur was rather high, '*this district was to an unusual degree emancipated from the strict theory of agnatic succession*' (emphasis added). Moreover, Leigh explained, cutting straight to the heart of the matter, the customs of the district had 'not been seriously modified [in the meantime], either by judicial decision or by general practice'.[81]

What Leigh failed to anticipate, however, in the context of his notes regarding the muted influence of 'tribal' custom, was the emerging shape of provincial *politics* and, more specifically, the emerging influence of party-based political competition *after* 1918. Indeed, within the space of just a few years after Leigh completed his 'revised' settlement report, prominent Shahpur-based politicians like Sir Umar Hyat Khan Tiwana had emerged as leading figures within the politics of the Punjab as a whole—particularly, but not exclusively, within an entirely new political formation known as the Punjab Unionist Party.

In fact, precisely insofar as politicians like Tiwana and the Punjab Unionist Party (est. 1923) came to dominate the political landscape, key districts like Shahpur came to be regarded, *not* as a beacon of adherence to the terms of Muslim personal law (as Leigh believed), but rather as a bulwark of *resistance* to that law—in fact the very definition of adherence to a provincial custom of agnatic (all-male) inheritance.

Party Politics in the Punjab, 1900–1947

Increasingly, as the twentieth century unfolded, the legal tensions lying at the very heart of colonial Punjab (custom v. *shari'ah*) were drawn out into the open and exposed. For the most part, these tensions were engaged at the level of private family disputes: Who owned which 'plot'? Who received which 'share'? Who owed which portion of the local government 'demand'? And so on. And, yet, 'by one of [those] curious chances which play such [an] unexpected part in politics', senior observers like Cyril P.K. Fazal had noticed that, over time, ostensibly 'private' family disputes had begun to attract a certain amount of public 'political' attention.[82]

In what can only be described as a growing synthesis of law and local politics, ostensibly private matters came to be seen, quite unintentionally, as a reflection of the communal politics unfolding in other parts of North India: educated urban professionals seeking to expand the reach of 'religious' personal law, on the one hand; countless rural peasants seeking to *avoid* that law (in an effort to preserve the terms of 'tribal' custom), on the other.

Like Lieutenant-Governor Sir Michael O'Dwyer, Cyril P.K. Fazal was acutely aware of the extent to which the political language prevailing in rural Punjab departed from the predominant forms of political expression in other parts of India: 'kinship' in rural Punjab; 'creed' or 'class' everywhere else. And, yet, even then, keen observers like Fazal clearly recognized that the political language of rural Punjab was never totally isolated. Indeed, when Raja Narendra Nath announced, in the spring of 1936, that the Punjab Unionist Party appeared to regard the Punjab Alienation of Land Act (1900) as the legal and, indeed, the moral equivalent of the Vedas and the Qur'an, Fazal understood exactly what he meant. In fact everyone understood that Raja Narendra Nath was simply using a bit of political shorthand to flesh out the conventional wisdom of his time—drawing attention to the parameters of an evolving political landscape in which, slowly but surely, the idiosyncracies of the Punjab were being drawn into contact with a wide range of religious-cum-political developments in other parts of India.

Throughout India, the basic terms of religious-cum-political identity were tied to diverse expressions of religious personal law. But even a cursory glance was enough to suggest that this rather simple set of religious-cum-political assumptions made for a rather poor fit in the context of colonial Punjab—particularly (but not exclusively) among rural Muslims. In fact, throughout the 1920s, 30s, and 40s, individual Muslims throughout the Punjab increasingly found themselves forced to confront what might be described as the conflicting terms their own internal desires—in certain respects, the conflicting terms of their own (rather complex) legal identities: 'Muslims who follow custom', on the one hand; 'Muslims who follow *shari'ah*', on the other.

These conflicts were never limited to the private legal choices made by individual Muslim litigants in the district and appellate courts. On the contrary, they surfaced quite explicitly in the confrontation between and among competing political factions *within* the local Muslim majority: the Punjab Unionist Party, on the one hand; the All-India Muslim League, on the other.

The Muslim Personal Law (Shariat) Application Act (1937)

In 1931, the terms of this political confrontation acquired a new level of urgency when Sir Umar Hyat Khan Tiwana of Shahpur, one of the largest and most influential landowners in the Punjab, introduced a bill in the Punjab Legislative Council seeking to make primogeniture the special custom of inheritance in his family.[83] The impetus for this bill is unclear, because primogeniture was already the rule of inheritance among the Tiwana chiefs of Shahpur. But, as David Gilmartin (1988b) points out, 'the real issue may have been the definition of Sir Umar Hayat's own position' in the context of local factional rivalry.[84] Whatever the case may be, the ensuing controversy pitted Sir Umar Hyat of Shahpur, who favoured a strict defence of 'tribal' custom, against the 'religious' posture adopted by Sheikh Mohammad Sadiq, representing the Muslims of Amritsar, who pressed for a more conventional interpretation of *shari'ah*.

As the historical record clearly demonstrates, however, the combined influence of Sir Umar Hyat and the Punjab Unionist Party was simply too much for Sadiq and his urban (religious) friends: 'Unfortunately', noted one member of the Legislative Council by the name of Mian Narullah, this bill 'relates to one of the most powerful *zamindars* in the province' and, notwithstanding the fact that most of the members of the Council were Muslims, he explained, 'nobody [had] the courage of [his] conviction[s] to rise to the occasion and say that [it] ... should not receive our support'.[85]

Almost immediately after Sir Umar Hyat's bill was passed within the Legislative Council, however, another member of the Council stepped forward to introduce a second bill calling for the complete abolition of custom throughout colonial Punjab. In fact this second bill, sponsored by a close ally of Mohammad Sadiq, namely Malik Mohammad Din, called upon the Legislative Council to adopt (for Muslims) an exclusive attachment to *shari'ah*.[86] Needless to say, this bill only reinforced the strength of existing divisions, pitting the views of the Punjab Unionist Party against those affiliated with the (Punjab) Muslim League.

Even as this second bill was marching towards its own rather swift demise in Lahore, however, a third bill, known as the Muslim Personal Law (Shariat) Application Bill, was just beginning to receive a very different response—in fact a far more nuanced response—within the All-India Legislative Assembly in Delhi. This third bill was not a product of the Punjab. It was, instead, a product of the All-India Muslim League and the rhetorical stratagems of its rather ambitious president, Mohammad Ali Jinnah.

Much like the bill introduced by Malik Mohammad Din in Lahore, this third and final bill sought to reinforce the terms of *shari'ah* over and above any formal legal reference to the specific terms of 'custom'. However, unlike the bill introduced by Malik Mohammad Din, Jinnah made no effort to stress the terms of legal 'exclusivity'. In fact the bill introduced by Jinnah was little more than a powerful political ruse—in many ways, the first articulation of a purely *symbolic* appeal to *shari'ah* wrapped up within an abiding commitment to the *de facto* persistence of specific 'tribal' norms.

The problem: female disinheritance. When the Muslim Personal Law (Shariat) Application Bill was first introduced in Delhi, the vast majority of South Asia's Muslims had been governed by the terms of Anglo-Mohammadan law (that is, Muslim personal law) for more than 150 years—ever since Warren Hastings, the Governor-General of India, stated that 'the laws of the Koran with respect to the Mahomedans and those of the *shaster* with respect to the Gentoos [Hindus]' should prevail 'in all suits regarding inheritance, marriage, caste, and other religious usages' (Rule XXIII, 1772). In fact, when Jinnah stepped forward to articulate his support for the Muslim Personal Law (Shariat) Application Bill during the mid-1930s, few were inclined to suspect an appeal for any dramatic 'legal' change. On the contrary, given the nature of existing legal practice throughout British India, only the *taluqdars* of Oudh and the agriculturists of the Punjab were expected to articulate any serious or sustained opposition and, even then, only in an effort to defend their own (countervailing) 'regional' or 'customary' norms.

To be sure, Jinnah did not underestimate these sources of resistance. But, as Jinnah himself was well aware, *the symbolic appeal of shari'ah* was enormous, providing precious little scope for the language of opposition on the part of 'faithful' Muslims.

Indeed, as M. Sultan Bakhsh, a *tehsildar* employed in District Gujrat, was quick to point out (explicitly reversing the quandary articulated by Mian Narullah in Lahore): 'the stigma of opposing ... a law sanctioned and sanctified by the Holy Qur'an' was extremely powerful.[87] In fact, on so many levels, the basic dilemma was clear: whereas, in Lahore, very few had the courage to *support* the enforcement of *shari'ah*, in Delhi few had the courage to *oppose* it.

'[This] bill proposes to make the most far-reaching changes in the law of succession governing the descent of agricultural land', observed the provincial government in Lahore, 'and [a] change from custom to Mohammadan Law must inevitably increase the fragmentation of holdings', which, they argued—clearly referring to the legacy of late-nineteenth-century rural indebtedness—is 'already one of the greatest ... problems in this province'.[88] In fact, as the Resident Magistrate of New Delhi pointed out, expressing an undeniable sense of alarm, 'if *shariat* comes into force ... the land [itself] ... will be reduced to petty holdings'. And this, he added, was 'bound to result in poverty'.[89]

Clearly, the rather dramatic implications of Jinnah's bill were very well understood—at least in the context of the Punjab. And, yet, a closer look at the historical record also reveals that ordinary Muslims were extremely reluctant to express any strong sense of opposition. In response to an initial draft circulated by the Government of India, for instance, the Legislative Assembly in Delhi received more than five hundred letters expressing a wide range of political views. Some supported the bill for ideological reasons tied to specific opinions about the unerring sanctity of Muslim personal law. But, of course, most were considerably more ambivalent. In fact, reading between the lines, the Government of India explained that several responses revealed 'a definite uneasiness' as to the effect of adopting *shari'ah* as the guiding rule—particularly 'in matters of inheritance'.[90]

'The supporters of the bill maintain that it would greatly improve the social and economic position of Muslim women', wrote W.T. Amman in his Executive Summary of the Legislative Assembly debates, adding that, more often than not, these women had been 'deprived by custom of the rights given to them by [the text of the Holy] Koran'.[91] Indeed, most of those who responded to the circular issued by the Government of India understood, only too well, that the proposed change in the law would have a profound, even revolutionary, effect on the structure of the rural economy. And of course they understood that this 'earth-shattering' effect would follow, quite directly, from the inheritance rights of women. '[Although] town Mohammadans are not really affected', noted the Deputy Commissioner of District Lyallpur, it was abundantly clear that 'rural Mohammadans will have no time for [this] Bill whatsoever'.[92]

Again and again, close observers noted that overt criticism of Jinnah's bill on the part of local Muslims (including rural Muslims) was extremely rare. But the provincial government hastened to dismiss this fact as 'a natural reluctance among Muslims to appear as [the] opponents of [an ostensibly immutable] ... law'.[93] Indeed, the Government appeared to regret the extent to which even the most prominent Muslim agriculturalists had been placed in a religious, legal, economic, and political bind. Many noted, for instance, that although the terms of the debate had been cast in terms of particular 'religious' injunctions, making 'economic' interests seem incongruous or even crass, the 'political' problem of inheritance vis-à-vis the ownership of agricultural land was clearly the most important feature of the bill—leaving many Muslims, and especially many *rural* Muslims, feeling rhetorically and politically trapped.

The truth of the matter, however, lay in the fact that Muslim opinion throughout British India was radically differentiated. Indeed, many were prepared to concede that, although Jinnah himself—frequently styled as 'the sole spokesman' of Muslim interests throughout British India—had emerged as the Bill's primary supporter, the studied silence emanating from so many of his fellow Muslims spoke volumes. In fact, at one point the Legal Remembrancer of the Punjab cut directly to the heart of the matter, noting that 'in spite of what [any] politician may say [or do], I do not believe there is any desire for this revolutionary [legal] change'.[94]

The solution: the Shariat Application Act of 1937. In the end, after more than five years of protracted political debate, the final form of the Muslim Personal Law (Shariat) Application Act (1937) was unveiled. This was an historic piece of legislation. But, in the context of colonial Punjab, it was *not* a transformative piece of legislation. In fact the final, rather anæmic form of this Act cannot be understood without taking into account two very different sets of sharply cross-cutting influences. The first involved the President of the All-India Muslim League (Mohammad Ali Jinnah); the second—in many ways the more important set of factors—involved a founding member of the Punjab Unionist Party (Mian Fazl-i-Husain).

Mohammad Ali Jinnah. In its original (draft) form, the Muslim Personal Law (Shariat) Application Bill was designed to apply 'notwithstanding any custom, usage, or law to the contrary'. In other words, the bill was designed to prevail over any existing law that sought to constrain the application of *shari'ah* within the realm of 'religious' personal law. In due course, however, the agriculturists of the Punjab joined the *taluqdars* of Oudh in objecting to the use of the word 'law' in the Bill, mostly because, they explained, female disinheritance was already protected by the Punjab Laws Act of 1872 (Section 5), just as the custom of primogeniture was protected by the Oudh Laws Act of 1876 (Section 3).[95]

Precisely insofar as prominent agriculturists in Muslim-majority provinces like the Punjab sought to retain their traditional practices, however, the core leadership of the All-India Muslim League sought to encourage, and preserve, their pivotal (provincial) support. Indeed Jinnah himself realized, almost immediately, that a superficial appeal to the political logic of 'religious' (or 'communal') solidarity did *not* require an inflexible approach to the provincial application of *shari'ah*. On the contrary, Jinnah was a shrewd politician; and, as the debate unfolded, he wasted no time at all in removing the word 'law' from the preliminary text of the bill, effectively preserving the status of the Punjab Laws Act (1872) even *within* the context of a much larger push for *shari'ah*.[96] In fact, in his concluding remarks, shortly before the final text of the bill was put up for a vote, Jinnah himself went so far as to say that, for all intents and purposes, nothing would be touched by the final terms of the bill.[97]

After more than five years of political agitation and legislative deliberation, then, Jinnah succeeded in having the Muslim Personal Law (Shariat) Application Act of 1937 enacted. The text of the Act itself, however, deserves a closer look, particularly insofar as it attempted to preserve the relationship between collective landed property relations, on the one hand, and female disinheritance, on the other, even *within* the terms of a more specific appeal to *shari'ah*. In particular, Section 2 of the Act stated that:

> Notwithstanding any custom or usage to the contrary, in all questions, *save questions relating to agricultural land*, regarding intestate succession, [the] special property of females, [and so on] ... the rule of decision in cases where the parties are Muslims shall be the Muslim Personal Law, (emphasis added).

Ironically, this rather exceptional treatment of 'questions relating to agricultural land' in the opening sentence of the Act owed less to the work of Mohammad Ali Jinnah than it did to the work of Mian Fazl-i-Husain. Indeed, it would hardly be an exaggeration to say that, whereas Jinnah succeeded in removing the word 'law' from the final text of the Act, Mian Fazl-i-Husain succeeded in removing something far more important. In particular, he succeeded in removing any connection to the subject of agricultural land—not directly, in terms of the Act itself, but rather, indirectly, through a series of carefully constructed modifications in a far more important piece of legislation, namely the 'proto-constitutional' Government of India Act (1935).

Mian Fazl-i-Husain. On 2 August 1935, the Government of India Act brought an end to more than fifteen years of power-sharing (or 'dyarchy') between the colonial administration and thousands of locally elected representatives. Greatly expanding the scope of self-rule throughout British India, this Act stressed the importance of provincial representation and provincial (as opposed to federal) control in several key areas—above all, in the administration and adjudication of provincial landed property rights.

This effort to cede control over several different areas of administrative responsibility amounted to an important expression of political reform in its own right. But, for present purposes, the most important feature of this ostensibly progressive legal change lay in the extent to which its delineation of special 'provincial subjects' reflected the political machinations of Mian Fazl-i-Husain, whose priorities were grounded first in the political concerns of the Punjab Unionist Party, which he helped to form in 1923, and, second, in the 'communal' politics of British India, for example, in the All-India Muslim Conference, which he established in 1929.

As one of the leading exponents of 'Muslim' public opinion in early-twentieth-century British India, Mian Fazl-i-Husain was deeply and, in many cases, often personally involved in a series of efforts to bridge the gap between the economic and political concerns of individual Muslims (especially individual Muslim landowners) living in (a) Muslim-majority provinces like the Punjab and (b) Muslim-minority provinces located in other parts of India. In fact a closer look reveals that it was precisely this combination of 'national' and 'provincial' concerns that allowed Mian Fazl-i-Husain to play such an important part in bringing the concerns of individual Muslim landowners from the Punjab to bear on the terms of the Muslim Personal Law (Shariat) Application Act when it finally emerged, for all of the Muslims in India, in the autumn of 1937.

Above all, the politics of Mian Fazl-i-Husain were grounded in an effort to balance the system of landed property relations in colonial Punjab against the political appeal of Muslim solidarity elsewhere in British India. This he did, primarily, by conflating the interests of Muslim agriculturalists in the Punjab with those of Muslims in general. Indeed the political logic of this strategy was never very subtle. As Mian Sahib was quick to point out, the former represented a healthy majority; the latter, a struggling minority. And, according to Mian

Sahib, this simple fact led to one rather unmistakable conclusion: what was good for the Muslim majority in the Punjab was also good for the Muslim community as a whole. In fact, as far as Mian Fazl-i-Husain was concerned, what was good for the Unionist Party in Lahore was also good for the Muslim League in Delhi.

Indeed the Government of India Act (1935) reflected this political logic in several important ways, the most dramatic and powerful of which was its delineation of an entirely new set of federal and provincial 'subjects'. The former included defence, diplomacy, and a common currency. The latter included health, education, and, above all, the regulation of agricultural land.[98] Clearly, Mian Sahib argued, the best way to help the Muslim minority of British India was to recruit the political support of those living in Muslim-majority provinces like the Punjab, and the best way to recruit the support of those living in Muslim-majority provinces like the Punjab was to ensure provincial control over the administration of agricultural land.

After the introduction of the Government of India Act in 1935, however, many argued that the Muslim Personal Law (Shariat) Application Act of 1937 reflected little more than a shadow of its initial aspirations.[99] 'On account of the introduction of provincial autonomy', reported H.M. Abdullah, referring to the implementation of the Government of India Act, 'the succession to agricultural land has gone out of the purview of the [Shariat Application] Bill'. 'I am really sorry', he added with a clear sense of disappointment, 'that by the exclusion of agricultural land from the scope of the bill, its real object has been frustrated'.[100]

Of course the 'real object' of the bill boiled down to a specific commitment to the inheritance of rights of individual Muslim women. And yet, as H.M. Abdullah's colleague, Mohammad Ahmed Kazmi, pointed out, this 'real object' was almost entirely crushed by the terms of the Government of India Act. In fact, Kazmi explained, the 'real object' of the Shariat Application Bill had been almost completely annihilated by the Government of India Act, as '[the bill itself] did not apply to agricultural land, which constituted about 99.5 percent of all [of the] property ... in India'.[101]

After 1937: The Punjab Unionists v. the All-India Muslim League

Among historians, the Muslim Personal Law (Shariat) Application Act (1937) tends to be regarded as an enormous political achievement for the All-India Muslim League. In particular, many insist that the Shariat Application Act marked the beginning of a major discursive transformation in the history of South Asian Islam—for some, the first appearance of a coherent, cohesive, 'all-India' Muslim politics.[102]

In many ways, however, a closer look suggests a rather different picture. In fact with the removal of 'agricultural land' from the final text of the Act itself, even Jinnah felt compelled to explain that nothing would be touched by its (ostensibly revolutionary) provisions. Even as it prompted a fundamental transformation in the terms of Muslim legal discourse and political rhetoric, arguably cultivating an entirely new appreciation for the possibility of 'all-India' Muslim solidarity, then, the final text of the Act clearly stressed the political importance of enduring *provincial* norms. In fact it would hardly be an exaggeration to say that, when it came to the underlying logic of local Muslim politics, the impact of this Act (1937) was almost entirely invisible.[103]

To be sure, the rhetorical landscape had changed. And, when it changed, it changed quite dramatically. But, in a pattern that would become increasingly apparent over time, the reality of the local legal landscape (at the level of individual estates) remained almost exactly the same—closely tied, as it had been since the earliest days of the colonial settlement, to enduring notions of *izzat*, or 'honour', *riwaj*, or 'custom', and the survival of 'agnatic' norms: 'Even when the Shariat Act of 1937 was enacted, supposedly for the protection of [Muslim] women', argues Shahida Lateef in her book, *Muslim Women in India* (1995), 'their inheritance rights were curtailed in the interests of men and the family'. 'This', she added, must be viewed within the parameters of existing social norms, 'which subsumed individual interests to those of the [agnatic] family'.[104]

Provincial Politics: 1937–1945. In a political sense, of course, Jinnah clearly expected the fortunes of the All-India Muslim League to improve after the promulgation of the Shariat Application Act in 1937—particularly, following the logic of Mian Fazl-i-Husain, in the context of Muslim-majority provinces like the Punjab, where so many concessions had been made to reduce the strength of any substantial backlash.

Unfortunately, this expectation was almost entirely misplaced. In fact the provincial fortunes of the All-India Muslim League continued to suffer quite severely. During the first round of provincial elections following the coming into force of the Government of India Act in

1937, for instance, the Muslim League fielded just eight Punjab-based candidates, winning only two seats in the Legislative Council of Lahore. And, even then, one of these two candidates, namely Raza Ghazanfar Ali, chose to abandon the League in favour of the Unionists within the space of just a few months, leaving Malik Barkat Ali, a close friend of Sheikh Mohammad Sadiq, to fend for himself as the sole member of the League in the Punjab Legislative Council.[105]

In fact throughout the 1930s the logic of local politics in the Punjab was so clearly dominated by the rural priorities of the Punjab Unionist Party that, more often than not, *all* of the candidates running for election from a particular rural constituency were provided with Unionist Party tickets, leaving little doubt as to the outcome of the election in conventional 'party' terms.[106] Even the Governor of the Punjab, Sir Herbert William Emerson, noted in 1936 that, as a general rule, local elections involved 'two or more Muslim candidates fighting [in] the same [rural] constituency, all of whom are prepared to support the Unionist Party if elected'. More specifically, he explained that 'the elections [are] fought on personal or tribal lines' and 'the fact that the candidates [happen to] subscribe to the same political creed [that is, the same party] will not mitigate [the] local animosity which will long survive as a result'.[107]

Even as the Unionists succeeded in posting an overwhelming number of electoral victories throughout the 1930s, then, their 'strength in victory' was severely limited by the 'tribal' divisions that seemed to play such an important part in the context of their initial success. Indeed, what drew the members of a particular 'tribal' community together (in opposition to the Muslim League)—namely, their common attachment to the parameters of 'tribal' kinship—also divided them, rather bitterly, against one another. In fact a closer look at the historical record clearly reveals that, throughout the Punjab, the strength of the Punjab Unionist Party was quite robust and quite fragile at exactly the same time. Each member of each local faction remained firmly united in his unflinching support for the terms of 'tribal' custom; and, yet, even so, each remained fiercely opposed to any strength on the part of his local rivals—*patti* v. *patti*; family v. family; brother v. brother; and so on. (See Chapters 4 and 5.)

For Mohammad Ali Jinnah and the All-India Muslim League, of course, the politics of the Punjab as a whole were always more important than the specific skirmishes unfolding between and among specific 'tribal' factions.[108] And, yet, following the League's poor performance in the elections of 1937, it was the politics of the province as a whole that forced Jinnah to consider an entirely new strategy grounded in the terms of what later came to be known as the Sikander-Jinnah Pact—a political pact with the Punjab Unionist Party marked by distinctly 'Faustian' implications.

Ostensibly, the Sikander-Jinnah Pact aimed to draw the Unionist Party into the electoral orbit of the All-India Muslim League, with those attached to the Unionist Party promising to commit themselves, in purely nominal terms, to a pattern of support for the Muslim League in several 'all-India' fora (including the Legislative Assembly in Delhi). In practice, however, at a *provincial* level, the Pact merely *replaced* the existing leadership of the Punjab Muslim League with prominent Punjab 'agriculturalists', shifting the agenda of the League toward an explicit pattern of support for existing agricultural 'tribes'.

Indeed, as Ian Talbot has noted, the presiding leader of the Punjab Unionist Party, Sikander Hyat Khan, 'lost nothing by this move, for whilst the All-India Muslim League's position was revitalized, [Sikander himself] assumed complete control of the ... League [in the context of colonial Punjab]'.[109] In fact, almost immediately after the 'old' League was dismissed, the inaugural meeting of the 'new' League was held—perhaps not surprisingly—in the home of Sikander Hyat himself.

Needless to say, neither the All-India Muslim League nor its provincial branch in Lahore was in a strong position to capitalize on the moment when, in 1942, British Prime Minister Winston Churchill dispatched a special commission from London to investigate the possibility of quitting India immediately after World War II.[110] In fact differences between Sikander Hyat's successor, Malik Khizr Hyat Khan Tiwana, and the president of the All-India Muslim League, Mohammad Ali Jinnah, led to the demise of the Sikander-Jinnah Pact in the spring of 1944, leaving the already-fragile position of the Punjab Muslim League in a truly desperate situation.[111]

Provincial Politics: 1945–1947. When the Punjab Muslim League rose like a phoenix from the ashes to prevail in the provincial elections of 1945–46, many believed that they had witnessed a miracle. And indeed they had. As D.A. Low (1991) points out, the revival of the Punjab Muslim League 'was essentially the product of an urgent but passing circumstance, which generated a great deal of enthusiasm, but entailed no sustained commitment, nor much institutionalisation either'. 'Once its great objective had been achieved', Low explains, referring to the creation of Pakistan in August 1947, 'it soon relapsed once again'.[112]

The details of this fleeting but dramatic political transformation, culminating in the provincial elections of 1945–46 and the formation of Pakistan on 14 August 1947, lie beyond the scope of this book (although they have been addressed, in considerable detail, by others).[113] Nevertheless, three brief comments are in order—three 'all-India' comments that, together, help to illuminate the critical combination of exogenous factors that, in the space of just a few months, converged to produce a precipitous decline in the political fortunes of the Punjab Unionist Party.

The first comment draws attention to the impact of considerable economic hardship throughout India in the final years of World War II, including aggressive military recruitment drives and, more importantly, the requisitioning of grain, not only for the war effort but also to alleviate some of the suffering wrought by a devastating famine in Bengal. The Unionist Party, reflecting its trademark focus on 'provincial' as opposed to 'federal' concerns, urged local agriculturalists to hoard their grain, noting that, eventually, this strategy would allow them to reap enormous financial benefits. But, in the end, they were wrong. In fact the colonial regime simply forced the Punjab to hand over a significant portion of its grain at extremely low prices, catching the Unionists off guard. Naturally, the Muslim League wasted no time in exploiting the resentment felt by thousands, if not millions, of discontented Unionist supporters.

The second comment concerns the collapse of a special conference known as the Simla Conference in June 1945. This conference was called to flesh out the political terms of independence—in effect, the political terms of a complete British withdrawal—following the end of World War II. But, as the conference drew to a close, a growing number of agriculturists became increasingly convinced that, for those with an interest in securing various types of political patronage in the years immediately following any award of independence, it was not the Punjab Unionist Party but rather the All-India Muslim League that offered the most reliable assurances.

The Indian National Congress, for its part, had shown itself to be astonishingly unsympathetic to the concerns of ordinary Muslims, particularly in the areas where it had obtained strong victories in the provincial elections of 1937.[114] And, yet, during the conference in

Simla, the Unionist Party was treated as little more than a provincial sideshow. In fact, when the conference in Simla finally adjourned, the leadership of the Punjab Unionist Party could only watch in horror as its supporters began to shift to the League in droves.[115]

The third and final comment concerns the conduct of the 1945–46 election itself—an election in which the rhetoric of 'tribal' kinship crumbled, however briefly, under a surge of support for the rhetoric of specific 'communal' demands. As David Gilmartin points out, describing the rhetorical underpinnings of this election, the prohibition regarding religious campaign speeches (what Gilmartin refers to as politically motivated 'threats of divine displeasure') was patently ignored in almost every constituency.[116]

Indeed, when the dust finally settled the All-India Muslim League rushed forward to claim a narrow victory. This victory, however, was not a direct result of the election itself, which ended in a draw. Instead it emerged as a result of local riots. The Muslim League, for its part, won seventy-five seats in the Punjab Legislative Council, including eleven out of eleven urban seats and sixty-four out of seventy-five rural seats, providing it with 87 per cent of the seats 'reserved' for local Muslims. But the Unionist Party and the Indian National Congress cobbled together a total of seventy-two seats (Unionist Party twenty-one, Congress fifty-one), leaving twenty-eight seats for assorted Sikhs and independents.[117] And, for more than a year after the election, Unionist Party leader Malik Khizr Hyat Khan Tiwana simply refused to relinquish his position as Head of the Punjab Legislative Council—eventually sparking violence and, in a rather swift response to this violence, the imposition of Governor's Rule.[118]

Finally, however, after more than twelve months of political uncertainty and public violence, Khizr Hyat abruptly resigned (2 March 1947). And, just six days later, the leadership of the Indian National Congress called for the partition of the Punjab in an effort to protect the interests—above all, the political interests—of local Hindus and Sikhs.

As Ian Talbot points out, the Punjab was always 'the key province for the success of the Pakistan demand'. In fact, he argues, 'there could be no separate Muslim state without it'.[119] And, so, with discussions regarding a formal partition of the Punjab now fully under way in Delhi, Pakistan itself emerged as a realistic possibility. Less than six months later, on 14 August 1947, independence was achieved amidst the triumph and the trauma of partition.

CONCLUSION

Even before the turn of the twentieth century, the relative importance of individual and collective landed property relations was rarely debated. 'Individual' rights were routinely dismissed as the naïve preoccupation of an earlier administrative era. 'Collectivities' were regarded as a simple empirical fact.

In fact the main question did not involve simmering disagreements regarding the extent to which 'individuals' might succeed in pulling themselves together in an attempt to overcome what social scientists often describe as 'the collective action problem'. On the contrary, few administrators believed that there was any collective action 'problem' to overcome. Some stressed the terms of religious personal law, drawing attention to the collective aspirations of Hindus, Muslims and Sikhs. Others stressed the enduring principle of village custom, for which 'the land itself' was expected to furnish 'an all-sufficient basis'. But, in the context of colonial Punjab, most were inclined to set (a) the *sastras* (Hindu law), (b) the *shari'ah* (Muslim law), and (c) the *wajib-ul-arz* (village custom) aside in favour of (d) 'tribal' custom and the terms of the *riwaj-i-am*.

Indeed, for late-nineteenth and early-twentieth-century colonial bureaucrats and judges, the question was not *whether* individuals would pull themselves together in the shape of specific 'collectivities'. The question was simply *how*.

For nearly a hundred years, from the latter half of the eighteenth century until the latter half of the nineteenth century, colonial administrators clung to conventional assumptions about the primacy of economic self-interest set apart from local concerns about the parameters of 'the village community' or the bonds of 'tribal' kinship. But, as 'the customary right of ejection' fell into dispute, following the work of E.A. Prinsep in District Sialkot (1865), many administrators were forced to concede that their guiding assumptions had been, at the very least, oversimplified. In fact a growing number began to realize that, even if their evolutionary assumptions made sense 'in general', they did not make sense in the context of colonial Punjab. Indeed, just as late-nineteenth-century concerns about the problem of rural indebtedness began to overlap with early-twentieth-century concerns about the relative importance of 'religious' and 'customary' laws, a growing number of administrators began to insist that the 'ownership' rights of local agriculturalists could not be apprehended or adjudicated without a more consistent approach to the 'inheritance' rights of married Muslim women.

Even a cursory glance at the historical record would indicate that fundamental concerns about the stability, the liquidity, the authority, and even the long-term viability of the colonial state were tied to enduring questions about the ownership of agricultural land. And, yet, throughout the early part of the twentieth century, it became increasingly apparent that these questions regarding the ownership of agricultural land were closely tied to questions about the inheritance rights of married women—not only in the Punjab, but throughout British India.

In Bengal, Madras and Bombay, efforts to clarify the relationship between 'ownership' and 'inheritance' had led to the standardization of ancient Hindu texts and elaborate strains of Islamic jurisprudence. But, in the Punjab, these 'religious' traditions were often ignored. In fact what began with an effort to codify the *sastras*, the *shari'ah*, and the terms of 'village' custom ultimately concluded, in the Punjab, with an effort to clarify the logic of (agnatic) 'tribal' norms. 'We should not be introducing any novel or distasteful legislation', argued W.H. Rattigan (1878), but rather 'doing our best to maintain ... [that] which was suited to the people'. 'We should', he added, 'have certainty for uncertainty', and, thus, a 'stable' *customary* law.[120]

Unfortunately, as Rattigan himself was quick to point out, few things were 'certain' when it came to the specific terms of late-nineteenth and early-twentieth-century tribal customary law. In fact, as interpreted by the district and appellate courts of Lahore, Sialkot, and Sargodha, the terms of 'tribal' custom rarely amounted to anything more than a mélange of 'mischievous uncertainties'.[121] And, yet, amongst all of these 'uncertainties', one thing remained abundantly clear: the existence of a clear and consistent link between (a) vertically segmented landed property relations, (b) exogamous marriage patterns, and (c) the disinheritance of married Muslim women.

Social scientists and historians often insist, with considerable attention to the nuances of historical change, that late-nineteenth and early-twentieth-century adjustments in the colonial bureaucracy encouraged a heightened sense of religious or 'communal' identity. This is, in some sense, undoubtedly true, but a closer look at the history of colonial Punjab (1849–1947) appears to encourage a very different pattern of interpretation. Indeed, even if the colonial state produced a heightened sense of religious or 'communal' identity in the Muslim-minority districts of North India, the very *same* colonial state appeared to struggle, quite relentlessly, to *limit* the growth of 'communalism' in the districts of colonial Punjab. In fact to insist that the logic of late-nineteenth- and early-twentieth-century political debate was framed or constructed, in every case, by the rhetoric of state-sponsored 'communalism' would be to ignore almost everything we know about the shape of the provincial economy, the work of the colonial courts, and the terms of rural 'agency' in the context of colonial Punjab.

It is of course important to keep in mind that Muslims in particular were deeply concerned about the extent to which a wave of support for the All-India Muslim League would force them to confront an excruciating choice between the ecumenical terms of 'tribal' custom, on the one hand, and a conventional interpretation of the Holy Qur'an, on the other. And yet, precisely insofar as that was the case, a closer look at the historical record clearly reveals that, although some Muslims *were* inclined to promote the inheritance rights of Muslim women (as these were defined in the context of 'Muslim personal law'), *most* were not.

If the British were committed to the reinforcement of some groups but not others (and of course they were), a number of questions arise about the precise nature of the groups they sought to reinforce. More specifically, given what we know about the nature of colonial efforts to codify the terms of agnatic kinship, one could be forgiven for asking about the extent to which colonial efforts to sanction, recognize, or enforce the disinheritance of Muslim women amounted to a case of 'pushing against the grain'. Indeed, how much resistance did British colonial administrators actually encounter in the context of their daily efforts to reinforce the terms of custom (as opposed to *shari'ah*) in the context of rural Punjab? The answer, I would argue, is 'not very much'.

Indeed, even if D.A. Low and many others are correct when they note that the demand for Pakistan was inextricably bound up with the support of those based in (Muslim-majority) provinces like the Punjab, a closer look at the historical record reveals that, when it came to the final push for Pakistan, the Muslim majority in places like Lahore, Sialkot and Sargodha was considerably more ambivalent.[122] In fact the question for most Muslims did not boil down to the outcome of any particular election or, for that matter, even the question of partition.

By and large, it concerned their ties to the patronage of the state and, more directly, the immediate fate of their beloved 'ancestral' estates.

During the 1920s, 30s, and 40s, the rhetoric of provincial politics was transformed. And, when it changed, it changed quite dramatically (custom → *shari'ah*). But, as I will explain, the reality 'on the ground' was more enduring. In fact, the reality on the ground remained almost exactly the same.

PART TWO

CHANGING THE 'LAW OF THE LAND' (1947–1999)

Part Two: Summary

As noted above, the central theme of this book grows out of a pattern in which ordinary Muslims attempt to engage the state (both formally and informally) in a persistent effort to avoid the implementation of Islamic laws of inheritance—in effect, a persistent effort to 'circumvent *shari'ah*' (*'ilm al-fara'id*). The first part of this book sought to provide a detailed response to two important questions: first, why do they do this? And, second, what do they want instead?

Drawing attention to the shifting terms of landed property relations in the Muslim-majority districts of western (colonial) Punjab, Chapters 1 and 2 examined the inner workings of the colonial land revenue administration in an effort to explain exactly 'what people wanted' and 'why they wanted it' following the annexation of the Punjab by the British in 1849. Chapters 3 and 4 simply *extend* this investigation, using an account of evolving postcolonial institutions to address the implications of this local preference structure for the underlying terms of electoral 'accountability', as it emerged, in relation to the terms of 'Islamic law', *after* 1947.

After the independence of India and the formation of an independent 'Dominion' of Pakistan in August 1947—later redefined as an 'Islamic' Republic (1956), then as a 'Republic' (1962), and, finally, as an 'Islamic Republic' (1973)—the underlying conflict between the terms of custom, on the one hand, and those of 'religious' personal law (*shari'ah*), on the other, came to be associated with a number of rather specific debates, most of which concerned the introduction of 'Islamic' laws governing inheritance (*'ilm al-fara'id*) as well as taxation (*ushr*). Chapters 3 and 4 provide a detailed account of these debates, focusing, primarily, on their implications for the emerging relationship between local politicians and the demands of their landowning constituents—a relationship that, I will argue, acquired a rather unexpected shape (after 1947) *in the shadow of shari'ah*.

The implications of this relationship for those with an interest in the link between Islam, Islamic law, and democracy will be taken up, rather briefly, in Chapter 4, before being examined, in somewhat greater detail, in Part Three and, finally, in the Conclusion.

3

FROM COLONIAL PUNJAB TO POSTCOLONIAL PAKISTAN

INDEPENDENCE, PARTITION, AUTHORITARIANISM AND DEMOCRACY

Even before the independence and partition of British India in 1947, the rhetorical importance of 'Islam' had begun to overshadow that of 'custom' in the Muslim-majority districts of western Punjab. Eventually, however, this religious rhetoric appeared to advance well beyond the culturally and historically embedded language of Mohammad Ali Jinnah and his party, the (newly reconstituted) *Pakistan* Muslim League, becoming one of the most important and ubiquitous features of the postcolonial political landscape.

Before 1947, the Punjab Unionist Party struggled persistently on behalf of countless rural elites to hold the terms of *shari'ah* at bay. But, after the formation of Pakistan in August 1947, the Punjab Unionist Party was disbanded. And, increasingly, this tenacious defence of custom (*qua* 'custom') slowly began to fade. In fact within less than ten years Pakistan had emerged as one of the few countries in the world with an explicit constitutional commitment to the enforcement of Islamic law.

Even despite this rather explicit turn in the direction of Islam (and Islamic law), however, few were prepared to deny that—detailed calculations regarding specific Qur'anic 'shares' notwithstanding—individual Muslim women continued to enjoy precious little control over the land that, legally speaking, they were now entitled to receive through inheritance. In fact, for those with an interest in the logic of local politics as it actually unfolded 'on the ground', the challenge did not lie in any attempt to chart the shifting terrain of existing postcolonial 'laws'. (On the contrary, this terrain tended to unfold, almost invariably, within a rather specific understanding of Islam.) The challenge lay in accounting for the shape of an increasingly significant gap—what I will describe as an increasingly significant pattern of legal and political *estrangement*—between the 'law', on the one hand, and the parameters of political 'practice', on the other.

Before I proceed to illuminate the underlying implications of this gap for those with an interest in the relationship between Islam, Islamic law, and democracy, however, a brief account of several events unfolding between 1947 and 1999 is in order. In fact, without a basic understanding of these events—in many ways, the key events that propelled and refined the postcolonial history of Pakistan—the fundamental terms of my argument and, indeed, the remainder of this book, would remain almost completely indecipherable.

What follows is, therefore, merely a brief historical introduction to several well-known events, one that aims to present the names, dates, and places that, I feel, readers will need before they are in a position to proceed. Throughout this chapter basic features of the existing historiography will be examined with special reference to (a) the politics of postcolonial *Punjab* and (b) the postcolonial politics of *Islam*. In both cases, elements of a process that I will describe with reference to patterns of postcolonial state centralization will figure prominently. In the first case, the politics of Pakistan (as a whole) will be shown to reserve a special place—in many ways a central place—for the provincial politics of the Punjab. And, in the second case, the politics of Pakistan (as a whole) will be shown to reserve a special place for the rhetorical appeal of Islam. The challenge of course lies in drawing these two features together. Indeed, even a cursory glance at the issues raised in Chapters 1 and 2 would suggest that, notwithstanding specific moments of political interaction over time, these two features of the political landscape—the provincial and the religious—had a rather specific tendency to differ or diverge 'on the ground.'

What follows is merely an attempt to bring a more refined account of both features forward in time, moving beyond the provincial politics of colonial Punjab toward a more sophisticated understanding of religious-cum-political 'practice' in the context of Pakistan. How did the historical tension between the 'Punjab' and 'Islam' unfold *after* 1947? Indeed, how did those with a specific attachment to the preservation of 'agnatic' estates actually proceed, *politically*, in an environment (by all accounts, an historically alien environment) increasingly defined by 'Islam'?

In keeping with the chronology of the existing historiography, my response to such questions will be structured around four key moments. The first concerns the rather tumultuous years between 1947 and 1958, after the departure of the British but before the military coup led by Field Marshal Mohammad Ayub Khan. The second concerns the period between 1958 and 1977, beginning with the military regime of Ayub Khan and ending, quite abruptly, with the execution of Prime Minister Zulfiqar Ali Bhutto. The third will take up the period between 1977 and 1999, beginning (once again) with a military dictatorship—this time, the dictatorship of General Mohammad Zia-ul-Haq—and ending with a period of protracted political instability under Prime Ministers Mohtarma Benazir Bhutto and Mohammad Nawaz Sharif.

The fourth and final part will function chiefly as an epilogue, drawing special attention to the conclusion of my argument following the military coup led by General Pervez Musharraf in the autumn of 1999.

Independence and Partition: 1947–1958

As Ayesha Jalal explains in her book *The Sole Spokesman: Jinnah, the Muslim League, and the Demand for Pakistan* (1985), the shift from 'custom' to *shari'ah* that occurred throughout the Punjab during the final years of British India was, primarily, a shift in political rhetoric. 'Vague appeals to [even] vaguer [religious] ideals', she writes, 'might have rallied some popular enthusiasm', particularly during the final stages of the election campaign that unfolded during the winter of 1945. But even so, she argues, this dramatic *rhetorical* shift was never able to constitute 'a serious threat' to the dominant *political* order.[1]

'No one can argue that, in the heady winter of 1945', Jalal explains, referring to the anticipated implications of a *de facto* shift in favour of Islam, 'Punjab's rural nobility decided severally and collectively to commit *hara-kiri*'. And, 'equally', she notes, no one can argue that 'the [Muslim] League ... surreptitiously discovered and openly propagated a popular programme' which 'hurled the base against the top'. On the

Fig. 14. Political history of Pakistan (1947–1999)

National leaders	*Elections and coups*	*Elections (party/non-party)*
I. 1947–1958		
MOHAMMAD ALI JINNAH (d. 1948)		
NAWABZADA LIAQAT ALI KHAN Governor-General Khwaja Nazimuddin	1951 PM Liaqat Ali Khan *assassinated*; (Replaced by Khwaja Nazimuddin)	
KHWAJA NAZIMUDDIN (PML) Governor-General Ghulam Mohammad	1951 Punjab Assembly (P.A.) Election (PML) 1953 Khwaja Nazimuddin *dismissed*; (Replaced by Mohammad Ali Bogra)	Party
MOHAMMAD ALI BOGRA (PML) Governor-General Ghulam Mohammad	1954 Indirect C.A. Election (via P.A.) (PML) 1955 Ghulam Mohammad *resigns*; (Replaced by Iskander Mirza)	Party
Governor-General Iskander Mirza * *extended period of political instability …*	1955 Mohammad Ali Bogra *dismissed*; (Replaced by Chaudhry Mohammad Ali, then Hussein Shaheed Suhrawardy, then Firoz Khan Noon) …	

II. 1958–1977	1958 *military coup* (Field Marshal Mohammad Ayub Khan)	
Field Marshal Mohammad Ayub Khan	1959 Basic Democracy Elections (local)	Non-party
	1960 Basic Democracy Election (presidential)	Non-party
	1961 National Assembly (N.A.) Election; P.A. Election	Non-party
	1964 Basic Democracy Elections (local)	Non-party
	1965 Basic Democracy Election (presidential)	Non-party
	1969 Field Marshal Mohammad Ayub Khan *resigns*; (Replaced by General Agha Mohammad Yahya Khan)	
General Agha Mohammad Yahya Khan * *formation of Bangladesh* …	1970 N.A. Election (Awami League); P.A. Election (PPP)	Party
ZULFIQAR ALI BHUTTO (PPP)	1977 N.A. Election (PPP); P.A. Election (PPP) …	Party
III. 1977–1999	1977 *military coup* (General Mohammad Zia-ul-Haq)	
General Mohammad Zia-ul-Haq	1979 Local Bodies Elections (local)	Non-party
	1983 Local Bodies Elections (local)	Non-party
	1984 Presidential Referendum	Non-party
	1985 N.A. Election (PML PM Junejo); P.A. Election (PML)	Non-party
	1987 Local Bodies Elections (local)	Non-party
	1988 General Mohammad Zia-ul-Haq *killed* …	

III. 1977–1999 (*continued*)		
BENAZIR BHUTTO (PPP)	1988 N.A. Election (PPP PM Bhutto); P.A. Election (PML)	Party
	1990 Benazir Bhutto *dismissed* …	
NAWAZ SHARIF (PML-N)	1990 N.A. Election (IJI PM Sharif)	Party
	1991 Local Bodies Elections (local)	Non-party
	1993 Nawaz Sharif *dismissed* …	
BENAZIR BHUTTO (PPP)	1993 N.A. Election (PPP PM Bhutto); P.A. Election (PML)	Party
	1997 Benazir Bhutto *dismissed* …	
NAWAZ SHARIF (PML-N)	1997 N.A. Election (PML-N PM Sharif); P.A. Election (PML-N)	Party
IV. 1999–2008	1999 *military coup* (General Pervez Musharraf) …	
General Pervez Musharraf	2001 Local Bodies Elections (local)	Non-party
	2002 Presidential Referendum	Non-party

N.b. Left-hand column: UPPER-CASE denotes *elected* leaders; lower-case denotes *unelected* leaders. Middle column: C.A. denotes Constituent Assembly; N.A. denotes National Assembly; P.A. denotes (Punjab) Provincial Assembly. Parties include: PML (Pakistan Muslim League); PML-N (PML 'Nawaz' Faction); PPP (Pakistan Peoples Party); IJI (Islami Jamhoori Ittihad / Multi-Party Islamic Democratic Alliance)—see 1990 (above).

contrary, Jalal explains, the incongruous result of this momentous election during the final days of British India 'owed much, [and] perhaps all' to a series of opportunistic decisions taken by a significant group of established rural elites—a mélange of party-based defections that was, in fact, clearly 'dedicated to the single-minded pursuit' of individual political survival. These elites, Jalal insists, 'were not rebels against their fathers' cause; nor were they iconoclasts turning their backs on family tradition'. On the contrary, she argues, they were actually 'models of filial piety', models who simply calculated 'that the Unionists were about to lose'.

Of course this calcuation was entirely correct. The Unionists did lose, and, in due course, the Muslim League cobbled together a fragile but enduring victory. The rural elites who defected from the Unionist Party to join the Muslim League at the last possible moment, however, did not aim to 'abandon the past' with plans to support an ambitious programme of bold 'religious' reforms. On the contrary, they merely aimed to preserve their existing ties of patronage—ties of state-based patronage that had sustained their families for years. And of course, the urban stalwarts of the Muslim League were only too happy to welcome them. Indeed, it was an electoral alliance of convenience dedicated (overwhelmingly) to a passing set of 'communal' patron-client bonds.

Almost immediately, however, bitter disagreements about the parameters of these newly established 'communal' bonds emerged to threaten their pragmatic political foundations. In fact most historians agree that the fragile 'communal' fabric of Pakistan encountered its first major crisis, just a few years later, during the spring of 1953, when the All-Pakistan Muslim Parties Convention (based in Lahore) threatened violence if the Government of Pakistan, led by Pakistan Muslim League (PML) Prime Minister Khwaja Nazimuddin, failed to brand the Ahmadiyya sect as *kafirs*, or infidels, owing to their rather unconventional approach to the notion that Mohammad was in fact the final Prophet of God.[2] Indeed, when Prime Minister Nazimuddin ultimately rejected this demand and refused to brand the Ahmadiyya as *kafirs*, the leadership of the Muslim Parties Convention initiated a series of deadly riots in Lahore (and elsewhere)—riots the Lahore High Court Chief Justice Mohammad Munir described as 'widespread' hostilities of a truly 'menacing' character.

These riots were, of course, significant on their own. But, in a larger sense, their primary significance lay in the fact that, after more than a week of murder, arson, and general unrest, the existing (civilian) regime was simply unable to restore a basic sense of order. And, on 6 March 1953, the provincial executive intervened to declare 'martial law'.[3]

This period of martial law, ostensibly intended to restrict the scope of the riots, carried on for nearly two months, during which time Prime Minister Khwaja Nazimuddin moved to dismiss *the elected* Chief Minister of the Punjab, Mian Mumtaz Khan Daultana—not merely for his role in failing to *prevent* the riots, but also for his role in *promoting* them.[4] Indeed, despite his reputation as a leading figure within the Punjab Unionist Party before 1947, Daultana was accused of using the 'religious' tenor of the anti-Ahmadiyya riots to shore up his own political career, becoming, in some sense, 'even more Catholic than the Pope' in a bid to exploit the prevailing religious-cum-political winds.

This effort to dismiss Daultana was regarded as an important victory for those who wished to oppose the forces of religious authoritarianism. But Daultana's dismissal was not the end of the story. In fact, less than two weeks later, Prime Minister Khwaja Nazimuddin himself was dismissed—ostensibly for his role in removing Daultana—by the Governor-General of Pakistan, Malik Ghulam Mohammad.[5]

The final outcome of the anti-Ahmadiyya riots that unfolded during the spring of 1953, in other words, was not confined to a simple declaration of 'martial law'. In fact the final outcome was defined by the removal of one ex-Unionist Chief Minister (Daultana) in favour of another (Malik Firoz Khan Noon of Shahpur), followed, almost immediately, by the removal of the Prime Minister himself—a Prime Minister with family roots in Bengal (Khwaja Nazimuddin)—by a powerful Governor-General with family roots in the heart of colonial and postcolonial Punjab (Malik Ghulam Mohammad of Lahore).[6]

Indeed, in a purely political sense, the historical record clearly reveals a pattern in which the anti-Ahmadiyya riots of 1953 succeeded in combining *both* aspects of the 'postcolonial state-centralization process' mentioned above: on the one hand, a dramatic rhetorical bid to promote 'centralized' approach to the specific terms of 'Islam' and, at the same time, a dramatic political shift in which the surviving leadership of the Punjab Unionist Party, now joined together at the very pinnacle of the Pakistan Muslim League, was carefully and deliberately reinforced.[7]

In fact in this sense the final outcome of the anti-Ahmadiyya riots only seemed to set the stage for several subsequent events, even after

Map 5. Pakistan: 1947–1971 East Pakistan, West Pakistan (with provinces)

Ghulam Mohammad (falling prey to poor health shortly before his removal of Khwaja Nazimuddin) quietly resigned on 6 October 1955.

Ghulam Mohammad was replaced by his Interior Minister, Iskander Mirza, who wasted no time at all in resuming his predecessor's attention to the importance of 'centralized' (Punjab-based) politics. In particular, Mirza rushed to address what he had come to regard as a rather irksome administrative-cum-political anomaly, namely the fact that, although the bureaucratic machinery of Pakistan retained a close attachment to the administrative traditions of colonial Punjab, the weight of the population as a whole (roughly 54 per cent) clearly favoured Bengal (see Map 5, above). In fact, in a rather extraordinary attempt to 'correct' this anomaly, Mirza set out to extend the ambitions of his predecessor, Ghulam Mohammad, with an elaborate plan to reconstruct the existing map of the country.

This plan contained two key components, both of which clearly aimed to reinforce a special role for the provincial politics of the Punjab. First, Mirza sought to erase the administrative boundaries of the Punjab, Sindh, Balochistan, and the Northwest Frontier Province (NWFP), recasting the provinces of West Pakistan as 'one' provincial unit. (In fact Mirza simply extended the district-level administrative structures of the Punjab throughout the western half of the country, introducing what can only be described as a radical transformation of the postcolonial administrative order.[8]) But this was only the first part of Mirza's elaborate two-part plan. The second part—in many ways the more ambitious part—led Mirza to reconfigure the two remaining provinces as politically equal 'units'. In other words, having already collapsed the constituent parts of West Pakistan into just one unit, Mirza went on to declare that the voting strength of West Pakistan would equal that of *the de facto majority* in the East.

Unfortunately for Mirza, this policy of administrative-cum-political 'harmonization' (interpreted, by many, as a centralizing push for 'Punjab-ification') was not enough to unite the elected members of Pakistan's Second Constituent Assembly. In fact, as Figure 14 (above) clearly reveals, the Second Assembly (1954–58) was unable to produce anything more than a political three-ring circus, involving three prime ministers from three different parties in three years: Chaudhry Mohammad Ali (Muslim League, 1955–56), followed by Hussain Shaheed Suhrawardy (Awami Party, 1956–57), followed, eventually, by the already familiar Firoz Khan Noon (former Chief Minister of the Punjab) (Republican Party, 1957–58).[9]

After three years of political turmoil and uncertainty, then, Mirza decided to bring this circus to an end. Suspending the constitution on 7 October 1958, he dissolved the Constituent Assembly, banned political parties, and returned the country to 'martial law', naming Field Marshal Mohammad Ayub Khan of District Haripur (NWFP) as his Chief Martial Law Administrator. Within a matter of weeks, however, Ayub Khan decided to send Mirza himself into exile, assuming complete control of the government.

Authoritarianism and Democracy: 1958–1977

For ten years, Ayub Khan chose to preserve the 'one-unit' system introduced by his predecessors, Ghulam Mohammad and Iskander Mirza.

But, even as he held fast to this highly centralized administrative and political structure, Ayub went on to promote two rather dramatic pieces of 'executive legislation' in a carefully controlled effort to chart what he expected to be an entirely new course for the country.

The first of these two pieces of legislation, known as the West Pakistan Land Reforms Regulation (1959), sought to limit (however modestly) the size of the landed estates still held by thousands of politically influential agriculturists—not only in the Punjab, but throughout Pakistan. The second, known as the Muslim Family Laws Ordinance (1961), sought to expand the reach of 'religious' and, more specifically, 'Muslim' personal laws in several key areas, namely marriage, divorce, maintenance, and, above all, inheritance. Clearly, Ayub Khan was not a traditional Punjabi agriculturalist.

The full extent of these two new pieces of legislation will be examined in Chapter 4, particularly insofar as they sought to introduce or extend specific adjustments in what many considered to be the remarkably persistent landscape of the *ancien* (colonial) *régime*. For the time being, however, it is sufficient to note that these two new laws did *not* succeed in disrupting (or dislocating) that regime—particularly in the context of the Punjab. In fact, as I will explain in Chapter 4, these two new laws merely succeeded in combining the politics of the Punjab, following in the footsteps of Mian Mumtaz Khan Daultana, with an explicit 'rhetorical' appreciation for the ideological appeal of Islam.

Even before the full impact of these two pieces of executive legislation could be fully examined (let alone appreciated), however, Ayub Khan saw his reputation severely tarnished by the fate of the Pakistan Army during a disastrous war in Kashmir (1965). In West Pakistan, the underlying thrust of the ensuing disenchantment was led by Ayub Khan's own Foreign Minister, Zulfiqar Ali Bhutto of District Larkana (Sindh), who resigned from his post in the government to found the Pakistan People's Party (PPP) under the populist motto 'Islam is our Faith, Democracy is our Polity, Socialism is our Economy: All Power to the People'. In East Pakistan, however, popular frustration was framed by the leadership of Sheikh Mujibur Rahman, who relied on his own party, the Awami League (AL), to channel a series of Bengali protests against the country's ruling Punjabi elite. Indeed, by the winter of 1968, enormous demonstrations throughout the country had led to the reimposition of martial law, the resignation of Ayub Khan, and, finally, the installation of General Agha Mohammad

Yahya Khan of District Chakwal (Punjab) as the country's new Commander-in-Chief.[10]

Surprisingly, Yahya scheduled national elections for the autumn of 1970. And, for the first time since 1951, the Government of Pakistan permitted these elections to proceed with the support of numerous political parties. Unfortunately, the ensuing victory obtained by the Awami League was not honoured. And, within less than three months, the whole country found itself plunged into a gruesome and tragic civil war.

The catastrophic events of 1970 and 1971, culminating in the separation of East Pakistan and the formation of Bangladesh, have been addressed in several well-known books.[11] For present purposes, however, it should be sufficient to note that, when the civil war finally ended, Zulfiqar Ali Bhutto was named Prime Minister of a truncated Pakistan while Sheikh Mujibur Rahman became the first Prime Minister of a triumphant Bangladesh.

As an elected Prime Minister from Sindh, Zulfiqar Ali Bhutto was believed to represent an important democratic departure from the persistent military regimes of the preceding decade. But, again, every indication seemed to suggest that Bhutto was equally if not more obsessed with the terms of postcolonial state 'centralization'. In fact, throughout the 1970s, the terms of 'controlled democracy' under Ayub (1958–69) were surprisingly difficult to distinguish from what came to be known as a pattern of 'populist authoritarianism' under Bhutto (1971–77).[12] Indeed, when provincial efforts to *resist* Bhutto's rapidly centralizing regime emerged in Balochistan, Bhutto himself wasted no time at all in responding with military force. The provincial government of Balochistan was summarily dismissed, and, in due course, the government in Peshawar (NWFP) resigned.

Apparently, if the separation of East Pakistan (1970–71) taught Bhutto anything at all, it seemed to be that the people of Pakistan required a highly centralized political apparatus bound together by the politics of state patronage and nourished by a specific appreciation for the 'integrative' aspirations of Islam. In fact, to the surprise of many, Bhutto's foreign policy throughout the 1970s was dominated by a specific effort to strengthen ties with the Islamic Middle East, even as his domestic policy, focused on the promulgation of a new constitution, saw the introduction of a special constitutional amendment specifically designed to define Pakistan's beleaguered Ahmediyya minority as, by law, a 'non-Muslim' minority—by all accounts a rather cynical effort to exploit the 'integrative' potential of Islam through the gratuitous excommunication of 'others'.

The focus, in any event, was familiar. The focus remained firmly tied to a pattern of exclusive (and exclusionary) control. Indeed, throughout the 1970s, the most surprising feature of the political landscape did not grow out of any special effort to avoid the terms of state centralization. On the contrary, the most surprising feature grew out of the fact that this rather familiar pattern of state *centralization* was politically concentrated in *Sindh*.

Few were surprised when, following the announcement of fresh elections in the spring of 1977, nine different political parties led by the Punjab-based Pakistan Muslim League came together to form a new coalition known as the Pakistan National Alliance (PNA), an entirely new political formation espousing a firm commitment to the rhetorical appeal of 'Islam'.[13] Unfortunately, Bhutto was accused of rigging the elections that followed in March 1977. And, shortly thereafter, the leadership of the PNA took to the streets in protest, using hundreds of local mosques to supply their supporters with a steady stream of zealous 'religious' reinforcements.

By July, enormous riots had spread throughout the country. And, on 5 July 1977, 'martial law' was declared (once again), allowing Chief of the Army Staff Mohammad Zia-ul-Haq of District Jullundur (East Punjab) to seize political control.[14]

Authoritarianism and Democracy: 1977–1999

If Bhutto tends to be remembered for his commitment to the familiar cause of state centralization tinged with (Sindh-based) provincial parochialisms, General Zia-ul-Haq tends to be remembered for his efforts to *reinforce* Bhutto's attachment to the rhetorical appeal of 'Islam' while, at the same time, seeking to *replace* Bhutto's interest in Sindh-based politics with a renewed appreciation for the homogenizing potential of non-party (village-based) elections.

Beginning in 1979, Zia-ul-Haq went out of his way to reinforce the universalizing religious rhetoric of the PNA with a series of dramatic legal reforms, including the rather notorious Hudood Ordinances (1979), which sought to reconfigure and, in many ways, reduce the legal status of Muslim women, as well as the equally notorious Zakat and Ushr Ordinance (1980), which attempted to revise the mechanisms, as well as the content, of the postcolonial tax regime.

Even as Zia set out to smash the legal idols of the *ancien* (colonial) *régime* with a series of references to the specific terms of Islam, however, he also sought to move beyond this focus on 'religion' with an effort to revive the logic of local 'politics'. In fact, throughout the late-1970s (and then continuing throughout the 1980s), Zia routinely sought to shore up his ostensibly 'Islamizing' regime with an elaborate sequence of what came to be known as local 'union council' elections.[15]

Much like Ayub Khan during the autumn of 1965, however, Zia found that the full impact of his religious-cum-political agenda was still unfolding when, in December 1979, Pakistan was caught up in the middle of (yet another) major military conflagration—this time in conjunction with the Soviet invasion of Afghanistan.

Thrust into the role of a 'frontline' leader in the context of an all-encompassing, international, anti-Soviet *jihad*, General Zia quickly discovered that his appreciation for the rhetorical appeal of Islam was not confined to his domestic religious advisers. On the contrary, his pious posturing appeared to enjoy an international dimension as well. In fact, even as the war in Afghanistan sent millions of Afghan refugees pouring across the border into Pakistan, Zia scheduled a national referendum in the autumn of 1984 to assess the state of public opinion regarding his push for 'Islamization', safe in the knowledge that the outcome of this referendum depended less on the 'reformist' orientation of his own population than the cold religious pragmatism of specific supporters abroad.

The referendum itself, completed on 20 December 1984, was a sham. In fact, even apart from the problem of extremely low voter turnout (roughly 10 per cent), *The Economist* in London called it 'an exercise so absurdly rigged that most communist countries would have been ashamed to mount it'.[16] And yet, precisely insofar as this pattern of widespread rigging succeeded in producing an overwhelmingly 'positive' result, Zia went on to embrace the outcome as a ringing endorsement of his own highly centralized regime.

On 17 August 1988, however, the centralizing politics of General Zia-ul-Haq—in effect, the centralizing politics of an Islamic reform agenda pursued by an all-powerful General from Jullundur—came to an end, as Zia was unexpectedly killed, along with the American ambassador, in a mysterious plane crash. (Conspiracy theories abound, but, even today, this crash remains unexplained.) In any event, the military chose to retreat (politically), and a fresh round of elections was scheduled just three months later on 16 November 1988.

At this point, the daughter of Zulfiqar Ali Bhutto, Mohtarma Benazir Bhutto of the PPP, was drawn out of exile and catapulted into office on a wave of sympathy for her deposed (and executed) father. Unfortunately, the finer points of the voting process that unfolded during the autumn of 1988 meant that the PPP was left with an extremely weak majority and a host of challengers, not only in Islamabad but throughout Pakistan.

The focus of the assault on Benazir Bhutto and her rather feeble government in Islamabad did not come from her own province of Sindh. Instead it came from the Provincial Assemblies in Quetta, Peshawar, and above all Lahore, where the provincial Chief Minister, Mohammad Nawaz Sharif (PML)—for many years an important protégé of General Zia-ul-Haq (and, like Zia, born into a family with roots in East Punjab)—emerged to lead the erstwhile supporters of the Pakistan National Alliance, now joined together in a political formation known as the Islami Jamhoori Ittehad (IJI), that is, the Islamic Democratic Alliance, against the PPP. In fact for two years (1989–90), economic and political development throughout Pakistan ground to a halt as the PPP in Islamabad battled the IJI in Lahore.

The PPP, for its part, following in the footsteps of Benazir Bhutto's late father Zulfiqar, struggled to retain exclusive control over the levers of power at the centre. And, of course, the IJI struggled to wrest that control away, using increasingly strident forms of religious rhetoric to demonize (and silence) their opponents.[17] In fact Nawaz Sharif was keenly aware of the extent to which the rhetoric of *religion* had the power to paralyze his opponents while, at the same time, shifting the attention of the public away from Islamabad towards an alternative based in *Lahore*.

The rivalry between the PPP in Islamabad and the IJI in Lahore was, however, devastating for the country as a whole. And, after just twenty-two months in office, the Chief of the Army Staff instructed President Ghulam Ishaq Khan to dismiss Benazir Bhutto on charges of corruption and political incompetence, allowing caretaker Prime Minister Ghulam Mustafa Jatoi to call for fresh elections on 24 October 1990.

Perhaps not surprisingly, these elections provided the IJI with an overwhelming victory, including 105 out of 207 seats (51 per cent) in

Islamabad and an astonishing 208 out of 234 seats (89 per cent) in Lahore. In fact Nawaz Sharif himself shifted from a rapidly industrializing and religiously conservative constituency in District Sialkot (NA-88) to an isolated agricultural constituency in District Shahpur, renamed Sargodha in 1950 (NA-48), in a deliberate effort to highlight the shifting parameters of his evolving political support—a rapidly shifting base of support in which several different aspects of the post-colonial political landscape came together in a number of surprising ways. Indeed, when Nawaz Sharif emerged from the notoriously rural milieu of Sargodha to support the promulgation of a new religious law known as the Enforcement of Shariat Act in 1991, few were inclined to see his efforts as anything more than a carefully calibrated (Sikander-style) attempt to balance the religious rhetoric of the Muslim League with the more traditional concerns of an (ostensibly defunct) Unionist Party.

The terms of this new Shariat Act were almost entirely toothless, leading many of the country's most prominent religious leaders to reject it out of hand.[18] In fact, many of these leaders went on to suggest that Nawaz Sharif and his party, the PML, simply aimed to subordinate the sacred language of 'Islam' to a cynical bid for unfettered Punjab-based power.

Just two years later, however, in 1993, the Chief of the Army Staff was found dead (quite unexpectedly), leading his widow to suggest the possibility of a politically motivated poisoning. Nawaz Sharif expressed his dismay in a nationally televised speech. But, the following day, his government was dismissed by President Ghulam Ishaq Khan, who noted that, once again, the parameters of political power had come to be associated with rampant forms of patronage and party-based political abuse.

The elections of 6 October 1993 were difficult for Nawaz Sharif, primarily because the caretaker Prime Minister, Moinuddin Ahmed Qureshi, took a special interest in exposing the corruption of his government and the members of his deposed regime. In fact for precisely this reason the PPP was soon returned to power in a loose coalition formed by Benazir Bhutto and PML dissident leader Mohammad Khan Junejo of District Tharparkar (Sindh).

Unfortunately, violence and administrative malfeasance soon resurfaced as the principal features of local politics; and, three years later, on 5 November 1996, President Farooq Ahmed Leghari moved to dismiss the PPP for a second time, once again citing charges of corruption, incompetence, and extrajudicial killing—including, most famously, a conspiracy to murder Mir Ghulam Murtaza Bhutto, the brother of the Prime Minister herself.

The Pakistan Muslim League (Nawaz) or PML-N was subsequently returned to power following the elections of 3 February 1997, this time with an even more overwhelming majority. In Islamabad, for instance, the PML-N secured 135 out of 214 seats (63 per cent), and, in Lahore, recalling the deeply factionalized 'success' of the Punjab Unionist Party, 211 out of 248 (85 per cent). This time, Prime Minister Sharif contested the elections from the provincial capital of Lahore—NA-95—effectively completing his romp through each of the districts featured in the context of this book.

Unfortunately, few were surprised when this landslide victory was interpreted, once again, as a mandate for massive corruption—although, in the end, it was more than two years before Nawaz Sharif was embroiled in yet another conflict with the Army. In the wake of this new conflict, however, Nawaz Sharif was not merely compelled to resign. This time he was ousted in a military coup.

Authoritarianism and Democracy after 1999

When General Pervez Musharraf seized power on 12 October 1999, his plans were uncertain. In fact, until 11 September 2001, they remained fairly obscure—hidden for the most part behind a smokescreen of palaver manufactured by the international development establishment. The earliest illustration of his plans, however, appeared in a brief report published by the Government of the Punjab, entitled, simply, *Devolving the State: A Model for Empowering the People* (2000): 'We are at the threshold of a new beginning', argued provincial Information Minister Shafqat Mahmood in Lahore. 'For the first time in our history, *objective conditions favour the devolution of power to the people*' (emphasis added).[19]

Unfortunately, and despite several attempts to clarify the 'democratic' importance of devolving administrative power to the people via representative local institutions, the initiatives undertaken by General Musharraf and his international allies in Islamabad failed to reflect even the slightest hint of familiarity with the historically embedded logic of local politics as it had emerged in the context of postcolonial

Punjab. In fact a closer look suggests that General Musharraf simply expected to follow in the footsteps of General Ayub Khan and General Zia-ul-Haq, treating a carefully calibrated return to (non-party) village-based elections as the best hope for a carefully controlled return to postcolonial civilian rule.[20]

Indeed, much to the chagrin of General Pervez Musharraf and his technocratic allies in Islamabad, repeated efforts to stress 'the devolution of administrative authority' while, at the same time, preserving an ostensibly 'immutable' understanding of Islam (or Islamic law) did *not* succeed in producing any new political 'beginnings'.[21] On the contrary, such efforts merely enhanced the rent-seeking opportunities available to those with enough leverage to manipulate the strength of existing laws—including, above all, those with sufficient leverage to manipulate (or avoid) existing 'Islamic' laws: *ushr*, *'ilm al-fara'id*, and so on.

Pervez Musharraf may have believed that a simple devolution of administrative authority to representative local institutions would be enough to inspire a dramatic process of postcolonial legal-cum-political change. But, in practice, this was not the case. In fact, as I will explain in greater detail in Chapter 4, the task of devolving administrative (as opposed to legislative) authority to representative local institutions merely led to the political *estrangement* of 'participatory' and 'legal' reforms.

CONCLUSION

As the twentieth century progressed, the terms of *shari'ah* became increasingly important as a symbol for the transformation of the postcolonial state. And, yet, throughout the Punjab, leading politicians sought new ways to 'support' this transformation in purely 'symbolic' ways. The Muslim Personal Law (Shariat) Application Act of 1937 provided one very early example of this trend. But, in due course, postcolonial efforts to promote the Muslim Family Laws Ordinance of 1961 and the Zakat and Ushr Ordinance of 1980 emerged to provide several additional examples. In fact, even after the specific terms of *shari'ah* found their way into the language of existing postcolonial laws, they were, in many ways, merely 'rhetorical'.

This pattern of postcolonial state centralization grounded in a purely 'symbolic' or 'rhetorical' attachment to Islam did not diminish the political power of the Punjab—at least not initially (1947–99). On the contrary, the impact of this pattern was far more diffuse. In fact persistent references to the terms of Islam (on the part of ex-Unionist elites and their political allies in the newly reconstituted Pakistan Muslim League) merely served to advance the cause of state centralization—centralizing a 'state' that the Punjab, in turn, controlled. Indeed the goal, throughout the latter half of the twentieth century, did not lie in 'Islamizing' the state (in practice). Instead it lay in placing the rhetoric of Islam (and Islamic law) in the service of a rapidly *centralizing* state; and, then, having done so, locating that 'state' (as a whole) within a pattern of enduring *provincial* control.

At a national level, politicians arranged themselves into rival factions, seeking either to reinforce the power of the Punjab (for example, the PML) or to restrain it (for example, the PPP). But, in both cases, the goal was largely the same. The goal lay in seizing control over an increasingly centralized state and, then, having done so, exploiting the character of that highly centralized state to rule by executive 'decree'.[22] In fact ordinary 'legislation' was often seen as deeply compromised (or constrained) by the terms of Islamization itself—if not directly, in the form of specific constitutional limits, then indirectly, in the form of a much larger sense that the logic of Islamization imposed a series of implicit restrictions on the consolidation of 'man-made' rules.

This sense of implied religious constraint was extremely widespread throughout the latter half of the twentieth century. And, as time passed, this sense of religious constraint began to affect the logic of local politics itself. In fact local notions of political accountability began to turn away from any special focus on the task of politically accountable 'legislation' in favour of a rather more creative appreciation for the value of accountable 'enforcement': in effect, a more creative appreciation for the ways in which various forms of privileged access *to* state power (including electoral access) could be converted into a more consistent pattern of protection *from* the enforcement of unpalatable 'rules' (including, of course, standard Islamic rules like the Islamic Law of Inheritance).

Indeed what follows, first in the context of Chapter 4 and then throughout Part Three, is, in many ways, a detailed examination of this pattern—this pattern of *political participation, accountability, and enforcement* (or non-enforcement as the case may be). How did this pattern actually work in practice? How did it take shape on the ground? These are, in effect, the questions that I will address in the remainder of this book. How were the terms of Islamic law brought to bear on the shape of landed property relations throughout postcolonial Punjab? How were these terms brought to bear on the lives of individual Muslims? And, finally, how did those Muslims respond—legally, politically, and so on?

4

WHO CONTROLS THE LAND? (1947–1999)

LAND REFORM, LAW REFORM, AND THE LOGIC OF LOCAL POLITICS

For several years after independence and partition, there were many in the Punjab who continued to stress the importance of village and tribal 'custom'. At the same time, however, there was also an increasingly vocal urban minority that sought to replace the language of custom with a countervailing interpretation of 'Islam'. This minority did not succeed in transforming the institutional landscape of the Punjab right away. But, as I will explain, their influence did expand throughout the latter half of the twentieth century (1947–99). In fact, as the twentieth century came to an end it would hardly be an exaggeration to say that, when it came to the content of existing laws, their influence was impossible to ignore.

What follows is merely an attempt to account for the nature, the scope, and ultimately, the implications of the influence exerted by this increasingly vocal urban minority, focusing specifically, on two rather ambitious sets of reforms—one concerning land; one concerning religious personal law. The most important reforms sought to introduce the terms of *shari'ah* in the context of (a) rural taxation (*ushr*) and, especially, (b) female (Qur'anic) inheritance (*'ilm al-fara'id*). But, as I will explain, the impact of these reforms also extended much further, steadily encroaching upon virtually every aspect of every ancestral estate.

The specific implications of these reforms for those with an interest in the fate of democracy and, more specifically, local notions of electoral 'accountability', will be examined in two parts. In the first part, my comments will be restricted to a brief assessment of the link between specific legal reforms (for example, the shift from 'custom' to *shari'ah*) and the logic underlying local union council elections in Lahore, Sialkot, and Sargodha. This assessment will appear at the end of this chapter in a short summary entitled 'The Logic of Local Politics'. The second part—the more detailed part—will appear in Chapter 5.

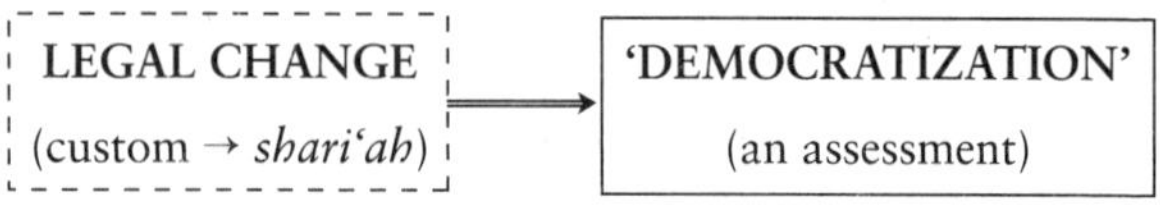

After the independence of British India, the trauma of partition, and the formation of Pakistan in 1947, the formal administrative landscape governing individual ancestral estates was slowly but surely transformed, with enormous implications for the logic of local politics and, eventually, the fate of democracy as a whole. This chapter aims to document the nature of this institutional and political change, drawing special attention to a wide range of dramatic legal reforms: land reforms, law reforms, and so on.

If, as noted above, political patterns in Pakistan (1947–99) were closely bound up with the politics of postcolonial *Punjab*, even as prevailing patterns *within* the Punjab were (increasingly) bound up with the rhetorical demands of *Islam*, the question is: How did these two aspects of the postcolonial landscape come together? How did they meet 'on the ground'? This is, very briefly, the question that I will take up and address in the context of this chapter: How did the expanding influence of Islam and, more specifically, the expanding influence of Islamic law, affect the shape of concrete political practices throughout postcolonial Punjab? How did the expanding influence of 'Islamic' law intersect with, and transform, local expressions of political participation, accountability, and 'democracy'?

LAND REFORM

For nearly 150 years (1849–1999), the structure of the district administration in colonial and postcolonial Punjab remained more or less the same. Even in 1999, more than fifty years after the formation of Pakistan itself (not to mention several decades of formal legal change—see below), the district *kachehri*, or headquarters, appeared almost entirely unchanged, right down to the forms filled in by local officials and clerks.

Within the district administration three officials were especially important. And, in what follows, these three officials will receive quite a lot of attention. Indeed what follows is merely a brief assessment of the work undertaken by these three officials—one that aims to set the stage for a more detailed discussion of their role in the reforms addressed below. Indeed, as I will explain, these three officials were, for all intents and purposes, the formal administrative functionaries through whom each decision—legal, quasi-legal and otherwise—was formally expected to pass.

The first and by the far the most prominent of these three officials was the Deputy Commissioner, or 'DC', whose position, *even after 1947*, continued to combine both revenue and judicial functions. The second, and in many ways the most notorious, was the *patwari*, or village accountant, whose position at the bottom of the administrative hierarchy allowed him to serve as a critical link—indeed, *the* critical link—between (a) the district administration and (b) the public at large. The third, and arguably the most obscure, was the local (often *patti*-based) *lambardar*, who served as a government functionary in the context of the local revenue administration, an expert witness in the district and appellate courts, and, more often than not, a vigorous contender in the context of local elections.

As I will explain, a certain familiarity with these three officials is absolutely essential for anyone with an interest in the formal legal landscape within which postcolonial property owners struggled—often quite creatively—to protect their 'agnatic' estates.

The District Administration

For more than fifty years after independence and partition (1947–99), the work of the Deputy Commissioner, the *patwari*, and the local *lambardar* continued to reflect the priorities of the colonial state as expressed by Sir John Lawrence shortly after the defeat of Maharaja Ranjit Singh in 1849.[1]

The Deputy Commissioner

As Sir William Hunter reminded his superiors in 1892, for instance, the work of the Deputy Commissioner was really twofold. On the one hand, he was said to be 'a fiscal officer charged with the collection of [the district land] revenue'. But, at the same time, he was also defined as a judge, 'both of [the] first instance and in appeal'.[2] Indeed, this was the meaning of his official designation: *Collector-Magistrate*.

Clearly, the DC was expected to be a busy man (and, as I encountered him in the course of my field research, he certainly was). As a 'jack-of-all-trades', however, the DC was also, too often, 'the master of none'. 'The nature of his business is so varied', wrote A.H. Aslam in a rather helpful survey entitled *The Deputy Commissioner: A Study in Public Administration* (1957), that, more often than not, the one who seeks 'to acquaint himself with the details of all will be unwise, not to say incompetent'.[3]

Not surprisingly, concerns about the multiple overlapping responsibilities of the DC were fairly widespread. In fact, by 1953, the Chief Minister of the Punjab, Malik Firoz Khan Noon, was keen to highlight emerging demands for 'an immediate separation of powers'.[4] In particular, Noon alerted his fellow politicians to a growing interest in separating (a) the Commissioner's role as a District Collector (DC), who served as a superior tax collector under the provincial Board of Revenue, from (b) his role as a District Magistrate (DM), who served as a public prosecutor under the Provincial Inspector General as well as a criminal magistrate under the Lahore High Court.

Indeed, as A.H. Aslam (1957) was quick to point out, just a few months before Malik Firoz Khan Noon became Prime Minister (1957–58)—the last Prime Minister, as it happens, before the military coup led by Field Marshal Ayub Khan—it had become increasingly difficult to justify this combination of executive and judicial functions in the same person to the point where 'the officer responsible for collecting evidence and prosecuting through the police should [also] be the judge who tries the case'.[5] This, Aslam noted, was an intolerable legacy of the colonial regime. And, as time passed, he could see no reason to preserve it in the context of Pakistan.

Given the underlying demands of postcolonial provincial politics, however, few were surprised when these concerns regarding the overlapping powers of the District Commissioner were simply ignored. In fact it was not until the spring of 1993—nearly fifty years after the formation of Pakistan itself—that the country's highest court finally stepped in and ordered 'the immediate separation' of executive and judicial functions in all areas of the district administration.[6]

Even then, however, a special (internal) memorandum produced by the office of the provincial Law Secretary in Lahore emerged to explain exactly why this order of the court—indeed, the Supreme Court—was likely to remain unimplemented.[7] In fact, according to the provincial Law Secretary, any effort to separate the functions of the District Collector from those of the District Magistrate would result in 'a drastic qualitative change' in the nature of the district administration and, thus, a threat to the province as a whole—something the Government of the Punjab was not, as yet, even remotely prepared to consider.[8]

As the Law Secretary pointed out, the real value of 'non-separation' lay in the adjudication of local agrarian disputes: evictions, partitions, inheritance mutations, and, more often than not, the 'law and order' concerns that surrounded them. In fact, drawing attention to the importance of local patterns of dispute resolution, the Secretary focused his comments on the competing jurisdiction of the 'revenue' and the 'civil' courts: 'With the weakening of the executive [magistrates]' (that is, the weakening of the District Magistrate or DM), he warned, 'ordinary citizens will have to ... move for judicial relief'. And this, he argued, would amount to a most unpopular change. The executive, he noted, is 'direct and prompt', since it 'cuts across the formal [legal] channels', whereas the judiciary is 'formal', 'slow' and 'channelled'.[9]

Needless to say, these comments led a certain number of observers to ask why a 'channelled' approach to the enforcement of existing postcolonial laws was so undesirable. Indeed, why were ordinary citizens so interested in a process of dispute resolution that promised to 'cut across' the substance of existing laws?

According to the Law Secretary, many litigants preferred the summary decisions of the Deputy Commissioner, because, compared with the civil courts, they were more accessible, cheaper, and less time consuming (at least in theory). But, at the same time, he also noted that the civil courts remained extremely unpopular because, for the most part, they had a tendency to 'proceed according to the prescribed laws' both in a procedural and in a substantive sense 'without taking [into] account the inconvenience being caused' to so many members of the public.[10]

What the Secretary suggested, however, was actually something quite important about the work of the Deputy Commissioner himself. Indeed the Secretary seemed to suggest that the appeal of the 'revenue' courts and the 'executive' magistracy did not lie in their ability to enforce existing laws more quickly, more consistently, or more effectively. Rather, it lay in their ability to 'cut across' existing channels and, thus, in their ability to *circumvent* existing laws—laws that in practice, were said to cause a great deal of 'inconvenience' to the public.

'Executive magistrates work under the ... scrutiny of [the] higher courts', noted the Secretary, coming straight to the heart of the matter, but they also worked under 'the political accountability of public representatives'.[11] The courts, he observed, may have taken an interest in the enforcement of existing laws. But, in conjunction with various locally elected representatives, the priorities of the bureaucracy lay somewhere else—indeed, somewhere closer to *the interests of the public at large*. 'The situation is currently on an even keel', argued the Secretary, adding that, under the circumstances, 'it would not be prudent to rock the [administrative] boat'.[12]

The *Patwari*

Interestingly, and despite a well-documented pattern of frustration with the district-level administration, most villagers were inclined to regard the Deputy Commissioner with a certain amount of indifference. In fact, although the DC/DM was a prominent official, he was also rather 'remote' and, therefore, relatively 'unimportant'. In the context of their daily lives, most villagers insisted that the *patwari* was far more influential.[13]

Like the DC, the *patwari* was involved in a wide range of administrative departments affecting countless areas of postcolonial policy concern. Above all, he served as the village registrar, recording routine 'mutations' or changes in the official records that sought to document the 'ownership' and 'tenancy' of land. But, as many scholars have pointed out, his duties (like those of the DC) also extended well beyond this.[14] In his book entitled *Expanding Role of Patwaris in Revenue Administration* (1966), for instance, S.M. Haider compiled a list of more than fifty departments to which the *patwari* was expected to respond.[15] (See Fig. 15 below.)

Needless to say, given the extent of this list, Haider found that most of the reports compiled by local *patwaris* were 'incomplete and

Fig. 15. *Patwaris*: records and duties (abbreviated)

Records	*Duties*
*Jamabandi*s	Prepare *jamabandi* every four years
List of sales and mortgages	Enter mutations as they occur
Digest of property boundaries	Complete surveys of agricultural land
Record of *patti*s and kin groups	Collect land revenue
List of *badmash* (i.e. 'vagrants')	Report crimes
Constituency lists	Assist union councils
List of debtors and absconders	Assist with collection of arrears
List of *lambardar*s	Attend the district courts

unreliable'.[16] In fact, recalling the work of Deputy Commissioner C. Minchin in District Dera Ghazi Khan (1863), Haider reported that it was 'really amazing' to see how often the *patwaris* themselves were prepared to step forward and confess their crimes—in many cases expressing no hesitation whatsoever when it came to recounting various strategies of corruption, harassment and abuse, including: (a) delaying or cancelling mutations, (b) collecting excess land revenue, (c) misrepresenting the value of property held by insolvent owners, (d) making unsolicited changes in the *haqdaran-e-zamin*, (e) failing to enter the names of specific heirs and (f) dividing the villagers into factions.[17] The list went on and on.

Fortunately for those of us with an interest in the link between land, law, and the logic of local politics, Haider went on to provide twenty-nine case studies to document the nature of the disputes that emerged from this pattern of administrative malfeasance, noting (perhaps not surprisingly) that every single one of the *patwar* circles included in his study contained several families—what Haider described as 'a large percentage' of the total population—involved in litigation.[18]

Drawing attention to the enduring importance of ancestral ties in the context of landed property disputes and, more specifically, the importance of 'agnatic' attachments to the land, for instance, Haider began with the rather compelling case of Ms Nasim and her husband, Hakim Khan.[19]

'It was in 1956', Haider explained, that Ms Nasim was married to Hakim, 'her relative of the same village'. Unfortunately, he noted, the fate of Ms Nasim, as a married Muslim woman, was not at all unusual. In fact 'her younger brother, known as Riaz, contacted the *patwari* ...

and got [a plot of ancestral] land measuring 16 *kanals* belonging to [Ms Nasim] transferred in his name'. As a matter of fact, 'Riaz managed to produce some other woman who deposed before the *tehsildar* that she was Nasim and she had no objection to the transfer'. (And, of course, Haider noted, 'the *patwari* was given Rs. 100 ... for this service').

After a few years, however, Haider explained that a new *patwari* was assigned to the same village. And, in due course, this new *patwari* informed Ms Nasim of all that had 'conspired' [*sic*]. Unfortunately, this new *patwari* demanded Rs. 500 from Ms Nasim, claiming that, if she paid this amount, '[her] land would be restored'. Still, '[Ms] Nasim could not make [any] arrangement for the payment of Rs. 500 as illegal gratification'. And, as a result, Haider explained, 'the land was ... still in the possession of Riaz'.

Clearly, when it came to the enduring shape of landed property relations in the context of postcolonial Punjab, it would be extremely naïve to emphasize the fact that *patwaris* occupied the lowest rung on the local bureaucratic ladder. In fact, as Haider (1966) clearly points out, the *patwari* was rather important, particularly when it came to the registration of rights and, ultimately, the control of agricultural land. Indeed a closer look at the empirical record unambiguously reveals that, throughout the latter half of the twentieth century, *the role of the patwari was dramatically enhanced as the 'law of the land' slowly changed* (1947–99).[20]

In theory, of course, the Deputy Commissioner controlled the *patwari*. But in practice this relationship was often turned upside down. In fact, owing to the nature of their relationship with prominent local landowners, *patwaris* frequently found ways to curry favour with influential members of the postcolonial political establishment. Indeed, as A.H. Aslam (1957) pointed out, referring specifically to the most corrupt *patwaris*, 'the subordinates of the Deputy Commissioner [often] have direct contacts with [incumbent] ministers'.[21] And more often than not, he noted, these ministers were keen to support 'their' local *patwaris* over and above the DC.

Whereas, in theory, then, the bureaucratic chain of command descended straight from the DC, at the top, all the way down to the *patwari*, at the bottom, the facts on the ground were different. In fact, owing to the influence of intervening *political* elites, this chain of command often began with the *patwari*, at the top, and then proceeded, all the way down, to each local Commissioner.[22]

The *Lambardar*

Both the *patwari* and the Deputy Commissioner were, in some sense, 'accountable' officials. Both were accountable to elected National Assembly members, Provincial Assembly members, union council members, and so on. In fact the possibility of a purely administrative realm (set apart from the logic of local politics) was extremely difficult to locate—increasingly, as the twentieth century unfolded, 'the 'administrative' was also 'political'.

Within this complex administrative-cum-political environment, however, few officials were able to claim the same level of versatility as the local (often *patti*-based) *lambardar*: he was, quite literally, part bureaucrat, part politician, part local 'tribal' chief. And, as I will now proceed to explain, his position was absolutely central.

'The *patwari* is, of course, the boss', noted Kamal Siddiqui (1997), returning to many of the issues raised above. But, in the end, he explained, the *patwari* 'has to depend on the *lambardar* for ... his office, [his] residence, and other essential amenities'.[23] As a matter of fact, Siddiqui explained, coming straight to the heart of the matter in his book *Land Management in South Asia* (1997), there was a carefully constructed 'balance' in the relationship between the two.

As a member of the district administration, for instance, the village *lambardar* was entitled (like the *patwari*) to retain a share of the revenue that, together, they collected from each member of the village proprietary body—what Siddiqui described as 'a paltry 6 percent'.[24] But, at the same time, Siddiqui explained, the village *lambardar* was also entitled—as he had been for more than a hundred years—to a role in the management of village affairs. And, in this context, the *lambardar* was frequently summoned to the district *kachehri* as a character witness in the district and appellate courts.

Even apart from his official responsibilities within both the revenue administration and the district courts, however, the local *lambardar* was also (rather frequently) elected by the members of his 'shareholding' *patti* to serve as an official member of the local union council. In fact, as Siddiqui went on to explain, the role of the local *lambardar* in the context of electoral politics was frequently his most important role of all: '[He] is there for the prestige', Siddiqui noted, and, more often than not, he simply 'uses' his administrative position as 'a stepping-stone' in the context of his political career.[25]

Needless to say, this combination of bureaucratic and political functions—so well reflected in the work of the village *lambardar*—came to play an extremely important role in the politics of postcolonial Punjab. In theory, of course, the Deputy Commissioner controlled the *patwari*, the *patwari* controlled the revenue records, and the revenue records controlled 'all that is wholesome and profitable in that great principle of association' for which 'the land itself' was expected to furnish an 'all-sufficient' basis.[26] But, in practice, this hierarchy was often reversed. In fact, the district *bureaucracy* was often left to the mercy of a much larger and more powerful logic of local *politics*—one in which, I argue, local *lambardars* remained active as a powerful binding force.

In practice, the revenue records were controlled by the *patwari*. But, more often than not, the *patwari* remained closely bound up with the enduring demands of the 'village proprietary body'. In fact the value of the salary that each *patwari* received from the Deputy Commissioner often paled in comparison to the value of the amenities he received from neighbouring *zamindars*. The village *zamindars* were, however, deeply divided; and of course, as noted above, they were divided into factions—factions bound up with local *pattis* represented, in practice, by politically 'accountable' *lambardars*.

A closer look at the empirical record, in other words, typically reveals that the *patwari*, just as much as the Deputy Commissioner, did not exist in a political vacuum. On the contrary, he often functioned, quite literally, as a village servant 'in the service of the village *zamindars*' (and, thus, in the service of specific *lambardars*). Indeed it would hardly be an exaggeration to say that, throughout the latter half of the twentieth century, any autonomy the district-level state may have enjoyed was, in practice, little more than a 'Poulantzian' autonomy pinched in between the interests of competing ancestral estates. The driving force, one may say, was not the Deputy Commissioner. It was, almost invariably, a logic of local politics inextricably bound up with specific 'agnatic' estates.

Land Reform

The rigidity of landed property relations after the independence of British India and the formation of Pakistan in 1947 is routinely explained in terms of the enduring influence of 'formal legal institutions' and, above all, the stickiness of the district-level bureaucracy.[27] This is understandable, given the extent to which formal legal institutions have been lionized in the context of the existing literature.[28] But, in many ways, this (rather narrow) focus has made it extremely difficult to account for the nature of what happened next—that is, what happened when, for all intents and purposes, the formal legal landscape was slowly but surely *changed.*

Fig. 16. Postcolonial Punjab: reconstructing the status quo (1947–1999)

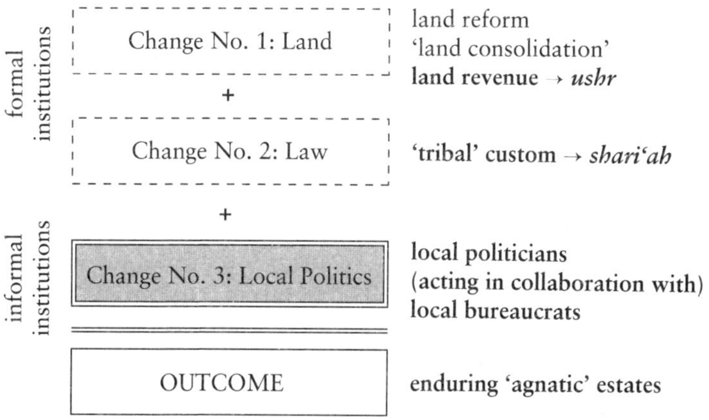

In fact, as the twentieth century unfolded, what we find throughout the Punjab is actually a pattern of dramatic *legal* change (land reform, law reform, etc.) followed, almost immediately—in fact simultaneously—by a pattern of elaborate *political* adjustment. In fact what we find is very much a pattern in which, following in the footsteps of Mian Mumtaz Khan Daultana and many others, numerous political adjustments emerged to preserve and protect a particular status quo. (See Fig. 16 above.)

The law changed. And, when it changed, it changed quite dramatically. But, even as the law changed, every indication seems to suggest that the integrity of many ancestral estates—many 'agnatic' estates—endured. In fact, as the twentieth century unfolded, the challenge lay in explaining exactly how existing forms of 'agnatic' interaction were systematically reproduced over time. How did local 'bureaucrats' connect with local 'politicians'? How did local politicians succeed in attracting local voters? Indeed, how did postcolonial *patwaris* succeed in working together with local politicians (for example, *patti*-based *lambardars*) to meet the demands of their most influential landowning constituents? How did these *patwaris* succeed in meeting the demand for (postcolonial) 'agnatic' estates?

Land Reform (1947–1977): Ceilings, Floors

Shortly after the formation of Pakistan in 1947, a series of rather ambitious reform initiatives were introduced to tackle the problems surrounding two groups of landowners throughout postcolonial Punjab, namely the largest and the smallest. With respect to the former—that is, the largest landowners—progressively lower 'ceilings' were introduced to limit the size of individual holdings. And, with respect to the latter—that is, the smallest landowners—so-called 'consolidation' schemes were introduced to gather locally scattered plots into larger and more efficient estates. Land reforms (targeting the largest owners) have always received more attention in the context of the existing literature. But, as I will explain, land 'consolidation' schemes were never any less important when it came to the preservation of specific 'ancestral' estates.[29]

What is interesting about the history of both sets of reforms, however, at least in the context of postcolonial Punjab, is not merely their common goal—namely, the promotion of a more sustainable form of individual peasant proprietorship—but also, and perhaps more importantly, the common trajectory of their respective failures. Indeed, both sets of reforms failed for two very similar reasons, mostly related to the manipulation of the existing revenue records by individual *patwaris* acting on behalf of prominent (elected) elites.[30]

Postcolonial land reform: ceilings. Responding to the legacy of the colonial regime and, more specifically, the Punjab Alienation of Land Act (1900), the transformation of postcolonial laws governing the ownership of agricultural land advanced in two stages, each of which sought to introduce progressively lower ceilings on the terms of 'individual' (as opposed to 'group-based') proprietorship. The first phase culminated in 1959, when Field Marshal Ayub Khan promulgated the West Pakistan Land Reforms Regulation, also known as Martial Law Regulation (MLR) 64. The second reached its peak under Prime Minister Zulfiqar Ali Bhutto, first in 1972 and then in 1977.

As noted above, both of these two phases stressed the value of individual peasant proprietorship. But, as I will now proceed to explain, this (rather narrow) focus on the rights of *individual* proprietors merely reinvigorated a series of remarkably familiar debates regarding the relative status of individual 'owners' and 'tenants'.

1947–1958. Rejecting earlier reports issued by the Sindh Hari Committee (1930) and the Sindh Tenancy Legislation Committee (1945), the postcolonial Government Hari Enquiry Committee of 1947–48, chaired by an independent English landlord named Sir Roger Thomas, adopted an extremely conservative position—one that sought to distance itself from several of the reforms recommended in Sindh just a few years before (for example in 1945).[31] Above all, following in the footsteps of Lord Cornwallis in Bengal (1793) and, more specifically, E.A. Prinsep in the Punjab (1865), Sir Roger Thomas sought to resist the extension of occupancy rights to individual 'tenants-at-will', preferring, instead, to reinforce the rights of local *zamindars*. In fact the only significant changes recommended by Sir Roger's Committee involved the abolition of so-called 'auxiliary' or 'undocumented' obligations like *abwab* (water rents), *haboob* (miscellaneous cesses), and *begar* (forced labour).

Less than a year later, however, in the summer of 1949, the Agrarian Reforms Committee of the Pakistan Muslim League, led by none other than Punjab Chief Minister Mian Mumtaz Khan Daultana, reached a very different set of conclusions regarding many of the same issues. In fact, finally agreeing with a note of dissent submitted the previous year by Mr M. Masud, a Deputy Commissioner from Sindh, Daultana surprised his ex-Unionist colleagues with an explicit effort to press for (a) the extension of ownership rights to occupancy tenants, (b) the enhancement of security for tenants-at-will, and (once again) (c) the immediate abolition of *begar* (forced labour). In fact, in the long run, Daultana even suggested a permanent ceiling of 150 acres 'irrigated' land, 300 acres 'semi-irrigated' land, and 450 acres 'unirrigated' land, as well as legislation designed to prevent the acquisition of land beyond these limits by purchase, gift, or inheritance.

As landowners throughout the Punjab began to hear about these recommendations and, more specifically, the possibility of extending ownership rights to ostensibly 'inferior' occupancy tenants, however, the number of evictions soared.[32] In fact, recalling the experience of E.A. Prinsep in Sialkot (nearly one hundred years before), landowners throughout the Punjab retaliated in ways that can only be described as familiar. To be sure, this new wave of evictions was no longer discussed in terms of the relative strength of 'village' and 'tribal' custom, as it had been, for instance, in the days of Sir Henry Sumner Maine. But, even so, the parameters of the debate did seem to invoke an almost unmistakable sense of administrative *déjà vu*.

On the one hand, following Sir Richard Temple and the terms of the Punjab Tenancy Act (1868), Daultana's Agrarian Reforms Committee sought to enhance the rights of local tenants—for example, through the abolition of *begar*. And, yet, at the same time, following in the footsteps of Prinsep, the Punjab Laws Act (1872), and the Punjab Alienation of Land Act (1900), Daultana's Committee went out of its way to ensure that the extensive rights of ancestral owners were carefully and consistently preserved. Whereas the rights of individual owners were in one sense more limited (for example, through restrictions on the possibility of 'forced labour'), then, the introduction of a prohibition on 'evictions' was recommended only insofar as existing tenants (a) refrained from subletting their plots and (b) carried on with their cultivation in keeping with 'the customary manner'.[33] Indeed, the meaning of enhanced 'security' for existing tenants was still rather severely constrained by the possibility of their periodic—indeed, the possibility of their customary—eviction.

The recommendations made by Chief Minister Daultana and the Agrarian Reforms Committee, in other words, like so many reforms in the past, were largely 'rhetorical'.[34] The extension of ownership rights to occupancy tenants, in particular, emerged as an altogether insignificant concession, mostly because, as Viqar Ahmed and Rashid Amjad explained in their book *The Management of Pakistan's Economy* (1984), a careful landlord would never allow a tenant employed on his property to cultivate the same plot for more than three consecutive years, knowing full well that, if he did, the tenant in question would be allowed (by law) to claim the land as his own.[35] Indeed, as Ahmad and Amjad pointed out, 'even the limited rights conferred on the [labourers] could not be enjoyed by them' owing to the 'customary' influence of the landlords.[36]

1958–1970. In the autumn of 1958, however, almost immediately after seizing power, Field Marshal Ayub Khan appointed a new land reforms commission headed by the incumbent Governor of West Pakistan, Akhtar Hussain. And, just three weeks after Hussein submitted his final report, Ayub went on to promulgate MLR 64 (1959), otherwise known as the West Pakistan Land Reforms Regulation—by all accounts, a landmark piece of work.

In many ways, MLR 64 (1959) merely revisited the ideas expressed by several earlier committees, ordering the conversion of 'occupancy' rights into 'ownership' rights and (once again) demanding the complete abolition of *begar*. Even beyond these routine measures, however, MLR 64 went on to articulate one rather notable innovation. Briefly stated, it sought to introduce a formal legal limit on individual landholdings, finally drawing the line at 500 acres 'irrigated' land and 1,000 acres 'unirrigated' land—a threshold commonly described in terms of 36,000 'Produce Index Units' (PIU).

Unfortunately, this change was almost completely ineffective owing to a series of loopholes within the Regulation itself. The first of these many loopholes provided a general exemption of 150 acres for 'orchards', as well as unlimited exemptions for 'livestock' farms, 'stud' farms, and *shikargahs*, or 'hunting grounds'.[37] A further loophole, however, stated that individual owners would be permitted to hold land in excess of the stipulated acreage (500 or 1,000 acres) up to a parallel limit of 36,000 Produce Index Units—a measurement that varied enormously with soil quality, cropping patterns, and irrigation systems. In fact this second loophole encouraged thousands of landowners to conspire with their local *patwari* to adjust the description (and, thus, the valuation) of their land.[38]

There was, however, a third and final loophole—in many ways the most important one of all. This loophole drew attention to the fact that, technically speaking, MLR 64 (1959) targeted individual holdings rather than joint family holdings. In other words, alienations involving more than 500 acres 'irrigated' land or 1,000 acres 'unirrigated' land were strictly prohibited as per the terms of Paragraph 7, because, by definition, they led to the creation of estates in violation of the Regulation itself. But, then, having said this, a further portion of the law went on to allow a number of special exceptions in cases involving (a) gifts made to 'relatives' after 1947, (b) alienations made to 'heirs' up to 18,000 'PIUs', and finally (c) alienations involving 'female dependents' (for example, unmarried daughters and widowed sisters) up to 6,000 PIUs. (In fact MLR 64 was later amended, in the form of MLR 64-B, to introduce several additional exceptions.)

According to many critics, however, the exceptions outlined in MLR 64-B (1959) were already unnecessary by the time they were introduced. 'Large owners', noted Syed Nawab Haider Naqvi in his book *Land Reforms in Pakistan* (1987), 'ha[d] already distributed their property among as many real or imaginary ... heirs as they could trust to hold the land'.[39]

Indeed, as an editorial in *Dawn* (Karachi) pointed out, most *zamindars* had already distributed their rights to a wide assortment of dependents, including wives, unborn children, servants, even livestock. The combined effect of these three loopholes, in other words, ensured that even as MLR 64 and MLR 64-B (1959) altered existing patterns of formal legal *ownership*, existing patterns of *control* remained firmly intact: '[The] net effect ... for a long time to come', wrote the future President of Pakistan, Ghulam Ishaq Khan, 'will be to leave the concentration of land in [the hands of local] families instead of individuals'.[40]

1970–1977. On 1 March 1972, less than ten weeks after taking office, however, Zulfiqar Ali Bhutto sought to advance the process of land reform well beyond the point where Field Marshal Ayub Khan had left it, targeting the holdings of prominent individuals *as well as* their families.

Above all, Bhutto introduced Martial Law Regulation 115 (1972) in an effort to lower the ceiling on individual ownership from 500 to 150 acres (irrigated) and 1,000 to 300 acres (unirrigated) land, promising that all of the resumed land would be redistributed among landless tenants 'free of charge'.[41] In fact, just five years later, in an attempt to shore up his own rapidly declining popularity, Bhutto reduced these ceilings once again—this time, to just 100 and 200 acres (respectively).

The most important changes, however, did not involve the definition of specific ownership 'ceilings'. Instead they involved a series of modifications in the protocol of exemptions—modifications that attempted to shift the focus away from hereditary 'owners' to their 'tenants'.

Abolishing the exemption for orchards, livestock farms, and *shikargahs*, for instance, Bhutto tried to break the *de facto* bonds of enduring family estates.[42] But, in the end, he failed, and he failed for two main reasons. The first concerned the emergence of 'alternative alienations' *within* landowning families. The second concerned enduring notions of 'preemption'. In fact, as Ahmed and Amjad explained in their assessment of Bhutto's land reforms, 'the reforms in the seventies were [always] more egalitarian regarding the limit on ceilings and ... exemptions'. But even so, they noted, Bhutto's reforms were always more generous to 'heirs'.[43]

In order to understand exactly why this was the case, it is important to highlight the fact that, according to MLR 115 (1972), gifts made to family members were included in a special framework of exemptions (see MLR 115 Paragraph 7). In fact, even beyond this framework of exemptions, MLR 115 had a tendency to shift family-based alienations away from intra-family 'gifts' to intra-family 'sales' and, especially, unregistered (oral) sales involving fathers, their sons, and in some cases even their grandsons. Indeed, even those who failed to accommodate the second wave of land reforms with a focused effort to 'give' their land away still managed to circumvent the underlying purpose of the law. They simply redefined their 'gifts' as 'sales', requiring individual (typically male) beneficiaries to pay a small amount for the purchase of what was, at least 'customarily', their own 'ancestral' land.

Furthermore, turning away from intra-family 'sales' to local patterns of 'preemption', Bhutto's government sought to grant the right of first refusal (in the case of any 'sale') not to individual co-sharers, but rather to their tenants.[44] As Ahmed and Amjad went on to explain, however, this carefully targeted adjustment in the existing law of preemption appeared to fail just as miserably as the government's half-hearted approach to 'gifts', mostly because, in practice, this newly redefined right of preemption was rarely used to achieve the purpose for which it was ostensibly intended. In fact, in the wake of this reform, most tenants simply used their newly acquired right of first refusal to secure a special form of 'hush money', accepting a small token (in cash) in return for their willingness to step aside in favour of a more acceptable bid from among the existing 'co-sharers'.[45]

'The legal remedies are there', explained an editorial in *Dawn* (1976), 'but very often the unprivileged and pauperized tenant lacks the resources, and often even the will, to invoke these remedies'. In particular, the editorialist went on to explain, 'a harassed tenant would much ... prefer to return to "his" *zamindar* and seek his forgiveness in exchange for work and continued dependence on his land than go to the nearest town ... to obtain redress through litigation'.[46]

Indeed, as Ahmed and Amjad were quick to point out, 'the entire task of implementing the land reforms fell on the bureaucracy', allowing most officials to rely on what Ahmed and Amjad described as '[their] old contacts ... [within] the rural elite'.[47] In fact, more often than not, *patwaris* who set out to implement each new batch of post-colonial land reforms 'on paper' (allocating hundreds of acres to local tenants while, at the same time, failing to speak up when those acres were resumed by way of force or harassment) were handsomely rewarded ... twice. In the first instance, they were rewarded for their 'administrative' efficiency. And, in the second, they were rewarded for their subversive 'political' awareness.

Postcolonial land reform: floors. Typically, studies regarding the failure of postcolonial land reforms assume that the primary source of rural disaffection lay in the behaviour of local *patwaris* collaborating with 'large' landowners. And, to a certain extent, it did. But a closer look at the empirical record indicates that the terms of rural disaffection were also tied to 'small' owners: fragmentation, if you will, more than feudalism.

Even before the emergence of Pakistan in 1947, and partially in response to studies conducted by the Punjab Board of Economic Inquiry, colonial officials attempted to stem the tide of village fragmentation throughout rural Punjab. Initially, these efforts were launched after obtaining the consent of the village proprietary body as a whole. But, after 1936, a two-thirds majority was considered sufficient. In fact, owing to the strength of local factions, even this majority was rarely achieved. And, for the most part, consolidation proceedings remained exceedingly rare.[48]

Finally, however, in 1960, compulsory consolidation schemes were introduced in conjunction with the West Pakistan Consolidation of Holdings Ordinance—a companion ordinance designed to accompany MLR 64 (1959). This ordinance stipulated that gifts, sales, and the partition of joint family property would be *forbidden* if they threatened to reduce the size of any plot below what had (by then) come to be known as a 'subsistence' holding (12.5 acres). In fact, recalling the rules governing *taqsim*, or partition, in the context of colonial Punjab, this new ordinance declared that whole *khatas*, jointly held, could be alienated *in toto* within the limits defined by existing 'ceilings' and 'floors', but, in the end, it also declared that these *khatas* could *not* be partitioned beyond the level of a subsistence holding (not even to facilitate the sale of a particular plot of land by one of the recognized 'co-sharers').

Much to the surprise of those who drafted this Consolidation Ordinance (1960), however, the introduction of specific 'floors' did not succeed in encouraging any increase in the sale of larger plots. Instead it merely succeeded in encouraging the preservation—and, in some cases, even the expansion—of existing 'family' estates.

'It has been noticed that many irregularities of [a] grave nature are being committed during consolidation operation[s]', noted A.K. Khalid in 1998, adding that these irregularities created significant 'difficulties for landowners, involving protracted litigation and resulting in financial liabilities both for the village community as well as the government'.[49] In particular, Khalid explained, *patwaris* were encouraged to falsify the revenue records in ways that allowed influential families (as opposed to individuals) to expand their holdings through fraudulent forms of consolidation-friendly 'exchange'.

The land consolidation scheme in Sialkot, for instance, was completely derailed when members of the local Consolidation Board were accused of diverting plots to their own family members, conspiring with the local *patwari* to overvalue their land in such a way that, as the scattered plots in each village were slowly reassigned, any future 'exchange' would produce a financial gain.[50]

For those with an interest in the terms of 'efficiency' (considered in isolation), of course, this pattern of abuse was quite surprising, mostly because, in a purely technical sense, there should be nothing objectionable about the consolidation of agricultural land. In fact, through the exchange of (honestly valued) 'equivalent plots', everyone in the village should benefit (for example, in terms of increased productivity). But of course, as A.K. Khalid pointed out, returning to his own experience as a member of the Board of Revenue: 'it is a matter of common knowledge that the consolidation programme in [each] village is undertaken ... on the move of [large families] ... rather than ... small owners, because it is always the former who, being more influential and assertive and possessing more resources to win [the] favours of the corrupt underlings in the consolidation staff, can maneuver the choicest of land ... in excess of their entitlements to the disadvantage of [the] other [owners]'.[51]

The goal, in other words, was not 'efficiency', defined in terms of 'productivity' (or, for that matter, the well being of the village as a whole). The goal was simply 'power', defined in terms of local factions and enduring 'ancestral' control.

Land Reform (1977–1999): Agricultural Income Tax, *Ushr*

For a number of reasons, including the transfer of land to (real or imaginary) heirs, postcolonial land reforms were expected to boost the number of individuals with 'rights' in agricultural land—leading, in due course, to more intensive forms of cultivation and (more often than not) a steady increase in the value of the land itself. This increasing value of land was, in turn, expected to boost the amount of revenue collected by the state as 'rent'.

In the context of postcolonial Punjab, however, this interconnected sequence of events did not emerge. In fact, throughout the 1970s, 80s, and 90s, a steady *increase* in the value of land came to be associated with a steady *reduction* in the amount of revenue collected by the state as 'rent'. Indeed, as the value of land increased, the power of the existing revenue administration—by all accounts, the centrepiece of the *ancien* (colonial) *régime*—slowly but surely *declined*.

One reason for this shift boiled down to the enduring problem of fragmentation. Indeed, most of the plots in postcolonial Punjab, both on paper and in practice, had long since fallen well below the level of a 'subsistence' (12.5 acre) holding, meaning that, for all practical purposes, they were considered too small to merit any government 'demand' at all. Before 1947, individual owners had routinely paid less than Rs. 5 every year in land revenue. (In fact, even as late as 1938, the largest portion of the colonial budget was collected from an average revenue payment of less than Rs. 2.) But, increasingly, after the formation of Pakistan in 1947, any effort to collect such a small amount was considered extremely inefficient. And, by 1977, the reach of the postcolonial land revenue administration had declined to such an extent that most landowners paid nothing at all for their land—no rent, no revenue, no formal 'tax' at all.

Needless to say, this led many policy makers to search for alternative forms of rural taxation, focusing, primarily, on two main options, namely (a) a special agricultural income tax and (b) a special tax on agricultural productivity, known as *ushr*, derived from the specific terms of Islam.

Agricultural income tax. The possibility of an agricultural income tax first emerged during the Great Depression under Financial Commissioner Malcolm Darling. But, after independence and partition in 1947, several additional committees returned to reconsider this option, including (a) the Taxation Enquiry Committee (1957), (b) the Fact-Finding Committee on Agricultural Taxation (1963), (c) the National Taxation Reform Commission (1986), and, finally, (d) the Committee of Experts on the Taxation of Agricultural Income (1989).

The most illuminating study, however, was undertaken in 1997 by a group of bureaucrats at the National Institute of Public Administration (NIPA) in Lahore.[52]

'A number of big landowners have escaped the two land reforms by various devices', the group explained, and '[there] is now a class of wealthy landowners who reside in urban centres and have made substantial investments in real estate'. '*Since they pay no income tax*' (emphasis added), the group pointed out, referring to some of the exemptions included in the Second Schedule of the Pakistan Income Tax Ordinance (1979), 'they have created jealousies among the trading and industrial classes'. In particular, the group went on to explain, 'the exemption of agricultural income' had enabled a new class of so-called 'agriculturalist businessmen' to avoid the payment of any income tax at all, mostly 'by showing their "commercial" ... income as "agricultural" income'. As a matter of fact, they noted, this pattern merely encouraged a growing number of urban industrialists 'to purchase agricultural lands' as well, mostly in an effort 'to whiten their (untaxed) black income'.[53]

Digging even deeper, the NIPA group went on to note that several urban businessmen had entered into 'collusive arrangements' with local landowners. In fact these businessmen were known to 'obtain fictitious leases of lands, from which they show enormous amounts of agricultural income, which in fact is their business income'.[54] And, in this way, the group explained, many prominent businessmen living in urban areas had also managed to escape the introduction of a progressive income tax. In fact, they noted, 'a large number of corrupt government ... employees have also either purchased agricultural land or obtained fictitious leases'. And, increasingly, they reported, these officials were 'declaring [even their] graft money as [tax-free] agricultural income'.[55]

Notwithstanding this rather extensive and elaborate indictment of the existing tax regime, however, the value of an 'agricultural' income tax—as reflected, for instance, in the promulgation of a new Punjab Agricultural Income Tax Act in 1997—was expected to be quite negligible, not only because, under the First Schedule of this new Act, those with 'less than a subsistence holding' (in effect, more than 90 per cent of all owners) were considered tax-exempt, but also—and perhaps more importantly, recalling the challenges faced by late-nineteenth-century administrators like G. Ouseley and W.G. Davies—because it was extremely difficult to construct reliable estimates regarding the 'productivity' and, hence, the income-based 'taxability' of land.[56] Indeed, where absentee landowners used small plots 'below the subsistence limit' to hide large non-agricultural incomes, the team at NIPA realized that it would be extremely difficult, if not impossible, to describe the proper level of assessment without an elaborate and costly 'resettlement':

'Serious consideration should be given to one single direct tax on agriculture in the interest of transparency and simplicity', argued the team at NIPA, adding that, in the end, '[the existing] land revenue as one single direct tax' was still the most compelling and attractive option.[57]

'Islamic' ushr. Even before this effort to reconsider the possibility of a tax on exploding agricultural incomes gained pace during the late 1990s, however, provincial debates regarding the most appropriate form of rural taxation had begun to struggle with the introduction of *ushr* as an 'Islamic' alternative to the existing tax regime.[58] In fact, when General Zia-ul-Haq promulgated the Zakat and Ushr Ordinance, again by executive 'decree', in the summer of 1980, it would hardly be an exaggeration to say that the entire history of the colonial land revenue administration was dramatically (and decisively) transformed.[59]

Basically, *ushr* amounts to a tax of 5 per cent on all agricultural produce. The tax itself is collected in cash (except for wheat and paddy, on which it is collected in kind). In Islamic Arabia, *ushr* amounted to a tax of 10 per cent, or a tithe, paid directly to the state; but, elsewhere, in *kharij* or 'conquered' lands, this tax was reduced to 5 per cent, and it was collected as a form of *bait-ul-mal* 'for the benefit of the community as a whole'.[60]

After the promulgation of the Zakat and Ushr Ordinance in 1980, however, the meaning of this '5 per cent' was left to the interpretation of individual landowners, most of whom simply began by deducting the largest portion of their taxable profits as routine production expenses. In fact, as many observers pointed out, recalling some of the fieldwork concerning *zakat* and *ushr* undertaken by James C. Scott in Malaysia (1987), most landowners simply failed to deposit any part of their *ushr* assessment at all.[61]

'In practice', noted the study group at NIPA, 'the *ushr* system ... is dependent on the goodwill of a few individuals in the village'. And of course, they added, this merely implied that the system was poorly institutionalized and extremely ineffective.[62]

The most important consequence of the Zakat and Ushr Ordinance, however, was not confined to its faulty implementation. Instead it boiled down to the status of the land revenue itself and, more importantly, the ways in which this ordinance (as a 'prior' form of taxation) affected the status of the land revenue collected from each local estate.

According to the study group at NIPA, the introduction of *ushr* deprived the provincial government of a substantial amount of land revenue.[63] But of course, they noted, this was just the tip of the iceberg. In fact a closer look revealed that this move away from existing forms of rural taxation in favour of an 'Islamic' tax on production very nearly redefined the primary function of the district administration as a whole, pulling it away from the adjudication of 'revenue' rights toward a special focus on the battles unfolding between and among individuals seeking to obtain a larger share of (effectively) 'tax-free' land.[64]

In fact, increasingly after 1980, it would hardly be an exaggeration to say that Zia's 'Islamizing' effort to introduce a 'religious' tax on agricultural production (*ushr*) slowly tipped the balance away from any focus on the problem of rural taxation altogether, effectively encouraging a fevered push to acquire small plots of land (including 'unproductive' plots) as an increasingly acceptable form of 'tax evasion'. This in turn pushed the price of land even higher, increasing local expressions of demand without any of the benefits that increasing 'prices' might have been expected to yield in the form of higher levels of taxation, revenue, or 'rent'.

Indeed, as the burden of the colonial revenue administration was, for all practical purposes, not simply reduced (as it had been during the 1850s) but rather slowly removed, the incentive to acquire agricultural land increased dramatically; and, as the value of the land increased, the pressure to acquire it increased even more quickly, launching what can only be described as an entirely new wave of violent and disruptive evictions.[65]

At one point these evictions might have been regarded as an acute political risk—a contested expression of 'customary' norms with specific implications for the stability of the state itself. But, as the twentieth century drew to an end, this sense of political 'risk' no longer seemed to obtain. In fact, as the twentieth century drew to an end, the violent *qabza* or 'possession' groups that emerged to advance this new wave of evictions were not regarded as a source of political 'instability'. Instead they came to be regarded as a novel source of 'revenue' for the *patwari* and his political patrons—increasingly (and ironically) a source of 'irregular' rents!

LAW REFORM AND THE LOGIC OF LOCAL POLITICS

The Zakat and Ushr Ordinance (1980) remained firmly in place throughout the twilight years of the twentieth century, even as earlier initiatives designed to promote (a) land reform and (b) land consolidation were overturned—struck down by the Supreme Court following the advice of a newly established Shariat Appellate Bench, which described their efforts to adjust existing patterns of land ownership as 'contrary to the injunctions of Islam'.[66]

To be sure, disagreements about the best way to introduce, enforce, interpret and apply the terms of Islamic law were nothing new in Pakistan. Mian Fazl-i-Husain, for instance, famously set the stage during the 1930s, before the creation of Pakistan, when he asserted that the application of Islamic laws concerning the ownership of agricultural land should be defined, not by the priorities of the nation as a whole, but rather by the priorities of each individual province. And, yet, even as the laws of British India gave way to those of Pakistan, specific disagreements regarding the introduction of *shari'ah* continued. In fact, as the colonial 1930s gave way to the postcolonial 1950s and 60s, the question for many policy makers did not concern *the extent to which* the terms of *shari'ah* might be introduced (for example, at a 'provincial' level). No, the question was simply *how* to introduce the terms of *shari'ah* (at a 'national' level) more effectively.

Proceeding with caution, so-called religious 'modernists' tended to place their faith in the power of public opinion—for example, in the views expressed by ordinary Muslims and their elected representatives in the National and Provincial Assemblies. But, as the twentieth century unfolded, these religious modernists were never able to advance their ideas in isolation. They were, almost invariably, challenged by the views of religious 'traditionalists', including those who placed their confidence in the cloistered wisdom of the religious scholars ensconced in prominent *madrasas*.[67]

Throughout Pakistan, a substantial majority sought to embrace and advance the terms of Sunni (Hanafi) Islam. They simply disagreed about the underlying *meaning* of those terms and, more importantly, the best way to address 'the problem of disagreement' itself. In fact, despite a certain measure of broad doctrinal agreement (notwithstanding the persistence of considerable interpretative diversity even among local Sunnis), the two groups mentioned above—namely, the modernists and the traditionalists—maintained sharply divergent views regarding the practice of religious 'politics' and, more specifically, the most acceptable parameters of religious *difference*, political *disagreement*, and ongoing legal *debate*.

Each of these two groups sought to articulate a particular attachment to the specific terms of Islam and, within this, the specific terms of Sunni (Hanafi) jurisprudence—in this case, a Sunni (Hanafi) interpretation of *'ilm al-fara'id*, or the Islamic Law of Inheritance. They simply disagreed about the best way to do this; and, of course, over time, their enduring disagreements came to reflect several rather important debates. What did the terms of *'ilm al-fara'id* mean in practice—for example, at the level of (ancestral) agricultural land? And, more importantly, how did those with different responses to this question understand, and engage, the possibility of (ongoing) legal debate?

Law Reform

When the Constituent Assembly declared, in the spring of 1949, that local Muslims throughout Pakistan would be 'enabled to order their lives ... in accordance with the teachings and requirements of Islam as set out in the Holy Qur'an', few were surprised.[68] But, at the same time, many observers were quick to point out that the meaning of this statement (the so-called 'Objectives Resolution' situated within the Preamble of the Constitution itself) remained rather obscure. In fact, as the twentieth century unfolded, the meaning of this statement continued to generate a fair amount of disagreement and, ultimately, two rather important debates.

The first of these two debates concerned the teachings and requirements of Islam itself and, within this, 'the meaning of Islamic law'. This debate was, primarily, a debate regarding the issue of interpretation: did the teachings and requirements of 'Islam', for instance, permit the promulgation of a policy—say, MLR 115 (1972)—according to which land could be resumed (without compensation) and, then, redistributed to landless labourers? Or, phrased somewhat differently, did the teachings of Islam *permit* 'compulsory' land reform? Some argued that the teachings of Islam *did* permit this type of reform. But of course, others disagreed. And, in 1986, the Supreme Court of Pakistan decided to agree with the latter (*Said Kamal Shah vs. Pakistan*), generating an unmistakable sigh of relief on the part of several powerful landowners throughout postcolonial Punjab.

(Perhaps not surprisingly, disagreements regarding the narrow terms of *'ilm al-fara'id* persisted as well, focusing, specifically, on the extent to which the teachings of Islam actually 'required' the *de facto* possession of specific Qur'anic 'shares'. Did the teachings of Islam, in other words, permit the *de jure* distribution of specific Qur'anic shares followed, in due course, by a certain distance from the *de facto* 'control' of those shares? Again, the terms of consensus remained elusive; see Chapter 5, below.)

Moving away from this basic issue of exegetical interpretation, however, the second debate was, in many ways, the more important debate. This debate concerned the extent to which all of those who sought to participate in the first debate (regarding interpretation) might be permitted to acknowledge that they were, in fact, involved in any 'debate' at all. Here the primary issue concerned the existence of competing ideas regarding the various ways in which 'the teachings and requirements of Islam' might be understood or examined in relation to the problem of 'politics.' Were the 'teachings' of Islam and, ultimately, the 'requirements' of Islamic law, for instance, open to the influence of disagreement and debate ... or not?

Typically, those who tended to see themselves as religious 'modernists' were prepared to concede that, yes, 'religion' on the one hand and 'politics' on the other were largely inseparable. Drawing attention to the importance of *ijtihad*, or interpretative 'reason' (grounded in the terms of individual or collective 'opinion'), for instance, they held that, as a general rule, mere mortals were not in a position to know or declare, in any definitive sense, the transcendant 'mind of God'. In fact, for them, the problem of public (or private) 'opinion', and thus the problem of 'politics', was simply omnipresent.

Those who tended to see themselves as religious 'traditionalists', however, disagreed. In fact they often appeared to reject the dynamic terms of popular 'reason', focusing, instead, on the principle of *taqlid* or 'following' grounded in the terms of an ostensibly unthinking attachment to the work of established (Sunni) *imams*. For them, 'religion' (or 'religious law') and 'politics' were simply opposites—in many ways, a basic contradiction in terms.[69]

This was of course an important religious-cum-political distinction. And, yet, throughout the latter half of the twentieth century, conventional ideas regarding the Islamic Law of Inheritance (*'ilm al-fara'id*) tended to provide the 'traditionalists' with an enormous boost of support. In fact, throughout the latter half of the twentieth century, those who sought to define themselves as religious traditionalists drew considerable support from the unusual clarity commonly associated with specific Qur'anic 'shares', noting that, when it came to the question of inheritance, the mind of God was, in effect, actually knowable in a specific mathematical sense. And of course, these traditionalists insisted that those with an elaborate and extensive religious education (namely, the *ulema*) were privileged in their ability to know it.

The power of this traditionalist perspective would be difficult to overstate—and, as I will explain, it became even more powerful throughout the latter half of the twentieth century, with enormous implications for 'the logic of local politics' in the context of postcolonial Punjab. Indeed, as the terms of Islamic law came to be viewed as lying 'beyond' the realm of religious (or political) debate, the logic of local politics itself was slowly but surely transformed, moving away from any specific interest in the construction of 'new' or 'better' laws toward a more limited focus on the law's irregular enforcement.[70] In fact, throughout the latter half of the twentieth century, the logic of local politics slowly began to stress the emergence of a pattern in which the ostensibly 'inaccessible' laws of Islam were actively *acknowledged* (at the level of legal rhetoric) and, then, simply *ignored* (at the level of local practice).

In other words, as the postcolonial legal landscape was, in due course, reconfigured to permit local Muslims 'to order their lives ... in accordance with the teachings and requirements of Islam', the question remained: How did this transformation affect the parameters of personal 'practice'? How did it shape existing patterns of postcolonial *political* reform?

Introducing *Shari'ah*

Almost immediately after the formation of Pakistan in 1947, the Muslim Personal Law (Shariat) Application Act of 1937 was replaced, first with the West Punjab Muslim Personal Law (Shariat) Application Act of 1948, and then, just three years later, with the Punjab Muslim Personal Law (Shariat) Application (Amendment) Act of 1951.

Bringing an end to what might be called 'The Mian Fazl-i-Husain Exception' pertaining to the inheritance of ancestral (agricultural) land, these two acts reinvigorated what can only be described as a rather protracted effort to purge the terms of customary law from the courts of postcolonial Punjab. They did not, however, bring an end to the influence of kinship-based ('tribal') custom. In fact they provided one rather important escape clause—one clause that delayed the *de jure* application of *shari'ah* for another forty years.

The West Punjab Muslim Personal Law (Shariat) Application Act (1948). The West Punjab Muslim Personal Law (Shariat) Application Act of 1948 indicated that the Islamic Law of Inheritance (*'ilm al-fara'id*) would apply in every case of inheritance throughout Pakistani Punjab, but only *after* the termination of existing lifetime estates—that is, after the death or remarriage of women widowed (within the terms of 'tribal' custom) before 1948. 'Limited' lifetime estates 'inherited' from the colonial past, in other words, were carefully and consistently preserved.

The only exception to this provision involved the terms of individual mortgages. In colonial Punjab, for instance, a widow holding a 'limited' lifetime estate within the terms of tribal custom was permitted to mortgage, 'temporarily', *all* of the property once owned by her deceased husband. But, according to this new Act (in 1948), a surviving widow was permitted to construct a mortgage (within the terms of her 'limited' lifetime estate) *only* to the extent of her specific Qur'anic share (that is, one quarter of the estate or, in the presence of a child, as little as one eighth).[71] In addition, suits filed by remote reversioners to challenge these widow-based mortgages—for example suits filed by surviving male heirs—were permitted, even as the subsequent distribution of the widow's estate by inheritance was made to descend, not to the heirs of the widow herself, following *shari'ah*, but rather, following custom, to the heirs of her deceased husband (that is, to the heirs of what had come to be known as 'the last full male owner').

Even as this new Shariat Act in 1948 sought to recognize widows as 'Qur'anic heirs' with respect to any possible mortgage, then, it went out of its way to deprive them of the ancestral property that they might have distributed, as full-fledged 'owners', through inheritance. Of course this new Act (1948) was clearly intended to limit the terms of 'tribal' custom.[72] But, even so, a closer look clearly reveals that, in practice, it only reinforced the limitations affecting those with an interest in advancing the enforcement of specific Qur'anic shares.

Indeed, even *after* 1948, questions concerning the application of customary law and, especially, the status of 'limited' lifetime estates, persisted. The Punjab Muslim Personal Law (Shariat) Application

(Amendment) Act of 1951, for instance, continued to stress a pattern of inheritance tied to the rights of 'full male owners', once again reinforcing the legal constraints confronting those with 'limited' lifetime estates. And, of course, the basic tenacity of this situation was only reconfirmed when Field Marshal Ayub Khan went on to promulgate the West Pakistan Muslim Personal Law (Shariat) Application (Amendment) Ordinance of 1963, explicitly seeking to finalize the termination of 'limited' lifetime estates with clear and immediate effect.[73]

Indeed, even *after* 1963, Zulfiqar Ali Bhutto found himself forced to revisit exactly the same topic in two further pieces of legislation, namely (a) the Punjab Muslim Personal Law (Shariat) Application (Removal of Doubts) Ordinance (1972), and, finally, (b) the Punjab Muslim Personal Law (Shariat) Application (Removal of Difficulties) Act (1975).[74] Clearly, the transition from custom to *shari'ah*, particularly as this related to the question of 'limited' lifetime estates, required far more than a simple declaration of formal legal intent.

In fact it was not until 1981, shortly after General Zia-ul-Haq seized control in Islamabad, that the Federal Shariat Court and, eventually, the Supreme Court of Pakistan, actually returned to settle the question of 'limited' lifetime estates once and for all, drawing special attention to the case of *Federation of Pakistan vs. Mohammad Ishaq*.[75] Indeed, even this decision had to be revisited, in 1990, when the case of *Ghulam Ali vs. Mst Ghulam Sarwar Naqvi* provided the Supreme Court with an opportunity to declare, more than four decades after the formation of Pakistan, that 'the rights of widows, ... as per the terms of *shari'ah*, should not [in practice] be infringed'.[76]

Finally, just a few months after the *Mohammad Ishaq* decision was announced in the autumn of 1983, the provincial Government of the Punjab went on to promulgate the Muslim Personal Law (Shariat) Application Act Punjab (Amendment) Ordinance in an effort to ensure that, henceforth, male and female owners inheriting from the deceased husband of any woman in possession of a 'limited' lifetime estate would be (a) treated as 'full' Muslim owners in their own right and (b) protected from 'the claims of remote reversioners'.[77] In other words, individual women still in possession of a 'limited' lifetime estate would not be regarded as full-fledged Muslim owners; but, in the wake of this new law, *the heirs of their deceased husbands would inherit, according to shari'ah, with no encumbrance whatsoever.*

In fact, strictly speaking it was not until the 1980s and, in some senses, even the 1990s—fully forty years after the formation of an ostensibly 'Islamic' Republic—that the terms of 'tribal' custom were finally removed (in an official sense) from the courts of postcolonial Punjab.

Initially, of course, each of these new laws, beginning with the West Punjab Muslim Personal Law (Shariat) Application Act of 1948, was designed to replace the terms of 'tribal' custom with the specific terms of *shari'ah*. In fact, in a certain sense, each and every one of these new laws (1948–1983) was specifically designed to chip away at the most controversial provisions of the Punjab Laws Act (1872) (Section 5), with its special appeal to the terms of 'tribal' custom, and, especially, the Muslim Personal Law (Shariat) Application Act (1937) (Section 2), with its rather notorious effort to 'protect' all matters relating to '[the] question ... [of] agricultural land'.

As time passed, however, several of these new laws were also motivated by a special interest in addressing the specific terms of a new law known as the Muslim Family Laws Ordinance (1961)—arguably the most important piece of legislation concerning the introduction and enforcement of *shari'ah* in the context of postcolonial Punjab.

The Muslim Family Laws Ordinance (1961). On 4 August 1955, the Second Constituent Assembly summoned a special Commission on Marriage and Family Laws to address the legal status of Muslim women throughout Pakistan.[78] This Commission began with a series of questions regarding marriage and divorce, but, eventually it sought to push beyond this rather limited focus in an effort to engage a number of closely-related problems concerning the issue of inheritance.

As one leading member of the Commission pointed out, recalling the work of men like W.T. Amman in the context of the Legislative Assembly debates surrounding the Muslim Personal Law (Shariat) Application Act of 1937, the Commission on Marriage and Family Laws was convened to bring the substance of existing postcolonial laws into conformity with the *shari'ah*, while, at the same time, 'suggest[ing] new laws', so that, in the end, 'the women of [Pakistan might] be freed from the age-old disabilities under which they have groaned', and, in due course, 'secured their proper and lofty place in society, which Islam has given them'.[79]

The work of the Commission on Marriage and Family Laws (1955) has been carefully documented in the existing literature.[80] In fact, for the time being it should be sufficient to note that, in its attempt to 'bring the substance of existing laws into conformity with the *shari'ah*', this Commission merely succeeded in drawing the views of various legal-cum-political 'modernists' into a pattern of bitter and protracted conflict with one (rather energetic) 'traditionalist'.

The majority of the Commission, headed by former Supreme Court Chief Justice Mian Abdul Rashid, favoured an explicity 'modernist' approach to the introduction of *shari'ah*, drawing special attention the principle of *ijtihad* and the terms of public consensus. This approach, however, did not advance unopposed. In fact the dissenting voice of Maulana Ehtisham-ul-Haq Thanvi soon emerged to articulate a very different approach—one that focused, primarily, on the value of *taqlid* and the 'educated' understanding of specific (*madrasa*-based) *ulema*.

Chief Justice Mian Abdul Rashid. Tracing their lineage, and that of Pakistan as a whole, to the legacy of Sir Syed Ahmed Khan (1817–98), the Commission's 'modernist' majority focused on the terms of *ijtihad*, noting that, for all intents and purposes, the terms of *ijtihad* could be defined as 'interpretive intelligence working within the broad framework of the Qur'an and the *sunnah*' (although a much longer definition was also drawn from the well-known work of Allama Mohammad Iqbal).[81]

At the same time, however, the 'modernist' majority went on to criticize two very different traditions of Islamic jurisprudence, which, they argued, *opposed* the terms of *ijtihad*, namely 'Anglo-Mohammadan' jurisprudence on the one hand and the notion of *taqlid* on the other. 'What was accepted as the personal law of the Muslims [within the colonial state]', they wrote, referring to the terms of Anglo-Mohammadan law, 'was conservative, rigid, and in many respects undefined'.[82] And, yet, even beyond this, they argued, the terms of *taqlid* were *even more inflexible* (routinely suggesting what they described as '[an] unquestioned following of the previously established authority of a great jurist *imam*').[83]

According to the modernist majority, both of these traditions were plagued by a certain legal paralysis—a paralysis they intended to overcome with an appeal to the dynamic terms of contemporary 'public opinion'. 'Law is ultimately related to life experiences, which are not a monopoly of [the] theologians', they argued.[84] 'Some may be more learned in Muslim law than others, but that does not constitute them as a separate class; they are not vested with any special authority, and they enjoy no special privileges'.[85]

Of course, Chief Justice Rashid took special care to note that the terms of *ijtihad* were always circumscribed by the Qur'an, the *sunnah* and *ijma* or 'consensus'.[86] He simply noted that there were 'hundreds of Muslims who ha[d] answered the questionnaire issued by the Commission', adding that '[these Muslims could be taken to represent] the terms of *ijma*' and, therein, the all-important 'will of the [political] majority'.[87]

Maulana Ehtisham-ul-Haq Thanvi. Naturally, the dissenting response submitted by Maulana Ehtisham-ul-Haq Thanvi, drawing special attention to the value of *taqlid*, was perfectly clear.[88] In fact Thanvi was incensed. 'What greater outrage can there be', he thundered in defence of the *ulema*, 'than that those who have never read a single word of the Qur'an in all their life, who do not know Arabic, and who have not received any grounding ... in any of the sciences necessary for a proper understanding of the Qur'an, would have us believe that the *ijtehad* of Razi, Imam Ghazali, Abu Hanifa, and Abu Yusuf was wrong, so that we may swallow down their own *ijtehad*'? According to Thanvi, this was just the Committee's way of lashing out against those who consistently sought to stifle 'the will of the majority' in their bid to 'change' Islam.[89]

'As a matter of principle', Thanvi argued, rejecting the views articulated by the Committee's 'so-called majority', '*reference to public opinion on purely shariat questions amounts to trifling with [the] Islamic shariat and ridiculing the religion, which can never be tolerated*' (emphasis added.)[90] In fact, he declared, the terms of *taqlid*—and, more specifically, the authority of 'properly qualified' *ulema*—were absolutely indispensable.

In the end, of course, the views expressed by the Chief Justice and the remaining members of the Committee prevailed by majority vote, and the terms of *shari'ah* (that is, Muslim personal law) passed into the statute books via the Muslim Family Laws Ordinance of 1961. But, even then, the views articulated by Maulana Ehtisham-ul-Haq Thanvi were not forgotten; in fact for the next forty years the terms of the debate were routinely framed by 'modernist' and 'traditionalist' approaches to postcolonial legal reform. Both sides sought to introduce the terms of *shari'ah*. Both sought to embrace the language of the Holy Qur'an. They simply disagreed about the best way to go about doing this. And of course they disagreed about the religious-cum-political 'legitimacy' of their competing points of view.

Whereas one side appealed to the language of the public at large (and the value of a certain 'flexibility'), the other insisted on closer ties to the conservative views articulated by cloistered 'scholar' *imams*.

Enforcing *Shari'ah*

Even in the midst of their (partial) disagreement, however, neither the so-called 'modernists' nor the so-called 'traditionalists' seemed to appreciate the magnitude of the challenges associated with the pursuit of a truly successful leap from formal legal 'rhetoric' to practical (or enforceable) 'reality'. To be sure, the final report submitted by the Commission on Marriage and Family Laws in 1955, followed by the promulgation of the Muslim Family Laws Ordinance in 1961, dramatically refocused the formal institutional framework within which the process of postcolonial legal change could occur. But, even then, several rather important questions remained—above all, questions regarding the problem of practical (day-to-day) *enforcement*.

These questions, regarding the need for a more effective pattern of enforcement, were finally taken up, several years after the promulgation of the Muslim Family Laws Ordinance (1961), by the Ministry of Law under Prime Minister Zulfiqar Ali Bhutto, focusing specifically on the work of an ambitious new committee known as the Pakistan Women's Rights Committee.

Submitting its final report to the Attorney General of Pakistan, Yahya Bakhtiar, in 1975, the members of this newly established Women's Rights Committee quickly succeeded in promoting an entirely new level of empirical sophistication within the context of ongoing legal debates. Turning specifically to the complex problem of basic implementation, for instance, the members of this new Committee cut straight to the heart of the matter: 'These laws have been in force for quite some time', they noted, drawing attention to Section 4 of the Muslim Family Laws Ordinance (regarding inheritance), 'but in actual practice it has been found that even now women do not get their due share in the property, ... *particularly where it is agricultural land*, because the male heirs of the deceased either suppress information about the existence of female heirs or otherwise manipulate statements by or on their behalf', claiming, for instance, '[that] the female heirs have relinquished their right ... in favour of the male heirs' (emphasis added).[91]

Clearly, the members of this new Committee perceived an important problem—in many ways the very same problem that S.M. Haider had illuminated in his study of the role played by local *patwaris* several years before (focusing on the case of 'Ms Nasim'). According to the final report submitted to the Attorney General, however, the solution to this problem—in effect, this problem of endemic non-enforcement—was not likely to involve any effort to bolster the work of local *patwaris*. Instead, they argued, the most effective solution would require a concerted effort to move *away* from the *patwari* altogether, focusing, instead, on the work of the district and appellate courts—a dramatic shift, if you will, away from the realm of the village proprietary body (and the domain of local 'politics') toward a more explicit focus on (autonomous) 'religious' rights: 'No authority should accept any statement to the effect of relinquishing a share of any property, either on inheritance or otherwise, by a *woman*', they argued, 'unless such [a] statement [has been] attested by a common civil *judge*' (emphasis added).[92]

Throughout their final report, the members of this newly established Women's Rights Committee were keen to stress the fact that the laws of inheritance had changed: 1948, 1951, 1961, 1963, 1972, 1975, and so on. In fact the law itself had changed in ways that explicitly aimed to sweep away the last vestiges of 'tribal' custom and, with this in mind, several features of the *ancien* (colonial) *régime*. But, even in 1975, the members of this new committee felt compelled to note that, practically speaking, the impact these changes remained almost entirely 'rhetorical'. As a matter of fact, they noted, the *de facto* shape of landed property relations remained almost exactly the same nearly thirty years after the formation of an independent 'Islamic' Republic. The problem, they argued, could not be found in the specific terms of the 'law'. On the contrary, the problem lay at the level of local *patwaris* and their attachment to the practice of local 'politics'.

Indeed, even as the rhetorical landscape began to overflow with formal legal references to the specific injunctions of Islam—for example under Zia-ul-Haq (1977–88)—the situation 'on the ground' remained almost entirely unchanged: 'The Qur'anic precepts do receive lip service', noted the members of a special follow-up commission convened to examine the status of Muslim women in 1983. But, even then, the specific influence of these precepts was still 'greatly masked by centuries-old cultural patterns alien to the spirit of Islam', patterns that led countless women, throughout Pakistan, to remain 'dispossessed and disinherited' even despite the presence of explicit legal 'safeguards'.[93]

Drawing special attention to the issue of inheritance as it actually unfolded on the ground, for instance, the members of this special follow-up commission (1983) went on to explain that 'the Islamic right to own property for women [is] very often ... merely theoretical and not matched by any actual access to the property which they may, on paper, be [the] owners of'. 'While a perusal of the ... real estate records would indicate that at least one third of all privately owned urban and rural property is registered in the name of women', they noted, '*the control of these properties is invariably under the exclusive control of men*' (emphasis added).[94]

'The land is transferred in [the] women's name in [the] *jamabandi*', noted the chair of this commission, 'but possession is not handed over'.[95] 'Women's names are entered against their share, [but] they are not given the possession, for which they have to turn to the courts'. And, even then, the chair explained, cutting straight to the heart of the matter, 'it takes as long as ten to fifteen years [to receive a] final court verdict'.[96] (See Chapter 5.)

Women were consistently 'deprived of their share', the chair concluded, because any effort to provide them with their share would, almost invariably, lead to '[a] division of [the] land, which most families avoid'. In fact, throughout the Punjab, she noted, most families sought to maintain a *de facto* attachment to the 'custom' of female disinheritance, because, even in 1983, the terms of economic and political status were still very much defined by the magnitude of the (agnatic) family's 'landholding'.[97]

The Logic of Local Politics

Considered in isolation, of course, neither land reform nor the introduction of *'ilm al-fara'id* was enough to change the shape of landed property relations in the context of postcolonial Punjab. But, together, I would argue, their effect was considerably more significant, particularly—in fact, primarily—at the level of local politics.

It would of course be naïve to conclude that the deterioration of the colonial land revenue administration in favour of *ushr*, combined with the formal legal demise of 'tribal' custom, for example, in the context of the postcolonial district courts, might have led (automatically) to any practical demise in the status of female disinheritance. On the contrary, as Bina Agarwal explains in her well-known book, *A Field of One's Own* (1994), the deprivation of women's access to land continued in a spectacular form even despite dramatic changes in the law.[98]

Indeed, even as the terms of *de jure* 'ownership' were extended (at least on paper) to countless women, the terms of *de facto* 'possession' were withheld. And, of course, precisely insofar as this was the case, existing patterns of (agnatic) 'control' largely survived. In fact, as I will now proceed to explain, moving beyond the basic assumptions that drive the work of scholars like Bina Agarwal, existing patterns of control had a tendency to survive as the direct result of an entirely new logic of 'participatory' and 'accountable' local *politics*.

The formal introduction of Islamic law, as a form of *'siyasa' shari'ah*, in other words, was never the most important part of the story. In fact the most important part of the story was not defined by the introduction of any new 'laws' at all. Instead it was defined by the emergence of an entirely new logic of postcolonial political accountability specifically designed to circumvent the substance of existing laws—in many ways, a logic of political accountability specifically designed to circumvent *shari'ah*: 'accountability' *versus* the 'law'.

With respect to the survival of existing agnatic estates, the question was no longer confined to a simple account of local preferences: why did local families *prefer* agnatic estates? No, the question concerned the basic underpinnings of individual *actions* as they actually took shape on the ground: how did individual owners actually manage to *preserve* those estates (politically)? Where did they go? What did they do? Who did they meet? And why?

The Logic of Local Politics: Local Politicians

For decades (1947–1999), the primary debate concerning 'the logic of local politics' in Pakistan focused on the relative importance of 'modern' and 'traditional' factors in the context of local elections.

Some, arguing in favour of 'modern' factors, stressed the role of local politicians when it came to the delivery of material goods and, more specifically, the provision of improved access 'to' basic public services. In fact throughout this period a substantial majority insisted that, with respect to the question of local electability, factors like party membership, links to senior politicians, wealth and achievement in the context of various development initiatives mattered more than competing factors like kinship and the influence of rival *pattis*.

Others, however, disagreed. Stressing local patterns of landownership in the context of existing *pattis*, for instance, many held fast to the notion that the geography of village politics—*khewats, khatas*, *pattis*, and so on—still mattered. At the very least, they noted, *patti*-based kinship factions tended to *precede* and, in many ways, also *explain* the 'patterned' delivery of goods and services that did so much to account for the 'electability' of individual (*patti*-based) elites.

The challenge, of course, does not lie in discrediting one or the other of these two views so as to expose a single (unidimensional) driver of political practice: performance, if you will, versus *pattis*. In fact, more often than not, the challenge lies in an effort to expose exactly how these two views come together to 'explain' the work of *patti*-based politicians as it actually unfolded on the ground.

A simple survey (Part I). Some insist that, throughout the latter half of the twentieth century, local politicians attempted to secure the support of their constituents via their 'performance' in the context of various development initiatives—focusing, specifically, on the construction of new roads, new schools, and new technology (for example, electricity, tubewells, and drainage systems). But, as my research unfolded, I quickly discovered that this emphasis on the provision of access 'to' basic public services was often less important than the provision of a carefully constructed pattern of protection 'from' the application of existing laws.

To illuminate this point, I proceeded to conduct a simple survey in Lahore, Sialkot, and Sargodha regarding the daily conduct of local politicians. This survey, involving a total of 281 respondents (ninety-five in Lahore, ninety-three in Sialkot and ninety-three in Sargodha), focused on two simple questions. First, I sought to discover what local politicians actually 'did' for their constituents. And, second, I sought to discover whether or not this activity on the part of local politicians actually served to 'preserve' the integrity of specific agnatic estates. (And, if it did, I wanted to know exactly how this outcome was achieved.)

To begin, I asked my respondents to identify two things that local politicians actually 'did' in reality (that is, *haqeeqat mein*), drawing special attention to a brief list of options that included (a) providing personal 'assistance' or *safarish* in the context of local government offices, (b) providing personal assistance in the context of local private offices, (c) promoting basic infrastructure improvements (for example, better roads), (d) helping individual citizens in their search for better jobs, and, finally, (e) resolving local disputes.

The most common response, I found, was (a) 'providing personal assistance or *safarish* in the context of local government offices', although, in the course of my research, this response was closely followed by a popular write-in response drawing special attention to the fact that, *haqeeqat mein*, or 'in reality', local politicians 'did' *kuchh bhi nahin*, that is, 'nothing at all'.

In several further questions, however, I pressed for additional information, and, ultimately, this information clarified the work undertaken by local politicians in a number of important ways. First and foremost, I asked my respondents to tell me exactly what they meant when they mentioned the provision of personal assistance or *safarish* in the context of local government offices: 'Many people say that they receive personal "assistance" in the context of local government offices', I noted. 'So the question is: What does this actually mean? Where are local politicians expected to show that they are being "helpful"'?

Above all, I wanted to know whether local politicians were expected to 'help' in the context of (a) offices related to basic infrastructure improvements—education, electricity, water, and so on—or (b) offices related to the adjudication of local property matters and (at least potentially) the resolution of 'factional' disputes.

Many respondents were (understandably) reluctant to tell me about their personal experiences with *safarish*—a term with specific connotations of 'corruption'. In fact nearly 30 per cent refused to respond at all (a figure that increased quite dramatically among the landless poor). (See Table 1 below.) Among those who *did* respond, however, the answer was perfectly clear: local politicians were expected to provide personal assistance or *safarish* in two places, namely (a) the local *thana* (that is, the local police station) (32 per cent) and (b) the local district courts (12 per cent).

In fact, among those holding at least 1 acre of land, the office of the local *patwari* was also quite important. And, among those holding 1–5 acres of land, the domain of the *patwari* was only slightly less important than that of the district courts. Indeed, among those holding *more* than 5 acres, the role of the *patwari* actually outranked that of the courts, leading me to observe that the role of *safarish* in the context of

Table 1. *Safarish* in government offices (choices 1 and 2) (%) v. landownership

	WAPDA	***thana***	*patwari*	**courts**	schools	PakTel	tax	other	—
No land	2.2%	**21.8%**	6.5%	**8.7%**	2.2%	4.3%	6.5%	2.2%	**43.5%**
0–1 *kanal*	9.0	**32.0**	5.8	**9.9**	5.3	2.5	0.0	0.8	**34.0**
1 *kanal*—1 acre	8.7	**32.6**	4.4	**10.8**	6.5	4.4	0.0	0.0	**32.6**
1–5 acres	3.6	**35.8**	10.7	**12.5**	1.8	5.4	0.0	1.8	**28.6**
6–10 acres	6.3	**31.3**	16.7	**12.5**	6.3	6.3	0.0	0.0	**20.8**
11+ acres	6.6	**40.8**	15.8	**14.5**	4.0	2.2	0.0	0.0	**15.8**
OVERALL	6.1	**32.4**	10.0	**11.5**	4.4	4.2	1.1	0.8	**29.2**

Abbreviations:
WAPDA: Water and Power Development Authority
PakTel: Pakistan Telecom
— I don't know/no answer

Fig. 17. Landownership v. *safarish* in the the district *kachehri* (%)
(derived from Table 1, above)

Size of holding	*Location of* safarish: kachehri
No land	37.0 per cent (*Kachehri*: *Thana* + Courts + *Patwari*)
0–1 *kanal*	47.7
1 *kanal*–1 acre	47.8
1–5 acres	59.0
6–10 acres	60.5
11+ acres	71.1

the district *kachehri* (as a whole) increased, quite consistently, with the size of individual *landholdings*. (See Fig. 17)

With this in mind, I decided to pose one final question. Fully aware of the fact that civil disputes regarding landed property were the most common type of dispute by far (often spilling over into the local *thana* and, in due course, the criminal courts as the intensity of the dispute increased), I asked: 'If you were involved in a dispute regarding landed property, would you be inclined to contact an elected leader for help'?

Not surprisingly, 73 per cent said 'yes, they would consider turning to an elected leader for help'.[99] In fact it is important to stress that this 'help' was *not* provided—at least not primarily—in the context of local government offices devoted to the provision of access 'to' specific development initiatives (water, electricity, schools, and so on). Instead it was provided in the context of local government offices specifically devoted to the adjudication of local disputes.

A simple survey (Part II). At this point, however, I found myself searching for a more compelling way to draw two very different pieces of information together. On the one hand, I knew that individuals confronted with landed property disputes were inclined to contact their elected leaders for 'help'. And, yet, at the same time, I knew that local politicians were expected to provide their constituents with 'personal assistance' in the context of specific government offices—above all, in the context of the district *kachehri*.

The question was: How did those with 'landed property disputes' link *those disputes* (specifically) to existing forms of *safarish*? What did the terms of *safarish* actually 'mean' with respect to those disputes in the context of the district *kachehri*? And, cutting straight to the heart of the matter, how did the terms of *safarish* intervene, *within the kachehri*, to reinforce—or not—the specific substance of existing postolonial laws? Indeed, how did the terms of *safarish* work to reinforce—or not—the underlying substance of *shari'ah*?

My response to these questions will be taken up primarily in the context of Chapter 5 (below). But, for the time being, it is important to note that the terms of *safarish* were never actually confined to the work of the district *kachehri*. Instead, within the framework of my brief survey, I was informed that, more often than not, those embroiled in landed property disputes (specifically) had a tendency to visit not one but two institutions (simultaneously), namely (a) the district *kachehri* and (b) the local *panchayat*, that is, the local (village or kinship-based) 'council of elders'.

This was, of course, an extremely important point. In fact, to the extent that those embroiled in landed property disputes were inclined to avail the services of more than one institution at exactly the same time, several questions emerged regarding the role of local politicians when it came to stitching those institutions together. How did the practice of postcolonial *safarish* serve to support the work of the district *kachehri*? How did it work to support—or derail—the work of the district courts? How did it serve to advance the enforcement of *shari'ah* (if at all)? And, finally, how did it serve to achieve the *preservation* of existing 'agnatic' estates?

The Logic of Local Politics: Local Voters

Naturally, few of my respondents were prepared to admit that local patterns of dispute resolution were systematically set 'apart from' or 'against' the substance of existing laws (particularly when it came to postcolonial landed property disputes and the terms of *'ilm al-fara'id*). In fact, when a senior lawyer in Sialkot closed the door to his office and whispered, in response to my questions, that, more often than not, local disputes regarding the inheritance of ancestral land were resolved within the terms of 'Mitakshara' (Hindu) custom rather than the specific terms of *shari'ah*, I was amazed—vindicated, perhaps, but, recalling the muted tones of those who struggled to oppose the promulgation of the Muslim Personal Law (Shariat) Application Act in 1937, still somewhat amazed.

Fortunately, one final piece of evidence emerged from my brief survey to reinforce the terms of this otherwise rather unconventional, even 'unspeakable', confession. This piece of evidence concerned the fact that, notwithstanding the work of countless local politicians seeking to provide their constituents with various types of *safarish* in the context of the district *kachehri*, most of the cases filed in the district courts were *not* resolved with the help of any substantive decree. Instead, as I will explain, in Chapter 5, most were resolved with the help of a *razeenama* or 'compromise' rendered *outside of*—and, in many cases, *against*—the work of the courts themselves.

Not surprisingly, those embroiled in landed property disputes generally agreed that the likelihood of obtaining a speedy and enforceable decision rendered by a district judge within the terms of existing postcolonial laws was actually extremely small. In fact, when I asked my respondents how long it would take them to obtain an enforceable decree within the specific terms of existing postcolonial laws (including existing Islamic laws), most of them simply rolled their eyes and said, '*Hai, hai! Kam-az-kam das saal*', or 'Heavens! At least ten years'. In fact, within the space of a decade, fewer than 20 per cent appeared to expect any decision at all. (See Table 2 below.)

Table 2. Dispute resolution (full judgment) (%) v. education: Lahore, Sialkot, Sargodha

	Less than 2 years	2–5 years	5–10 years	More than 10	—
No education	1.6%	7.9%	6.3%	54.0%	30.2%
Primary	5.1	6.4	10.3	51.3	26.9
Matriculation	3.0	3.0	13.4	59.7	20.9
Intermediate	0.0	7.1	9.5	66.7	16.7
University	0.0	6.9	6.9	65.5	17.2
OVERALL		—— 18.1 ——		57.3	24.2

When I asked my respondents how long it would take them to reach an acceptable 'compromise' *outside* of the district courts (albeit, more often than not, in conjunction with some form of 'ancillary' or 'strategic' litigation), however, not even one expected this process to take ten years. In fact, nearly 70 per cent noted that it would take them 'less than two'.[100] (See Table 3.)

Indeed, the closer I came to an account of the relationship between (a) the courts and (b) the production of local 'compromises' outside of

Table 3. Dispute resolution (*razeenama*) (%) v. education: Lahore, Sialkot, Sargodha

	Less than 2 years	2–5 years	5–10 years	More than 10	—
No education	63.5%	4.8%	0.0%	0.0%	31.7%
Primary	66.7	3.8	0.0	0.0	29.5
Matriculation	74.6	0.0	1.5	0.0	23.9
Intermediate	78.6	2.4	0.0	0.0	19.0
University	72.4	0.0	0.0	0.0	27.6
OVERALL	**69.8**	2.5	0.0	0.0	27.4

the courts themselves, the more I began to see exactly how the work undertaken by local politicians—not only in the context of the district courts, but also in the context of local *panchayats*—was related *both* to the production of local 'compromises' *and* to the preservation of existing 'agnatic' estates.

Again, I knew that individuals with landed property disputes were inclined to take these disputes both to the district *kachehri* and to the local *panchayat* (simultaneously) (and, within this process, I knew that the very same individuals were inclined to contact their elected leaders for 'help' with different types of *safarish*). And, yet, even then, it was still difficult to confirm exactly what the nature of this *safarish* actually involved in specific 'substantive' terms. In fact the question remained: What was the nature of the 'help' that locally elected leaders were actually expected to provide? And, more specifically, how was this 'help' related to the satisfaction of local constituent 'demands'? If, having arrived in the district *kachehri*, most people did *not* expect their elected leaders to facilitate the production of a substantive judicial 'decree', what *did* they expect? What did they want *instead*?

As I will explain, in Chapter 5, the challenge for most politicians did not lie in constructing new and better laws. Nor did it lie in promoting a more rigorous pattern of enforcement for the laws that (for better or worse) already appeared to exist. In fact, as I will explain, local politicians were simply expected to apply themselves *within* the district *kachehri*—for example, *within* the district courts—to facilitate the production of a more acceptable 'compromise': in effect, a more thoroughly 'custom-friendly' *razeenama* outside of the courts themselves.

CONCLUSION

Given what we know about the nature of historically embedded preferences in the context of colonial and postcolonial Punjab—particularly insofar as these preferences concerned the preservation of 'customary' landed property relations and the reinforcement of local kinship factions—the challenge for most politicians did not lie in mobilizing the courts to uphold or enforce the law. After all, any effort to do so would have implied (a) the strict application of landed property ceilings specifically designed to dismantle existing ancestral estates, (b) the rapid extension of land consolidation schemes with the potential to unsettle existing agnatic *pattis*, and (c) the immediate implementation of *shari'ah* (including, above all, the specific enforcement of inheritance rights for countless Muslim women).

Indeed, the challenge for most politicians did not lie in any effort to 'enforce' the law. Nor did it lie in making 'new' laws. Instead, I would argue, the challenge lay in a seeking to *acknowledge* the substance of existing laws (in court) while, at the same time, working to ensure that those laws were *avoided* (in practice).

Certainly, when it came to the satisfaction of local constituent demands, Deputy Commissioners and district-level judges played an extremely important role. After all, they controlled the police, the record of rights in land, and the adjudication of disputes in court. And, yet, having said this, few would deny that, throughout the Punjab, these officials were often regarded as little more than petty pawns in a much larger political game—petty pawns, if you will, in a much larger political pagaent performed by postcolonial *patti*-based proprietors.

To be sure, many insist that this assessment of the political landscape 'in practice' turns the story upside down. Far from calling the shots, they argue, *patti*-based proprietors were frequently held at bay by powerful local *patwaris*. Far from defining local outcomes, they note, individual *zamindars* were routinely crushed under the thumb of commanding Deputy Commissioners. And so on and so forth. Indeed, in a purely 'technical' sense, this view of the district administration was (at least partially) correct. In a purely 'technical' sense, Deputy Commissioners did control the *patwari*, *patwaris* did control the revenue records, and, even after more than 150 years, the revenue records were still believed to control 'all that is wholesome and profitable in that great principle of association' for which 'the land itself' was still believed to furnish an 'all-sufficient' economic and political basis.

And, yet, having said this, it is equally clear that, throughout postcolonial Punjab, this purely 'technical' sense had a tendency to ignore several important facts. Indeed, as my work unfolded, first in Lahore, then in Sialkot, and, finally, in Sargodha, I quickly realized that, bureaucratic technicalities notwithstanding, it would be extremely difficult, if not actually impossible, to find even one district-level official who believed that his administrative-cum-political relationship with local landowners was, in any way, hierarchically 'unidirectional'.

Indeed, those who insist that local politicians were consistently 'held at bay' by powerful local *patwaris* would do well to remember that these politicians were, in fact, frequently in a position to press for the transfer of an offending *patwari* with the assistance of their allies in Islamabad. And, of course, those who believe that national or provincial politicians were, themselves, all-powerful, would do well to remember that, in practice, even these politicians were often severely constrained by the need to spend considerable amounts of time chasing fee-based 'favours' in the context of the district *kachehri*.

The challenge for those with an interest in the logic of local politics, in other words, did not lie in drawing local bureaucrats and politicians into separate analytical spheres in a schematic effort to measure their relative 'statutory' strength. On the contrary, the challenge lay in developing a more nuanced and sophisticated appreciation for the administrative-cum-political logic that emerged to structure their interaction over time.[101]

Broadly speaking, this historically embedded administrative-cum-political 'logic' was closely tied to a specific understanding of *shari'ah*. In fact, as the twentieth century progressed, few would deny that extraordinarily generous rent-seeking opportunities accrued to those with some ability to ameliorate the enforcement of existing postcolonial laws. Indeed, even apart from the formal legal demise of 'limited' lifetime estates and the introduction of Islamic laws of inheritance (*'ilm al-fara'id*)—1948, 1951, 1961, 1963, 1972, 1975, and so on—it is impossible to deny the extent to which the promulgation of the Zakat and Ushr Ordinance (1980) engendered an enormous demand for the 'services' of those with an ability to control the allocation of what many had come to regard as effectively tax-free land.

Clearly, for those with an interest in the work undertaken by local *patwaris*, it would be impossible to ignore the ways in which, following this step-wise shift in favour of *shari'ah*, the level of support for politically 'accountable' forms of postcolonial law enforcement (or non-enforcement, as the case may be) expanded by leaps and bounds.

'Politicians never help the help the people,' noted one of my respondents in Sialkot, drawing special attention to a rather common expression of local 'anti-incumbency' sentiment. 'They only work for *aapna mufaad*,' that is, their own (private or factional) benefit. And, yet, as Anjum Altaf (2004) pointed out in a brief article prepared for *The Daily Times* in Lahore, the terms of a politician's *mufaad* and that of his most influential landowning constituents were never very far removed. On the contrary, he explained, these terms were often inseparable.

Indeed, as Altaf pointed out, politicians (like *patwaris*) routinely extracted enormous fees for their services. But the demand for those 'services' (for example, the demand for 'personal assistance' in the context of the district *kachehri*) was never in short supply. On the contrary, Altaf explained, 'voters regularly elect representatives who[m] they know to be dishonest.'[102] And, as voters, they did so with an interest in the advancement of their own *mufaad*, that is, their own private 'benefit'.

Indeed, as the twentieth century came crashing to an end in a complex jumble of overlapping local norms ('custom' v. *shari'ah*), a politician's *mufaad* and that of his most influential landowning constituents were often extremely difficult to disentangle. The question—among local shareholders—was rarely 'who benefited' from the preservation of the *ancien* (colonial) *régime* in the face of postcolonial 'Islamic' reforms. The question for local shareholders was often, simply, 'who didn't'?

PART THREE

UNDERSTANDING ISLAM, ISLAMIC LAW, AND DEMOCRACY IN PRACTICE

Part Three: Summary

As noted above, the central theme of this book grows out of a pattern in which ordinary Muslims call upon their elected representatives in an effort to acknowledge and, yet, at the same time, also avoid the consistent implementation of specific Islamic laws—in effect, a persistent effort to 'circumvent *shari'ah*' (*'ilm al-fara'id*).

Drawing special attention to the shifting terms of landed property relations in the context of colonial Punjab, Chapters 1 and 2 drew upon an historically embedded account of the colonial land revenue administration to explain exactly 'what people wanted' *instead of shari'ah* and, more importantly, 'why' they wanted that alternative—namely, 'tribal' custom—after the conquest of the Punjab in 1849. Chapters 3 and 4 then went on to address the implications of this preference structure for the logic of political participation and electoral accountability as it actually emerged, *in the shadow of shari'ah*, after 1947.

While Chapters 1–4 were concerned with a detailed account of what happened in various parts of the Punjab between 1849 and 1999, focusing in particular on the terms of one rather specific legal change (custom → *shari'ah*), Chapters 5 and 6 seek to illuminate the larger implications of this change on two levels. In Chapter 5, the implications of this change will be addressed at the level of specific *empirical* trends: what did this change imply for local landowners; how did it affect their relationship with the formal institutions of the postcolonial state; and, above all, how did it affect their relationship with the underlying terms of democracy? In Chapter 6, the implications of this legal change will be addressed at the level of specific *theoretical* concerns. Here I ask what an account of land, law, and the logic of local politics in colonial and postcolonial Punjab (1849–1999) might begin to reveal about the connection between Islam and democracy in general: how is an account of Islam, Islamic law, and local forms of electoral accountability in just one place related to an account of the connections—in effect, the 'compatibility' connections—between 'Islam' and 'democracy' in general?

5

THE LOGIC OF LOCAL POLITICS IN LAHORE, SIALKOT AND SARGODHA

For more than three years (1998–2000), the newspapers in Lahore ran the same minor headlines every day. Unfortunately, these headlines read like the body count in a low-intensity civil war. 'Man kills brother', for instance, was often followed by 'Tribal feud claims two lives'. Indeed, the numbers kept growing. 'Two uncles axed' in Faisalabad, for instance, merely set the stage for 'Three shot dead' in Jhang. Or, 'Four die' in Okara. The list went on and on. Sadly, all of these headlines ended with exactly the same words: '*Over land dispute*'.[1]

Occasionally, local reporters dug a bit deeper, exposing the conflicts that lay behind these headlines with stories like '[A] comparison between customary and Islamic law in the Punjab' or 'Brothers continue to gobble up sisters' inheritance'. In fact, every now and then, some of the most intrepid reporters managed to follow the specific logic of these headlines straight to the top, implicating the most prominent national politicians in some of the most parochial landed property disputes: 'Land fraud gang busted, councillor arrested', for instance, or 'Land-grabbing case [lodged] against PML leader [and] his brothers'.[2]

What follows is merely an attempt to illuminate the basic analytical drivers behind these headlines, focusing specifically on the relationship between (a) postcolonial patterns of formal legal change (custom → *shari'ah*) and (b) the logic of local politics that emerged to accommodate that change over time (1947–99).

At this point the most important questions do not concern the extent to which individual landowners attempted to circumvent existing postcolonial laws. Instead, I would argue, the most important questions concern the strategies whereby those landowners actually managed to accomplish their goals 'in practice'. (See Fig. 18 below.) Where did they go? Who did they meet? What, exactly, did they do?

Fig. 18. From preferences to strategies

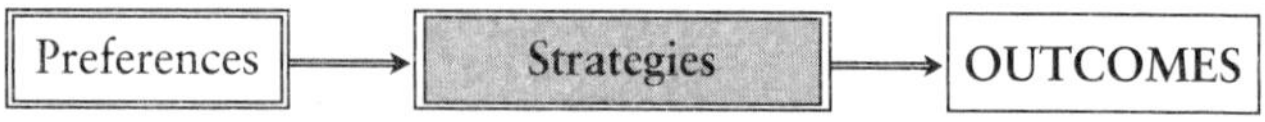

When I arrived in Lahore, Sialkot, and Sargodha to conduct my research, I expected to encounter a long list of people grappling with the terms of 'Islamic' law. In fact, as the terms of Islamic law became more and more prominent (at an official level) throughout the latter half of the twentieth century, I expected to encounter a growing sense of apprehension regarding the shifting terms of the law and, thus, a steadily declining level of postcolonial litigation concerning the ownership and inheritance of land—a halting pattern of decline, at least initially (1947–1983), followed by a more precipitous pattern of decline somewhat later on (1983–99).

What I found, however, was something else entirely. In fact what I found was *not* a steadily declining pattern of litigation—if anything the number of cases continued to increase throughout the latter half of the twentieth century. What I found was actually a puzzle. In fact what I found was a steadily *increasing* number of cases combined with a steadily *declining* attachment to the pursuit of substantive and enforceable decrees.

As my work unfolded, first in Lahore, then in Sialkot, and finally in Sargodha, I quickly discovered that, more often than not, those who found themselves embroiled in a typical dispute regarding immovable property—one side seeking to defend the terms of custom; one side seeking to advance the specific terms of *shari'ah*—these people did not shy away from the courts. In fact it would hardly be an exaggeration to say that, over time, they traveled to the courts in droves.

And, yet, having said this, I also found that, even after they decided to take their disputes to court, ordinary litigants did not always do so with any expectation of resolving their disputes 'in court'. On the contrary, the party with an interest in defending the terms of 'tribal' custom often seemed to visit the courts with just one thing in mind—namely, 'time'. In fact, more often than not, 'custom-friendly' litigants simply 'used' the courts to *detain* their opponents—in effect, to *delay* the resolution of their disputes—until, slowly but surely, a more acceptable *razeenama* or 'compromise' could be reached outside of the courts themselves.

As noted above (for example in Chapter 4) few disputes were confined to the district and appellate courts alone. Instead, most were pursued in (a) the district courts and (b) the local *panchayat* (simultaneously). In fact I quickly discovered that a comprehensive understanding of postcolonial patterns of dispute resolution would be almost impossible to construct without a specific understanding of the interaction, not only *between* these two very different forums, but also between these forums and the work that *patti*-based *politicians* did to stitch these forums together.

Prominent landowners did not seek to abandon or reject the formal institutions of the postcolonial state. They simply 'used' these institutions to achieve diverse and, in many cases, deeply conservative economic and political ends. Indeed, local politicians were not expected to construct 'new' and 'better' laws. They were simply expected to *engage* the substance of existing laws—including existing Islamic laws—in court, while, at the same time, providing their constituents with new and better ways to control the enforcement of those laws as they actually took shape on the ground—providing their supporters with new and better ways to lower the cost of enforcement (or non-enforcement, as the case might be) while, at the same time, raising those costs for opponents.

The courts were, in effect, just one small part of a much larger postcolonial strategy designed to *avoid* the practical implications of a legal environment that, many believed, they were not in a position to *amend*. In fact the issue for those with an interest in constructing a more complete understanding of the relationship between Islam, Islamic law, and democracy was not an issue defined by the terms of political accountability (full stop). It was, primarily, an issue of political 'accountability' closely tied to enduring questions regarding the alleged 'immutability' of existing Islamic laws.

PREFERENCES 'IN THEORY'

Those with an interest in the work of the postcolonial district courts, as well local *panchayats*, often begin their work with a set of *a priori* analytical assumptions—assumptions regarding the endemic inefficiencies of the courts, for instance, or the intrinsic inequalities associated with *patti*-based rural *panchayats*. The 'inefficiencies' of the district courts, for instance, tend to be evaluated in light of specific conventions regarding the reach of an ostensibly universal interest in limiting various transaction costs. And of course, the 'inequalities' associated with the postcolonial *panchayat* tend to be evaluated in light of specific assumptions regarding the overwhelming (albeit informal) power exerted by dominant rural factions.

These *a priori* assumptions are thought to serve the cause of parsimonious explanation insofar as they reveal something about the nature of empirical reality and, especially, the nature of empirically embedded *motivations*—suggesting, for instance, that landowners who find themselves confronted with landed property disputes might be inclined to settle their disputes out of court (in an effort to avoid the transaction costs associated with a protracted course of litigation) just as landless labourers might be expected to *approach* the courts in an effort to offset the informal strength of specific 'feudal' lords.[3] In fact this analytical shorthand is really the primary virtue of all motivational assumptions. They simply aim to illuminate (or explain) 'why people do what they do'.

Unfortunately, the nature of empirical reality frequently departs from the specific substance of these (rather conventional) assumptions. In the case of District Sialkot, for instance, even a cursory glance would reveal that, although the district courts remained extremely slow throughout the latter half of the twentieth century—indeed, roughly 14 per cent slower than the average articulated in Table 4 (below)—those with landed property disputes in District Sialkot were, in fact, three times *more* likely to proceed directly to court than those in District Lahore.[4] Clearly, this pattern cannot be said to conform to the expectations of those who begin their work with a set of *a priori* assumptions regarding the 'universal' pull of formal institutional 'efficiency'. In fact the virtue of this example is closely related to the fact that, with reference to its rather dramatic non-conformity, it seems to demand an entirely different account of local motivations—a more thoroughly nuanced, empirically grounded, and historically specific account of 'why people do what they do'.

Of course the same principle applies to *a priori* assumptions grounded in the motivational imperatives of 'class', the essential injunctions of 'Islam', and so on.

Table 4. Institutional 'inefficiency' in the district courts: Lahore, Sialkot, and Sargodha

	Case Disposal Rate (Months)							*Average*
	1–3	4–6	7–12	13–24	25–60	60+	—	
Lahore (N = 85)	41%	20%	18%	13%	8%	0%	0%	9.7 months
Sialkot (N = 179)	26	10	17	16	16	2	12	14.4
Sargodha (N = 104)	39	6	11	21	12	2	11	12.9
AVERAGE	**33**	**11**	**15**	**17**	**13**	**1**	**9**	**12.6**

Why is it, for instance, that, throughout the latter half of the twentieth century, individual landowners throughout the Punjab routinely sought to create alliances with the members of their own *patti*—including many of their most impoverished relatives—at the expense of any close relationship with the comparatively affluent owners of adjacent (or neighbouring) estates? Indeed, why did they opt to privilege the terms of *kinship* over and above the assumed 'imperatives' of *class*? And, turning to the injunctions of Islam, why did local Muslims, as 'Muslims', appear so keen to undermine the specific terms of *shari'ah* (for example, *'ilm al-fara'id*)? Why did they appear so keen to *avoid* the 'essential' injunctions of Islam?

Clearly, the challenge does not lie in rejecting the value of *a priori* assumptions outright. Instead it lies in developing a more thoroughly nuanced perspective—one that might allow us to construct a more thoroughly grounded understanding of the strategies that individuals use to pursue a particular set of interests (for example, 'tribal' interests) within a particular time and place.

Formal Institutions and the Question of Efficiency

Typically, those with an interest in the work of the district and appellate courts begin their research with a set of *a priori* assumptions regarding the ostensibly universal value of 'efficiency'. In fact, drawing attention to the power of an apparently unavoidable aversion to mounting 'transaction' costs, they routinely assume that endemic courtroom delays will have a tendency to discourage, dishearten, and perhaps even derail the efforts of those who (in the absence of such delays) might attempt to resolve their disputes in court.

As my research unfolded in Lahore, Sialkot, and Sargodha, however, I soon discovered that this assumption was no match for the actual process of litigation taking shape in the district courts. In fact, far from discouraging most litigants, the problem of endemic institutional inefficiency actually seemed to encourage the most powerful and persistent among them. (Indeed, one study conducted by the Asian Development Bank found that, even among those who chose to *avoid* the district courts, nearly half—48 per cent—believed that an ability to *delay* the resolution of their dispute would serve as a powerful incentive to *engage* the courts at some point in the future.[5])

In theory, of course, most litigants were expected to prefer 'quicker' courts. And for the most part they were expected to prefer these courts en route to the production of a formally demarcated, legally substantive, and fully enforceable decree. But, in practice, I found, this was only rarely the case. In fact, many of the most powerful litigants I encountered in the context of the district courts (typically those with an interest in protecting or preserving the specific constraints of custom) were drawn to a considerably more lackadaisical process—one that generally culminated, after several months, in a perfunctory judicial notation stating that, for reasons that almost always remained undisclosed, the initial plea was no longer under trial. It was in fact simply 'dismissed' (or 'withdrawn') owing to the emergence of an informal 'compromise'.

The conclusion of the trial, in other words, was not defined by the terms of any substantive decree. It was defined, instead, by a politically strategic dismissal.

The Politics of Delay: a Closer Look at the Courts

As is well known, the district courts of postcolonial Punjab were consistently overwhelmed throughout the latter half of the twentieth century (1947–99). Serving several thousand citizens apiece, for instance, district-level judges routinely faced a daily docket with more than fifty cases; and, in some parts of the Punjab, this figure climbed to more than 100. Not surprisingly most of these cases were postponed. But, even when the formalities of a particular trial actually managed to proceed, most of the witnesses failed to appear for the hearings. And, even when they did appear, most of them failed to produce any evidence. In fact most of the cases that appeared before the district courts of postcolonial Punjab were simply adjourned—often more than fifty times.

In Sialkot and Sargodha, for instance, fewer than 15 per cent of the cases I encountered in the district courts actually managed to conclude with anything even remotely resembling a 'substantive' judicial decree. (See Table 5 below.) As noted above, most were simply 'withdrawn' independently (or 'dismissed') because the parties themselves simply failed to press on with the trial. Indeed, even among those that actually managed to obtain a 'substantive' decree, few succeeded in obtaining a decree that was, in the end, fully or effectively enforced.[6]

Table 5. 'Fully contested' cases: Sialkot, Sargodha

	Decisions	*Decisions (%)*	*Decision Favouring:*	
			Plaintiff	*Defendant*
Sialkot (N = 179)	26	14.5%	22 (85%)	4 (15%)
Sargodha (N = 104)	12	11.5%	10 (83%)	2 (17%)
Total/Average	**38**	**13.4%**	**32 (84%)**	**6 (16%)**

The courts, in other words, were extremely slow. And, at the end of the day, their work was often set apart from the production of any 'substantive' decrees. Needless to say, this prompted a simple question: If the chances of receiving a substantive decree were so small (and, even then, if the process itself was so extraordinarily slow and expensive), why did so many individuals choose to take their disputes to court? Why were the courts so consistently overwhelmed with landed property disputes throughout the latter half of the twentieth century?

Naturally, this question is particularly intriguing for those with an interest in the implications of postcolonial 'Islamic' laws. *Why did so many landowners rush to obtain the services of a court that was, in certain respects, guided by laws that distressed them?*

Fortunately, the Asian Development Bank (ADB) set out to address several different aspects of this question in the context of one of the most elaborate and ambitious legal reform projects ever undertaken.[7] In fact within its project, launched in 1998, the ADB appeared to take a particular interest in the problem of courtroom delay, noting that, in a clear deviation from the celebrated norm of formal institutional 'efficiency', cases that managed to complete all of the steps in the litigation process were, as a general rule, likely to linger in the district courts for at least three years—indeed, according to the ADB, *exactly* 41 months.[8]

Unfortunately, the study used to produce this estimate—a study of 968 cases drawn from several different courts throughout Pakistan (including more than 500 cases drawn from the district courts of Lahore, Sargodha, Rawalpindi, and Jhelum in the context of postcolonial Punjab)—was somewhat flawed. Its flaws, however, were not completely debilitating; and, upon closer inspection, I discovered that many of its flaws were actually quite illuminating.[9]

Briefly stated, the study conducted by the ADB focused on a carefully selected sample of 'fully contested cases' (that is, cases completing all of the steps in the litigation process) while, at the same time, excluding those cases that were, in the end, simply 'dismissed' or 'withdrawn' before the production of any substantive decree. In effect, the ADB chose to bifurcate the daily docket of the district courts, distinguishing those few cases that managed to obtain a substantive judicial decree (roughly 10–15 per cent) from the overwhelming majority (85–90 per cent) that ended with a perfunctory dismissal followed by an alternative conclusion outside of the courts themselves.[10]

The significance of this division, of course, lay in the fact that cases completing all of the steps in the litigation process tend to take more time—effectively increasing any estimate of delay.[11] In fact, as my research unfolded I quickly discovered that, if the sample collected by the ADB had been extended to include *all* of the cases in the district courts, including *both* 'fully contested' cases *and* 'not fully contested' cases—for an indication of this latter sample (see Table 4 above)—the average lifespan of a civil case would have been, not 'more than three years' (41 months), but rather scarcely one (12.6 months).

Pushing back against several common assumptions, in other words, I found that the problem of delay did not involve an enormous number of earnest litigants lingering in the district courts for decades. On the contrary, it involved something far more specific. In effect, it involved a situation in which, over time, thousands and perhaps even millions of litigants were permitted to indulge themselves for a few months and (in rare cases) several months or years.

Indeed, with this more refined account in mind, it may be worth recalling that, when I conducted my brief survey in Lahore, Sialkot, and Sargodha (Chapter 4), asking people to tell me just how long it would take them, having arrived in the district courts, to produce either (a) a substantive judicial 'decree' or (b) an alternative informal 'compromise' (see Tables 2 and 3 above), fewer than 20 per cent felt that a substantive judicial decree could ever be reached in less than ten years (although, having said this, nearly 70 per cent believed that an informal 'compromise' could be reached in 'less than two').

Perhaps they were simply guessing when they mentioned this rather protracted timeframe for the production of a substantive decree. (After all, this was a highly unusual outcome, accounting for just 10–15 per cent of the total caseload burden.) But, when it came to the production of an informal 'compromise', their guess was remarkably accurate. As a matter of fact, their guess was empirically spot-on.

The Politics of Delay: a Closer Look at Local Clients

In their book *Game Theory and the Law* (1994) Douglas G. Baird, Robert H. Gertner, and Rundel C. Picker joined the ADB in positing a strong set of assumptions regarding the (allegedly universal) value of 'efficiency'. 'In addition to ... direct costs', they explained, 'litigation consumes [both] the time and [the] energy of the litigants'. And, *as a result*, they noted, 'rational' litigants would '[probably] find it in their [best] interest to settle [out of court]' *before* the start of a trial.[12] In fact, they explained, the merits of a 'pre-trial settlement' were, as a matter of common 'rationality', routinely taken for granted.

Unfortunately, these expectations regarding the assumed value of 'time-based' efficiency did not appear to hold up particularly well in the context of postcolonial Punjab. In fact, throughout the district courts, I quickly discovered that the total number of 'settled' cases (defined as the total number of cases settled outside of the district courts *before* the start of a trial) tended to lag far behind the total number of (fully or partially) 'litigated' cases. And, of course, the total number of 'settled' cases trailed far behind the total number of 'litigated' cases precisely *because* the 'rationality' of most litigants was not constructed in the way that Baird, Gertner, and Picker were generally inclined to expect. The rationality of these litigants, one might say, was counter-intuitive and, in keeping with the specific terms of my argument, historically 'context-specific'.[13]

Throughout postcolonial Punjab, the process of pre-trial discovery was almost never used to formulate a pre-trial settlement. In fact the process of pre-trial discovery was almost never attempted at all.[14] And even when it was attempted, it often failed, mostly because individual litigants simply refused to disclose their 'evidence' before the start of the trial: 'Most people refuse to show their cards all at once', noted one civil judge, responding to my questions regarding local notions of 'discovery', adding that, more often than not, any effort to do so 'would ruin their strategy'.[15]

Of course the most straightforward explanation for this rather telling observation lay in the fact that, as a general rule, so-called 'evidence' was simply created as the need for it arose in the context of a particular trial: 'Where data on the recording of evidence is available, it is alarming', noted one report issued by the ADB, referring to some of the data presented in Table 6 (below). But when these numbers 'are combined with the paltry number of cases in which *discovery* is taken', the report explained, these figures were 'even more disturbing'.[16]

Table 6. 'Inefficiency' in the courts: completing a 'fully contested' case[17]

Case Elements	***Property Cases***		*Family Cases*	
	Punjab	*Pakistan*	*Punjab*	*Pakistan*
Summons	1.6 months	2.8 months	2.7 months	2.6 months
Pleadings	1.7	3.5	1.8	1.9
Issues	3.4	3.0	1.1	1.8
Evidence	**17.7**	17.4	13.7	13.3
Arguments	2.1	2.9	0.9	2.5
Judgment	0.2	0.5	n.d.	1.1

According to the ADB, most plaintiffs had a tendency to 'embark upon litigation and proceed to trial even before they [had] decide[d] upon the specific contours of their case'. And, as the case proceeded (for example, with the summons, the pleadings, and the framing of issues), they noted, most litigants simply began to 'conjure up their evidence'. In fact, 'even when they [did] not actually fabricate [that] evidence', noted the Bank's final report, many litigants found that 'essential documents [were] difficult to procure for reasons of poor record management and severe bureaucratic intransigence'.[18]

Table 7. 'Inefficiency' in the courts: the problem of case adjournments[19]

Case Adjournments	***Property Cases***		*Family Cases*	
	Punjab	*Pakistan*	*Punjab*	*Pakistan*
0 – 15	16.5%	48.5%	8.6%	18.5%
16 – 50	**48.8**	35.2	76.6	68.5
51 – 100	25.2	11.8	12.3	10.9
101 or more	9.4	4.4	0.0	0.0

The ADB's data regarding the process of discovery pointed to extremely low rates of (otherwise ostensibly 'rational') 'pre-trial' settlement. But even beyond these data—in fact even *after* the start of an average trial—the ADB found that the data regarding adjournments were often even worse. In fact, even after a given trial was well under way, the Bank reported that most cases suffered from at least fifteen adjournments. And, in the Punjab, many suffered from 50, 100, or more. (See Table 7, above.)

Unfortunately, in its effort to understand this proliferation of adjournments, the ADB threw up its hands, noting that, more often than not, it was extremely difficult to explain exactly why the number of adjournments was so high—particularly, albeit perhaps not surprisingly, in the context of postcolonial Punjab.[20]

For the most part, the final report issued by the ADB sought to blame this proliferation of adjournments on district-level judges, citing an apparently arbitrary abuse of their formal institutional 'discretion'. But, as I will explain, a more compelling explanation is also possible—one that begins to stress the terms of a more sophisticated and strategic relationship involving 'the politics of informal institutions'.[21]

'There are several adjournments', noted Mohammad Azam Chaudhary in his book *Justice in Practice* (1999), 'sometimes due to ... the laziness of the judges or [the] magistrates who do not finish their job and simply tell the parties to come back the next time'. But 'the most frequent reason', he noted, 'especially if one party is rich and influential, ... is that [the richer party] has a better "senior" lawyer, and [it] is interested in prolonging the case till eternity to make the other party bankrupt'.[22]

In fact, Chaudhary explained, drawing special attention to the 'custom-friendly' logic of protracted litigation, many of the most powerful litigants sought to prolong their disputes with the help of multiple adjournments—not until a formal judicial decision could be reached, but rather until their opponents were financially ruined, at which point the case in the courts could be rendered *dastbardar*, or 'withdrawn', owing to the production of a *razeenama* or 'compromise' outside of the courts themselves.[23]

Indeed it was here, in the practice of prolonged (but officially 'inconclusive') litigation, that, I found, the survival of so many 'agnatic' estates was carefully and consistently preserved. The point, of course, did not lie in avoiding the district courts. Nor did it lie in the production of any substantive or enforceable decree (rendered, as quickly as possible, within the terms of existing postcolonial laws). On the contrary, the point lay in the protracted process of postcolonial litigation itself—a complex process specifically designed to preserve enduring forms of *patti*-based power with the help of an informal 'compromise' rendered outside of the district courts.[24]

Again, the courts did not determine the final substantive outcome in most cases. Instead they merely detained those cases—holding them in abeyance, in a sense, until a more enduring 'compromise' could be reached beyond the corridors of the district *kachehri*. Refusing to confine themselves to the district and appellate courts, in other words, most landowning litigants simply went on to engage multiple dispute resolution forums simultaneously. Indeed this was an indispensable part of the process—moving *beyond* the realm of the district courts to the realm of the local *panchayat*; *beyond* the problem of 'delay' to the practical implications of that delay in the production of a negotiated 'compromise'; and, finally, *beyond* the formal institutions of the state itself in the direction of a purely 'informal' recapitulation of specific 'agnatic' norms.

Most cases were not 'decided' by the courts. They were simply *delayed* in the courts and, then, dismissed or abandoned as 'withdrawn'.

Informal Institutions and the Question of Inequality

Typically, in their study of local forms of postcolonial dispute resolution and, more specifically, the consolidation of postcolonial 'compromises', those with an interest in moving 'beyond the district courts' have sought to shift their attention away from the courts in favour of a special emphasis on the work undertaken by local *panchayats* (traditionally albeit somewhat flexibly defined as community-based 'councils' of *panch*, or 'five', male elders).

These *panchayats*, deeply rooted within specific communities, have been applauded for their ability to coax otherwise recalcitrant parties to accept the terms of a negotiated settlement or 'compromise' (at a comparatively low cost) while, at the same time, remaining subject to relentless academic criticism for their notoriously conservative attachment to specific forms of economic (and gendered) inequality.

The most common expression of this criticism has been tied to a set of class-based assumptions regarding the link between (a) grossly unequal forms of *patti*-based landownership, on the one hand, and (b) specific forms of *panchayat*-based dispute resolution, on the other.[25] These assumptions, grounded in a familiar set of concerns regarding the content of unwritten (class-based) norms, are certainly understandable. But of course, the problem lies in the fact that, even as early as the nineteenth century (and continuing thereafter), the work of local *panchayats* was almost never defined—neither by the *panchis* themselves nor by their clients—with any reference to the specific terms of 'class'. On the contrary, just as E.A. Prinsep discovered, upon reviewing the work of his predecessor, Sir Richard Temple, in Sialkot (1865), the language of the *panchayat* (as an empirically embedded language of 'custom') was almost invariably embedded within the aspirations of particular (agnatic) 'clans': clans, if you will, over class; *pattis* over possession; kinship over capital; and so on.[26]

In fact—just as many 'neoinstitutionalist' scholars began their work in the district courts with an elaborate set of assumptions regarding the universal value of 'efficiency', only to discover that, *in practice*, much of the work undertaken in the courts was guided by an historically embedded attachment to the specific terms of 'delay'—those with a more explicitly 'neo-Marxist' orientation have often begun with a set of universal assumptions regarding the specific compulsions of 'capital' ... only to discover that, *in practice*, the work of the local *panchayat* has been guided by an enduring attachment to kinship, custom, and the preservation of persistent (agnatic) 'clans'.[27]

From Class to Kinship

When Alain Lefebvre (1999) set out to examine the economic implications of international labour migration in 'Chahiwala' (a pseudonym), District Sialkot, for instance, he firmly believed that the compulsions of international capital would drive local patterns of decision-making. In particular, he expected local landowners to use any remittances they received to pursue higher levels of rural productivity—for example, with the help of mechanized cultivation. And, in due course, he believed that this reconfiguration of 'production' would shift the balance of power in the context of local disputes. (After all, Lefebvre noted, the benefits of international labour migration were not confined to rural elites; on the contrary, these benefits extended to small owners, and, in some cases, even local tenants as well.)

Unfortunately, when Lefebvre completed his work in District Sialkot, he found that his expectations regarding the motivations of many villagers were (often quite dramatically) misplaced. In fact, more often than not, he found that overseas remittances were not used to fund rural 'production'. Instead they were used to fund so-called 'unproductive' purposes like the installation of televisions in homes without electricity or the spectacle of more extravagant weddings.[28] And, even when these remittances *were* used to support the local agricultural economy, Lefebvre went on to explain that, in most cases, they were used to buy more land—not for strictly 'productive' purposes but, again, as a fillip for local patterns of 'prestige'. 'Whatever money is saved is used for social investments which are necessary for the ... reaffirmation of the villagers' cultural identity', Lefebvre reported, 'even if their cost is a burden for the domestic economy'.[29]

In fact, throughout Chahiwala, Lefebvre discovered that the primary goal for most villagers did *not* involve increased 'productivity' in any 'capitalist' sense. On the contrary, the primary goal lay in the expansion of existing *pattis* and, therein, the reinforcement of cultural *prestige*: *patti*-based 'prestige', if you will as an expression of Punjab-based 'power'.

To flesh out the larger implications of this point, Lefebvre went on to examine the nature of local disputes and, within these disputes, the logic of *patti*-based politics, providing numerous illustrations with the help of a concise genealogy of local kinship factions. (See Fig. 19, below.) According to Lefebvre, Chahiwala had four *pattis*—*patti* Matto, *patti* Malik, *patti* Kala, and *patti* Dhedo.[30] In fact he noted that (*bhaiachara* tenures and expanding forms of property-based 'individualization' notwithstanding) these four *pattis* continued to represent the most important lines of social and political cleavage in the village.

As Lefebvre went on to explain, however, recalling some of the conflicts mentioned at the beginning of this chapter ('Man kills brother',

Fig. 19. Chahiwala (Lefebvre 1999): four *pattis*, four factions

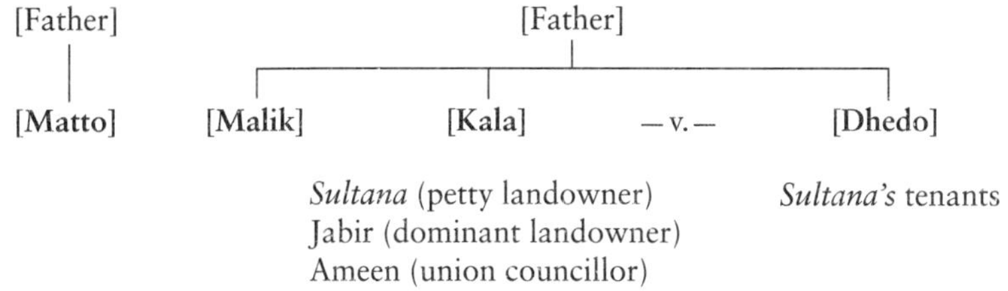

for instance), these four *pattis* were especially well known for their violent political rivalries—violent prestige-based rivalries focused on (a) the landed property rights of married women and (b) the outcome of local elections.

To illustrate this connection—this connetion between the landed property rights of married women and the logic of prestige-based politics—Lefebvre went on to provide a rather detailed account of some of the difficulties experienced by a local widow named 'Sultana' based in *patti* Kala.

According to Lefebvre, Sultana inherited eight acres of agricultural land from her husband in 1966—presumably in accordance with Section 4 of the Muslim Family Laws Ordinance (1961). But, in a pattern reflecting the sort of harassment faced by many female owners, Lefebvre discovered that the dominant landowner in the village—a Kala 'co-sharer' by the name of Jabir—generally refused to release any of the water that Sultana required for her land (despite the fact that, at the end of each harvest, Jabir continued to demand nearly all of Sultana's crops as a form of 'payment for services rendered').[31]

'I don't want to go to the city', Sultana cried, referring to her visits to the district *kachehri*. But of course she had no choice. 'They want me to leave this village so that they can take my land'.[32]

Adding insult to injury, however, Sultana also fell prey to a pair of her tenants (based in *patti* Dhedo)—tenants who took advantage of her illiteracy by obtaining her thumbprint on a blank piece of paper, which they later used to fabricate a bogus lease agreement. This agreement resurfaced, several months after its registration, when Sultana entered her fields to cut some fodder for her cow. Her tenants objected, claiming that, by 'trespassing' on her very own fields, Sultana had violated their lease agreement. And, in due course, they proceeded to beat Sultana, leading her to call upon the family of her 'co-sharing' patron

(Jabir) for help. In fact, upon hearing Sultana's cries, Jabir's sons arrived on the scene with a rifle and some bricks, accompanied by Ameen, the chairman of the local union council.[33]

At this point, however, drawing special attention to the escalation of the conflict and the intervention of an elected politician (Ameen), Lefebvre cut straight to the heart of the matter: 'In order to understand the [ensuing] ... conflict', he noted, 'other elements must be considered'. In particular, he explained, the first cause of the conflict surrounding Sultana did not involve Sultana's tenants or the production of a bogus lease agreement. Instead it involved '[a] rivalry between the headman of *patti* Kala and the headman of *patti* Dhedo—a [*patti*-based] feud which ha[d] existed for many decades'.[34]

The first cause of the conflict, in other words, did not begin with the 'economic' friction between Sultana and her tenants. Instead it began with the underlying terms of a *patti*-based 'political' rift between two of the most powerful kinship factions in the village. This was, in fact, a *patti*-based conflict tied to the terms of a familiar competition for ancestral agricultural land. Which *patti* controlled which land? And how?

According to Lefebvre, both factions harrassed Sultana in an effort to seize her land. In the case of *patti* Dhedo, Jabir's rivals manoeuvred to secure a larger share of ostensibly 'tax-free' land (notwithstanding the specific terms of *ushr*). And, in the case of *patti* Kala, Jabir's sons, together with Ameen, jockeyed to overcome the implications of the Muslim Family Laws Ordinance (1961) and, thus, the *de jure* rights of a female 'interloper' like Sultana.[35] In fact a closer look clearly reveals that both factions sought to remove Sultana for reasons closely tied to their purely strategic posture vis-à-vis the practical implications of *shari'ah*.

'Jabir's sons help Sultana' (for example, in her case against her tenants), noted one villager. '[B]ut it is not real help. They will write down all [of] their expenditures for defending her, [but] these are false expenditures. They will say, "we have spent so and so with so many officials, and you have to pay us back", [but] Sultana won't be able to pay them back, and [in the end] she will be compelled, [for example, in the context of a *patti*-based *panchayat*]', to hand over some of her land.[36] In fact the *panchayat* was rarely (if ever) defined as a simple 'class' *panchayat*. It was, more often than not, defined as a 'caste' *panchayat* firmly devoted to the preservation of existing (agnatic) 'clans'.

Indeed the point of Lefebvre's account did not lie in describing the strength of Sultana's economic or religious 'rights'. Instead it lay in providing a more detailed account of the ways in which—economic or religious rights notwithstanding—competing elites collaborated with their political allies (allies like Ameen) across a wide range of institutions, both formal and informal, to preserve (and, in some cases, to promote) the specific parameters of their enduring ancestral estates. Of course this complex mélange of informal community-based interests was never totally removed from 'that great principle of associaton' for which 'the land itself' was expected to furnish 'a real, permanent, and all-sufficient basis'. But, even for Lefebvre—so keen to trace the economic drivers behind local patterns of decision-making—it was simply impossible to ignore the trends first articulated by E.A. Prinsep more than one hundred years before. Indeed, as Lefebvre discovered, upon returning to Sialkot, even 'the land itself' was embedded *within* the work of patti-based *panchayats* and the preservation of specific (agnatic) 'clans'.

Kinship, Custom and the Courts

This effort to highlight the enduring importance of local agnatic clans was also taken up and extended, to great effect, by Mohammad Azam Chaudhary in his closely related book *Justice in Practice: Legal Ethnography of a Punjabi Village* (1999). Drawing attention to the village of Misalpur, District Faisalabad, Chaudhary went out of his way to highlight the ways in which the procedures of the district courts and the deliberations of the local *panchayat* were brought together and, in due course, strategically combined by the 'political' machinations of Misalpur's two major kinship factions: one dominated by a prominent member of the local union council named 'Naeem' (PML-N) and one dominated by his political archrival 'Karim' (PPP).[37]

(N.b. In Misalpur, these factions were not defined by the parameters of competing local *pattis*; instead, they were defined by rival castes. Naeem represented the dominant caste of landowning *zamindars*; Karim represented the largest caste of *kammis*.)

Like Lefebvre in 'Chahiwala', however, Chaudhary noted that nearly all of the conflicts in Misalpur were derived from local skirmishes between and among these two factions. And, like Lefebvre, Chaudhary went out of his way to explain that the resolution of these disputes (typically, disputes regarding *zan, zar* and *zamin*, or 'women', 'wealth' and 'land') was generally related to the collaborative intervention of (a) the district *kachehri* and (b) the local *panchayat* (simultaneously).[38] In fact, recalling some of the results outlined in Chapter 4 (above), Chaudhary noted that 'all [of] those conflicts and quarrels which are brought before the *panchayat* ... are, at the same time, brought to the police and [the] courts'. And, over time, he explained, returning to the question of final outcomes, '[either] a decision or [a] compromise is arrived at with the cooperation of [both] systems'.[39]

Coming straight to the underlying politics of the matter, however, Chaudhary set out to illuminate the emergence of increasingly complex forms of interaction involving the district *kachehri*, on the one hand, and the local *panchayat*, on the other, noting that, more often than not, this connection was constructed with the help of competing political elites. In Misalpur, for instance, recalling the experience of Sultana and Ameen, Chaudhary observed that '[Naeem and Karim were keen to] help people in different ways, in return for which they [expected to] receive ... [a certain number of] votes'. In fact 'in each and every conflict', Chaudhary explained, Naeem and Karim were 'directly or indirectly involved', working to provide the members of their own political faction with various types of *safarish*—*safarish* vis-à-vis the local *patwari*, the local *thana* (that is, the local police station), and specific district courts—en route to the production of a satisfactory final settlement.[40] As a matter of fact, Chaudhary noted, both men sought to provide this *safarish* in an effort enhance the terms of *aapna mufaad* (that is, 'their own private benefit') while, at the same time, seeking to enhance the *mufaad* of those who called on them for 'help'.

Interestingly, this pattern resurfaced quite explicitly in the context of my own field research when, quite by accident, I was provided with an opportunity to observe the distribution of *safarish* as it was undertaken by the *munshi*, or aide, of a local politician in Sargodha. This *munshi's* appearance in the district record room, where I was reading the files of old cases, was extremely brief, lasting just two or three minutes. But of course its brevity was no indication of its significance; in fact, if anything, its brevity was probably an indication of its rather subtle strength.

After a flurry of questions regarding the health and wellbeing of the local staff, the *munshi* posed just one final query almost in passing. '*Ji Sir*', he said, reaching for his notebook. '*M Sahib ki muqadama*'? ('Yes, the case of Mr M'?) '*Kyaa hua? Kahan ho gaya*'? ('What happened?

Where did it go'?) And, then, even before he had received a reply, he turned around and left.

As the superintendent of the record room later explained to me, the case of 'Mr M' had been 'dismissed as withdrawn' owing the production of a *razeenama* or 'compromise'. But the plaintiff (Mr M) was attempting to reinstate it. And, as the superintendent was quick to point out, that alone was the problem. Given the shape of local political rivalries, local kinship factions, and so on, everyone knew that Mr M was affiliated with the chief rival of the *munshi's* politician-employer. (For convenience, he might be described as Mr X.) In fact, precisely insofar as Mr M was keen to revive his case against Mr X, everyone knew that the *munshi's* primary task lay in ensuring that X (not M) would prevail.

With this in mind the staff of the record room leapt into action. Fearing that the *munshi's* employer (X) and his senior political allies in Islamabad might proceed with a 'transfer order' drawing them away from family, friends, and a comfortable relationship with the president of the district bar, the offending files were swiftly recovered from the inner sanctum of the record room. And, after checking to make sure that no stone had been left unturned, the relevant staff members went on to ensure that each file was systematically transferred into oblivion by a 'peon' who could, of course, be fired at the drop of a hat.

And that was that—briefly stated, the practice of *aapna mufaad* as an expression of postcolonial political 'accountability'. The superintendent of the record room kept his job; the *munshi* appeared to reinforce the terms of an otherwise unstable 'compromise'; and, in due course, the *munshi's* employer (Mr X) probably succeeded in shoring up more than one hundred local votes, including those of his loyal brothers, at least fifteen of their cousins, more than twenty of their deeply impoverished tenants, and over sixty female dependents.

In reality (that is, *haqeeqat mein*), Chaudhary explained once again recalling the data I collected in Lahore, Sialkot, and Sargodha (Chapter 4)—the villagers gave their votes 'in return for favours', noting that, for many 'custom-friendly' landowners, these favours did not always lie in the speedy or consistent enforcement of existing postcolonial laws.[41]

'Generally', Chaudhary explained, members of the local community travelled to the district courts to appear as witnesses, 'not for the sake of truth or [the] love of justice', but rather, on the basis of 'who ha[d] helped [them] in the past', 'who could be of help in the future', and, especially, who was the closest 'relative'.[42] In fact, Chaudhary noted, coming straight to the heart of the matter, key decisions were made on the basis of formal and informal expressions of institutional, political, and familial reciprocity, for example, 'who escort[ed] whom to the *police*', 'who [gave] evidence against whom [in the *courts*]', 'who support[ed] whom in the *panchayat*', and, in a natural extension of this pattern, *'who vot[ed] for whom' in the context of the village elections* (emphasis added).[43]

In Misalpur, Chaudhary explained, both Naeem and Karim '[took] an active part in village affairs and quarrels'.[44] And, again, they did so in the expectation that, on election day, their efforts would yield '[a certain number of] votes'. Naeem, for instance, was 'known to pay a monthly fee to the police on account of which he [had] good connections', while Karim was known to maintain strong 'connections with the police' even as he employed a dedicated team of violent *goondas* or 'thugs'.[45]

These affiliations were not always associated with the enforcement of existing laws. In fact, as the twentieth century unfolded, bringing innumerable 'agnatic' affiliations into contact with a rapidly shifting body of ostensibly 'immutable' laws, a growing number of co-sharers found that their relationship with various conduits of violence—including both the police and local thugs—was increasingly set apart from any attachment to the enforcement of existing laws. As the twentieth century came to an end, rifles came to replace the rule of law as the refuge of last resort: 'Tribal feud claims two lives', 'Three shot dead' in Jhang, 'Four die' in Okara—the list went on and on.

'First the brothers, then the other immediate relatives, then the ... friends, neighbours, and distant relatives', Chaudhary noted, shifting his attention away from the specific constraints of 'class', all were bound together by a web of institutional, political, and, in some cases, explicitly coercive forms of obligation—what Chaudhary referred to as 'the mutual obligations of the kinsmen'.[46] The law, he explained, was one thing. But the logic of local politics, as a deeply conservative logic tied to enduring expressions of *patti*-based obligation, was something else entirely. Justice was not always the first priority, Chaudhary argued. The focus was clan-based 'reciprocity'.[47]

Political 'reciprocity' and thus 'accountability', if you will, set apart from any support for the consistent enforcement of 'law'. This was the language of postcolonial politics: 'accountability' *versus* the 'law'.

PREFERENCES 'IN PRACTICE'

What Chaudhary revealed, throughout Misalpur, was of course the nature of local preferences as they actually emerged in practice—historically embedded expressions of *patti*-based 'reciprocal obligation' that did most of the work when it came to sustaining the link between landed property, private litigation, and the logic of local politics in the context of postcolonial Punjab. Indeed what Chaudhary revealed in his account of 'the mutual obligations of local kinsmen' was nothing less than the microfoundational mechanism that allowed for the preservation of 'customary' landed property relations in Lahore, Sialkot, and Sargodha even *after* the emergence of several rather dramatic postcolonial legal *reforms*.

As the terms of Islamic law (for example, the terms of *'ilm al-fara'id* and the specific constraints of *ushr*) became increasingly well established throughout the latter half of the twentieth century, the terms of postcolonial political accountability were not defined, at least not primarily, by the formulation of 'new' and 'better' laws. On the contrary, expressions of political accountability frequently shied away from the terms of 'legislation' in favour of what I have chosen to describe as entirely new forms of subversive (extralegal) 'protection'.

These increasingly elaborate forms of 'protection', focusing on the *de facto* preservation of existing agnatic estates, were not set apart from the work of the district courts—at least not entirely. In fact, as I began to suggest in my discussion of emerging expressions of 'delay', they often *involved* the courts in ways that reinforced, however surreptitiously, the specific constraints of 'custom' outside of the courts themselves.

What follows is merely an attempt to illuminate the underlying mechanics of this legal-cum-political process with the help of six examples drawn from the district courts of Lahore, Sialkot, and Sargodha—first in the context of three 'fully contested' cases from the district courts of Sialkot and Sargodha and, then, finally, in the context of three 'not fully contested' cases from the district courts of Lahore.

The first three examples—that is, the 'fully contested' cases—must be regarded, in the first instance, as an important *exception* to the general postcolonial trend. In fact, as noted above, 'fully contested' cases represented less than 15 per cent of the total caseload burden throughout the latter half of the twentieth century. The cases that I have selected are, however, even *more* unusual than this larger trend might suggest.

In fact, whereas *most* 'fully contested' cases came to embrace the specific terms of *shari'ah*—indeed, additional time-series data would probably show an ever-expanding number of fully contested cases moving in this direction throughout the latter half of the twentieth century—the examples that I have selected *depart* from this trend insofar as they reveal some of the ways in which the parameters of 'tribal' custom were, in fact, occasionally *sustained* even *within* the terms of a 'substantive' judicial decree . Indeed the 'fully contested' cases that I have selected point to the fact that, even in the rather unusual event of a substantive postcolonial decree, *some* cases still managed to emerge with formal decisions that continued to support the specific constraints of 'custom', not only in 1950 or 1970 but, as one of these cases reveals, even in 1995.

The final three cases (that is, the 'not fully contested' cases) are, however, considerably more conventional. In fact these cases should be taken to represent the overwhelming majority of the total caseload burden throughout the latter half of the twentieth century—as much as 85–90 per cent—clearly reminding us that, by and large, most of those who found themselves embroiled in disputes regarding immovable property did *not* travel to the district courts with any expectation of receiving a 'substantive' decree. Instead they simply expected to spend a bit of time in the courts (typically, about a year) en route to the production of a *razeenama*, or compromise, outside of the courts themselves.

The nature of these compromises was of course rather difficult to determine without a specific investigation of each outcome as it actually took shape 'on the ground'. In fact, as I will explain, this effort to connect the work of the district courts to a definitive account of each estate (in *de facto* as opposed to purely *de jure* terms) must be regarded as an excellent avenue for future sociolegal research—future research grounded in an account of late-twentieth-century disputes far beyond the 'decisions' of the district courts.

Microfoundational Mechanisms: 'Fully Contested' Cases

Each of the 'fully contested' cases I have selected from the courts of Sialkot and Sargodha speaks to the enormous tension that existed between the terms of 'tribal' custom, on the one hand, and those of *shari'ah*, on the other. (See Tables 8 and 9.)

The first of these three cases, recalling headlines like 'Brothers continue to gobble up sisters' inheritance', concerns the basic microfoundational mechanism underlying frequent attempts to shift specific forms of immovable property away from 'Qur'anic' to 'agnatic' heirs—and, of course, the tensions that surrounded such attempts—in District Sialkot. (This example, like so many others, concerned an ostensibly innocuous 'gift'.)

The second example, recalling frequent efforts to provide '[A] comparison between customary and Islamic law in the Punjab', takes up the terms of a rather protracted bid to ensure the survival of a particular 'agnatic' estate long after the promulgation and, in due course, the formal statutory assimilation of *shari'ah*—this time, in a rather complex suit for 'inheritance' filed in District Sargodha. (This example emerged, for the first time, in 1957, before being decided, in a *de facto* nod to 'custom', nearly four decades later, in 1995.)

The final example, recalling headlines like 'Land fraud gang busted, councillor arrested' or 'Land-grabbing case [lodged] against PML leader and his brothers', concerns the basic implications of this enduring tension between 'custom' and *shari'ah* for the conduct of local *elections*. In fact this third case, which began with a rather simple dispute regarding the inheritance rights of an ordinary Muslim grandmother ('custom' v. *shari'ah*), clearly reveals what the underlying terms of this dispute really meant for the unfolding 'political' competition between and among rival kinship factions. (This case emerged in District Sargodha during the late 1950s; but, as I will explain, its basic parameters were revisited, several times over, in countless villages throughout postcolonial Punjab.)

Table 8. 'Fully contested' cases: Sialkot, Sargodha (courts and context)

Case Number	1	2	3
District	Sialkot	Sargodha	Sargodha
Jurisdiction	*Tehsil* (civil)	Division (revenue)	District (civil)
Plaintiff	Female	Female	Male
Year	1976	1995	1960
Ruling party (Islamabad)	PPP	PPP	Military
District-level MNA	PML (1976)	PML-N (1995)	N/A

Table 9. 'Fully contested' cases: Sialkot, Sargodha (issues and outcomes)

Plaintiff	*Formal Issue*	*Underlying Issue*	*Decision Favors*	*Outcome*
1. Female	declaration/permanent injunction	disputed gift	defendant male	disinheritance
2. Female	inheritance	custom v. *shari'ah*	defendant male	disinheritance
3. Male (union councilor)	allegations of election fraud	custom v. *shari'ah*	plaintiff	fresh polls

Case Number 1: 'Female Disinheritance' Revisited

In colonial Punjab (1849–1947), the preservation of 'agnatic' *pattis* was routinely reinforced by a pattern of formal legal recognition targeting specific expressions of 'tribal' custom—for example, the custom of female disinheritance. Following the formation of Pakistan in 1947, however, the laws of custom were dismantled and, in due course, the formal legal landscape began to embrace a specific interpretation of *shari'ah*: 1948, 1951, 1961, 1963, 1972, 1975, and so on.

As legally sanctioned forms of female disinheritance slowly disappeared from the courts of postcolonial Punjab, however, a growing number of families sought to reinforce the terms of custom by other means. In particular, a growing number sought to reconfigure the practice of female disinheritance within a series of formal and informal, consensual and coerced, legal and quasi-legal 'gifts' made by Muslim daughters in favour of their brothers. This first case (below) provides a brief illustration of this strategy, focusing, specifically, on the disputes that emerged when, in some cases, daughters refused to comply.

Concluded in 1976 in the *tehsil*-level civil court of a Class II Magistrate by the name of MH, this case was filed by a Muslim daughter named *HB* against her brother, AD. (See Fig. 20 below.) To make a long story short, the father of *HB*—a man by the name of FA—died. And, in accordance with the terms of the Muslim Family Laws Ordinance (1961), his estate was divided according to a rather conventional interpretation of *shari'ah* between his daughter, *HB*, as a 'Qur'anic' heir, and his son, AD, as an 'agnatic' co-sharer.

In the wake of FA's death, however, and in keeping with the specific constraints of custom, AD claimed that his sister, *HB*, had decided *not* to retain her 'share'. Instead, AD argued, *HB* had decided to *gift* her share to him. *HB*, however, emphatically denied this. In fact she argued

Fig. 20. 'Fully-contested' Case Number 1: '*HB* vs. AD'

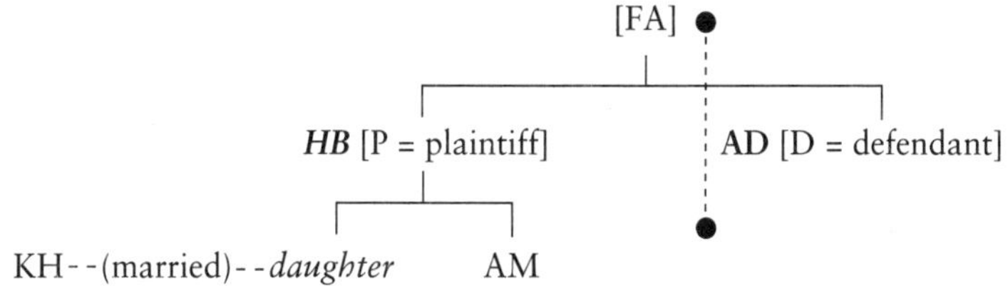

that the gift mutation allegedly obtained by her brother, AD, had been obtained through fraud and deception. In particular, she claimed that she had never appeared before any revenue official or any court whatsoever to sanction any 'gift' at all. And, charging AD with impersonation—in effect, suggesting that her brother had recruited the help of another woman, probably hidden behind a *burqa*, to 'impersonate' her in the office of the village *patwari*—*HB* proceeded to file a suit for 'declaration' with an additional claim for 'permanent injunction' in an effort to recapture, and control, her Qur'anic 'share' of the family's ancestral land.

(In effect, *HB* filed a suit for 'declaration', hoping that the court would declare that, according to every available record, the disputed land was hers. And, having done so, she appealed for a legally sanctioned injunction—in effect, a 'restraining' order—in order to ensure that her brother, AD, would not be in a position to seize her land at any point in the future.)

In due course, *HB* called two witnesses to support her 'Qur'anic' claims. The first was her son-in-law, a man by the name of KH, who, in an effort to bolster *HB's* statement that the 'gift' described by AD had never actually been made, denied that he (KH) was actually present, as alleged, on the day the disputed 'gift' mutation appeared in the local *haqdaran-e-zamin* (that is, the record of rights in land). The second witness was not a member of *HB's* family. In fact he was not a member of the village proprietary body at all. Instead he was a private fingerprint expert who denied that the fingerprints on the disputed gift mutation were those of any woman known as '*HB*'. As a matter of fact, he argued, there was no physical evidence linking the plaintiff to the promulgation of any (custom-friendly) 'gift' whatsoever.

The testimony brought before the court by *HB* was, however, systematically discounted by the presiding judge (MH). As a 'family-based' witness with a personal interest in the fate of the disputed land, for instance, MH explained (drawing attention to some of the pitfalls surrounding 'the mutual obligations of the kinsmen' reported by Chaudhary above) that the testimony provided by *HB's* son-in-law (KH) was unreliable. And, in due course, he noted, the testimony provided by the fingerprint expert was also deeply flawed. As a matter of fact, MH explained, the final report submitted by the fingerprint expert was not actually prepared by the fingerprint expert at all; instead it was prepared (and signed) by two other men, neither of whom had been called to explain their work in open court. In fact, MH explained, every indication seemed to suggest that the final report submitted by the fingerprint expert was suspicious—that, in the end, the impugned mutation was still very much 'in dispute'.

Turning to the witnesses for the defence, however, the court was invited to examine a body of evidence submitted by the village *patwari*. This *patwari* began by claiming that, when the time came to enter the disputed gift mutation in the 'record of rights in land', he simply entered it 'on the instructions of [*HB*]'. The impugned mutation, in other words, was not a matter of 'coercion'. It was, at least ostensibly, a clear-cut case of 'consent'.

As the case proceeded, however, the decisive issue did not appear to involve the origins of the disputed gift 'mutation' or the question of 'consent' at all. Instead it concerned the possession of the land itself.

As the judge pointed out, the burden fell on *HB* to prove that, if, as alleged, she had *not* made the disputed 'gift', she should still be in possession of 'her' land. And, yet, according to the records maintained by the village *patwari* and, in due course, confirmed by his superior, the local *lambardar*—presumably acting on behalf of the village proprietary body and, thus, the agnatic community as a whole—the defendant was actually in possession of the land. In fact the defendant (AD) had been cultivating that land, as a member of the village proprietary body, for quite some time.

The implication, of course, was that, if, as *HB* alleged, no 'gift' was ever made, *HB* should have either remained in possession of the land itself or included a demand for 'possession' (*dakhliabi*), as a form of judicial relief, in her framing of the 'issues' at the start of the civil trial. Because *HB* failed on both of these two accounts, however, the judge decided that the impugned mutation was, in fact, fully valid. And of course, in doing so, he refused to accept that *HB* was entitled to any 'share' of her family's ancestral land.

'Women do not get their ... share in the property', noted the Women's Rights Commission of the Ministry for Law and Parliamentary Affairs (1975) just a few months before this decision was issued. As a matter of fact, they added, drawing attention to specific provisions within the Muslim Family Laws Ordinance (for example, Section 4), 'the male heirs of the deceased either suppress information about the existence of female heirs or ... manipulate statements by or on their behalf', claiming, for instance, '[that] *the female heirs have relinquished their right ... in favour of the male heirs*' (emphasis added).[48]

Indeed, like the case of Ms Nasim (1956) outlined by S.M. Haider in his study of local *patwaris* (1966), the case of *HB* (1976) illuminated just exactly this sort of trend. In some cases, of course, gifts of ancestral land passing from sisters to their brothers were undertaken with the full and enthusiastic consent of absolutely everyone involved (including the husbands of the sisters). But, according to many observers, this was not always the case. More often than not, the Qur'anic shares of local women were removed, through fraud and deception, by the village *patwari* and his local patrons (for example, the local *lambardar*) in keeping with a pattern of 'custom-friendly' coercion, *patti*-based persuasion, and surreptitious administrative *safarish*.[49]

In this case, MH felt compelled to rule in favour of AD on the basis of AD's 'possession'. Of course he may have made the right decision according to a strict understanding of the law; after all, possession *is* regarded as the most reliable indication of a valid 'Islamic' gift. And, yet, having said that, it is entirely possible that MH was complicit in a much larger, more complex, and politically protracted fraud—effectively providing the constraints of 'custom' with a certain measure of postcolonial legal cover even after local reformers sought to promote an exclusive (postcolonial) attachment to *shari'ah*. In fact it should not be forgotten that, just a few years before this case was decided in District Sialkot, the Punjab Assembly went out of its way to introduce the Punjab Muslim Personal Law (Shariat) Application (Removal of *Doubts*) Act (1972) before, shortly thereafter, seeking to shore up this Act with a further measure known as the Punjab Muslim Personal Law (Shariat) Application (Removal of *Difficulties*) Act (1975).

The point, of course, lies in realizing that, even when the custom-friendly terms of administrative-cum-political *safarish* were challenged with a direct appeal to the work of the district courts, the success of women like *HB* could not be assured. On the contrary, the 'proof' of the matter lay in the problem of 'possession', meaning that, without a deliberate effort to secure 'possession' first, even the courts were rarely in a position to prevent a suspicious 'gift-based' transfer from 'Qur'anic' to 'agnatic' heirs. The *de facto* disinheritance of *HB* did not rely on a legal defence of 'tribal' custom. It relied on a pattern of *patti*-based *possession* permitted (and endorsed) by the work of the district courts.

Case Number 2: 'Tribal' Custom, c. 1995

The second case merely reiterates this point regarding the enduring legacy of 'tribal' custom throughout the latter half of the twentieth century.

This case was concluded nearly fifty years after the formation of Pakistan, in 1995, in the revenue court of AK, the Commissioner of Sargodha Division. In this case a woman by the name of *FB* filed a suit against the grandchildren of her father's second wife—grandchildren known as R1, R2, R3, and *R4*—arguing that, as a Qur'anic heir, she should have inherited a portion of the land once owned by her late father, MB (d. 1934). (See Fig. 21 below.)

Fig. 21. 'Fully-contested' Case Number 2: '*FB* vs. R1'

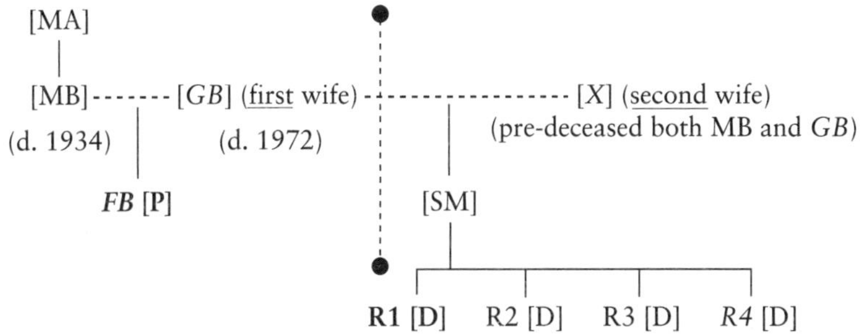

Two factors, however, appeared to limit *FB's* ability to inherit this land. The first involved an earlier dispute in which (for reasons that were never fully disclosed) the eldest of MB's four grandchildren, namely R1, sued his father, SM (the consanguine half-brother of *FB*), to secure a portion of the estate once held by R1's grandfather (MB). This dispute ended in 1957, when R1 received a formal decree entitling him to a certain amount of MB's estate. (The size of this portion, vis-à-vis the enumeration of specific ancestral 'shares', was, however, not described in the context of the case itself.)

Unfortunately, the terms of this decree (1957) were not enforced for more than fifteen years—not until the beginning of 1973, when, at last, a formal mutation (*intiqal*) was made in the local *haqdaran-e-zamin* (that is, the record of rights in land) to transfer the proper amount of land in R1's name.

According to *FB*, however, this much-delayed mutation (1973) was actually fraudulent, because, instead of receiving a portion of the land formerly owned by R1's father (SM)—as per the terms of the 1957 decree—R1 was (quite unexpectedly) given a portion of the land formerly owned by MB's first wife (namely, *GB*). And of course, *FB* explained, this was precisely the land that she herself claimed, on the basis of *shari'ah*, as a portion of her own inheritance. In fact, *FB* explained, the practical effect of this 1973 mutation lay in its apparent effort to transfer a portion of her own Qur'anic 'share' quite erroneously to her consanguine half-brother (SM).

As a woman who observed the norms of *pardah* or 'seclusion', however, *FB* claimed that she was quite unaware of this much-delayed mutation until several years later, when, in due course, recalling the fate of 'Sultana' (above), she was prevented from harvesting a portion of the crop within a plot that she believed was hers. This inability to enjoy the benefit of her own private property alerted *FB* to the existence of the 1973 mutation. And, in due course, *FB* explained, she was finally spurred into action.

As the judge himself pointed out, however, the relevant issues were not confined to the possibility of a 'fraudulent' mutation in 1973. Instead, he explained, the most important issue concerned the relative ownership rights of (a) SM and (b) MB's first wife, *GB*. Did *GB* own her 'share' outright, in which case she might have passed that share directly on to *FB* via inheritance? Or did she merely 'hold' her share in the form of a 'limited' lifetime estate with no possibility of passing that share, as a fully-fledged 'legator', on to her own 'legatees' or heirs?

This question effectively constituted the second factor affecting *FB's* inheritance rights. In fact the eldest son of SM maintained that *FB* had no right to 'inherit' the land in question, because, historically, the estate of MB (who died in 1934) was not governed by the terms of *shari'ah* at all. Instead, he noted, MB's estate was governed by a specific attachment to the terms of 'tribal' custom.

In short, the defence argued that, after MB's death, his ancestral land was equally divided, following the 'tribal' custom of the Khokhar Makhdooms living in *tehsil* Bhalwal (District Sargodha), between his surviving widow (*GB*) and his son (SM). His surviving widow (*GB*) received one half of MB's estate as a 'limited' lifetime interest; and, following custom, his son (SM) received the remaining half as a full-fledged male owner.

Furthermore, the defence noted that, after the death of MB's first wife (*GB*) in 1972, the land simply passed—in keeping with the specific constraints of custom—to the descendents of 'the last full male owner', that is, the descendants of SM. (Hence the 1973 mutation transferring all of the land formerly owned by MB to SM's descendants, R1, R2, R3, and *R4*.) In short, the defence explained, *FB* was not excluded from her father's estate by the production of a 'fraudulent' mutation (1973). Instead, she was excluded by the terms of 'tribal' custom, even *after* the promulgation of the Muslim Family Laws Ordinance in 1961. In fact, even as late as 1995, the defence explained, *FB's* rights were still constrained by the custom of the Khokhar Makhdooms as defined by the colonial land revenue administration and, then, in due course, by the postcolonial district courts.

Turning to his final decision, however, the Divisional Commissioner (AK) did not rely on the strength of R1's evidence regarding 'the custom of the Khokhar Makhdooms'. Instead, referring to a more contemporary expression of local efforts to preserve the terms of 'tribal' custom, the Commissioner indicated that the fate of *FB's* claims rested on what might be described as the protracted history surrounding the case itself.

In particular, the Commissioner noted that, even though she observed the norms of *pardah*, *FB* was not entirely unaware of the disputed 1973 mutation affecting the land in question. This much was clear from the fact that she had already filed two suits to contest that mutation. The first, filed immediately after the mutation itself, in 1973, was dismissed. (No explanation for this dismissal was available in the surviving documentation.) But the second, filed two years later, in 1975, was withdrawn—this time owing to the production of an extra-judicial 'compromise'. The specific terms of this compromise cannot be determined without a special effort to visit the disputed plot of land, but the fact that *FB* felt compelled to return to the courts more than twenty years later, in 1995, could be taken to suggest that, at least from *FB's* perspective, those terms were never entirely satisfactory. In fact the substance of this compromise (1975) was probably in keeping with 'the custom of the Khokhar Makhdooms' and, thus, 'the custom of female disinheritance'.

In any case, the Divisional Commissioner took the pattern of recidivist litigation surrounding *FB's* case, stretching across nearly four decades, to suggest that, despite apparent limitations owing to the norms of *pardah*, *FB* was not a helpless pawn. In fact *FB* appeared to be a rather persistent litigant—one who, even in 1995, decided to file her case in two courts simultaneously (namely, the revenue courts and the civil courts), stating that her civil suit would be withdrawn if, in the end, she were able to 'cut across' the civil process to obtain 'a more attractive settlement' from the (quicker) revenue courts.

As the Divisional Commissioner presiding over those revenue courts pointed out, however, this intention to withdraw one of the two suits in the event 'a more attractive settlement' was 'obviously unacceptable'. In fact, as a result of this claim (described as a claim of legal insincerity), the Divisional Commissioner decided that he was not in a position to provide *FB* with any access to any portion of her father's (MB's) land. Of course the Commissioner may have followed the law, drawing special attention to emerging patterns of purely 'strategic' litigation. But, even in 1995, this meant that, broadly speaking, *the terms of 'custom' prevailed.*

Case Number 3: From the *Patti*...to the Polls

The third and final case indicates the extent to which these and many other similar disputes regarding the contested terms of 'tribal' custom were, in fact, closely related to the consolidation of competing kinship factions and, in due course, the conduct of postcolonial elections. Decided by an *ad hoc* election tribunal based in *tehsil* Bhalwal, District Sargodha, in 1960, this case featured a bitter rivalry between distant cousins, each of whom represented a specific faction within the same extended family.

The core issue in this case, known as *GJ vs. MR* (1960), concerned the use of illegal polling procedures in the first (non-party) local elections of the postcolonial period—the 'basic democracy' elections of 1959. As my reading of this case progressed, however, I quickly came to understand that the underlying problem actually predated those elections. In fact the underlying problem grew out of a rather specific colonial-era conflict—one in which (as noted above) the landed property rights of an ordinary Muslim grandmother played an extremely important role.

For all practical purposes, this case began when a man by the name of MY (see Fig. 22 below) appeared in a separate trial, several years earlier, to enumerate the 'Qur'anic' shares held by his surviving Muslim grandmother—the only child of a prominent Muslim landowner (the namesake of *patti* 'B'). In effect, MY argued that, colonial notions of 'tribal' custom notwithstanding, his grandmother was in fact entitled to a particular plot of 'ancestral' agricultural land.

It is unclear exactly when this testimony was provided, but in any case its success clearly angered MY's distant cousin, GJ. In fact GJ

Fig. 22. 'Fully-contested' Case Number 3: 'GJ vs. MR' (Part One)

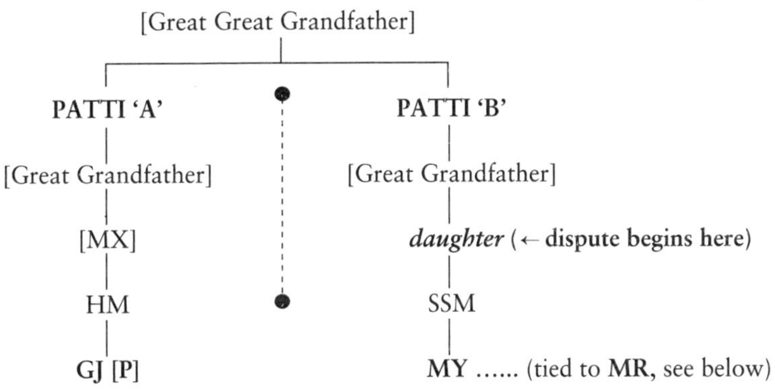

clearly expected the disputed land to remain, not in the hands of MY's Muslim grandmother, but rather, following 'custom', in the hands of that grandmother's father (and, hence, in the hands of that father's surviving male relatives)—that is, within the parameters of 'agnatic' kinship and, thus, the parameters of *patti* 'A'.

(N.b. As in the previous case, involving MB and his daughter *FB*, the grandmother may have been entitled to the terms of 'limited' life-time interest. But, in the event of her death, GJ clearly believed that the disputed plot would pass to the grandmother's father's surviving male relatives—that is, to the agnatic heirs of 'the last full male owner' according to 'tribal' custom.)

Owing to an apparent failure on the part of *patti* 'A' to prove the existence of any countervailing 'tribal' custom, however, the inheritance of the disputed plot did *not* adhere to the strictures of agnatic kinship. Instead, reflecting a specific attachment to the female-friendly terms of *shari'ah*, the disputed plot was held by the grandmother herself and, in due course, by her son, SSM, then his son, MY, and so on.

This was of course a rather unusual outcome (albeit by no means impossible) in the years preceding the promulgation of the Muslim Family Laws Ordinance in 1961. But the significance of this outcome was not confined to the nature of its implications for the distribution, so many years later, of particular 'ancestral' shares ('GJ' v. 'MY'). In fact, as a reflection of emerging *political* trends, the real significance of this outcome lay in the extent to which it appeared to provoke and then, later on, to aggravate an emerging *factional* rivalry between the partisans of *patti* 'A' and those of *patti* 'B'. Indeed, as the remainder of this case revealed, the 'successful succession' of MY's Muslim grandmother effectively split the village (known as GM) into two hostile factions. And, eventually, it was these two factions that clashed in the first (non-party) local elections of the postcolonial period (1959).

As soon as the date for these non-party elections was announced, GJ stepped forward to challenge the candidate put forward by his archrival MY. This candidate, known as MR, was a 'proxy' candidate. In fact this candidate was the adult son (MR) of a tenant (AR) employed by MY's oldest son (MA). (See Figure 23, below.)

Fig. 23. 'Fully contested' Case Number 3: 'GJ vs. MR' (Part Two)

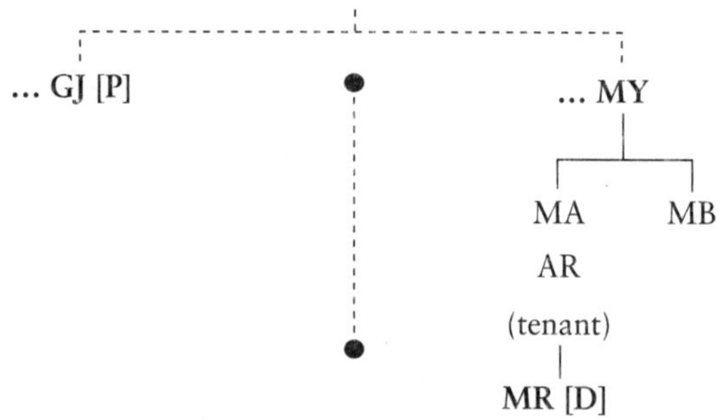

The case itself, regarding allegations of illegal polling procedures in GM (Ward Number 6), included an unusual amount of detailed testimony submitted by various local residents—far more than in most of the files I encountered in the context of the district courts. But, within this testimony, which included numerous accusations of bribery and sectarian harassment (or 'threats of divine displeasure'), one aspect stood out. This aspect involved an accusation made by GJ regarding the location of the ballot box on election day.

According to several witnesses the votes had been cast, not in the local primary school, as ordered by the election commissioner, but rather in a private *dera*—in effect, the private (usually *patti*-based) political salon—owned by MY and his oldest son MA.[50]

Consider, for example, the following testimony submitted on behalf of the plaintiff (GJ):

Prosecution Witness No. 1: GJ (Zamindar). 'I and MA, [as well as] his father [MY], have been on inimical terms due to our old political alignments and also due to litigation over land'.

Prosecution Witness No. 2: X (Kammi). 'MR said to me that, as I am related to him, I should vote for him. He gave me Rs. 10 as the price of my vote, and I voted for him'.

Prosecution Witness No. 3: S (Zamindar). 'The polling station was situated at the *dera* of MA. In the adjoining room, there were MA, MB, and their father, MY. ... They could see the voters putting their papers in the ballot boxes. [And], at the time of casting votes, these three persons were asking the voters to vote for MR'.

Apparently, the voting process in GM was somewhat less than 'free and fair'. But the testimony offered on behalf of the plaintiff, GJ, was not the only suspicious feature of this case. In fact, even as the testimony offered on behalf of the defendant, MR, seemed to confirm certain things about the location of the ballot box, it also seemed to raise a certain number of questions regarding the nature of the 'offending' local *dera*.

Defence Witness No. 1: MR (Kammi). 'It is incorrect to suggest that MA and MB [the sons of MY] are on inimical terms with [GJ]. ... [In any case], I did not influence the voters'.

Defence Witness No. 2: G (Kammi). 'The polling station was situated in a school. The room in which the polling took place had two doors. [One 'was used as an entrance'; 'the other as an exit'.] ... It is incorrect [to say] that MA, MB, and MY were sitting in that room'.

Defence Witness No. 3: N (Primary School Teacher). 'The *dera* of MA has six rooms ... out of which one is used as [the school and one is used as] the *dera*'.

According to the judge, most of the testimony offered on behalf of GJ and MR was suspicious or incomplete. But, even so, he explained,

Fig. 24. 'Fully contested' Case Number 3: polling station/*dera*/school

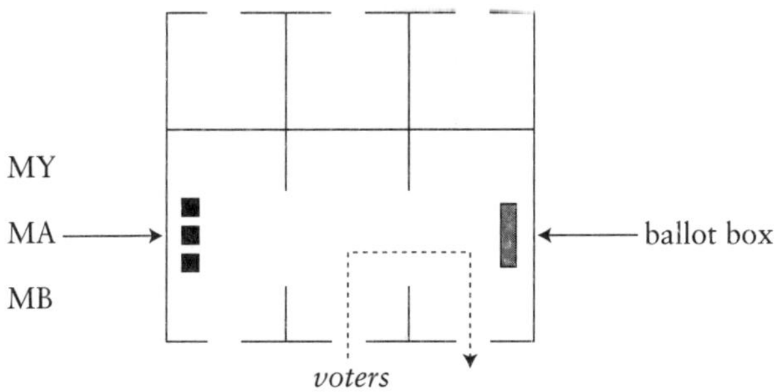

it was probably safe to say that the ballot box *was*, in fact, located in the same building as the *dera* owned by MY and his son MA. (See Fig. 24 above.) And, ultimately, he argued, this was enough to prove that 'undue influence' had been a factor in the outcome of the election. In fact, as the judge was quick to point out, *where* votes were cast—for example, in the private *patti*-based salon of *patti* B—often had a lot to do with *how* they were cast.

The election was declared invalid, in other words, because, heeding the plea submitted by GJ, the judge believed that the votes had been cast, not in secrecy, but in full view of MY and his sons MA and MB. And, on this basis, the judge ordered an entirely new round of voting.

Unlike most cases, this case was blessed with an unusually definitive outcome. But, even apart from its unusually definitive outcome, this case was exceptionally revealing. It was revealing because, far more than most of the cases I encountered in the context of the district courts, this case illuminated several closely related features of my larger story all at once, particularly insofar as it appeared to stress the postcolonial political legacy of a simple disagreement regarding inheritance (*'ilm al-fara'id*) and, within this, the specific *political* legacy of one woman's bid to secure her Qur'anic share.

When MY's Muslim grandmother secured her ancestral share in accordance with the specific terms of *shari'ah*, the ostensibly hegemonic terms of 'tribal' custom appeared to falter—at least for a moment. And of course they appeared to falter, within a prominent landowning family, even *before* the promulgation of the Muslim Family Laws Ordinance (1961). In fact, when MY's grandmother obtained her Qur'anic share in accordance with the specific terms of *shari'ah* the underlying landscape of Ward Number 6 appeared to shift—and, when it shifted, it appeared to shift in ways that left the village of GM (as a whole) both legally and politically divided.

Drawing special attention to the *political* implications of this shift in the direction of *shari'ah*, this was *not* a case in which the terms of *patti*-based political power were in any way dismissed or superseded. On the contrary, this was a case in which (one Muslim grandmother notwithstanding), the terms of *patti*-based influence were powerfully and predictably reinforced.

When MY appealed to the terms of *shari'ah* on behalf of his Muslim grandmother (the only child of a prominent local *zamindar*), for instance, we should not assume that he did so out of any deeply held religious conviction. He was not, as it were—recalling the words of Ayesha Jalal (1985)—a renegade 'iconoclast' who sought to turn his back on family 'tradition'. On the contrary, he was, just as easily, 'a model of filial piety', one who recognized that his *patti* (*patti* B) was teetering on the edge of collapse. When MY appealed to the terms of *shari'ah* on behalf of his Muslim grandmother, in other words, he did so primarily as a matter of political survival. In fact he did so in an effort to resuscitate the parameters of his own 'agnatic' *patti* while, at the same time, weakening his most important political rival. This was not an intrinsically reformist religious strategy. It was, primarily, a deeply *conservative* strategy, grounded in 'the politics of enduring *pattis*'.

As noted above, the case of *GJ vs. MR* (1960) was unusual for two reasons. First, it was unusual because, unlike most of the cases I encountered in the context of the district courts, this case ended with a 'substantive' (and 'enforceable') decree. But, even more importantly, I would argue, this case was unusual because, even *within* this decree, the case of *GJ vs. MR* (1960) succeeded in reinforcing 'the political importance of *pattis*'. Indeed, far from uniting the residents of GM within a specific attachment to *shari'ah*, the enforcement of *shari'ah* only seemed to divide them: 'A' v. 'B' and so on.

Microfoundational Mechanisms: 'Not Fully Contested' Cases

When *FB* (*FB vs. R1*, above) finally emerged from the district courts of Sargodha with a 'substantive' judicial decree in 1995, it is important to stress that *FB* had already shared the experience of most postcolonial litigants on two previous occasions—first in 1973, when her case was dismissed, and then again in 1975, when her case was duly withdrawn. In fact, as noted above, 'fully contested' cases culminating in a 'substantive' judicial decree accounted for just a tiny percentage of the total caseload burden throughout the latter half of the twentieth century. Most of those who travelled to the district courts did not do so with any expectation of a substantive (or enforceable) decree. They simply expected to spend a bit of time in the courts en route to the production of an informal *razeenama*, or compromise, outside of the courts themselves .

The persistence of 'tribal' custom after 1947, in other words, was not related—at least not primarily—to a pattern of substantive judicial decisions. On the contrary, it was rooted in a dynamic cycle of harassment and purely 'strategic' delays—delays involving, for example, innumerable adjournments combined with a veritable avalanche of irritation perpetrated by 'custom-friendly' clerks. Indeed, persistent forms of 'agnatic control' were not sustained, at least not primarily, through substantive judicial decisions; instead they were sustained by what might be described as an expanding *deficit* at the level of such decisions.

In 1983, some indication of this pattern was highlighted by the members of a special Women's Rights Commission, who noted that, increasingly, as the formal legal landscape began to change (in favour of *shari'ah*), women's names were 'entered against their share[s]' (for example, in the *haqdaran-e-zamin*). But even then, as the members of this Commission went on to explain, women were not provided with 'possession', for which 'they had to turn to the courts'. And of course, recalling the experience of *HB* (above), they noted that this appeal to the courts often amounted to just one more nail in the coffin surrounding their 'shares'.

Claiming that it took 'as long as ten to fifteen years [to receive a] final court verdict', the chair of this new Commission (Begum Sarfaraz Ali) noted that, as a general rule, women were unable to survive the process of securing and defending their shares. In fact, she noted, most female litigants were slowly compelled to quit. And this, she noted, was the primary source of 'custom-friendly' continuity in the context of postcolonial Punjab—this legacy of 'strategic' delays adding up to a corrosive pattern of (so-called) 'not fully contested' litigation.

The 'not fully contested' cases that I have chosen to examine from the district courts of Lahore (below) clearly conform to this pattern of purely 'strategic' delays. In fact all three of these cases appear to involve some element of tactical deferral or delay.

Sometimes the party with an interest in prolonging the case was the 'plaintiff'. Sometimes he (or she) was the 'defendant'. But, in the end, my research revealed that, more often than not, the party with an interest in 'delay' was also the party with an interest in sustaining the specific parameters of 'custom'. (See Table 10, below.) In fact, in most cases, the party with an interest in the specific terms of 'custom' was also the party that prevailed—typically, in conjunction with an extra-judicial compromise rendered outside of the district courts (for example, within a *patti*-based *panchayat*).

Table 10. 'Not fully contested' cases: Lahore

Plaintiff	*Formal Issue*	*Underlying Issue*	*Formal Decision*	*Outcome*
1. Female (sisters)	mutation (*intiqal*)	disputed gift	dismissed (no show)	disinheritance
2. Family of heirs	injunction (*hukm imtinai*)	disputed gift	dismissed (no fee)	compromise
3. Male co-sharers	partition (*taqsim*)	joint family ownership	withdrawn	compromise

This, I discovered, was the empirical expression of *patti*-based 'continuity' in the context of postcolonial Punjab. This was the practice-based *response* to a climate of 'immutable' laws.

Case Number 1: Avoiding *'ilm al-fara'id'*

The first case was concluded in 1997 in Tokkar Niaz Beg, a congested suburb not far from the New Campus of Punjab University. This case began when a group of sisters sued their brothers after the brothers lodged a mutation in the revenue records transferring 121 *kanals* of land in their own name. As the sisters pointed out, however, this transfer was legally suspect because, according to an earlier 'gift' mutation, the brothers controlled only 109 *kanals* of land. In fact, recalling the case of *HB vs. AD* (1976), above, the sisters intervened to accuse their brothers of manipulating the revenue records in an effort to seize an illegal share of their family's 'ancestral' land (12 *kanals*).

Unfortunately, in what can only be described as a strong indication of harassment, obfuscation and delay, the sisters found that, even after several months, they were unable to procure the evidence they needed to defend their claims. And, in due course, they failed to turn up for their trial.

Like so many files, the file in this case was extremely thin: just a few pages with dates recording unspecified adjournments followed, eventually, by a perfunctory notation announcing a simple 'no-show' dismissal. (See Table 10, above.) But, as my work unfolded, I quickly discovered that, even without the benefit of a fully developed 'decree', the inner dynamics of this case were not at all invisible. On the contrary, some insight could be gained from a careful effort to read between the lines, particularly with the help of several examples prepared by careful investigators like S.M. Haider (for example, the case of 'Ms Nasim') and, in due course, several additional files of a remarkably similar nature, including one that emerged, more than twelve years earlier, in the courts of District Sialkot.

Taking up exactly the same set of issues as this case from Tokkar Niaz Beg (District Lahore), this case in Sialkot emerged with a decision that might be described as 'formulaic' for cases of this type: 'In fact it is very strange', noted the presiding judge, 'that ... a suspicious mutation [was] effected in the very important and permanent revenue records without any lawful authority by the revenue officials' (that is, by the *patwari*), thereby depriving the plaintiff woman of 'her due right, which she got out of [the] inheritance of her father'. Indeed, he continued, turning to a statement of judicial censure, 'the revenue staff ... have exhibited the height of irresponsibility by scoring out [a] genuine entry on their own, thereby depriving one co-sharer of her due right and showing undue favour to the other[s]'. And for this, he explained, the concerned officials should be called upon 'to explain their opprobrious conduct'.

It is of course impossible to know exactly why the sisters in Tokkar Niaz Beg (District Lahore) failed to press on with their trial—even despite the existence of several parallel examples drawn from several different courts throughout postcolonial Punjab. But, given all that has come before, it may be safe to suggest that one of two outcomes seems likely. On the one hand, the sisters may have been offered a small piece of land as an incentive to drop their case. On the other, they may have been threatened with violence or financial ruin if they continued to press on with their trial. Either way, however, the outcome was largely the same; the sisters were almost certainly prevented from defending their claims within the parameters of existing (Islamic) laws. And of course their 'custom-friendly' brothers were probably successful in using a climate of 'strategic' harassment to appropriate the sisters' shares.

Again, the final outcome is impossible to determine without a specific effort to visit the disputed piece of land. But, if I had to guess, I would guess that, in this case, the specific terms of *shari'ah* (*'ilm al-fara'id*) were probably disregarded. Indeed, the courts were rarely in a position to counter a coordinated appeal to 'custom'.

Case Number 2: Preserving Ancestral Shares

The second case, also filed in 1997, merely extended this pattern of 'custom-friendly' harassment, drawing special attention to enduring concerns regarding the potentially unsettling implications of *shari'ah*.

This case did not involve a disputed 'gift' between 'Qur'anic' and 'agnatic' heirs. Instead, it began when an elderly man gifted some of his property to his lifelong servant. And it continued, three years later, after the elderly man had died, when this (rather poor) servant tried to rent the property to a stranger. When he did so, however, he found that the surviving heirs of the (now deceased) elderly man were keen to frustrate his intentions. And, deploying one of the two most common types of postcolonial civil litigation, they applied for a 'permanent injunction'.[51] (N.b. The other type was tied to suits for 'declaration'.)

The servant testified that the plaintiff's heirs had personally witnessed the registered deed of gift entitling him to own (and 'alienate') the disputed property. But in due course the heirs proceeded to challenge that testimony, arguing that the deed of gift held by the servant was, in fact, completely fraudulent, because, once again recalling the case of *HB vs. AD* (1976), *possession was never given.* (And, even if it had been given, they noted that the servant was not in a position to prove it.)

Six months later, however, the plaintiff's case was simply dismissed owing to the non-payment of any official 'fees'. Of course this may have been due to ordinary negligence: perhaps the heirs simply 'forgot' to pay their fees; perhaps, when these fees were finally due, they found that they were suddenly short of cash; perhaps, in the end, they simply decided to allow the servant to claim the property as his own.

Another, more plausible explanation, however, concerns the possibility of purely 'strategic' litigation. Indeed it is entirely possible that the plaintiffs simply sought to intimidate the servant. And, after six months, when the servant was sufficiently humbled, beaten or bankrupt, they simply dropped their case in favour of a more acceptable 'compromise', one that, presumably, ignored the specific legal claims of the servant in an effort to keep the estate intact. This much, at least, seemed perfectly obvious to the clerk who retrieved this case from the stacks of the district record room in the Lahore Secretariat. As he pointed out, every indication seemed to suggest a process of simple 'harassment' followed by an extra-judicial 'compromise' designed to protect 'the interests of the ancestral family'.

Again, the final outcome of this case was impossible to ascertain without a further effort to examine the fate of the property itself. Still, this case was an absolutely perfect illustration of what actually happened in the context of the district courts. More often than not, litigants did not emerge from the courts with any substantive judicial decree. Instead they simply emerged with a notation explaining that their case had been dismissed (or withdrawn) owing to the production of a *razeenama*, or compromise, *outside of the courts themselves*.

Case Number 3: Protecting the Joint Family Coparcenary

The final case, for 'partition' (*taqsim*), was concluded in 1997 in a neighbourhood known as Sanda Kala locatd in the centre of Lahore not far from the Lahore Secretariat. In this case the plaintiffs were *zamindari mushtarka* 'co-sharers' and, as such, they applied to the court for permission to divide their joint family estate on the basis of each fractional share: *zamindari mushtarka* → *pattidari*. (For a more complete account of the issues surrounding this process, see pages 24–26.)

Unfortunately, the judge pointed out that it had been more than forty years since the preparation of the last *jamabandi* in Sanda Kala. So, rather than referring to the written record of the postcolonial revenue administration—including, perhaps, the terms of an extant *shajra nasb*—the partition-seeking plaintiffs were informed that they would be forced to rely on the oral testimony of a *naib* (assistant) *tehsildar*.

Much to the chagrin of the plaintiff co-sharers, however, this assistant *tehsildar* seemed to favour the defendants—that is, those who sought to *defend* the 'joint family' estate *against* any bid for 'partition'. In fact, after more than four years of delay, the partition-seeking plaintiffs found that they were simply not in a position to prove their case; and, eventually, their case was reluctantly withdrawn (*dastbardar*).

As the presiding judge went on to explain, however, this rather familiar outcome was something of a surprise. It was a surprise because, recalling the case of *FB vs. R1* (1995) (Round Two: 1975), above, *the parties themselves had already secured the terms of an informal 'compromise'*, stating that, despite specific frustrations within the estate, all of the related co-sharers were prepared to cooperate as 'joint' owners. In fact the judge explained that this compromise had been drafted four years earlier, almost immediately after the case itself was filed!

Perhaps, upon reflection, four years of purely 'strategic' delays were required to persuade the parties of the merits associated with their commitment to 'custom' and, thus, their commitment to the preservation of an existing 'joint family' estate. Indeed, even if the terms of partition were still regarded, by some, as 'a sure sign of economic and social progress,' the co-sharers of Sanda Kala were not entirely convinced. 'We are not concerned with the individual,' they seemed to say, echoing so many of their colonial forebears. 'Our sole object is to save the land of the family'.

CONCLUSION

When I arrived in Lahore to begin my research in the district courts, the 'rhetoric' of Islam was inescapable. But, at the same time, I discovered, the language of 'tribal' custom was never completely absent. It simply existed 'behind the scenes' at the level of innumerable adjournments and, ultimately, 'adjacent' to the courts themselves. In fact as my work unfolded the challenge seemed to lie in reconciling two very different elements of the same story—two elements that appeared to move in opposite directions at exactly the same time.

The first element involved an increasingly consistent record of 'substantive' legal decisions spelt out in prominent legal publications like the *Pakistan Law Digest* (PLD)—in many ways an increasingly consistent record of Lahore High Court decisions in which the rights of Muslim women were formally acknowledged, legally recognized, and (almost invariably) preferred. But, of course, the second element, moving in precisely the opposite direction, involved the terms of what might be described as an exceptionally tenacious reality—a reality in which, hundreds of thousands of landed property cases notwithstanding, Muslim women continued to enjoy precious little control over the land that, legally speaking, they were formally entitled to 'inherit'.

Time and again, as I met with local judges to discuss my research, I was told that the terms of 'tribal' custom were long since dead and buried throughout postcolonial Punjab: 1948, 1951, 1961, and so on. Time and again I was told that women were never deprived of their 'shares'. And, of course, time and again I was told that, with respect to the question of inheritance, a deeper understanding of local reality lay in a more intensive reading of specific *suras* within the Holy Qur'an—for example, Suras 4:11, 4:12, and 4:176.

But of course the terms of local reality did not flow directly from the text of the Holy Qur'an. Nor did they lie in a simple reading of the *Pakistan Law Digest*. On the contrary, a deeper understanding of local reality clearly lay in a more sophisticated appreciation for the historically embedded motivations of individual Muslims in the context of countless disputes. These disputes were not confined to the district courts. In fact they involved a wide range of institutions, a host of different laws, and several tiers of overlapping legal (and political) practice.

As the language of *shari'ah* became more and more thoroughly established, in a formal legal sense, throughout the latter half of the twentieth century, disputes regarding the ownership and inheritance of ancestral agricultural land were extremely widespread. And of course, in the context of these disputes, many Muslims (73 per cent) confessed that they were inclined to call upon their elected leaders for 'help' (see Chapter 4, above). But, as my work unfolded, I began to see that the nature of this 'help' (as a form of electoral 'accountability') had a rather ambiguous link to the law. In fact, as my work unfolded, first in Lahore, then in Sialkot, and, finally, in Sargodha, I began to develop a special interest in this relationship—this rather unexpected (political) relationship—between 'accountability' and the 'law'.

For several reasons—reasons that lie beyond the specific reach of this book—the statutory expression of *shari'ah* was generally regarded (by lay Muslims) as inflexible, unchanging, and largely immune to any sort of interpretative or political intervention. Indeed, as political intermediaries, elected leaders were rarely called upon to 'amend' or 'improve' existing Islamic laws.[52] By and large, they were simply called upon to assist those who found themselves embroiled in conflicts—conflicts that (for better or worse) routinely *involved* those laws. In fact, departing from a conventional understanding of electoral accountability, most representatives were not expected to translate the substance of local concerns into 'new' or 'better' laws. They were simply expected to hold specific laws (for example, specific Islamic laws) in abeyance.

This legally 'protective' pattern of postcolonial political accountability was often expressed through the provision of *safarish*, or 'assistance', in the context of the district *kachehri*. In fact, as locally elected leaders became involved, either directly or indirectly, in various conflicts, they were often called upon to deploy specific types of *safarish* in a bid to produce, as Chaudhary explained, either a 'decision' or a 'compromise' within *both* the courts *and* the local *panchayat* (simultaneously).

To be sure, very few conflicts managed to emerge from this multifaceted process with a 'substantive' decree reflecting the specific terms of Islamic law. On the contrary, most cases simply lingered in the district courts for a few months (typically, 12 months) en route to a perfunctory dismissal through the production of a *razeenama* outside of the courts themselves. In fact, throughout the Punjab, most of those who sought to *avoid* the 'law' did *not* seek to avoid the postcolonial district courts—they simply sought to engage the courts while, at the same time, seeking to *avoid* the articulation of any substantive or enforceable decision.

'Suppose we ... are told to come [in] on a certain date', noted one lawyer in Misalpur, referring to one rather common expression of this pattern. But, on that date, 'the judge is not present [and] we need a new date'. Well, he noted, 'it costs anything between Rs. 20 and 100, depending on the date you want to have, early or late'. (Apparently, the later dates were more expensive because the demand for those dates was so much greater.) There was, he explained, 'a proper procedure for [everything]'. 'But ... if we follow it we will also make the subordinate staff angry'. 'We have to deal with them every day', he shrugged, and, in the end, 'it is not always the legal jobs [that] we want from them'.[53]

Of course this pattern of evasive legal manoeuvring—a pattern in which various forms of *safarish* were called in by individual voters to lower the cost of 'strategic' litigation for political allies (while, at the same time, raising those costs for opponents)—was not always in keeping with conventional assumptions regarding the 'universal' value of efficiency or, for that matter, the 'essential' injunctions of Islam. In fact, if anything, this legal-cum-political manoeuvring reflected little more than an historically embedded strategy designed to embrace the introduction of *shari'ah* while, at the same time, finding new ways to 'manage' its *de facto* postcolonial enforcement.

These manoeuvres were not at all irrational. They were simply context-specific. In fact, in a purely 'political' sense, the result of these manoeuvres generally lay in the production of a narrow but 'accountable' process set apart from the enforcement of the law. Indeed a closer look reveals that, in a purely political sense, those with greater access to incumbent *patti*-based politicians were simply in a better position to achieve the ends they desired: protecting their *pattis* from the implications of *'ilm al-fara'id*; expanding their access to effectively tax-free land; and so on. The politics of the postcolonial Punjab were, in other words, 'participatory', 'competitive', and 'accountable'. But they were also accountable in ways set apart from the negotiation of alternative 'laws'—raising several questions about the extent to which prevailing patterns of political 'accountability' were in fact 'democratic' patterns (involving, more specifically, a democratic approach to the 'law').

This issue was taken up quite explicitly by Partha Chatterjee in his book *The Politics of the Governed* (2004) and, more recently, in a book entitled *Lineages of Political Society* (forthcoming). Drawing special attention to those living 'on the margins of legality' within what he refers to as 'political society', Chatterjee argues that most citizens 'make their claims on government, and in turn are governed, not within [a] framework of stable ... rights and laws', but rather through a pattern of 'unstable arrangements' arrived at through 'direct' political negotiations—direct negotiations that involve the 'tacit acknowledgement of various illegal practices' by a state that agrees to recognise these practices as regularized-but-revocable 'exceptions'.[54] When people living on or cultivating 'illegally occupied land' claim 'the right to continue', for instance, Chatterjee argues that 'they are in fact inviting the state to declare their case as an exception'. They do not demand that existing laws—for example, existing laws of property (or inheritance)—should be 'abolished'. They simply demand that, with respect to the content of the laws in question, their cases should be treated as 'exceptions'.[55]

The political negotiations that produce these 'exceptional' arrangements, Chatterjee argues, frequently overlap with the work of postcolonial political parties and the domain of ongoing electoral mobilization. As a matter of fact, he notes, these arrangements are often facilitated by the work of elected elites, effectively constituting what Chatterjee calls 'the vast bulk of democratic politics' around the world today.[56] Indeed, for Chatterjee there is no sense in which these 'unstable' arrangements might be renegotiated as legally differentiated and, thus, formally defensible 'rights'. They are, for Chatterjee, simply arbitrary arrangements set apart from the rule of 'law'. In fact this basic 'arbitrariness' is, for him, one of their key virtues, with the social legitimacy of arbitrary power constituting what he describes as a 'new' and potentially 'richer' form of *democracy*.[57]

Of course the extrajudicial manoeuvring that accompanied most forms of postcolonial dispute resolution in Lahore, Sialkot and Sargodha throughout the latter half of the twentieth century is closely related to the underlying terms of Chatterjee's argument: ostensibly 'inaccessible' laws, regularized but revocable 'exceptions', ongoing electoral 'participation', unstable political 'settlements', and so on. But again the question arises: How do these interconnected elements of legal-cum-political manoeuvring relate to the question of 'democracy' and, more specifically, *a 'democratic' approach to the 'law'*?

The focus of my concern is not Chatterjee's interest in informal settlements as a site of ongoing political contestation, negotiation and accountability. On the contrary, my concern lies with Chatterjee's eagerness to equate these (exclusively) 'informal' arrangements with an alternative form of 'democracy'. As I understand it 'democracy' is not concerned with arbitrary and revocable settlements set apart from the rule of 'law'. It is in fact concerned with reiterative patterns of participation, competition, and negotiation focused on the delineation of 'law' itself. Indeed, for those with an interest in illuminating postcolonial processes of democratization, the challenge does not lie in replacing the negotiation of existing 'laws' with an appreciation for informal (*patti*-based) 'exceptions'. On the contrary, the challenge lies in understanding how local exceptions are related to, or separated from, the specification of statutory 'laws'. Democracy is not about opposing or avoiding ostensibly inaccessible laws. It is in fact about supporting or opposing the law—and, *if opposing*, seeking perchance to change it.[58]

What Chatterjee describes is not a democracy, but a particular form of locally embedded despotism.[59] That despotism may be 'enlightened' insofar as it is reinforced by locally elected politicians; and, in this sense, it may be regularized, participatory, and 'accountable'. But, set apart from a process of specifying the content of existing (*de jure*) laws, accountability is not a synonym for democracy. Protection rackets are 'accountable'; they rest on a responsive recognition of regularized but revocable 'exceptions'. But of course protection rackets are not democratic. They are in fact merely despotic.

Throughout postcolonial Punjab, prevailing patterns of electoral accountability did *not* lie in promoting higher levels of formal institutional efficiency. Nor did they lie in constructing a more consistent approach to the enforcement of existing Islamic laws. In fact, for many voters, the primary objective lay in gaining access to postcolonial administrative control, using access 'to' the resources of the postcolonial state in an effort to secure higher levels of partisan or *patti*-based protection 'from' the enforcement of existing laws.

Briefly stated, this book aims to provide an historically embedded account of individual preferences, motivations, and strategies as they actually emerged 'on the ground'—an historically embedded account of what people 'wanted' bound up with an empirically nuanced account of what they actually 'did'. Chatterjee, turning away from any special interest in the ongoing redefinition of (*de jure*) laws, sees the informal patterns of extralegal political accountability that lie at the very heart of this account as a plausible foundation for 'democracy'. I, on the other hand, do not.

6

MICROFOUNDATIONAL MECHANISMS AND COMPARATIVE POLITICS

When I arrived in Lahore to begin my research, I was struck by a number of things, not the least of which was an epidemic of purely strategic litigation growing out of an endless parade of landed property disputes in the district and appellate courts. Above all, I was struck by the fact that, despite a series of rather dramatic institutional reforms designed to undermine the legacy of the colonial administration—indeed, despite a series of formal legal changes designed to *replace* both (a) collective land revenue obligations with a special Islamic tax on 'production' and (b) 'tribal' customs regarding female disinheritance with a conventional interpretation of *shari'ah* (*'ilm al-fara'id*)—the shape of landed property relations in Lahore, Sialkot, and Sargodha *remained* largely unchanged.

Some have insisted that, throughout the late-nineteenth and early-twentieth centuries, an uncompromising colonial state struggled relentlessly to impose an alien property regime in South Asia, achieving 'dominance without hegemony' throughout the subcontinent. And of course, others have argued that, even after the departure of the British, the most important features of the colonial regime were sustained by formal incentive structures and the raw coercive power of an isolated (authoritarian) bureaucracy.

As my work unfolded, throughout the Punjab, however, I began to see something else. In fact, the closer I came to a more complete understanding of land, law, and the logic of local politics in Lahore, Sialkot, and Sargodha, the more I began to realize that *critical features of the colonial regime endured long after many of that regime's most important institutions had been dismantled.* The closer I came to a deeper understanding of the relationship between *zan*, *zar*, and *zamin* in places like Lahore, Sialkot, and Sargodha, in other words, the more I began to appreciate the extent to which the terms of postcolonial continuity lay *beyond* the scope of any account focusing purely on 'formal' institutions.

Slowly but surely, as my research unfolded, I began to realize that the hegemonic apparatus of the colonial state was not sustained—at least not directly, by the formal institutional legacy of the colonial administration. It was in fact sustained by an active, deliberate, and conservative 'logic of local politics' firmly embedded within the competitive efforts of elected representatives struggling to promote the delivery of *safarish* within (and beyond) the local district courts.

Precisely insofar as this was the case, however, I quickly realized that my research had illuminated the parameters of a rather startling puzzle—a rather startling puzzle regarding the elaborate social embeddedness of the *ancien* (colonial) *régime*. In fact a detailed examination of my data raised two further questions—two questions that I have sought to engage at various points throughout the course of this book.

The first question concerned the formation of individual preferences in the context of the colonial state (and, especially, the formation of individual preferences favouring the preservation of kinship-based landed property relations and the terms of 'tribal' custom). This was, in many ways, *both* a preliminary historical question regarding individual preference formation and a theoretically significant question regarding 'what individuals wanted' (and 'why they wanted it') in a particular time and place. (See Fig. 25 below.)

Fig. 25. Question 1: individual preference formation

The second question was always closely related to this initial account of local preferences. This question concerned the (unintended) consequences of specific postcolonial reforms and, especially, the fact that postcolonial efforts to *replace* the terms of 'tribal' custom with those of *shari'ah* had produced an entirely new logic of postcolonial political accountability—one in which local representatives were often selected, not in an effort to improve, but, rather primarily, to avoid the enforcement of existing laws. In fact this second question boiled down to an account of the evolving postcolonial relationship between (a) local preferences, (b) local patterns of dispute resolution, and (c) the logic of local politics, moving *beyond* a preliminary account of 'why people wanted what they wanted' toward a more compelling account—a more compelling empirical account—of 'how individuals actually managed to *get* what they wanted' in a particular time and place.

This second question, regarding the unintended consequences of a dramatic shift in the direction of *shari'ah*, was, of course, particularly important for the practice-based underpinnings of my argument regarding the consolidation (or not) of 'democracy' in the context of postcolonial Punjab. In fact its importance lay in the extent to which it framed my analytical approach to the (dynamic) development of an entirely new logic of postcolonial political accountability. Indeed, as my research unfolded, I found that it was precisely this logic of post-colonial political accountability that worked to *undermine* the regular enforcement of *shari'ah*—indeed, the rule of law—and, in due course, the process of 'democratization' itself. (See Fig. 26 below.)

Fig. 26. Question 2: Islam, Islamic law, and 'democracy'

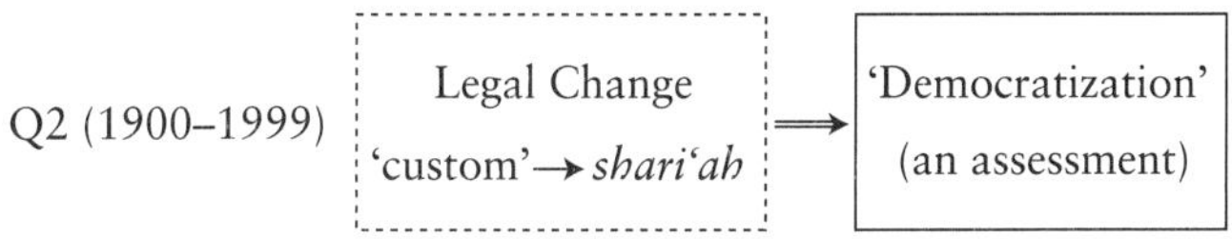

What follows is merely an attempt to illuminate exactly how I came to this historically embedded assessment of individual (landowner) preferences and, following on from this, my practice-based explanation for the non-consolidation of democracy in the context of postcolonial Punjab. Departing from convention, this chapter does not take the substance of individual preferences for granted. Instead, it comes to the issue of individual preferences as a question—a rather specific question, if you will, regarding the *theoretical* importance of particular *historical* events.

1849–1900: FROM HISTORY TO 'AGENCY'

Throughout the first half of this book (Chapters 1 and 2) a special effort was made to examine the impact of a particular sequence of late-nineteenth and early-twentieth-century debates, debates that came together in the context of the colonial revenue administration to forge a more narrowly defined and increasingly formalized expression of landowning Muslim 'self-interest'. In fact it would hardly be an exaggeration to say that what *began* with an historically embedded sequence of late-nineteenth and early-twentieth-century administrative debates regarding the ownership and inheritance of land eventually *concluded* with a notion of landowning Muslim self-interest grounded in the terms of (a) productive *pattis* and (b) specific 'tribal' customs.

This process was not confined to an elaborate sequence of colonial debates proceeding, as it were, from the 'top-down'. In fact with every passing moment my research revealed that late-nineteenth and early-twentieth-century colonial administrators were forced to move further and further away from the basic utilitarian priorities of their own bureaucratic antecedents. What began with a specific account of late-nineteenth and early-twentieth-century debates, in other words, led, somewhat sporadically, to entirely new forms of local Muslim agency—entirely new forms of landowning Muslim agency that emerged in the context of the colonial state and then endured long after that state was dismantled.

Microfoundational Mechanisms: Sequences and Logics

Shortly after the British conquered the Punjab in 1849 a series of disagreements emerged regarding the status of 'hereditary' cultivators with 'possession'. These disagreements were never pursued in isolation. In fact, from the very beginning, they were pursued within a setting strongly influenced by the substance of local 'family' laws.

Efforts to provide for the distribution of the land revenue within each village proprietary body, for instance, were always bound up with a series of closely related questions regarding 'inferior' (non-state) proprietorship. And of course, questions regarding inferior proprietorship were inextricably bound up with a series of questions regarding specific forms of 'inheritance'. As I explained in Chapter 2, however, this question of inheritance was, itself, never completely harmonized. In fact by 1912 the situation had become so complicated that judges like T.P. Ellis felt compelled to prepare lengthy digests to determine whether 'custom' or 'law' was the first rule of decision for each and every tribe: 'custom' for the Jats in Sialkot, 'law' for the Syeds in Gujrat, 'custom' for the Syeds of Multan, and so on. Indeed, throughout the latter half of the nineteenth century and, for that matter, even after 1900, 'proprietary' rights and 'personal' law were virtually indistinguishable. Each relied on the other.[1]

What began with a confident effort to *extend* the rights of landownership to those with cultivating 'possession', however, quickly re-emerged as an elaborate struggle to *limit* these rights to those with hereditary 'shares'. Indeed, as the colonial administration became more and more thoroughly entrenched, leading British officials began to argue that, for the most part, it was simply impossible to characterize the question of proprietorship as a purely *economic* question related to those with cultivating 'possession'. Increasingly, they argued, the question of proprietorship had become a *political* question related to the preservation of specific (agnatic) 'shares'.

Sequences and Logics: Preference Formation in the Punjab

To recapitulate, the consolidation of kinship-friendly preferences began shortly after Sir Richard Temple inaugurated the first (preliminary) settlement of District Sialkot in 1851. More specifically, it began when Temple's efforts to *reduce* the colonial demand produced a dramatic *increase* in the value of the land itself, followed, almost immediately, by an alarming wave of evictions—evictions in which those with specific 'ancestral' claims began to evict those with claims based solely on 'possession'.

Some, including Temple himself, were shocked by this development. But there were others, including the author of a revised (regular) settlement for Sialkot—namely, Edward Augustus (E.A.) Prinsep—who took these evictions in stride. In fact, pointing to information collected in the local *riwaj-i-am*, Prinsep argued that, according to the terms of 'tribal' custom, proprietorship based on heredity was generally 'more secure' than proprietorship based on possession. Moreover, he explained, the very success of the colonial regime implied that an increasing number of evictions would be almost impossible to avoid. The question, he noted, was not whether one villager would evict another, but rather whether the former was actually *entitled* (or, as the case might be, customarily *permitted*) to do so.

As Lord Dalhousie explained, in 1849, it was the policy of the British to 'uphold native institutions and practices' so long as these were able to preserve 'the distribution of justice' to all. And, more specifically, Dalhousie noted, it was the policy of the British to preserve the integrity of what had come to be known, throughout North India, as the local village 'coparcenary'. As Prinsep discovered, however, the most important questions did not concern the simple task of preserving these coparcenaries. The most important questions concerned the best way to define '[the] native institutions and practices' that held them together in the first place.

According to Temple, these native institutions and practices favoured the rights of individual cultivators with possession. But, according to Prinsep, this was not the case. He argued that landed property relations in the Punjab were bound up *neither* with the rights of individual *zamindars* (following Cornwallis in Bengal) *nor* with those of individual *ryots* (following Munro in Madras and Bombay). Instead, he suggested, 'native' property relations were defined by the institutions and practices associated with native agricultural 'tribes'.

The wave of evictions that emerged in District Sialkot, in other words, was not entirely unexpected. In fact, according to Prinsep, those with ancestral claims enjoyed a 'customary right' to evict those without such claims. And, of course, as the value of agricultural land increased, Prinsep explained that it was only natural to expect the holders of specific ancestral 'shares' to exercise their customary 'rights'. Moreover, Prinsep insisted, the ensuing wave of evictions merely sought to *correct* the errors of Temple's earlier (preliminary) settlement, moving away from an erroneous emphasis on 'productive' capacity towards a more compelling account of the institutions, practices, and customs associated with specific 'tribes'.

Needless to say, Prinsep's rather unconventional views might have been rejected (for instance, as a case of hostile or naïve insubordination) had it not been for (a) the particular form in which they were produced, namely, an extraordinarily detailed study of landed property relations in one rather innocuous *tehsil* (*tehsil* Shikargarh) and (b) the particular moment within which they were introduced—a moment charged with a sudden increase in the value of agricultural land, a wave of (often violent) evictions, and a growing sense of concern about the possibility of widespread rural unrest.

In fact what emerged, under the circumstances, was a critical administrative-cum-legal 'debate' (1865–1900) pitting those who placed their faith in the rights of individual 'cultivators' against those who cast their lot with the survival of specific agricultural 'tribes'.

When Prinsep cast his lot with the notion of 'tribal' custom, however, he did not merely extend the terms of an already existing debate.

Fig. 27. Colonial Punjab: sequences and logics (Part One)

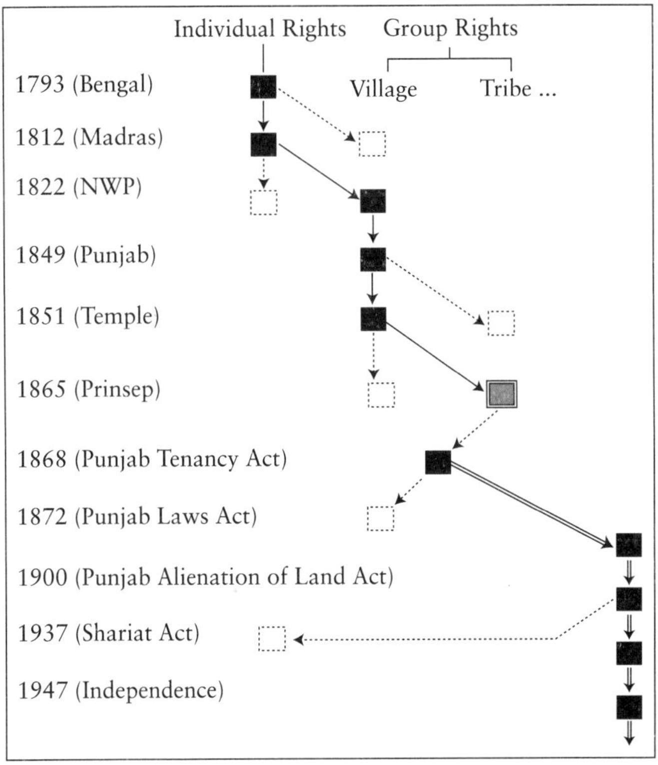

Instead he used the opportunity presented by a looming crisis of economic insecurity and political instability to transform the debate itself, moving away from any special emphasis on the value of 'individual' rights (for example, individual *zamindari* or *ryotwari* rights) toward a new discussion in which the rights of individuals were subordinated to those of agnatic (*mehalwari*) 'tribes'. In fact, when Prinsep began to stress the importance of 'agnatic' kinship, it would hardly be an exaggeration to say that he—perhaps unwittingly—challenged established bureaucratic notions with a set of ideas that many of his superiors regarded as a noxious defence of the rural aristocracy.

When Prinsep left Sialkot, in 1865, the full extent of what he had done was not yet known. But, at the same time, few were prepared to deny the profound implications of his work. In fact, when the Punjab Laws Act (1872) and, in due course, the Punjab Alienation of Land Act

(1900) were finally introduced, as a consequence of his work, some years later, few were prepared to deny that Prinsep's administrative attachment to the terms of 'tribal' custom had ushered in some of the most dramatic changes in the long and eventful history of British India—changes that echoed all the way from Lahore to London and beyond.

A complete account of these changes lies beyond the scope of this book, but the most important among them, I would argue, boiled down to some of the ways in which the Punjab Alienation of Land Act (1900) confirmed the demise of unrestricted individual ownership as the *raison d'être* of the British colonial administration—in effect, bringing more than a hundred years of clearly defined administrative priorities, economic assumptions, and political aspirations to an end (see Fig. 27 above). 'We are not concerned with the individual', noted one small group of colonial administrators in 1895. *'Our sole object is to save the land of the family'.*

Sequences and Logics: Preference Formation (Reconsidered)

The more I began to understand what had happened during the latter half of the nineteenth century, however, the more I began to wonder whether a different sequence of events might have produced a different configuration of local interests—replacing the interests of, say, agricultural 'tribes' with those of particular social 'classes'.

Consider, for instance, the years between 1849 and 1900. During the first regular settlement of District Lahore, in 1860, many local villagers had resisted colonial efforts to enter their names in the *haqdaran-e-zamin* (that is, the record of rights in land), expressing a clear inclination to view their newly defined landed property rights as an unwelcome revenue 'burden' rather than a propitious economic 'boon'. This in turn led Sir Richard Temple to cast his revenue net as wide as possible—up to and including occupancy tenants—just as he had, so many years earlier, in Sialkot.

When L.S. Saunders arrived to complete the *second* regular settlement of Lahore, in 1873, however, the advantages of a moderate rate of assessment were already widely known, leading many villagers to demand—in the form of violent evictions—the rights they had once denied. In fact the same colonial administration confronted the same people in the same villages at a different point in time. And, insofar as this was the case, Saunders found himself drawn toward an entirely different set of conclusions regarding core administrative issues like the relative importance of 'possession' (versus 'kinship') and 'village' (versus 'tribal') custom. In fact, like Prinsep, Saunders believed that, insofar as he was expected to honour the 'native institutions and practices' of the villagers themselves, he was also obliged to correct the 'errors' of his predecessors, moving away from cultivating 'possession' and the terms of 'village' custom toward a new appreciation for the rights of specific agricultural 'tribes'. Time T, if you will, produced one set of administrative conclusions. Time T + 1/8 quite another.

Having said this, however, it is important to point out that, throughout the Punjab, late-nineteenth-century efforts to provide for the preservation of specific agricultural 'tribes' (1865, 1872, 1873, etc.) emerged in conjunction with the arrival of locally elected institutions known as local district 'boards' (1882).[2] In fact, even *before* the Punjab Alienation of Land Act was promulgated in 1900, the membership of these boards was deliberately restricted to officially designated 'tribes'.

Indeed the question of historical sequence, as a basic *theoretical* question regarding the conduct of local politics, is almost impossible to ignore. If, for instance, local district boards had emerged just a few years earlier (for example in 1852), *before* agricultural 'tribes' had become such an important feature of the local administrative-cum-legal (and political) landscape, is it not possible that a different configuration of local interests might have come to frame the substance of local debates? Is it not possible that, following Sir Richard Temple, occupancy tenants with cultivating 'possession' might have come to play a far more important role? Indeed, if the inauguration of these district boards had been pulled forward in time, from, say, Time T + 1/4 (1882) to Time T+1/8 (1852), is it not possible that the politics of *kinship* might have been replaced with a politics defined by independent local *kisans* (farmers)?

Alternatively, if these district boards had emerged somewhat *later*, for example, after the formation of the Muslim League (1906) or the Hindu Mahasabha (1909), is it not possible that 'religious' factions could have come to play an entirely different role—indeed, a far more important role? To be sure, both the Muslim League and the Hindu Mahasabha enjoyed a certain amount of influence during the final months leading up to the independence of British India and the formation of Pakistan in 1947.[3] But, as I have tried to explain, the terms of 'religious' or 'communal' division were always less firmly entrenched, in the context of colonial Punjab (and particularly among the rural majority), than they were in other parts of North India. In fact it is entirely possible that the introduction of local district boards in 1882—rather than, say, 1852 or 1912—merely *reinforced* a logic in which *pattidari* tenures, female disinheritance, and the preservation of 'agnatic' estates were able to play an *especially* important role. (See, for example, the double-line 'logic' depicted in Fig. 28 below.)

Indeed, the analytical significance of the historical events that unfolded in Sialkot between 1849 and 1865 is really twofold. Empirically, these events unsettled existing patterns of thought within the

Fig. 28. Colonial Punjab: sequences and logics (Part Two)

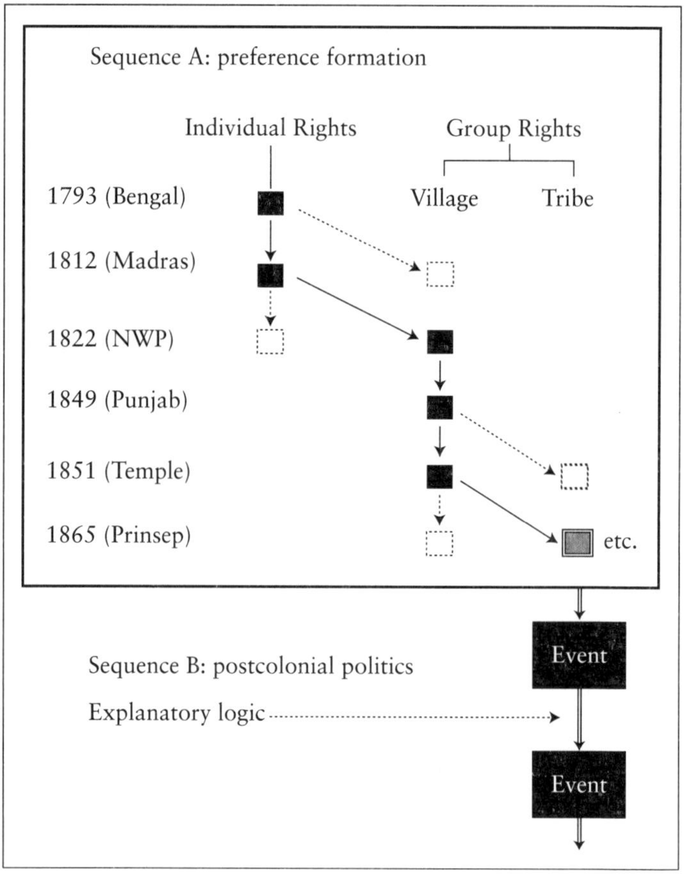

colonial administration, setting the stage for an entirely new debate between those who pressed for the promotion of 'individual' peasant proprietorship and those who lobbied (as it happens more successfully) for the preservation of 'tribal' shares. Theoretically, however, these events were also directly tied to the parameters of Q1 (above), providing a clear indication of exactly how it was that individual Muslims came to 'want what they wanted' in colonial and postcolonial Punjab.

Historical sequence, in other words, mattered *theoretically* in at least two ways. First and foremost, the sequence mentioned in Figure 27 (above) promoted the emergence of a particular administrative and political logic—reproduced as Sequence A in Figure 28—highlighting the importance of some conventions ('tribe') rather than others ('village'). But, as the second half of this book explains, Sequence A *also* mattered because it left an explanatory 'residue' of sorts at the level of individual preferences, one that militated against the emergence of alternative preferences while, at the same time, consistently pressing for the *de facto* preservation of the *ancien* (colonial) *régime*: Sequence B.

In fact it would hardly be an exaggeration to say that, precisely insofar as Chapter 1 took up the concerns addressed in Q1 (above), regarding preference formation, Chapters 2–5 were in a position to address the details of Q2 regarding the logic of local politics, emerging patterns of electoral accountability, and, ultimately, the 'practice-based' failure of democracy.

The answer to Q1 (▣), in other words, eventually reemerged in the context of Q2 at the level of a specific explanatory *logic*—one that helped me to illuminate, through a specific account of 'Muslim agency' (⇒), exactly how it was that a particular independent variable, namely the formal legal shift from custom to *shari'ah* (IV), eventually *produced* the political 'effect' that it did (DV).

Fig. 29. Accounting for the failure of democracy in postcolonial Punjab

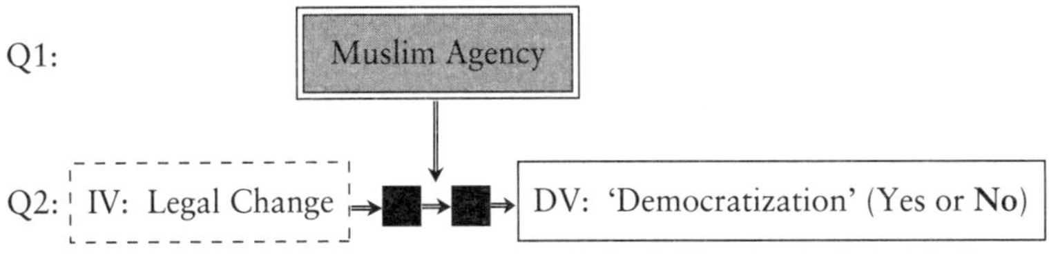

Microfoundational Mechanisms: Logics and Outcomes

As historical institutionalists have argued for quite some time, compelling explanations often have 'a sensitive dependence on initial conditions'.[4] And of course the historically embedded account presented in this book is no exception. But, then, having said this, it is important to recognize that we are confronted with a number of questions regarding the selection of a particular moment (say, 1849, 1865, 1872, or 1900) as our historical 'point of departure'. What makes this initial moment distinctive? What makes it theoretically significant? Indeed, how does this moment help to explain the particular phenomenon (for example, the process of postcolonial democratization) that concerns us?

Microfoundational Mechanisms: Origins and Outcomes

In recent years, political scientists have made great strides in their response to such questions, drawing special attention to the ways in which 'initial conditions' set the stage for theoretically relevant outcomes.

With respect to initial conditions, for instance, scholars like James Mahoney (2000) have gone to great lengths to highlight the ways in which initial moments of historical 'contingency' and 'uncertainty' can be shown to unsettle existing patterns of thought, opening up new trajectories, new sequences and new explanatory 'logics'.[5] In particular, Mahoney has stressed the ways in which specific moments of historical contingency can be used to highlight what Mark Bevir (2001) has described as dilemmas—that is, empirically observable moments when theoretically relevant patterns of thought become unsettled in ways that give rise to equally compelling (and, hence, competing) policy options.[6] These options, in turn, open up new ways of thinking, debating, and acting—new ways that, eventually, allow for the production of a theoretically 'divergent' sequence of historically specific events.

The work undertaken by E.A. Prinsep in *tehsil* Shikargarh (and its fallout after 1865) is of course an excellent illustration of this focus on destabilizing moments of 'uncertainty'. When Prinsep threw prevailing ideas about the relative importance of individual and collective landed property relations into question, not only in Sialkot but throughout British India, for instance, what mattered theoretically was not merely the presence of formal administrative uncertainty, but the rise of competing policy options and the emergence of a historically specific *debate*: 'village' v. 'tribal' custom, 'custom' v. *shari'ah*, and so on. What should the state promote? What did conditions demand? In fact, what began with a routine exercise in empirical observation quickly developed into an unanticipated 'critical juncture': theoretically speaking, the inauguration of a new explanatory 'sequence'. (See Figs. 27–29, above.)

Unfortunately, in their rush to acknowledge the importance of initial conditions, critical junctures, contingencies, dilemmas and debates, political scientists have paid somewhat less attention to 'the other side of the equation'. In fact, in their rush to highlight the 'beginning' of the story they have shown a remarkable tendency to underestimate the theoretical importance of the 'end'.

This is surprising, because it is actually here, in the relationship between 'origins' and 'outcomes', that one encounters the special significance of historical analysis itself. Indeed, when it comes to defining 'the thing to be explained' (that is, the *explanandum*) it is not the problem of initial conditions or the specification of a particular outcome but rather the problem of periodization that really matters.[7] As Peter Bearman (1999) explains: 'the central problem for historical social science is casing event sequences in order to induce beginnings and ends', because, in the final analysis, he notes, the specific 'meaning' of an event is conditioned by its unique position in a carefully differentiated 'sequence'.[8]

Consider, for example, an imaginary political party enjoying the support of 40 per cent of its potential membership. Naturally, interpretations of this statistic will differ (for instance among party strategists) depending on the initial level of support. If, for instance, during the previous two or three years, the 'initial' level of support had been just 10 or 15 per cent, then of course we might expect party strategists to carry on doing whatever it is they had been doing to boost their membership from 10 to 40 per cent. And, yet, if the 'initial' level of support had been around 75 or 80 per cent, a very different set of conclusions would emerge; indeed, as the party's support fell from 80 to 40 per cent, party strategists would probably be encouraged to consider a dramatic change of course.

Unfortunately, renewed attention to similar examples has tended to produce a greater appreciation for the theoretical importance of 'initial' conditions rather than a greater appreciation for 'ending' conditions, and, thus, an appreciation for periodization itself.[9] It is, however, worth recalling that, as Peter Bearman explains in his article 'Blocking the Future: New Solutions for Old Problems in Historical Social Science' (1999), 'different ends tell different stories'.[10] In fact it is 'only when we ... provide [*both*] a beginning *and* an end', he writes, that we can understand 'the meaning of an event', and, by extension, 'the meaning of the event sequence as a whole' (emphasis added).[11]

The problem of female disinheritance as it relates to overlapping expressions of customary and religious personal law in the context of colonial and postcolonial Punjab is, I would argue, a helpful illustration of precisely this point. In her study entitled *Muslim Women of British Punjab: From Seclusion to Politics* (1998)—a carefully edited version of her doctoral dissertation entitled 'The Changing Position of Muslim Women in the Punjab, 1872–1947' (1995)—for instance, Pakistani historian Dushka Saiyid attributes the scourge of female disinheritance in the Punjab to the debilitating terms of 'tribal' custom as these were expressed in the Punjab Laws Act of 1872. In fact Saiyid begins her study by treating the terms of the Punjab Laws Act as historically *sui generis*—an extension of specific *a priori* biases prevailing among British administrators—and, then, having done so, she proceeds to argue that, broadly speaking, it was this late-nineteenth-century colonial law that pulled Muslim women away from the special advantages of *shari'ah*.

Apparently overlooking an important body of work detailing persistent debates within the colonial state regarding the parameters of local practice in different parts of the Punjab *before* 1872, Saiyid blames the patriarchal apprehensions of specific colonial administrators (and judges) for the enduring fate of Muslim women.

Even beyond this rather sweeping indictment of colonial administrators and judges, however, Saiyid appears to *conclude* her study with the moment of partition in 1947—completely ignoring the improvements that should have been expected (as per the terms of Saiyid's own analysis) when in due course the Punjab Laws Act of 1872 was, in fact, *dismantled*: 1948, 1951, 1961, 1963 and so on.[12] This is of course an important oversight, because, as noted above (Chapters 4 and 5), dramatic postcolonial reforms designed to *replace* the terms of custom with those of *shari'ah*—especially in the context of disputes regarding inheritance—achieved almost nothing when it came to reversing the *de facto* disinheritance of women.

Indeed, even a cursory glance at the work undertaken by the postcolonial district courts would reveal that, notwithstanding numerous decisions specifically favouring *shari'ah*, the courts alone were largely ineffective when it came to revising (let alone improving) the status of Muslim women. In fact, *contra* Saiyid, the enduring problem of female disinheritance was not defined by the content of specific laws—at least not primarily. No, the problem of female disinheritance was defined by a deeply conservative logic of local politics closely tied to an historically embedded tussle between (a) powerful ancestral '*pattis*' and (b) politically 'inaccessible' laws.

When in due course the Supreme Court of Pakistan issued its landmark decision in the famous case of *Allah Rakha vs. Federation of Pakistan* (2000), however, this tussle was (officially) transformed.

Striking down the Muslim Family Laws Ordinance (MFLO 1961), the Supreme Court of Pakistan sought to clarify the meaning of a 'Qur'anic' share in the context of inheritance, drawing special attention to the need for a sharp distinction between (a) the legal shares enjoyed by individual Muslim women and (b) those enjoyed by a special class of heirs who appeared in the MFLO (Section 4) but *not* in the Holy Qur'an—namely, orphaned grandchildren.

Briefly stated, the Supreme Court did not suggest that orphaned grandchildren should be excluded from every case of inheritance. They simply noted that, legally speaking, these children should be 'excluded' from the list of 'Qur'anic' heirs. (In fact, having rejected the specific terms of the MFLO (Section 4), the Court went on to discuss the experience of several other Muslim-majority countries—countries like Algeria, Egypt and Iraq—noting that, in each and every case, orphaned grandchildren were protected by special legislation mandating the creation of a legally retroactive 'bequest'.)

Reaching beyond the specific language of the MFLO (1961), in other words, the Supreme Court went out of its way to stress the value of what might be described as alternative or compensatory *legislation*, noting that, with respect to the case of inheritance, the role of legislation was key.[13]

Indeed, with respect to the specific problem of inheritance, the significance of this case could hardly be overstated. *After 2000, the matter of inheritance was no longer politically 'inaccessible'. It was, at least ostensibly, a matter of routine 'legislation'.*[14]

Microfoundational Mechanisms: Intervening Steps

Clearly, when it comes to the issue of periodization, the traditional boundary between 'history' and 'theory' quickly begins to fade. And, yet, having said this, it is equally important to remember that theoretically rigorous approaches to the specification of beginnings and ends invariably rely on a parallel effort to expose and examine the 'intervening' parts of the story.[15] In fact, as James Mahoney (2000) points out, it is often the 'smaller sets of intervening steps through which initial breakpoints produce final outcomes' that are 'the central object of analysis'.[16]

Not surprisingly, in his efforts to account for the nature of these intervening steps, Mahoney draws particular attention to the importance of specific causal logics (⇒). However, in doing so, he also reflects the work of scholars like Peter Hedström and Richard Swedborg (1996) in reducing these logics to a set of *a priori* and, ultimately, 'unobservable' social facts.[17] Indeed, for Mahoney, the explanatory logics that lie at the very centre of every causal mechanism invariably unfold at the level of specific *a priori* assumptions—assumptions that he refers to as unobserved entities, processes or structures that act as 'ultimate causes' in generating outcomes, without, at any point, requiring verification themselves.

Of course, for those of us with an interest in overcoming the 'black box' dilemma so often associated with simple statistical correlations, the added value of this 'assumption-based' approach to intervening explanatory mechanisms is extremely difficult to ascertain. In fact, as completely unobservable 'ultimate causes' set apart from the task of empirical verification, the explanatory logics that Mahoney describes appear to reflect the *same* problem—namely, the 'black box' problem—they were ostensibly introduced to resolve.[18]

The weakness of this approach clearly lies at the level of empirical verification (and, thus, empirical testing). In fact, as Tim Büthe points out: '[any] model based solely on deduction from assumptions is [ultimately just] a shell consisting of "empty theoretical boxes"'. It invariably requires 'empirical *content* in order to make predictions about what we should [expect to] observe' (emphasis added).[19]

Again, returning to the specific focus of this book, the most instructive illustration of this point probably lies in the work of Dushka Saiyid (1998). In fact, whereas Saiyid attributes the problem of female disinheritance to a sense that colonial officials were motivated by specific *a priori* attachments to the preservation of agnatic copacenaries, a closer look at the empirical record clearly reveals that, in practice, colonial administrators arrived at these attachments with considerable historical reluctance. Indeed, even *after* the Punjab Laws Act of 1872 was promulgated by the colonial state (establishing the terms of 'tribal' custom as a complex array of specific 'rebuttable' presumptions), ordinary litigants were never actually compelled to embrace these presumptions. In fact, as litigants, ordinary Muslims were always presented with a complex legal choice: religious personal law, on the one hand; 'agnatic' tribal customs, on the other.

Clearly, conventional assumptions regarding the unrelenting biases of the colonial state have their limitations when it comes to illuminating the 'intervening' parts of a story regarding female disinheritance in the context of colonial Punjab.

And, yet, even after the terms of 'tribal' custom were slowly replaced (for instance, with a particular understanding of Islam), standard *a priori* assumptions regarding the value of things like institutional 'efficiency' would appear to obscure at least as much as they reveal about the intervening content of landowning Muslim 'agency' (1947–1999). Indeed a closer look clearly points to strategic patterns of delay in which stronger members of the village proprietary body simply ran circles around their victims in an effort to ensure that, even when the inheritance rights of Muslim women were duly *acknowledged* in court—as they were, almost without exception, in the published record of the *Pakistan Law Digest*—they were, nevertheless, systematically *ignored* 'on the ground'.

The suggestion, of course, is not that people in the 'middle' of the story simply 'got what they wanted' just because they wanted it. Nor is it that, given the nature of standard (*a priori*) assumptions, people simply failed to 'do what they were supposed to do' as faithful Muslims, independent (capitalist) landowners, or cost-conscious litigants. It is, rather, that if we aim to produce an account of how a particular legal X actually *produced* a particular political Y, at the level of precise explanatory mechanisms, we must be willing to pass through an account of individual motivations that is not merely 'assumed' but 'embedded'. In fact, if we seek to understand exactly how a particular process actually managed to produce a particular political outcome at the level of specific individual preferences, decision-making, or 'agency', we must be prepared to move beyond simple *a priori* assumptions in favour of a more specific account of historically specific demands.[20]

Standard *a priori* assumptions may lend themselves to out-of-sample testing and comparison in a way that detailed historical narratives do not. But, as Tim Büthe mentioned: '[any] model based solely on deduction from assumptions is [ultimately just an empty] ... shell'.[21] Indeed the explanatory value of such a model is really quite limited—hardly the sort of thing that scholars should be expected to rely upon if they wish to fill up the 'black box' of a convincing explanatory 'mechanism' in a particular time and place.

1849–1999: FROM 'AGENCY' TO EXPLANATION

Unfortunately, in their quest to address the endemic non-enforcement of specific (postcolonial) laws, scholars with an interest in the postcolonial politics of Pakistan have routinely succumbed to conventional explanatory assumptions regarding the importance of robust economic reforms (for example, land reforms) and, especially, neoliberal economic incentive structures. In fact many scholars continue to insist that landowning litigants filing purely 'strategic' cases should be identified, and, then, priced out of the litigation 'market' with higher court-based fees.

On the surface of course this appears to be a fine solution. But, in almost every case, a closer look reveals that many of those with an interest in delaying the resolution of their disputes (see Chapter 5) face extremely high costs already—so high, in fact, that many are forced to mortgage a portion of their property in an effort to pursue their 'strategic' goals. Indeed, as Marc Galanter reminded me (via email), it may be impossible to construct a financial barrier 'sufficient to deter those who use the courts specifically to defend their [honour]'.[22]

'With any other good', Galanter explained, 'you can play a strategy in which you maximize [your] gains and minimize [your] losses'. 'But with *izzat* [or honor]', he pointed out, you have to 'play to avoid losses entirely, even if that means foregoing the possibility of maximizing [financial] gains'.[23] As a matter of fact, Galanter noted, cutting straight to the heart of the matter, much of the litigation in the context of postcolonial Punjab had come to resemble 'a sunk-cost auction' in which 'parties have to keep on bearing tangible losses [in an effort to avoid] ... a (non-decomposable) loss of *izzat*'.[24]

This notion of 'a sunk-cost auction' strictly devoted to avoiding a 'non-decomposable' loss of *izzat* (read as a defence of 'tribal' custom) is of course extremely helpful. But, recalling the work of Douglas G. Baird, Robert H. Gertner and Rundel C. Picker in their book *Game Theory and the Law* (1994), Galanter went on to ask (rhetorically) whether those who chose to pursue this 'sunk-cost' option were in fact actually 'rational' in a specifically legal sense. Were the practical implications of *izzat*, he wondered, actually in keeping with those of a theoretically rational expression of modern legal 'self-interest'?

The answer, I would argue, is decidedly 'yes'. But, then, having said this, I must concede that this answer clearly depends on what one means by the terms of 'rationality' itself. Is one's understanding of rationality embedded or assumed? Abstract or contextualized? Empirically 'thick' or 'thin'? Are we referring to a general, even universal, form of rationality: Rationality with a Capital R? Or are we referring to something more specific—something like 'historically embedded' rationalities with a series of little r's?

Clearly, different scholars approach the question of rationality in different ways: instrumental rationality, value rationality, rationalities embedded in 'market' economies, 'moral' economies, 'mixed' economies, and so on. But the question is: which approach is best? Which approach is the most appropriate approach for those with an interest in the pursuit of microfoundational (mechanism-based) 'explanations'?

Typically, when it comes to the question of microfoundational mechanism-based explanations—that is, explanations constructed at the level of indvidual decision-making, individual strategizing, or agency—three schools of thought jockey for preeminence, each of which has emerged at various points in the context of this book. The first is dominated by rational choice theory; the second, by cultural theory; and the third, by historical institutionalism. Scholars often juxtapose these three traditions against one another in an effort to highlight their differences. But, as I will explain, my approach is somewhat different. In fact I stress a common thread of division *within* each school in an effort to highlight the differences between those who fall on either side of a particular (preference-based) divide.

Briefly stated, the dotted line demarcating this common thread of division (see Fig. 30, below) draws attention to (a) those who rely on abstract or *assumed* preferences (above the line) from (b) those who seek to rely on historically *embedded* preferences (below the line).

Within the rational choice tradition, for instance, the work of Robert Bates might be distinguished from that of Jon Elster. And, within

Fig. 30. Three traditions: assumed v. embedded preferences

A:	RATIONAL CHOICE THEORY	CULTURAL THEORY	HISTORICAL INSTITUTIONALISM
	Robert Bates	Aaron Wildavsky	Barrington Moore

ASSUMED PREFERENCES

EMBEDDED PREFERENCES

B:	Jon Elster	Clifford Geertz	Dipesh Chakrabarty
	generality v. validity	cultural theory v. cultural history	History v. 'translation' of history

the cultural theory tradition, that of Aaron Wildavsky might be distinguished from that of Clifford Geertz.[25]

The terms of this distinction apply to historical institutionalists as well. But, in this case, the line itself becomes somewhat more nuanced. (After all, historical institutionalists routinely claim to reject the notion of assumed preferences as a theoretical matter of course.[26]) Nevertheless, I would argue, important differences remain.

In an effort to account for the specific shape of individual preferences, for instance, some historical institutionalists are accused of suggesting that, owing to the history of global capitalism, a detailed account of the interests prevailing in modern Europe can be used to illuminate a historically embedded account of interests around the world.[27] In fact, with this in mind, a useful distinction might be drawn between (a) the universalizing 'core' of historical institutionalism, represented by the likes of Barrington Moore, and (b) the postcolonial 'periphery', recalling the work of prominent scholars like Dipesh Chakrabarty, Marshall Sahlins, and Sudipta Kaviraj. Indeed, whereas the former tend to stress the value of specific 'universal' categories—categories like social class—the latter aim to resist this impulse, focusing instead on an effort to *translate* otherwise familiar historical categories in ways that reflect the empirical concerns of individuals on the ground.[28]

Needless to say, all three of these traditions have informed various parts of this book. But, *within* each tradition, it should be fairly clear by now that some perspectives have been more influential than others. Indeed, the division between those who favour analytical assumptions and those who favour specific empirical evidence is obvious: both sides have their own advantages. But, as I will now proceed to explain, the latter have considerably *more* advantages when it comes to the specification of compelling explanatory 'mechanisms'.[29]

With respect to the case of purely strategic litigation, for instance, one might ask: Who is in a position to 'explain' the postcolonial politics of delay? Who can 'explain' the meaning of delay with respect to (a) the importance of *izzat*, (b) the notion of electoral accountability, and (c) the possibility of an 'Islamic democracy'?

Explanatory Logics: Assumptions v. Evidence

In his article 'Rational Choice History: A Case of Excessive Ambition' (2000), Jon Elster criticized Robert Bates and those attached to a special project known as The Analytical Narratives Project for taking rational choice approaches to the issue of microfoundational explanation too far.[30] In particular, Elster argued that Bates and his colleagues had extended the notion of rational choice explanation beyond what the discontinuous terms of empirical reality could reasonably be expected to bear.

Naturally, many rushed to characterize this exchange as yet another round in the debate between those who favour nomothetic 'covering laws' (in this case, Bates) and those who favour idiographic 'thick description' (in this case, Elster). In fact, by the time this debate appeared in the *American Political Science Review*, clashes of this type had become extremely common.[31] John R. Bowen and Roger Petersen, for instance, even went so far as to open their book *Critical Comparisons in Politics and Culture* (1999) with a statement to the effect that 'the social sciences ... are torn apart by a tension between two desires'. On the one hand, they explained, referring to the work of scholars like Margaret Levi (a member of Bates's Analytical Narratives Project), there was a desire 'to robustly model the world, showing its relationships and [its] regularities'. And, yet, at the same time, turning to the work of anthropologists like Fredrik Barth, they noted that there was an equally powerful desire 'to richly describe the world, showing its complexity and [its] variability'.[32]

Bowen and Petersen were not discussing a false dichotomy. In fact the chasm they sought to illuminate was indeed quite large—in many cases separating those who sought to embrace the analytical value of diverse expressions of 'interest' or 'value' from those who seemed to fear that any such effort might begin to draw our attention away from the 'universal' terms of Truth, Justice, and Equality. Indeed the problem that Bowen and Petersen identified could not be reduced to a simple question of methodology. Instead it grew out of a much larger and more enduring dispute between those with fundamentally different opinions regarding the analytical value of historically embedded preferences—in many ways, a fundamental disagreement regarding the theoretical value of accounts that sought to *acknowledge* and (in some cases) *explain* the substantive 'values' of their subjects.[33]

Much like scientific efforts to capture the essence of light as both a particle and a wave, these competing approaches were irreducibly bound up with the priorities of competing sets of observers.

Assumptions: Rational Choice Theory

Of course Robert Bates and his colleagues in the Analytical Narratives Project did not deny that rational choice theorists were inclined to gloss over specific historical questions regarding the substance of individual preferences. In fact they insisted that, as a general rule, there was no need to acknowledge the many and various ways in which individuals came to make sense, derive meaning, and construct order in their shifting perceptions of the world. 'Interests', they argued, were 'interests' pure and simple.[34]

Nevertheless, Bates and his colleagues went on to claim that, within the rational choice tradition, 'analytical narratives' represented an important step forward insofar as they sought to provide a renewed appreciation for the empirical sensitivities of the historian, the cultural sensitivities of the ethnographer, and the importance of area studies.[35] The goal, however, remained largely the same. The goal lay in drawing theoretical generalizations out of unique case studies and, in doing so, constructing what Bates and his colleagues sought to describe as 'systematic rational choice explanations'.[36]

If we take a closer look at the studies undertaken by Bates and his colleagues, however, we see that their approach was never quite as 'systematic' as they claimed. In the first instance, for example, those affiliated with The Analytical Narratives Project sought to take historically embedded individual preferences seriously in an effort to refine the scope of their models. This was of course a promising step. But, having done so, Bates and his team decided that, as they moved forward in the direction of 'comparison', they would simply hold the question of preferences constant to ensure that their models were able to travel more easily from one case to the next.[37] Needless to say, this was not terribly 'systematic'. Indeed, if Bates and his colleagues had been truly consistent, they would have either (a) held individual preferences constant from the very beginning (for example, with the help of assumed preferences) or (b) risked coming up with a different model based on an entirely different set of preferences in each and every case.

For precisely this reason, however, Bates and his colleagues chose to argue that, in the end, they were not really interested in the substance of historically embedded individual preferences: 'tribal', 'religious', and so on. In fact, like James Mahoney, they opted to shy away from any systematic account of historically embedded individual preferences altogether, precisely *because* they had no interest in providing an historically embedded explanation for what actually happened, at the level of individual 'decision-making', on the ground. The primary goal, in other words, was not related to the illumination of a 'valid' empirical explanation. It was in fact the construction of a 'reliable' model suitable for specific out-of-sample comparisons—the *sine qua non*, they argued, of rigorous empirical research.[38]

Leaving aside the question of doing better history, ethnography, or area studies, in other words, Bates and his colleagues insisted that, with respect to individual preferences, rational choice theorists should stand by their traditional claim that a deductive account of human behavior based on conventional (*a priori*) assumptions was probably 'good enough'.[39]

Assumptions: Cultural Theory

Needless to say, Aaron Wildavsky (1991) was not alone when he argued that the deductive assumptions of rational choice theory were not 'good enough'. In fact, according to Wildavsky, the most important question was not 'why people did what they did' at the level of specific actions (for example, 'strategic' delays), but, rather, 'why they wanted what they wanted' (for example, the preservation of agnatic estates) in the first place. Clearly, Wildavsky noted, taking aim at the deductive limitations of rational choice theory, 'a theory of human behavior that starts by ... saying "Assume Preferences!" leaves a lot to be desired'.[40]

In fact, turning away from Bates's attachment to assumed preferences—preferences in favour of formal institutional efficiency, for example—Wildavsky turned to the work of anthropologist Mary Douglas (1986) and, more specifically, to her notion that individual preferences were, themselves, 'socially constructed' within one of four clearly defined 'preference cultures', namely (a) 'individualistic' cultures, (b) 'hierarchical' cultures, (c) 'egalitarian' cultures, and (d) 'fatalistic' cultures.[41] These four cultures, Wildavsky argued, were important, because, following Douglas, they sought to replace the unacceptably narrow assumptions of rational choice theory with the more diverse and inclusive assumptions of cultural theory—not through any *ad hoc* reference to complex social norms but, rather, through a rigorous taxonomic illustration of 'universal' cultural patterns.[42]

Unfortunately, in his specific and persistent criticism of the deductive habits so common among rational choice theorists, Wildavsky may have protested too much. With his defence of Mary Douglas, for instance, Wildavsky appeared to have much in common with the work of Robert Bates—particularly with respect to the question of 'universal' patterns and *a priori* analytical assumptions.

To be sure, Wildavsky pressed for a more nuanced approach to culturally embedded forms of human motivation (seeking to move beyond some of the most thoroughly decontextualized applications of modern rational choice theory).[43] But, at the same time, following Bates, Wildavsky clearly relied on a view of individual preference formation that was, itself, ahistorical. In fact, even more than Bates, Wildavsky appeared to base his claims on a specific sense that human preferences conformed to 'universally demarcated patterns'.[44]

Explanatory Logics: The Task of Historical 'Translation'

Fortunately, historical institutionalists have followed historians in general in seeking to challenge Wildavsky's ahistorical (taxonomic) view, devoting far more attention to the (deeply historical) formation of individual preferences themselves. In fact, given the shifting terms of domination, accommodation, and creative resistance around the world, historians, anthropologists and political scientists like Dipesh Chakrabarty, Marshall Sahlins, and Sudipta Kaviraj have noted that globally 'standardized' notions of rational self-interest (Bates) or culture (Wildavsky) may be extremely difficult to come by.[45]

Even 'material self-interest' or, for that matter, 'egalitarianism', Chakrabarty argues, may imply one thing in London and then something else in Lahore. Indeed, being clear about the meaning of a conventional category like interest (even when it comes to something like an individual's interest in land) requires, as noted above, a carefully constructed process of historically embedded 'translation'.

In an effort to illuminate this process of translation, scholars like Dipesh Chakrabarty have not turned to the politics of landed property relations in the context of colonial and postcolonial Punjab. Instead they have turned to the work of scholars like Ranajit Guha and, more specifically, Guha's account of a miniature rebellion in colonial Bengal and Bihar. In particular, Chakrabarty explains that, within this rebellion, Guha ran across 'a phenomenon common in the lives of ... peasants', namely, the influence of 'supernatural beings'. In fact, Guha noted that *most* local peasants *explained* their actions—in this case their short-lived rebellion—as an act of resistance carried out at the behest of a god named 'Thakur'.[46]

Having said this, however, Chakrabarty notes that, within his work, Guha found himself in a rather complex theoretical bind.[47] After all, Chakrabarty notes, 'a principle aim of Guha's essay was ... [to make] the insurgent's consciousness [a] mainstay of [his] narrative about rebellion'.[48] And yet, Chakrabarty asks, what does it mean to (a) 'take the subaltern's view seriously' while, at the same time, seeking to (b) 'confer on the subaltern agency'—a status that, Guha found, most local peasants went out of their way to deny?[49] This was the question that brought both Guha and Chakrabarty back to the task of 'translation'.

Historians and social scientists will provide such things as 'the supernatural' with a place in somebody's belief system, Chakrabarty explains, 'but to ascribe to [such things] any real agency in historical events [would] be to go against the rules of evidence that give ... [historians and social scientists] procedures for settling disputes about the past'.[50] In fact, recalling the work of R.G. Collingwood (1946), Chakrabarty concludes that the most important task must lie in coming to know the 'motives' behind individual actions—not merely as a nuanced *historical* task, but rather, as a specific *theoretical* task.[51] Indeed the main task must lie in developing a more sophisticated understanding of individual *agency*—in effect a more refined account of 'why people do what they do'.

Certainly, different people want different things. (In fact my own work in the archives of District Sialkot revealed that the *same* people living in the *same* place may want *different* things at different points in time—for example, 1851 v. 1865.) But, of course, this is merely to illuminate the fundamental importance of history and, thus, the importance of 'validity' within the task of 'translation' itself.

'It is not just the idea of the exotic' that drives the search for historically embedded explanatory mechanisms, noted Bernard S. Cohn (1996). It is, rather, 'the sense one gets that other systems work, that there are such things as cultural logics', and, ultimately, 'that there is as much rationality in other societies as [there is, presumably,] in our own ... even though [it flows] from other principles'.

In fact, returning to the work of R.G. Collingwood (1946), Cohn noted that the challenge does *not* lie in drawing attention to the value of any 'reliable' *a priori* assumptions. Instead it lies in thinking oneself into a specific sequence of historical events so as to 'translate' and, thus, *explain*, the thoughts of local agents.[52]

'History', 'culture', and 'choice' do not exist as competing analytical frameworks. They simply overlap within an account of historically embedded motivation or agency—the *sine qua non*, I would argue, of 'mechanism-based research'.

CONCLUSION

In so many ways the benefits of a deeper appreciation for historically embedded individual preferences (in the context of microfoundational explanatory mechanisms) are perfectly clear. But, of course, the risks are no less apparent. Indeed, if the explanatory mechanism lying at the very heart of this book rests on a specific configuration of individual preferences grounded in a particular set of customary landed property relations (the consolidation of which was tied to a unique set of events in late-nineteenth and early-twentieth-century Punjab), the question arises: How would this explanatory mechanism hold up in a context defined by rigorous out-of-sample testing? How would it withstand the demands of a controlled cross-national research?

Initially, when I began this study of Islam, Islamic law, and democracy in the context of colonial and postcolonial Punjab, I was not concerned about any lack of comparative context. Instead I was concerned about the extent to which I might succeed in limiting my reach to just one or two comparative cases—cases like Senegal, Sudan, or Tajikistan, for instance, with large Muslim majorities, fragmented agricultural economies, complex local kinship networks, and a rich tradition of so-called 'tribal' laws.

In the end, however, as my research developed, I found that I was simply unable to locate even one comparative case with a sufficient number of similarities to allow for a suitable set of 'tests', particularly at the level of such critical explanatory elements as (a) precise historical 'sequences' or (b) historically embedded 'logics'.

More often than not I discovered that a different configuration of key explanatory elements—for instance, a different sequence or a different logic—produced a different outcome. But of course, recalling some of the patterns illuminated in the work of Partha Chatterjee (2004), I also encountered several cases in which a *different* set of events produced scattered elements of a remarkably *similar* logic: 'inaccessible' laws, exception-based patterns of electoral 'accountability', and so on. (See Fig. 31, below.)

Needless to say, this was an important discovery. It was particularly important because it raised a number of questions about the role of specific 'intervening' elements—for example, specific forms of historically embedded human *agency*—in the context of (a) microfoundational explanatory 'mechanisms' and (b) cross-national 'comparative' research.

Indeed, when social scientists claim that they are interested in formulating a microfoundational mechanism-based explanation, one might ask: What do they actually mean? Do they intend to account for the link between a particular set of independent and dependent variables: for example, **Event 2 → OUTCOME** (below)? Or do they intend to come up with a focused explanatory mechanism to illuminate the microfoundational *processes* that 'produced' that outcome (for example, 3A ⇒ 5A *or* 3B → 4B) in the first place?

Increasingly, I would argue, following in the footsteps of scholars like Lawrence Mohr (1996) and many others, social scientists are interested in the latter.[53] In short, they are interested in the specification of precise explanatory 'mechanisms'.

Fig. 31. Comparing explanatory mechanisms: A v. B

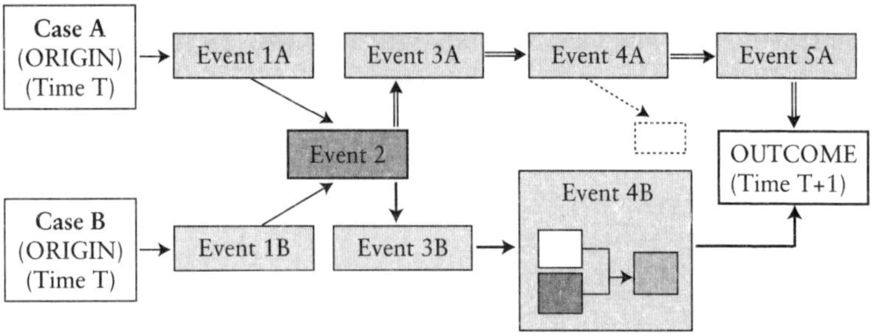

Again, those with an interest in the task of historically embedded 'explanation' rarely seek to examine cases in which there is 'a one-to-one correspondence' between X and Y. More often than not, Peter Hall (2000) explains, scholars seek to 'identify processes marked by extensive interaction effects in which X conduces towards Y but via a series of intermediary stages in which the interaction of other variables is [equally if not more] important'.[54]

Naturally, if social scientists limit their research to the study of outcomes set apart from the historically embedded processes that produce them, they will probably manage to get away with an appeal to standard assumptions regarding the substance of individual preferences. After all, when it comes to an evaluation of their work, they will be judged, not by the extent to which their arguments succeed in capturing the 'middle' of the story (1A ⇒ 5A; 1B → 4B), but rather, by the extent to which their measurement protocol succeeds in capturing a statistically significant correlation between the variables they describe at the 'beginning' (Time T) and those they describe at the 'end' (Time T + 1).

Insofar as social scientists begin to take an interest in the 'middle' of the story, however, standard assumptions regarding the nature of individual preferences will no longer seem to suffice. Instead, social scientists will find themselves forced to pry open the 'black box' of historically embedded individual preferences, motivations, or agency, recording what individuals actually 'say' and 'do' on the ground. In other words, taking up the challenge of historically embedded 'translation', social scientists will find themselves forced to move beyond the question of origins and outcomes toward a detailed understanding of the choices that people make—and the terms in which they make them—all along the way.[55]

For years, prevailing trends within the social sciences have stressed the importance of large-n correlations. But, increasingly, I would argue, scholars and policy makers alike have come to realize that, if we care about the question of 'validity' in a particular time and place (for example, colonial and postcolonial Punjab), the work of explanation must be redefined in ways that allow for the specification of intervening 'sequences' and, above all, the historically embedded 'logics' that drive them.

The challenge does not lie in an examination of outcomes based on standard *a priori* assumptions. Instead it lies in an effort to grasp the meaning of deeply contextualized 'decisions'. Explanations grounded in historically embedded notions of individual human agency are specific (even unique). But, as noted above, the role of human agency in the specification of microfoundational explanatory mechanisms is not unique at all.

CONCLUSION

ISLAM, ISLAMIC LAW, AND DEMOCRACY IN PAKISTAN AND BEYOND

This is a book about the relationship between Islam, Islamic law, and democracy. As I noted at the outset, however, it is also a book about the specific ways in which scholars and social scientists have studied and, ultimately, how they should study this relationship. In other words, this is a book about the relationship between Islam, Islamic law, and democracy wrapped inside a much larger book regarding specific methodological debates.

Along the way, considerable attention has been devoted to a detailed study of local customs regarding the inheritance of agricultural land, paying particular attention to the ways in which some of these customs—for example, the custom of female disinheritance—took shape in colonial Punjab (1849–1947) and, then, endured, long after the departure of the British and the formation of Pakistan in 1947. In fact, within this account of landed inheritance, the largest part of this book has been devoted to the terms of a rather specific shift 'from custom to *shari'ah*' (1947–1999). How did postcolonial efforts to replace the custom of female disinheritance with some acknowledgement of specific shares for individual Muslim women (that is, specific 'Qur'anic' shares) touch upon and, then, intervene to reconfigure, the logic of local politics? How did these efforts work to shape the logic of political mobilization, accountability, and voting? How did they shape the notion of political accountability vis-à-vis the delineation of state-based 'laws' and, thus, the shape of 'democracy' itself?

Throughout this book the relationship between Islam, Islamic law, and democracy has been addressed, almost exclusively, at the level of local 'practice'. In fact, with respect to the issue of methodology, considerable attention has been devoted to an understanding of the ways in which the postcolonial politics of *shari'ah* actually unfolded on the ground: who owns which plot; who inherits which share; who controls which votes (and why)?

In colonial and postcolonial Punjab (1849–1999) the landed property rights of Muslim women were a source of considerable and enduring tension: 'custom' v. *shari'ah*. This tension fuelled an enormous number of disputes. And, for the most part, this book has examined the ways in which these disputes were 'legally' and 'politically' resolved.

Following the demise of the colonial state and the formation of Pakistan in 1947, prevailing patterns of dispute resolution throughout the Punjab were, in many ways, 'politically accountable' patterns. However, having said this, it would be difficult to argue that these patterns were, in any way, 'democratic'. In fact, more often than not, postcolonial patterns of 'politically accountable' dispute resolution boiled down to a complex pattern of informal accountability *set apart from* (indeed against) the content of existing laws (with many citizens calling upon their elected representatives to manipulate the machinery of the state in ways that might begin to sustain, however informally, the countervailing substance of enduring agnatic norms: 'custom', not *shari'ah*). This was in fact an important feature of the logic surrounding local expressions of accountability in the context of postcolonial Punjab: 'accountability' *set apart from* the 'law'.

Partha Chatterjee (2004 and forthcoming) has argued that this pattern of informal extralegal accountability is, for all intents and purposes, a 'democratic' pattern. But, throughout this book, I have sought to disagree. In fact, as a general principle, I have sought to argue that democracy *itself* emerges *within* practices tied to the law. These practices may seek to enforce the law. They make seek to expand it, restrict it, amend it, or repeal it. But, in each case, I maintain that so-called 'democratic' practices remain closely tied to patterns of reiterative interaction with accountable expositors of the law. *There is, I argue, no such thing as a working democracy set apart from 'state-based rules of law'.*

After 1999, during the regime of General Pervez Musharraf, specific reforms were introduced in an effort to transform the underpinnings of local politics throughout Pakistan. I will examine these reforms in greater detail below. But, before I do, I would like to pause for just a moment to consider the relationship between the underlying concerns of this book and specific developments within the existing literature regarding Islam and democracy as a whole—specific developments pertaining to (a) the practice of 'Islamic law', (b) the practice of 'Muslim politics', and (c) the possibility of an 'Islamic democracy'. How do Muslim politicians understand, interact with, and shape, the terms of Islamic law? How might they begin to proceed, 'democratically', *within* 'the shadow of *shari'ah*'?

ISLAM, ISLAMIC LAW, AND DEMOCRACY: A CLOSER LOOK AT THE LITERATURE

Recent events in South Asia and across the Middle East—for example, in Afghanistan, Iraq, and Iran—have generated an enormous amount of interest in the relationship between Islam, Islamic law, and democracy. Studies of Islamic law lie at the very centre of this trend. But, so far, detailed studies of Islamic law as it actually unfolds in practice, vis-à-vis the work of local politicians (and the terms of electoral accountability), remain extremely rare. In fact, more often than not, studies of Islamic law and studies of the work undertaken by local Muslim politicians appear to occupy mutually exclusive spheres: *muftis*, on the one hand; Members of the National Assembly (that is, MNAs), on the other. One focused on the work of Islamic law; one focused on the delineation of state-based laws: east is east, west is west, never the twain shall meet.

For those with an interest in the relationship between Islam, Islamic law, and democracy, however, this bifurcation is actually quite surprising. Indeed, how might we begin to understand the meaning of an Islamic 'democracy' and, for that matter, the meaning of an 'Islamic' democracy, if the terms of Islamic law remain more or less completely set apart from any notion of electoral accountability and, then, in due course, if the work undertaken by locally elected representatives remains completely cut off from the practice of Islamic jurisprudence?

Clearly, for those with an interest in the relationship between Islam and democracy, some effort to address this bifurcation surrounding the terms of law-based accountability (both 'Islamic' and 'democratic') would appear to be quite helpful. What does it actually mean to examine contemporary forms of political accountability within the realm of Islamic law? When is the practice of 'Islamic law' also, at the same time, 'democratic'?

Islamic Law 'in Practice'

For decades, scholars with an interest in the terms of Islamic law have drawn our attention to the relationship between the practice of *shari'ah* and that of state-based *fiqh* or jurisprudence. The work of Joseph Schacht (1964), N.J. Coulson (1964), and J.N.D. Anderson (1976), focusing on what might be described as the politics of postcolonial '*shari'ah*-tization', has been particularly influential in this regard, as has the work of Wael B. Hallaq (2001 and 2005).

In recent years, however, several scholars have begun to move beyond this early focus on state-based efforts to 'formalize' the terms of *shari'ah* (as a form of state-based *siyasa shari'ah*) in favour of a more thoroughly focused effort to address the informal practice of *shari'ah* as it actually unfolds on the ground. (See, for example, Abbas Amanat and Frank Griffel 2007 as well as R. Michael Feener and Mark E. Cammack 2007.) This more recent body of informal 'practice-based' literature has generally sought to highlight the ways in which the terms of *fiqh* have been interpreted and, then, reinterpreted by local *qazis* and, especially, local *muftis* in the context of private local disputes. (See, for example, Gregory Kozlowski 1985, Lawrence Rosen 1989, Brinkley Messick 1992, and of course, Mohammad Khalid Masud 1996.[1]) In fact, within this expanding body of grassroots-oriented 'practice-based' literature, the recent work of Michael G. Peletz (2002), regarding *qazis* in Malaysia, and John R. Bowen (2003), regarding *muftis* in Indonesia, could be described as particularly striking, mostly owing to its astonishingly close relationship with the issues discussed in this book.

Broadly speaking, both Peletz and Bowen focus on the ways in which ordinary Muslims go out of their way to preserve and protect specific local customs—specific local customs of *inheritance* that tend to *depart* from a conventional reading of *shari'ah* (*ilm al-fara'id*).[2] In fact, for all intents and purposes, the only difference between the focus of their work and the specific focus of this book lies in the content of the customs in question: whereas, in Southeast Asia, the terms of local custom are largely 'matrilineal', in the Punjab these terms are mostly 'patrilineal'.

Specific empirical differences notwithstanding, however, both Peletz and Bowen go on to provide a remarkably nuanced analysis of the ways in which individual Muslim judges intervene to understand, engage, and accommodate the specific demands of their clients. In fact both Peletz and Bowen devote considerable attention to the ways in which a specific body of (in this case) matrilineal custom is, for the most part, preserved—not *apart* from the work undertaken by local 'Islamic' courts, but, rather, via ongoing patterns of 'informal' collaboration *within* them. Indeed, both Peletz and Bowen go out of their way to show how the daily practice of Islamic law is, in fact, the daily practice of a dynamic 'living' law. Individual judges do not simply apply the law (ahistorically). Instead they work to interpret it (historically). In fact, even as they seek to interpret the law, they seek to embed it *within* the contours of a particular case.[3]

Certainly, among those with an interest in contemporary scholarship regarding the practice of Islamic law, it is no longer unusual to read that individual *muftis* aim to bring the language of Islamic law to 'life' as an historical 'process' in ways that 'respond' to the historically embedded demands of their clients. It is simply unusual to read, within this emphasis on specific forms of contemporary legal 'responsiveness', that, moving forward, scholars might begin to reach *beyond* the responsiveness of local *muftis* toward an account of the *responsiveness* associated with elected MNAs. In fact, as noted above, the distinction remains perfectly clear: *muftis*, on the one hand; MNAs, on the other.

For those with an interest in the relationship between Islam, Islamic law, and democracy, however, this is the source of the problem. If, following Kozlowski, Rosen, Messick, Masud, Peletz, Bowen, and so many others, it is simply impossible to deny that the terms of Islamic law are, in some sense, historically and politically 'responsive', why have so few stepped in to examine what might be described as the *shari'ah*-based responsiveness (or not) of elected Muslim MNAs? Why have so few sought to connect the terms of Islamic law to the grassroots-level work of state-based Muslim politicians?

Clearly, this push in the direction of elected Muslim MNAs does not aim to reverse existing trends in the study of Islamic law. In fact, with reference to the notion of legal 'responsiveness', it simply seeks to expand them.

Muslim Politics 'in Practice'

By and large, the work of modern Muslim politicians (as 'politicians') has not been examined with reference to the 'practice' of contemporary Islamic law. In fact, for all intents and purposes, those with an interest in the work undertaken by elected Muslim politicians have sought to reduce the terms of Islamic law to the level of ‘ideology’ or ‘rhetoric’.

Within this more explicitly political branch of the literature, for instance, special attention has been paid to the development of an explicitly statist ideology of religious-cum-political authority known as ‘Islamism’. And, yet, even here, references to *shari‘ah* as ‘*fiqh*’ are rare. In fact the overwhelming majority of this literature has tended to unfold at the level of intellectual history or biography drawing special attention to the political sociology of abstract theocratic ‘ideas’. (See, for example, the work of S.V.R. Nasr 1996; Roxanne Euben 1999; and, more recently, Raymond Baker 2003.[4])

This literature, regarding the complex ideological landscape of Islamism, has been enormously influential. But, over time, a growing number of scholars have also sought to push beyond this focus on the formulation of Islamism as an abstract political ‘idea’ in favour of a closer look at its practical political application—for example, in the context of contemporary political ‘rhetoric’. Indeed a growing number of scholars have begun to focus on the special traction of modern Islamist rhetoric at the level of (a) modern Muslim social movements, (b) Islamic civil society organizations, and of course, (c) modern ‘Islamist’ political parties.

The outstanding work of scholars like S.V.R. Nasr (2001), regarding local patterns of Islamist political mobilization in Pakistan, is particularly notable in this regard, as is the work of Jillian Schwedler (2006) regarding the production of ideological ‘moderation’ among Islamists in Jordan and Yemen. In fact both Nasr and Schwedler provide extraordinarily nuanced accounts of the ways in which specific appeals to Islamist ‘ideas’ have been used to advance powerful strands of real-world political mobilization throughout the Muslim world.

What emerges from this focus on the real-world application of modern Islamist rhetoric is, of course, an exceptionally detailed understanding of the work undertaken by prominent Islamist ideologues, Islamist politicians, and their critics. What does *not* emerge is any special emphasis on the ‘application’ of specific Islamic laws. Indeed, what does *not* emerge is any special attachment to routine forms of engagement with the terms of *shari‘ah*, as *fiqh*, for example, at the level of local disputes. (For exceptions focused on the case of Iran see both Ziba Mir-Hosseini 1993 and Arzoo Osanloo 2006.)

To be sure, some insist that the aspirations of Islamism and the daily practice of *fiqh* diverge almost by definition. In fact, in a strictly historical sense, scholars of Islamic law routinely stress the extent to which, in a specific departure from the 'statist' rhetoric of Islamism, the practice of *fiqh* cannot be said to rely on the presence of any *state* at all. Indeed as John R. Bowen explains, drawing special attention to the 'classical' legal work of independent *qazis* and *muftis*: 'classical Islamic ideas ... are so strikingly different' that, for all intents and purposes, the Western notion of 'law' itself, 'with its prototypical meaning of positive or enacted law', has 'no real counterpart' in any conception of Islamic jurisprudence whatsoever.

Again, the basic impasse mentioned above—*muftis* v. MNAs—could hardly be stated more succinctly: *fiqh*, if you will, versus formal, positive, or enacted law; *shari'ah* versus the state . In fact for Bowen, like so many others, the very *raison d'être* of those with a responsive attachment to the state, namely positive or enacted law, would appear to remain completely set apart from the adjudicative underpinnings of *fiqh*. Indeed, for those with an interest in the relationship between Islam, Islamic law, and democracy, the question arises: how is the practice of 'democracy' possible, in any state-based 'Islamic' sense, without any access to responsive forms of *fiqh*?

Islamic Law, Muslim Politics, and the Possibility of an Islamic Democracy

This reference to an historically embedded wall of separation between the terms of *shari'ah*, on the one hand, and those of state-based forms of positive or enacted law, on the other, is of course rather common. (With reference to South Asia see both Michael R. Anderson 1999 and Scott A. Kugle 2001.) In fact, given the enduring value of the work undertaken by independent local *muftis*, some appreciation for this wall could be seen as quite understandable, even as a general principle, were it not for the fact that, historically speaking, state-based forms of *shari'ah* have in fact existed, in many cases quite prominently, for decades—and that too even apart from state-based forms of 'Islamism'. (See, for example, Daniel Lev 1972, Daniel Collins 1987, Mounira Charrad 2001, and Clark Lombardi 2006.)

Indeed, recent trends clearly point to the fact that state-based forms of *shari'ah* (as a form of '*siyasa*' *shari'ah*) are no longer uncommon or in any way incongruous—legally, politically, religiously, historically, and so on. On the contrary, the presence of *siyasa shari'ah* has emerged as a simple fact—a simple empirical fact with profound implications for the study of Islam, Islamic law, and the possibility of an Islamic democracy.

Opposing 'Islamic Democracy'

To be sure, many scholars are quick to reject this link between state-based forms of '*siyasa*' *shari'ah* and the possibility of an Islamic democracy. In fact the vast majority are inclined to reject it out of hand.

Some, like Carrie Rosefsky Wickham (1994) and Saba Mahmood (2004), aim to reject the study of democracy altogether, noting that, within the study of modern Muslim politics (for example, in Egypt), the existence of a parallel preoccupation with the study of democracy has too often pushed in the direction of analytically crude teleologies.[5] (In effect, they argue, Muslims as 'Muslims' begin as 'political' agnostics.)

Others, like Asef Bayat (2007 and 2010), insist that, when it comes to the possibility of 'democracy', the terms of '*siyasa*' *shari'ah* are simply irrelevant. In fact, for Bayat, democracy emerges from below—completely set apart from any '*siyasa*' or state whatsoever (for example, at the level of modern Muslim social movements and, more recently, at the level of quotidian 'non-movements' composed of 'everyday' interactions set apart from the state). Indeed, for Bayat, democracy unfolds within an environment that is, following Chatterjee (forthcoming), almost entirely 'informal'.

Some, like Robert W. Hefner (2000), focusing on the case of Indonesia, take a slightly different approach, noting that, when it comes to the possibility of 'democracy', the problem does not lie with the 'state' *per se*. Instead it lies with the terms of '*siyasa*' *shari'ah*. In fact, for Hefner, democracy would appear to rely (quite heavily) on a strict commitment to state-based forms of secularism—in many ways a specific commitment to shun any attachment to 'state-based forms of *fiqh*': Islam at the level of civil society, if you will, strictly set apart from the work of the modern state.

Indeed, the approach that Hefner describes is not confined to Indonesia. It has also emerged in cases as diverse as Turkey (with reference to specific secular accommodations embraced by the 'Islamist' Justice and Development Party—see Quinn Mecham 2004), as well as Egypt (with reference to the formation of an explicitly secular party known as

The Centre Party initially supported by a small group of dissident Muslim Brothers—see both A.R. Norton 2004 and Carrie Rosefsky Wickham 2004).[6]

In fact, what we see in the work of these scholars, each focusing on a very different empirical context, is really a common opposition to the notion of an 'Islamic' democracy. Some shy away from the study of democracy altogether. Others shy away from the fact that democracies rely on the state. And, of course, some embrace the possibility of a state-based democracy while, at the same time, rejecting the notion that a state-based 'democracy' might be tied to the language of '*siyasa*' *shari'ah*. In fact, with reference to the work of Hefner, Mecham, Norton, and Wickham what we see is an attachment to state-based forms of democracy categorically set apart from the politically 'responsive' processes that could be said to surround, at least historically, the 'practice' of Islamic law.

Supporting 'Islamic Democracy'

In so many ways, however, the terms of *siyasa shari'ah*—1948, 1951, 1961, 1963, 1972, 1975, and so on—these are the terms that define the heart of the issue. Some, anticipating the decision of the Supreme Court of Pakistan in the landmark case of *Allah Rakha vs. Pakistan* (2000), see the possibility of a close relationship between the terms of *siyasa shari'ah* and the work of elected MNAs. But, of course, many remain quite sceptical.

Among those who see the possibility of an Islamic democracy unfolding *within* the terms of *siyasa shari'ah*, the influence of would-be Pakistani scholars like Mohammad Iqbal (1934) is, of course, impossible to ignore.[7] As is the work of Pakistani philosophers like Fazlur Rahman (1982). In fact, both Iqbal and Rahman go out of their way to stress the possibility of an historically and politically dynamic connection between reiterative forms of 'law' and the dynamic 'process' of *fiqh*. Indeed, both go on to emphasize the dynamic processes long embedded within the practice of *fiqh* itself, noting that, when push comes to shove, the terms of *fiqh* are really just an an historically embedded 'project' within which the content of Islamic law is, itself, historically and politically 'produced'.[8] In fact, both Iqbal and Rahman appear to suggest that, in the context of an 'Islamic democracy', the work undertaken by local *muftis* and that of Muslim MNAs may be reconcilable after all—each engaged in their own way with an historically and politically 'responsive' approach to the application of Islamic law.

This is, of course, an alternative approach with dramatic implications for the study of Islamic law and the possibility of an Islamic democracy. In fact, even apart from the work of Iqbal and Rahman, in Pakistan, this approach has been taken up and elaborated by scholars like Abdolkarim Soroush in Iran, Rashid Ghannouchi in Tunisia, and Mohammad Arkoun in Algeria—each of whom, it must be said, struggled to find consistent backing on a 'practical' level given the religious conservatism prevailing in their home countries. (Rahman devoted the latter half of his career to the University of Chicago; Soroush spent several years at Harvard, Princeton, and Yale; Ghannouchi lives in London; Arkoun is based in Paris.)

Still, each of these scholars has gone to great lengths to stress the ways in which the terms of Islamic law are, in fact, the terms of a dynamic living law. And, having done so, each has opened up new ways to link the underpinnings of this law to the possibility of a dynamic, flexible, responsive, and accountable Islamic democracy.

The work undertaken by scholars like Iqbal and Rahman is clearly devoted to a deeper understanding of the linkages between Islam, Islamic law, and the possibility of an Islamic democracy. But, even so, when it comes to the 'practice' of modern politics—for example, in the context of Pakistan—few would deny that their ideas have failed to flourish. In fact few would deny that, practically speaking, their ideas have simply failed.

Returning to the experience of the Punjab during the latter half of the twentieth century (1947–1999), for instance, every indication seems to suggest that the terms of Islamic law were not regarded as an historically and politically dynamic 'project'. Nor were they, drawing attention to the experience of countries like Indonesia or Turkey, set aside in favour of any more explicitly self-conscious 'secularism'. In fact, for all intents and purposes, both of these options were ignored. For more than fifty years, the language of *shari'ah*—indeed, *siyasa shari'ah*—was seen as politically indispensable and, yet, at the same time, historically inflexible, with dramatic implications (dramatic *negative* implications) for the practice of democracy as it actually took shape on the ground.

Throughout the Punjab, local landowners rushed to embrace entirely new forms of private (extralegal) informal political exchange, hoping to preserve the content of their own local 'customs' within a formal legal context increasingly defined by an inflexible understanding of *shari'ah*. Of course scholars like Bayat (2010) and Chatterjee (forthcoming) maintain that this pattern of private extralegal exchange was, in and of itself, an important indicator of 'democracy'. But, again, I disagree. In fact, precisely insofar as prevailing patterns of political interaction came to reflect a pattern strictly *set apart from* the reiterative negotiation of existing laws, I argue that these patterns became increasingly set apart from the *de jure* imperatives of 'democracy'.

The central argument of this book, in fact, is directly related to this point. Indeed, what does it mean to speak of 'democracy' when the terms of electoral 'accountability' and the circulation of elites are related, not to the amendment of existing laws, but rather to their politically irregular enforcement? Is there really any reason to insist upon a more definitive link between the terms of 'democracy' and the reiterative negotiation of existing *de jure* laws? The answer, I argue, is 'yes'. In fact, for those with an interest in the relationship between Islam, Islamic law, and the practice of an Islamic democracy, the question is simply this: How are the terms of Islamic law related to local expressions of political 'accountability'? And, then, moving on to address the practice of Muslim politics, how is this 'accountability' related to the reiterative re-negotiation of (statutory) Islamic laws?

ISLAM, ISLAMIC LAW, AND DEMOCRACY IN PAKISTAN AFTER 1999

When General Pervez Musharraf launched himself into power on 12 October 1999, just a few months before the Supreme Court of Pakistan published its landmark decision in the case of *Allah Rakha vs. Pakistan* (2000)—a decision that finally set the stage for a 'negotiated' approach to the terms of Islamic law (with such negotiations unfolding between the superior judiciary and the work of an elected legislature)—Musharraf and his advisors were keen to unveil several rather ambitious plans. In particular, they sought to follow in the footsteps of Musharraf's military predecessors, Ayub Khan and Zia-ul-Haq, with a fresh round of local (non-party) elections—elections that aimed to marginalize Pakistan's historically ignominious civilian leaders while, at the same time, looking for new ways to cultivate alternative forms of dynamic grassroots support.

Insisting that 'objective conditions' favoured 'the devolution of power to the people', Musharraf and his team of technocratic advisors in Islamabad set out to redefine the structure of local politics (beginning with an attempt to reconfigure the structure of the district-level administration). In fact, recalling some of the ideas articulated by Punjab Assembly Chief Minister Malik Firoz Khan Noon in 1953, Musharraf set out to separate the work of the district-level judiciary from that of the district-level executive. And, then, having done so, he sought to subordinate the work of the *executive* to the demands articulated by an entirely new batch of district and village-level *politicians*.

Of course many believed that Musharraf's Local Government Plan—initially drafted in Islamabad with the help of the World Bank, the United Nations, and the ADB before being refashioned as a series of provincial plans to allow for the fact that local government was still (constitutionally speaking) a 'provincial' subject—represented the most important assault on the district-level administration (and the structure of local politics) since, perhaps, the postcolonial shift to *shari'ah*. This was particularly true insofar as it sought to dismantle the office of the Deputy Commissioner while, at the same time, seeking to place the departments *within* the office of each Commissioner firmly under the control of an elected local *nazim* or 'mayor'. In fact, broadly speaking, Musharraf insisted that all of the executive departments previously managed by the DC—for example, departments related to the police and local *patwaris*—would henceforth be placed firmly within a framework of local 'electoral' control.[9]

Local Politics (Revisited)

The reach of Musharraf's Local Government Plan was significant. But, in many ways, its full impact did not lie in the success of its attack on the office of the Deputy Commissioner. On the contrary, the full impact of Musharraf's plan lay in the rather dramatic failure of that attack and, more specifically, its surprising failure to apprehend the many different ways in which the office of the DC was, in fact, already bound up with (and, in many ways, subordinated to) the work of local politicians.

If the Deputy Commissioner held the key to local patterns of administrative-cum-political continuity in the context of postcolonial Punjab, then Musharraf's plan (2000) might have been associated with the introduction of several rather striking changes. But, if the office of the DC did *not* hold the key to local patterns of continuity—indeed, if the primary source of postcolonial continuity lay in a spectacular array of legally 'exceptional' arrangements negotiated (informally) with local *patwaris*, local *panchayats*, and the postcolonial district courts (indeed, if the primary source of that continuity lay in a pattern whereby the work of local politicians was closely bound up with a series of 'exceptional' arrangements completely set apart from any push to re-engage the meaning of *siyasa shari'ah* in the context of the postcolonial legislature)—well, in that case, it would probably be very difficult to claim that Musharraf's attempt to privilege the work of local politicians was likely to produce any 'change' at all.

In fact within the space of just a few years the World Bank teamed up with the ADB to note that 'political rather than institutional relationships' were still the most important 'explanatory variables' when it came to prevailing expressions of district-level administrative practice.[10] And, in 2004, both the World Bank and the ADB went on to publish a detailed assessment of Musharraf's plan in collaboration with the British Department for International Development (DFID), adding that, more often than not, 'direct interference by [local mayors]' was still the key factor when it came to explaining the 'weak enforcement' of existing postcolonial laws.[11]

Political tensions at the local level, in other words, were still the key factor leading most local representatives to provide 'private rather than public goods' for reasons of political 'visibility' and 'patronage'.[12]

Siyasa Shari'ah (Revisited)

Needless to say, the transformation that Musharraf sought to introduce shortly after he seized power during the autumn of 1999 did not occur. Instead, Musharraf found that his regime was strongly resisted, not only by the exiled leaders of Pakistan's leading political parties, and, then, by the leadership of Pakistan's (post-*Allah Rakha*) Supreme Court, but also, and, perhaps, more importantly, by an increasingly aggressive congeries of ostensibly 'religious' insurgents.

In fact, as Musharraf's agenda unfolded, particularly after 9–11, Pakistan as a whole found itself trapped within what might be described as 'a clash of competing despotisms', with one side, following Musharraf and his allies in Islamabad, representing the custom-friendly status quo, and the other, associated with various elements of the Taliban, representing an increasingly violent commitment to the strategic reassertion of *shari'ah*.

For many years, this battle had been associated with the machinations of the 'Afghan' Taliban. But, as the twentieth century gave way to the twenty-first, this conflict could be found in the heart of Pakistan as well—first in Pakistan's Federally Administered Tribal Areas along the border with Afghanistan, then in the settled areas of Pakistan's North-west Frontier Province, and, finally, within the Punjab itself, for example, in Bahawalpur, Mianwali, Jhang, Sargodha, Sialkot, and Lahore.[13]

Both sides spoke of their enduring commitment to the resolution of local disputes. Both sought to monopolize the modalities of the modern state. And, of course, appealing to the religious sensibilities of their constituents, both sought to defend an exclusionary attachment to the postcolonial interpretation of *shari'ah*. In fact, precisely insofar as each sought to claim an exclusive attachment to the terms of *'siyasa' shari'ah*, this clash of inflexible despotisms came to reflect what might be described as a pattern of newfangled 'Islamist' opposition to the failures of an 'Islamic' state.[14]

Whereas Musharraf and the defenders of the status quo sought to provide their *patti*-based supporters with the reinforcement of a 'custom-friendly' protection racket, in other words, the Taliban rushed forward to construct a more explicitly 'religious' racket, shielding their supporters from targeted attacks on the legacy of the colonial regime: *patti*-based landowners, 'tribal' elites, and the institutions of the state that supported them.

CONCLUSION

As I have sought to explain, throughout the course of this book, Islam and democracy are neither compatible nor incompatible in any permanent or specific sense. They simply become more or less compatible owing to the historically embedded choices that individual Muslims make with reference to their understanding of the 'law'. Different ideas make for different outcomes. And, moving forward, social scientists must look for new ways to capture the microfoundational mechanisms that underlie this empirical fact.

In recent years, a number of assumptions regarding the 'ahistorical' quality of *shari'ah* have re-emerged as questions. And, increasingly, these questions have engendered a specific set of ongoing 'practical' dilemmas. But, as it was in 1865, so it is today: dilemmas frame new options, and these options come to be associated with exciting new 'debates'.

It may be too early to draw any specific conclusions regarding the outcome of these debates vis-à-vis the terms of Islam, Islamic law, and democracy in general. But, as time passes, for example, in the wake of *Allah Rakha* (2000), the potential for dramatic realignments cannot be dismissed out of hand. What does 'Islam' promote? What does *history* demand?

If in fact the formal (statutory) laws associated with the state of Pakistan are regarded as an historically embedded project, and, within this 'project', as an expression of some historically embedded 'reason' (including religious reason)—indeed, if the law itself is seen as historically and politically dynamic (an option that, I would argue, remains very much in keeping with the history of Islamic law both within and beyond the parameters of the modern state)—then, of course, the possibility of a 'democratic' understanding of Islamic law (and its enforcement) would appear to remain quite strong.

But of course this is not the only option. If the laws of Pakistan are seen as impervious to any form of interpretive intervention—indeed, if the law itself is seen as completely set apart from any attachment to the terms of human engagement (or history)—the prognosis for a 'democratic' understanding would appear to be considerably reduced.

On some occasions the terms of Islam, Islamic law, and democracy are compatible. But on other occasions, as I have sought to explain, with particular reference to the Punjab, they are not. This is not an appeal to notions of democracy *set apart from* the rule of law (following Chatterjee). It is, rather, an appeal to *engage* the law and, then, having done so, to 'practice' democracy within it.

APPENDIX

DATA COLLECTION IN THE DISTRICT COURTS

Within each district court (Lahore, Sialkot and Sargodha) my data collection procedure followed four steps. The first step involved an attempt to link the 'settlement' pattern within the district as a whole to the system of record keeping in the context of the district courts. In Lahore, there were three district courts: one for the City itself, one for the military Cantonment, and one for a special subdivision known as Model Town. (I confined my efforts to the City itself.) In Sialkot, there was just one district court, but that court served three *tehsils*. (Within each *tehsil* cases were arranged according to villages, and the numbers presented here were drawn from a random sample of those villages.) Sargodha, too, was arranged according to *tehsils* and villages but, unlike Sialkot, the villages came in two varieties, namely 'original' villages and '*chak* numbers'. ('Villages' existed before the first colonial settlement of the district, whereas '*chak* numbers' were created as canal colonies during the late-nineteenth and early-twentieth centuries—the former have names like 'Ram Rehan' and 'Rawal' while the latter have names specifying their location, for example, 'Chak No. 161 South Branch'.) In any case, after determining the relationship between the district, its *tehsils*, and the villages within each *tehsil*, I attempted to locate the total number of cases consigned to the record room of the district courts (that is, the *mohafiz khana*) from each village in a given year. This figure was maintained by the court registrar along with a monthly enumeration of several different types of cases (including civil cases, family cases, succession certificates, and so on).

The second step involved the 'registers' maintained by the staff of each record room. Using my detailed list of the villages in each local *tehsil*, a limited number of villages were selected at random. This sample was then used to locate a specific set of *goshwaras*, or 'case registers', for each village. These registers contained a complete list of every case originating in the village as a whole; in fact, in some cases, the *goshwara* listed every case filed in the village since the establishment of the civil court in the middle of the nineteenth century. In most cases, however, the *goshwara* listed every case filed since 1947.

The third step involved an attempt to select civil cases concerning landed property rights in each of my randomly selected villages. Recognizing that these cases might appear in many different forms, I selected my sample from among the five most common types of civil litigation, including cases regarding (a) *haq-e-shufa* (preemption), (b) *istaqrar-e-haq* (declaration of title), (c) *hukm imtanai* (permanent injunction), (d) *dakhliabi* (possession), and (e) *jan-nashini* (succession). This procedure indicated that more than 40 per cent of all of the civil cases listed in the *goshawaras* pertaining to my randomly selected villages were related to property rights and, within this group, *most concerned land*: 43 per cent in District Sialkot, 49 per cent in District Sargodha, and so on. (For details from District Sialkot, see Table 11 below.)

Many criminal cases and many family cases—including adoption, custody, and divorce cases—grow out of landed property disputes as

Table 11. *Goshwara*: total cases v. property cases (District Sialkot 1947–99)

	Total	*Property*	*Property (%)*	*Cases Read**
tehsil Sialkot				
Pindi Laddo	80	31	39%	Maradpur 27
Rangpura Mohalla	c. 2,890	1,433	50%	31
tehsil Daska				
Daska Kot	c. 9,105	3,650	40%	21
Mussalmania	67	29	43%	47
tehsil Pasrur				
Dhol	73	34	47%	Pasrur 10
Dhalim	29	16	55%	Etc. 43
Bhagiardi	113	67	59%	
TOTAL	12,357	5,260	43%	**179**

*See Step Four (below). Where villages listed in the *goshwara* could not be located in the stacks, others from the same district were used as substitutes.

well; in fact, as Alain Lefebvre (1999) pointed out, 'women, land, and the struggle for power are the three intermingled elements behind [every] conflict in the village'.[1] Nevertheless, I chose to ignore these criminal and family cases in favour of a specific focus on so-called 'civil' cases.

The fourth and final step involved the transition from the *goshwaras* to the files themselves. In Lahore, this transition was remarkably straightforward. Given the limited number of files in the record room following a devastating fire shortly before my research began, it was possible to locate almost all of the cases I had identified in the *goshwara*. In Sialkot, however, the situation was very different (see photo).

District Sialkot: case files in the district record room (*mohafiz khana*)

While it was possible, in many cases, to locate files from the selected villages, it was not always possible, given the chaotic nature of the stacks, to locate the same files identified in the original set of *goshwaras*. As a result, the selected villages were located in the stacks, and then a new bundle of files (from the village) was chosen at random. At this point, a second round of winnowing was undertaken to select landed property cases; fortunately, this process produced nearly identical results, with the files concerning landed property relations amounting to nearly 50 per cent of the total number of cases in each bundle. In Sargodha, the situation was mixed. Again, it was possible to locate files from most of the selected villages, but it was not always possible to find the same files that I had identified in the *goshwara*. Where specific files could not be located, therefore, alternatives were substituted once again.

Ultimately, this procedure allowed me to gather basic data concerning the frequency of various types of cases (Table 12) and more detailed information about the process of litigation itself (Chapter 5).

Table 12. Landed property litigation: distribution of case types
District Sargodha

	I*	II	III	IV	V	VI	VII
tehsil Sargodha							
106 N.B. (11)		5	4		2	2	1
tehsil Bhalwal							
Ram Rehan (15)	2	8	2	3		4	
Chak Miana (17)	3	2	5	1		5	1
2 S.B. (10)	2	2	1	1	1		3
tehsil Shahpur							
Rawal (18)	1	5	6	3	2	3	
tehsil Silanwali							
61 S.B. (18)		2	1		1	2	
tehsil Sahiwal							
Bhochra (17)	5	6	2			7	
Sajoka (16)	4	2	3	3		5	
TOTAL (104)	17 (16%)	30 (30)	23 (22)	11 (11)	5 (5)	26 (25)	5 (5)

*I = Preemption (*haq-e-shufa*); II Declaration (*istiqrar-e-haq*); III Permanent Injunction (*hukm imtanai*); IV Possession (*dakhliabi*); V Succession Certification (*jan-nashini*); VI Arbitration (*salsi*); VII Execution of Decree (*ajra-e-degree*).

BIBLIOGRAPHY

Introduction

Bowen, John R., 'The Role of Microhistories in Comparative Studies' in John R. Bowen and Roger Petersen, eds., *Critical Comparisons in Politics and Culture* (Cambridge University Press, 1999), pp. 230–40.

Chatterjee, Partha, *The Politics of the Governed: Reflections on Popular Politics in Most of the World* (New York: Columbia University Press, 2004).

Collingwood, R.G., *The Idea of History* (London: Oxford University Press, 1946).

Erving Goffmann, *The Presentatin of Self in Everyday Life* (New York: Anchor Books, 1959).

Guha, Ranajit, *Dominance Without Hegemony: History and Power in Colonial India* (Cambridge, MA: Harvard University Press, 1998).

Hall, Peter A., 'Aligning Ontology and Methodology in Comparative Politics', paper presented at the Annual Meeting of the American Political Science Association in Washington, DC, September 2000.

Hasan, Arif, *The Unplanned Revolution: Observations on the Process of Socioeconomic Change in Pakistan* (Karachi: City Press, 2002).

Martin, Rex, *Historical Explanation: Re-enactment and Practical Inference* (Ithaca: Cornell University Press, 1977).

Zuckerman, Alan S., 'Reformulating Explanatory Standards and Advancing Theory in Comparative Politics' in Mark Irving Lichbach and Alan S. Zuckerman, eds., *Comparative Politics: Rationality, Culture, and Structure* (Cambridge University Press, 1997), pp. 277–310.

Chapter 1

British Library (Oriental and India Office Collection): L/PJ/7/943; Neg 5109; ST1530/PR/3; V/23/355; V/27/67/33–34, 46–49, 144; V/27/134/21–26, 49; V/27/247/2; V/27/310/51–52; V/27/311/489; V/27/313/1–3, 5; V/27/314/546–1, 567–571, 619–621, 624–627; V/27/335/1950; V/27/343/2004.

Ali, Imran, *The Punjab under Imperialism, 1885–1947* (Karachi: Oxford University Press, 2003).

Anand, C.L., *Sir Shadi Lal's Commentaries on the Punjab Alienation of Land Act XIII (1900)*, 5th Ed. (Lahore: University Book Agency, 1947).

Baden-Powell, B.H., *A Manual of the Land Revenue Systems and Land Tenures of British India* (Calcutta: Superintendent of Government Printing, 1882).

———, *The Land Systems of British India* (Oxford: Clarendon Press, 1892).

Bayly, C.A., 'Maine and Change in Nineteenth-Century India' in Alan Diamond, ed., *The Victorian Achievement of Sir Henry Maine: A Centennial Reappraisal* (Cambridge University Press, 1991), pp. 389–98.

Buck, C.H., *The Mutation Work in the Punjab* (Lahore: University Book Agency, 1937).

Chakravarty-Kaul, Minoti, 'The Commons, Community, and the Courts in Colonial Punjab', *The Indian Economic and Social History Review* 29:4 (Delhi: Sage, 1992).

———, *Common Lands and Customary Law: Institutional Change in North India over the Past Two Centuries* (Delhi: Oxford University Press, 1996).

Charlesworth, Neil, 'The Origins of Fragmentation of Landholding in British India: A Comparative Examination' in Peter Robb, ed., *Rural India: Land, Power, and Society Under British Rule* (Delhi: Oxford University Press, 1983), pp. 182–216.

Cunningham, J.D., *History of the Sikhs, from the Origin of the Nation to the Battles of the Sutlej* (London: John Murray, 1849).

Darling, Malcolm L., *The Punjab Peasant in Prosperity and Debt* (Oxford University Press, 1925).

De Soto, Hernando, *The Mystery of Capital: Why Capitalism Triumphs in the West and Fails Everywhere Else* (New York: Basic Books, 2000).

Dewey, Clive, *The Settlement Literature of the Greater Punjab: A Handbook* (London: The Riverdale Company, 1991).

———, 'The Influence of Sir Henry Maine on Agrarian Policy in India' in Alan Diamond, ed., *The Victorian Achievement of Sir Henry Maine: A Centennial Reappraisal* (Cambridge University Press, 1991), pp. 353–75.

Douie, J.M., *Settlement Manual*, 5th edition (Lahore: Mutaqi, 1899).

Dumont, Louis, 'The "Village Community" from Munro to Maine' in *Contributions to Indian Sociology* 9 (Paris: Mouton, 1966), pp. 67–89.

Embree, Ainslee T., 'Landholding in India and British Institutions' in Robert Eric Frykenberg, ed., *Land Control and Social Structure in Indian History* (Madison: University of Wisconsin Press, 1969), pp. 33–52.

Guha, Ranajit, *A Rule of Property for Bengal: An Essay on the Idea of Permanent Settlement* (Paris: Mouton, 1963).

Hambly, G.R.G., 'Richard Temple and the Punjab Tenancy Act of 1868', *The English Historical Review*, Volume LXXIX, ed. Denys Hay (1964), pp. 47–66.

Handa, Ram Lal, *Monography No. 2: A History of the Development of the Judiciary in the Punjab (1846–1884)* (Lahore: Punjab Government Record Office, 1927).

Ibbetson, Sir Denzil, *Panjab Castes* (Lahore: Government Printing Press, 1883).

Kaghzat-i-zamin-i-punjab ke intizam ka ibtadai risala (Lahore: Rai Sahib M. Gulab Singh, 1934).

Kapur, Daya Krishna, *Monography No. 4: A History of the Development of the Judiciary in the Punjab (1884–1926)* (Lahore: Punjab Government Record Office, [1926]).

Kessinger, Tom G., 'Sources for the Social and Economic History of Rural Punjab' in W. Eric Gustafson and Kenneth W. Jones, eds., *Sources on Punjab History* (Delhi: Manohar Books, 1975), pp. 9–44.

———, 'Indian Village Records and Historical Village Studies: A Reply to C. Dewey, "Annals of Rural Punjab"', *Modern Asian Studies* 11:4 (1977), pp. 615–22.

Lal, Rai Sahib L. Bihari, *A Handbook of Land Revenue Administration in the Punjab* (Lahore Law Depot, 1943).

'The Land Revenue of Madras', *Calcutta Review* 17:34 (1852), p. 327.

Malcolm, Sir John, *Sketch of the Sikhs; A Singular Nation Who Inhabit the Provinces of the Penjab, Situated Between the Rivers Junma and Indus* (London: John Murray, 1812).

Thomas R. Metcalf, 'The Struggle Over Land Tenure in India, 1860–1868', *Journal of Asian Studies* 21:3 (1962), pp. 295–307.

Mirza, Mukarram, *Alienation and Mutation of Land* (Lahore: Pakistan Legal Publishers, 1994).

Rattigan, W.H. and Charles Boulnois, *Notes on Customary Law as Administered in the Courts of the Punjab* (London: W. Clowes, 1878).

Robb, Peter, 'Land and Society: The British "Transformation" in India' in Peter Robb, ed., *Rural India: Land, Power, and Society Under British Rule* (Delhi: Oxford University Press, 1992), pp. 1–23.

———, 'State, Peasant, and Moneylender in Late-Nineteenth-Century Bihar: Some Colonial Inputs' in Peter Robb, ed., *Rural India: Land, Power, and Society Under British Rule*, (Delhi: Oxford University Press, 1992), pp. 109–51.

Siddiqui, Kamal, *Land Management in South Asia: A Comparative Study* (Karachi: Oxford University Press, 1997).

Singh, Deva, *Monograph No. 7: Colonization in the Rechna Doab* (Lahore: Punjab Government Record Office, [1929]).

Saumerez-Smith, Richard, 'Rule-by-records and Rule-by-reports: Complementary Aspects of the British Imperial Rule of Law', *Contributions to Indian Sociology* 19:1 (1995), pp. 153–76.

———, *Rule By Records: Land Registration and Village Custom in Early British Punjab* (Delhi: Oxford University Press, 1996).

Stokes, Eric, *The English Utilitarians and India* (Delhi: Oxford University Press, 1959).

———, *The Peasant and the Raj: Studies in Agrarian Society and Peasant Rebellion in Colonial India* (Cambridge University Press, 1978).

Thomason, James, *Translation of a Proceeding Regarding the Settlement of a Village, According to the System Pursued in the North Western Provinces and the Presidency of Bengal* (Agra: Secudra Orphan, 1847).

Tupper, C.L., *Customary Law I-III* (Simla: Government of India, 1881).

Van den Dungen, P.H.M., *The Punjab Tradition: Influence and Authority in Nineteenth-Century India* (London: George Allen and Unwin, 1972).

Chapter 2

Acharyya, Bijay Kisor, *Codification in British India* (Calcutta: S.K. Banerji, 1914).

Agarwal, Bina, *A Field of One's Own: Gender and Land Rights in South Asia* (Cambridge University Press, 1994).

———, 'Widows versus Daughters or Widows as Daughters? Property, Land, and Economic Security in Rural India', *Modern Asian Studies* 32:1 (1998), pp. 1–48.

Ali, Hamid, *Custom and Law in Anglo-Muslim Jurisprudence* (Calcutta: Thacker and Spink, 1938).

Ali, Shaheen Sardar, 'A Critical Review of Family Laws in Pakistan: A Women's Perspective' in Rubya Mehdi and Farida Shaheed, eds., *Women's Law in Legal Education and Practice in Pakistan: North-South Co-operation* (Copenhagen: New Social Science, 1997), pp. 198–223.

Ali, Syed Ameer, *Student's Handbook of Mahommedan Law* (Calcutta: Thacker and Spink, 1925).

Anderson, Michael R., 'Islamic Law and the Colonial Encounter in British India' in David Arnold and Peter Robb, eds., *Institutions and Ideologies: A SOAS South Asia Reader* (London: Curzon, 1993), pp. 165–85.

Anonymous ('An Eminent Lawyer'), *Customary Law in the Punjab* (Lahore: Jalali Art, [1942]).

Carroll, Lucy, 'The Hanafi Law of Intestate Succession: A Simplified Approach', *Modern Asian Studies* 17:4 (1983), pp. 629–70.

———, 'The Ithna Ashari Law of Intestate Succession: An Introduction to Shia Law Applicable in South Asia', *Modern Asian Studies* 19:1 (1985), pp. 85–124.

———, 'Daughter's Right of Inheritance in India: A Perspective on the Problem of Dowry', *Modern Asian Studies* 25:4 (1991), pp. 791–809.

Cohn, Bernard S., 'Law and the Colonial State in India' in June Starr and Jane F. Collier, eds., *History and Power in the Study of Law: New Directions in Legal Anthropology* (Ithaca: Cornell University Press, 1989), pp. 131–52.

Colebrooke, H.T., *Daya Bhaga of Jimuta Vahana*, ed. Girish Chundra Turkalankar (Calcutta: Sreenauth Banarjee, 1868).

Coulson N.J., *Succession in the Muslim Family Law* (Cambridge University Press, 1971).

Derrett, J.D.M., 'Justice, Equity, and Good Conscience' in J.N.D. Anderson, ed., *Changing Law in Developing Countries* (London: George Allen and Unwin, 1963a), pp. 114–53.

———, *Introduction to Modern Hindu Law* (Oxford University Press, 1963b).

———, *Religion, Law, and the State in India* (London: Faber and Faber, 1968).

Durai, J. Chinna, *Hindu Law in a Nutshell* (London: Sweet and Maxwell, 1933).

Ellis, T.P., *A Judge's Notebook, Being a Compilation of Notes on Customary Law in the Punjab, Part I* (Lahore: Civil and Military Gazette, 1912).

Fox, Richard, 'Urban Class and Communal Consciousness in Colonial Punjab: The Genesis of India's Intermediate Regime', *Modern Asian Studies* 18:3 (1984), pp. 459–89.

Fyzee, Asaf A.A., *Cases in the Mohammadan Law of India and Pakistan* (Oxford: Clarendon Press, 1965).

Gilmartin, David, *Empire and Islam* (Berkeley: University of California Press, 1988a).

———, 'Customary Law and *Shari'at* in British Punjab' in Katherine P. Ewing, ed., *Shari'at and Ambiguity in South Asian Islam* (Berkeley: University of California Press, 1988b), pp. 43–62.

———, 'Divine Displeasure and Muslim Elections: The Shaping of Community in Twentieth-Century Punjab' in D.A. Low, ed., *The Political Inheritance of Pakistan* (London: Macmillan, 1991), pp. 106–29.

———, 'A Magnificent Gift: Muslim Nationalism and the Election Process in Colonial Punjab', *Comparative Studies in Society and History* 40:3 (1998), pp. 415–36.

Gordon, Richard, 'The Hindu Mahasabha and the Indian National Congress, 1915–1926', *Modern Asian Studies* 9:2 (1975), pp. 145–203.

Hamilton, Charles, *Hedaya* (London: S.C. Grady, 1870).

Jalal, Ayesha, *The Sole Spokesman: Jinnah, the Muslim League, and the Demand for Pakistan* (Cambridge University Press, 1985).

Jones, Kenneth W., *Arya Dharma: Hindu Consciousness in Nineteenth Century Punjab* (Delhi: Manohar, 1976).

Jones, William, *Al-Sirajiyyah, or The Mahomedan Law of Inheritance*, ed. Shama Churun Sircar (Calcutta: Sanskrit, 1792).

Kishwar, Madhu, 'Codified Hindu Law: Myth and Reality', *Economic and Political Weekly* (13 August 1994), pp. 2145–61.

Lateef, Shahida, *Muslim Women in India: Political and Private Realities, 1890s-1980s* (London: Zed Books, 1990).

Lodhi, A.A.K., *Customary Law of the Punjab* (Lahore: The Caravan Book House, 1963).

Low, D.A., 'Introduction: Provincial Histories and the History of Pakistan' in D.A. Low, ed., *The Political Inheritance of Pakistan* (London: Macmillan, 1991), pp. 1–28.
Macnaghten, W.H., *Principles of Moohummudan Law*, ed. Shama Churun Sircar (Calcutta: Brahma Samaj, 1825).
Malik, Iftikhar, 'Identity Formation and Muslim Party Politics in the Punjab, 1897–1936: A Retrospective Analysis', *Modern Asian Studies* 29:2 (1995), pp. 293–323.
Mulla, D.F., *Principles of Mahomedan Law*, ed. M.A. Mannan (Lahore: P.L.D., 1995).
Norton, John Bruce, *A Selection of Leading Cases on the Hindu Law of Inheritance* (Madras: C. D'Cruz, 1871).
Pandey, Deepak, 'Congress-Muslim League Relations, 1937–1939: "The Parting of the Ways"', *Modern Asian Studies* 12:4 (1978), pp. 629–54.
Parashar, Archana, *Women and Family Law Reform in India: Uniform Civil Code and Gender Equality* (Delhi: Sage, 1992).
Prinsep, Henry Thoby, *History of the Punjab and of the Rise, Progress, and Present Condition of the Sect and Nation of the Sikhs* (London: W.H. Allen, 1846).
Qureshi, Badr-ud-din, *The Punjab Custom*, ed. Malik Ram Lal Anand (Lahore: University Book Agency, 1932).
Rattigan, W.H., *A Digest of Civil Law for the Punjab (Chiefly Based on the Customary Law)* (Lahore: University Book Agency, 1881).
———, 'The Possibilities of Codification in India', *The Law Quarterly Review* 14:56 (1898), pp. 367–78.
Roe, Charles A. and H.A.B. Rattigan, *Tribal Law in the Punjab, So Far As It Relates to Right in Ancestral Land* (Lahore: Civil and Military Gazette Press, 1895).
Rose, H.A., *A Compendium of the Punjab Customary Law*, 2nd Ed. (Lahore: Civil and Military Gazette, 1911).
Rosenthal, Erwin I.J., *Islam in the Modern National State* (Cambridge University Press, 1965).
Roy, Sripati, *Customs and Customary Law in British India* (Calcutta: Hare, 1911).
Saiyid, Dushka, *Muslim Women of the British Punjab: From Seclusion to Politics* (London: Macmillan, 1998).
Saksena, Kashi Prasad, *Muslim Law as Administered in British India* (Allahabad: Rai Sahib Ram Dayal Agarwala, 1938).
Scott, James, *Seeing Like a State: How Certain Schemes to Improve the Human Condition Have Failed* (New Haven: Yale University Press, 1998).
Select Cases in Hindu Law, Volume 2, ed. W.H. Rattigan (Lahore: Lawrence, 1871).
Sircar, Shama Churun, *The Muhammadan Law: A Digest of the Sunni Code in Part and of the Imamiyah Code* (Calcutta: Thacker and Spink, 1875).

Talbot, Ian, 'The 1946 Punjab Elections', *Modern Asian Studies* 14:1 (1980), pp. 65–91.

———, 'Muslim Political Mobilization in Rural Punjab, 1937–1946' in Peter Robb, ed., *Rural India: Land, Power, and Society Under British Rule* (Delhi: Oxford University Press, 1983), pp. 243–72.

———, *Provincial Politics and the Pakistan Movement: The Growth of the Muslim League in North-west and North-east India, 1937–1947* (Oxford University Press, 1988).

———, 'The Unionist Party and Punjabi Politics, 1937–1941' in D.A. Low, *The Political Inheritance of Pakistan* (London: Macmillan, 1991), pp. 86–105.

———, *Khizr Tiwana: The Punjab Unionist Party and the Partition of India* (London: Curzon Press, 1996).

Tuteja, K.L. and O. Grewal, 'Emergence of Hindu Communal Ideology in Early Twentieth Century Punjab', *Social Scientist* 20:7–8 (1992), pp. 3–28.

Chapter 3

Alam, Sardar Fakhre, Rashid Aziz Khan, and Hamid Ali Mirza, *General Elections Report, Volumes 1–2* (Islamabad: Government of Pakistan, 1997).

Ali, Christine Amjad and Charles Amjad Ali, *The Legislative History of the Shariah Act* (Rawalpindi: Christian Study Centre, 1992).

Dewey, Clive, 'The Rural Roots of Pakistani Militarism' in D.A. Low, ed., *The Political Inheritance of Pakistan* (New York: St. Martin's, 1991).

'Devolution in Pakistan: Reform or Regression?' (Islamabad and Brussels: International Crisis Group, 22 March 2004).

Jahan, Rounaq, *Pakistan: Failure in National Integration* (New York: Columbia University Press, 1972).

Jalal, Ayesha, *The State of Martial Rule: The Origins of Pakistan's Political Economy of Defence* (Cambridge University Press, 1990).

Kennedy, Charles H., 'Repugnancy to Islam: Who Decides? Islam and Legal Reform in Pakistan', *International and Comparative Law Quarterly* 41:4 (1992), pp. 769–87.

Mahmood, Shafqat, *Devolving the State: A Model for Empowering the People* (Lahore: Government of the Punjab, 2000).

Milam, William B., *Bangladesh and Pakistan: Flirting with Failure in South Asia* (London: Hurst & Co., 2010).

Report of the Court of Inquiry Constituted Under Punjab Act II of 1954 to Inquire into the Punjab Disturbances of 1953 (a.k.a. 'The Munir Report') (Lahore: Superintendent, Government Printing, 1954).

Sisson, Richard and Leo E. Rose, *War and Secession: Pakistan, India, and the Creation of Bangladesh* (Berkeley: University of California Press, 1990).

Syed, Anwar H., 'Factional Conflict in the Punjab Muslim League, 1947–1955', *Polity* 22:1 (1989), pp. 49–73.

Talbot, Ian, *Pakistan: A Modern History* (London: Hurst & Co., 2005).
Wilder, Andrew, 'Islam and Political Legitimacy in Pakistan' in Muhammad Aslam Syed, ed., *Islam and Democracy in Pakistan* (Islamabad: National Institute of Historical and Cultural Research, 1995), pp. 31–88.
Yusuf, Hamid, *Pakistan: A Study of Political Developments, 1947–1997* (Lahore: Sang-e-Meel, 1999).
Ziring, Lawrence, *Bangladesh: From Mujib to Ershad* (Karachi: Oxford University Press, 1992).

Chapter 4

Government Publications

Annual Report of the Proceedings of the Advisory Council of Islamic Ideology (Islamabad: Council of Islamic Ideology, Government of Pakistan, 1964, 1965, 1966, 1967).
Constitution-Making in Pakistan (Islamabad: National Assembly, Government of Pakistan, 1973).
Draft Law of Preemption (Islamabad: Council of Islamic Ideology, 1981).
Final Report on Examination of Laws (Islamabad: Council of Islamic Ideology, 1973).
First Five-Year Plan: 1955–1960 (Karachi: National Planning Board (Government of Pakistan), 1957). [Partially reproduced in Naqvi, *Land Reforms in Pakistan: A Historical Perspective* (Islamabad: Pakistan Institute of Development Economics, 1987).]
Injunctions of Islam (Islamabad: Council of Islamic Ideology, 1989).
Rehman, Tanzil-ur, *Implementation of Shariah in Pakistan* (Islamabad: Council of Islamic Ideology, 1982).
Report of the Agrarian Reforms Committee of the Pakistan Muslim League (Karachi: Pakistan Muslim League, 1949). [Partially reproduced in Naqvi (1987).]
Report of the Commission on Marriage and Family Laws (Islamabad: Law Division, Government of Pakistan, 1963).
Report of the Committee on Revitalization of the Revenue Administration (Islamabad: Government of Pakistan, 1978). [Partially reproduced in M. Ehsan-ul-Haq, 'Paper on Revitalization of Revenue Administration' (Lahore: National Institute of Public Administration, 1991).]
Report of the Government Hari Enquiry Committee 1947–1948 (Karachi: Government of Sind). [Partially reproduced in Naqvi (1987).]
Report of the Land Reforms Commission for West Pakistan (Lahore: Pakistan Land Reforms Commission, Government of Pakistan, 1959). [Partially reproduced in Naqvi (1987).]
Report of the Pakistan Commission on the Status of Women (Islamabad: Women's Division, Government of Pakistan, 1983).
Report of the Pakistan Women's Rights Committee (Islamabad: Law Division Government of Pakistan, 1976).

Report of the Special Committee of the Federal Council on the Form and System of Government in Pakistan from an Islamic Point of View (Islamabad: Federal Council Government of Pakistan, 1983).
'Subject: Separation of [the] Judiciary from the Executive', Files of the Additional Secretary Home and Judicial (Lahore: Government of the Punjab, n.d. [1994]), pp. 92–4, 223–41.
Zia, Shehla, Hina Jilani, and Asma Jahangir, *Muslim Laws and Their Implementation in Pakistan* (Islamabad: Women's Division, Government of Pakistan, 1984).

Books and Articles

Agarwal, Bina, 'Disinherited Peasants, Disadvantaged Workers: A Gender Perspective on Land and Livelihood', *Economic and Political Weekly* (28 March 1998), pp. A-2—A-14.
Ahmad, Khurshid, ed., *Studies in the Family Law of Islam* (Karachi: Chiragh-e-Rah, 1961).
Ahmad, Saghir, *Class and Power in a Punjabi Village* (New York: Monthly Review, 1977).
Ahmed, Khurshid, *Marriage Commission Report X-Rayed: A Study of the Family Law of Islam and a Critical Appraisal of the Modernist Attempts to 'Reform' It* (Karachi: Chiragh-e-Rah, 1959).
Ahmed, Viqar and Rashid Amjad, *The Management of Pakistan's Economy 1947–1982* (Karachi: Oxford University Press, 1984).
Alavi, Hamza, 'The Two Biraderies: Kinship in Rural West Pakistan' in T.N. Madan, ed., *Muslim Communities of South Asia* (Delhi: Manohar Books, 1995), pp. 1–62.
Anderson, J.N.D., 'Modern Trends in Islam: Legal Reform and Modernization in the Middle East', *International and Comparative Law Quarterly* 20:1 (1971), pp. 1–21.
Aslam, A.H., *The Deputy Commissioner: A Study in Public Administration* (Lahore: Punjab, 1957).
Balchin, Cassandra, ed., *Women, Law, and Society: An Action Manual for NGOs* (Lahore: Shirkat Gah, 1996).
Burki, Shahid Javed, 'Economic Management Within an Islamic Context' in Anita M. Weiss, ed., *Islamic Reassertion in Pakistan: The Application of Islamic Laws in a Modern State* (Syracuse University Press, 1986), pp. 49–58.
Cambridge University Asian Expedition, *The Bodhopur Report: A Study of the Forces of Tradition and Change in a Punjabi Village in the Gujranwala District, West Pakistan* (Lahore: Social Sciences Research Centre, 1962).
Coulson, N.J., 'Islamic Family Law: Progress in Pakistan' in J.N.D. Anderson, ed., *Changing Law in Developing Countries* (London: George Allen and Unwin, 1963), pp. 240–57.
Donohue, John J. and John L. Esposito, eds., *Islam in Transition: Muslim Perspectives*, (Oxford University Press, 1982).

Eglar, Zekiye, *A Punjabi Village in Pakistan* (New York: Columbia University Press, 1960).

Farani, Mohammad, *Manual of Family Laws in Pakistan* (Lahore: Lahore Law Times, 1997).

Feruki, Kemal, *Islamic Family Law in Pakistan* (Karachi: Government of Pakistan, 1964).

———, 'Pakistan: Islamic Government and Society' in John L. Esposito, ed., *Islam in Asia: Religion, Politics, and Society* (New York: Oxford University Press, 1987).

Gilani, Riaz-ul-Hasan, 'A Note on Islamic Family Law and Islamization in Pakistan' in Chibli, Mallat and Jane Connors, eds., *Islamic Family Law* (London: Graham and Trotman, 1990), pp. 339–46.

Haider, S.M., *Expanding Role of Patwaris in Revenue Administration* (Peshawar: Pakistan Academy for Rural Development, 1966).

Herring, Ronald, *Land to the Tiller: The Political Economy of Agrarian Reform in South Asia* (New Haven: Yale University Press, 1983).

Huntington, Samuel, *Political Order in Changing Societies* (New Haven: Yale University Press, 1968).

Hussain, Aftab, *Status of Women in Islam* (Lahore: Law Publishing Company, 1987).

Iqbal, Mohammad, *The Reconstruction of Religious Thought in Islam* (Oxford University Press, 1934).

Khalid, A.K., *The Agrarian History of Pakistan* (Lahore: Allied Books, 1998).

Khan, Hamid, *Islamic Law of Inheritance: A Comparative Study with Emphasis on Contemporary Problems* (Lahore: Law Times Publications, 1980).

Khan, Imdad Ali, *Rural Social Structure and Returning Councillors: A Pilot Study* (Peshawar: Pakistan Academy for Rural Development, 1989).

Kurin, Richard, 'Islamization: A View from the Countryside' in Anita M. Weiss, ed., *Islamic Reassertion in Pakistan: The Application of Islamic Laws in a Modern State* (Syracuse University Press, 1986), pp. 129–40.

Masihuzzaman, 'Separation of the Executive from the Judiciary at the District Level' in S.M. Haider, ed., *Public Administration and Police in Pakistan* (Peshawar: Pakistan Academy for Rural Development, 1961), pp. 11–28.

Mayer, Ann Elizabeth, 'Islamization and Taxation in Pakistan' in Anita M. Weiss, ed., *Islamic Reassertion in Pakistan: The Application of Islamic Laws in a Modern State* (Syracuse University Press, 1986), pp. 59–77.

Mehdi, Rubya, *The Islamization of the Law in Pakistan* (London: Curzon, 1994).

Metcalf, Barbara D., 'Islamic Arguments in Contemporary Pakistan' in William R. Roff, ed., *Islam and the Political Economy of Meaning: Comparative Studies of Muslim Discourse* (London: Croom Helm, 1987), pp. 132–59.

Naqvi, Syed Nawab Haider, Mahmood Hasan Khan and M. Ghaffar Chaudhry, eds., *Land Reforms in Pakistan: A Historical Perspective* (Islamabad: Pakistan Institute of Development Economics, 1987).

Nelson, Matthew J., 'Inheritance Unbound: The Politics of Personal Law Reform in Pakistan and India' in Sunil Khilnani, Vikram Raghavan, and Arun Thiruvengadam, eds., *Comparative Constitutionalism in South Asia* (Delhi: Oxford University Press, forthcoming).

North, Douglass C., *Institutions, Institutional Change, and Economic Performance* (Cambridge University Press, 1990).

Pal, Izzuddin, *Pakistan, Islam, and Economics: Failure of Modernity* (Karachi: Oxford University Press, 1999).

Powers, David S., 'Introduction: The Islamic Inheritance System', *Islamic Law and Society* 5:3 (1998), pp. 285–90.

Rana, Shaukat Ali, Zahur Iqbal Khan, Mohammad Arshad, Agha Sarwar Raza Qazilbash and Shaukat Ali Khawaja, 'Agriculture Income Tax: Syndicate Report (Syndicate C)' (Lahore: National Institute of Public Administration, 1997).

Scott, James, 'Resistance without Protest and without Organization: Peasant Opposition to the Islamic Zakat and the Christian Tithe', *Comparative Studies in Society and History* 29:3 (1987), pp. 417–52.

Shaheed, Farida, 'The Interface of Culture, Customs, and Law: Implications for Women and Activism' in Rubya Mehdi and Farida Shaheed, eds., *Women's Law in Legal Education and Practice in Pakistan: North-South Cooperation* (Copenhagen: New Social Science, 1997).

Siddiqui, Kamal, *Land Management in South Asia: A Comparative Study* (Karachi: Oxford University Press, 1997).

Rahman, Tanzil-ur, *Majmua-e-Qawanin-e-Islami* (Karachi: Markaz Idara-e-Tahqiqat Islami, 1988).

Waheed, Zuhra, *Contacts Between Villagers and Public Officials in Three Villages of Lyallpur Tehsil* (Lahore: Pakistan Administrative Staff College, 1964).

Weiss, Anita, 'Women's Position in Pakistan: Sociocultural Effects of Islamization', *Asian Survey* 25:8 (1985), pp. 863–80.

Wilder, Andrew R., *The Pakistani Voter: Electoral Politics and Voting Behaviour in the Punjab* (Karachi: Oxford University Press, 1999).

Zaidi, S. Akbar, 'Pakistan: Crisis of Governance', *Economic and Political Weekly* (14 March 1998), pp. 572–3.

Chapter 5

Baird, Douglas G., Robert H. Gertner and Rundel C. Picker, *Game Theory and the Law* (Cambridge: Harvard University Press, 1994).

Bates, Robert H., Rui J.P. de Figueiredo, Jr. and Barry R. Weingast, 'The Politics of Interpretation: Rationality, Culture, and Transition', *Politics and Society* 26:4 (1998), pp. 603–42.

Bevir, Mark, 'A Decentered Theory of Governance: Rational Choice, Institutionalism, and Interpretive Theory' (Berkeley: University of California,

Department of Political Science, unpublished, 2001). <http://igs.berkeley.edu/publications/working_papers/WP 2001–10.pdf>
Carroll, Lucy, 'Life Interests and Inter-Generational Transfer of Property: Avoiding the Law of Succession', *Islamic Law and Society* 8:2 (2001), pp. 245–86.
Chatterjee, Partha, 'Democracy and Economic Transformation in India', *Economic and Political Weekly* (19 April 2008), pp. 53–62.
———, *Lineages of Political Society* (New York: Columbia University Press, forthcoming), Chapter 1.
Chaudhary, Mohammad Azim, *Justice in Practice: Legal Ethnography of a Punjabi Village* (Karachi: Oxford University Press, 1999).
Cohn, Bernard S., 'Anthropological Notes on Law and Disputes in North India' in *An Anthropologist Among the Historians and Other Essays* (Delhi: Oxford University Press, 1987), pp. 575–631.
Galanter, Marc, 'Why the "Haves" Come Out Ahead: Speculations on the Limits of Legal Change', *Law and Society Review* 9:95 (1974), pp. 95–160.
——— and Mia Cahill, '"Most Cases Settle": Judicial Promotion and Regulation of Settlements', *Stanford Law Review* 46:6 (1994), pp. 1339–91.
———, 'Contract in Court; Or Almost Everything You May or May Not Want to Know About Contract Litigation', *Wisconsin Law Review* (2001), pp. 577–627.
Hansen, Thomas Blom, *Violence in Urban India: Identity Politics, 'Mumbai', and the Postcolonial City* (Princeton University Press, 2001).
Hoebel, E. Adamson, 'Fundamental Cultural Postulates and Judicial Lawmaking in Pakistan', *American Anthropologist* 67:6(2) (1965), pp. 43–56.
Humayun, Muhammad, *Land Disputes and Rural Development* (Peshawar: Pakistan Academy for Rural Development, 1992).
'Inception Report: Legal and Judicial Reform Project' (Islamabad: The Asia Foundation, 1998).
'Integrated Report: Part Five (Sociolegal Study)', *TA3015 Pakistan Legal and Judicial Reform Project Final Report* (Islamabad: The Asia Foundation, 1999).
Kritzer, Herbert M., 'Adjudication to Settlement: Shading in the Gray', *Judicature* 70:161 (1986), pp. 161–5.
Lefebvre, Alain, *Kinship, Honour, and Money in Rural Pakistan: Subsistence Economy and the Effects of International Migration* (London: Curzon, 1999).
Lyon, Stephen M., 'Local Arbitration and Conflict Deferment in Punjab, Pakistan', *Anthropologie* 40:1 (2002), pp. 59–71.
'Pakistan 2000: Reforming the Judicial System' (Islamabad: Government of Pakistan, 1997).
Sejersted, Francis, 'Democracy and the Rule of Law: Some Historical Experiences of Contradictions in the Striving for Good Government' in Jon Elster and Rune Slagsted, eds., *Constitutionalism and Democracy* (Cambridge University Press, 1988), pp. 131–52.

Sharma, Miriam, *The Politics of Inequality: Competition and Control in an Indian Village* (Honolulu: University of Hawaii Press, 1978).

Chapter 6

Abbott, Andrew, 'Conceptions of Time and Events in Social Science Methods: Causal and Narrative Approaches', *Historical Methods* 23:3 (1990), pp. 140–50.

Bates, Robert H., *Analytic Narratives* (Princeton University Press, 1998).

———, Avner Greif, Margaret Levi, Jean-Laurent Rosenthal and Barry Weingast, 'The Analytic Narrative Project', *American Political Science Review* 94:3 (2000), pp. 696–702.

Bearman, Peter, Robert Faris, and James Moody, 'Blocking the Future: New Solutions for Old Problems in Historical Social Science', *Social Science History* 23:4 (1999), pp. 501–33.

Becker, Howard S., 'Cases, Causes, Conjunctures, Stories, and Imagery' in Charles C. Ragin and Howard S. Becker, eds., *What Is a Case? Exploring the Foundations of Social Inquiry* (Cambridge University Press, 1992), pp. 205–16.

Bonnell, Victoria E., 'The Uses of Theory, Concepts, and Comparison in Historical Sociology', *Comparative Studies in Society and History* 22:2 (1980), pp. 156–73.

Bowen, John R. and Roger Peterson, 'Introduction', in John R. Bowen and Roger Petersen, eds., *Critical Comparisons in Politics and Culture* (Cambridge University Press, 1999), pp. 1–20.

Büthe, Tim, 'Taking Temporality Seriously: Modeling History and the Use of Narratives as Evidence', *American Political Science Review* 96:3 (2003), pp. 481–93.

Calhoun, Craig, 'Explanation in Historical Sociology: Narrative, General Theory, and Historically Specific Theory', *American Journal of Sociology* 104:3 (1998), pp. 846–71.

Carroll, Lucy, 'Orphaned Grandchildren in the Islamic Law of Succession: Reform and Islamization in Pakistan', *Islamic Law and Society* 5:3 (1998), pp. 409–47.

———, 'The Pakistan Federal Shariat Court, Section 4 of the Muslim Family Laws Ordinance, and the Orphaned Grandchild', *Islamic Law and Society*, 9:1 (2002), pp. 78, 80–1.

Chakrabarty, Dipesh, *Provincializing Europe: Postcolonial Thought and Historical Difference* (Princeton University Press, 2000).

Cohn, Bernard S., 'Comments on Papers on Land Tenure', *The Indian Economic and Society History Review* 1:2 (1963), pp. 177–83.

———, 'History and Anthropology: The State of Play' and 'Anthropology and History in the 1980s: Toward a Rapprochement' in *An Anthropologist Among the Historians and Other Essays* (Delhi: Oxford University Press, 1996), pp. 18–49, 50–77.

Dessler, David and John Owen, 'Constructivism and the Problem of Explanation: A Review Article', *Perspectives on Politics* 3:3 (2005), pp. 597–610.

Elster, Jon, *Nuts and Bolts for the Social Sciences* (Cambridge University Press, 1989).

———, *Alchemies of the Mind* (Cambridge University Press, 1999).

———, 'Rational Choice History: A Case of Excessive Ambition', *American Political Science Review* 94:3 (2000), pp. 685–95.

Ferejohn, John, 'Rationality and Interpretation: Parliamentary Elections in Early Stuart England' in Kristen Renwick Monroe, ed., *The Economic Approach to Politics* (New York: HarperCollins, 1991), pp. 279–305.

Friedman, Jeffrey, 'Accounting for Political Preferences: Cultural Theory vs. Cultural History', *Critical Review* 5:3 (1991), pp. 325–51.

Geertz, Clifford, *Negara: The Theatre State in Nineteenth-Century Bali* (Princeton University Press, 1981).

Goldstone, Jack, 'Initial Conditions, General Laws, Path Dependence, and Explanation in Historical Sociology', *American Journal of Sociology* 104:3 (1998), pp. 829–45.

Gondhalekar, Nandini and Sanjoy Bhattacharya, 'The All-India Hindu Mahasabha and the End of British Rule in India, 1939–1947', *Social Scientist* 27:7–8 (1999), pp. 48–74.

Green, Donald and Ian Shapiro, *The Pathologies of Rational Choice: A Critique of Applications in Political Science* (New Haven: Yale University Press, 1994).

Greif, Avner, 'Cultural Beliefs and the Organization of Society: Historical and Theoretical Reflections on Collectivist and Individualist Societies', *Journal of Political Economy* 102:5 (1994), pp. 912–50.

Hasan, Mushirul, 'The Muslim Mass Contact Campaign: An Attempt at Political Mobilization', *Economic and Political Weekly* 21:52 (1986), pp. 2273–5, 2277–82.

Hedström, Peter and Richard Swedberg, 'Social Mechanisms', *Acta Sociologica* 39:3 (1996), pp. 281–308.

Herring, Ronald, 'Review of Amrita Basu and Atul Kohli, *Community Conflicts and the State in India* (Oxford 1998) and Ashutosh Varshney, *Democracy, Development, and the Countryside: Urban-Rural Struggles in India* (Cambridge 1995)', *American Political Science Review* 94:4 (2000), pp. 958–60.

Jalal, Ayesha, 'Nation, Reason, and Religion: Punjab's Role in the Partition of India', *Economic and Political Weekly* 33:32 (1998), pp. 2183–90.

Katznelson, Ira, 'Structure and Configuration in Comparative Politics' in Mark Irving Lichbach and Alan S. Zuckerman, eds., *Comparative Politics: Rationality, Culture, and Structure* (Cambridge University Press, 1997), pp. 81–112.

———, 'Periodization and Preferences: Reflections on Purposive Action in Comparative Historical Social Science', in James Mahoney and Dietrich Rueschemeyer, eds., *Comparative Historical Analysis in the Social Sciences* (Cambridge University Press, 2003), pp. 270–301.

Kaviraj, Sudipta, 'Modernity and Politics in India', *Daedalus* 129:1 (2000) pp. 137–62.

Khan, Foqia Sadiq and Shahrukh Rafi Khan, 'A Benchmark Study on Law and Order and the Dispensation of Justice in the Context of Power Devolution' (Islamabad: United Nations Development Programme, 2003).

Kiser, Edgar and Michael Hechter, 'The Role of General Theory in Comparative Historical Sociology', *American Journal of Sociology* 97 (1991), pp. 1–30.

Kohli, Atul, Peter Evans, Peter J. Katzenstein, Adam Przeworski, Susanne H. Rudolph, James C. Scott and Theda Sckocpol, 'The Role of Theory in Comparative Politics: A Symposium', *World Politics* 48:1 (1995), pp. 1–49.

Laitin, David, 'Political Culture and Political Preferences', *American Political Science Review* 81:1 (1997), pp. 589–93.

Levi, Margaret, 'A Model, a Method, and a Map: Rational Choice in Comparative and Historical Analysis' in Mark Irving Lichbach and Alan S. Zuckerman, eds., *Comparative Politics: Rationality, Culture, and Structure* (Cambridge University Press, 1997), pp. 19–41.

———, 'Producing an Analytic Narrative' in John Bowen and Roger Petersen, eds., *Critical Comparisons in Politics and Culture* (Cambridge University Press, 1999), pp. 152–72.

Lichbach, Mark Irving, 'Social Theory and Comparative Politics' in Mark Irving Lichbach and Alan S. Zuckerman, eds., *Comparative Politics: Rationality, Culture and Structure* (Cambridge University Press, 1997), pp. 239–76.

Lustick, Ian, 'History, Historiography, and Political Science: Multiple Historical Records and the Problem of Selection Bias', *American Political Science Review* 90:3 (1996), pp. 605–18.

MacDonald, Paul K., 'Useful Fiction or Miracle Maker: The Competing Epistemological Foundations of Rational Choice Theory', *American Political Science Review* 97:4 (2003), pp. 551–65.

Mahoney, James, 'Path Dependence in Historical Sociology', *Theory and Society*, 29:4 (2000), pp. 507–48.

———, 'Revisiting General Theory in Historical Sociology', *Social Forces* 83:2 (2004), pp. 459–89.

Mandelbaum, Maurice, *The Anatomy of Historical Understanding* (Baltimore: Johns Hopkins University Press, 1977).

Matthai, John, *Village Government in British India* (London: J. Fisher, 1915).

Mohr, Lawrence, *The Causes of Human Behavior: Implications for Theory and Method in the Social Sciences* (Ann Arbor: University of Michigan Press, 1996).

Moore, Barrington, Jr., *Social Origins of Dictatorship and Democracy: Lord and Peasant in the Making of the Modern World* (Boston: Beacon Press, 1966).

Norman, Andrew P., 'Telling It Like It Was: Historical Narratives on Their Own Terms', *History and Theory: Studies in the Philosophy of History* 30:2 (1991), pp. 119–35.

Petersen, Roger, 'Mechanisms and Structures in Comparisons' in John R. Bowen and Roger Petersen, eds., *Critical Comparisons in Politics and Culture* (Cambridge University Press, 1999), pp. 61–77.
Porter, Dale H., *The Emergence of the Past: A Theory of Historical Explanation* (University of Chicago Press, 1981).
Quadagno, Jill and Stan J. Knapp, 'Have Historical Sociologists Forsaken Theory? Thoughts on the History-Theory Relationship', *Sociological Methods and Research* 20:4 (1992), pp. 481–507.
Ragin, Charles C., '"Casing" and the Process of Social Inquiry' in Charles C. Ragin and Howard S. Becker, eds., *What is a Case? Exploring the Foundations of Social Inquiry* (Cambridge University Press), pp. 217–26.
Roy, Beth, *Some Trouble With Cows: Making Sense of Social Conflict* (Berkeley: University of California Press, 1994).
Rudolph, Susanne Hoeber, 'The Imperialism of Categories: Situating Knowledge in a Globalizing World', *Perspectives on Politics* 3:1 (2005), pp. 5–14.
Sahlins, Marshall, 'Cosmologies of Capitalism: The Trans-Pacific Sector of the World System' in Nicholas Dirks, Geoff Eley and Sherry B. Ortner, eds., *Culture/Power/History: A Reader in Contemporary Social Theory* (Princeton University Press, 1993), pp. 412–55.
Sarkar, Sumit, *Writing Social History* (Delhi: Oxford University Press, 1997).
Stein, Burton, 'Notes on "Peasant Insurgency" in Colonial Mysore: Event and Process' in David Arnold and Peter Robb, eds., *Institutions and Ideologies: A SOAS South Asia Reader* (London: Curzon, 1993), pp. 186–200.
Stryker, Robin, 'Beyond History Versus Theory: Strategic Narrative and Sociological Explanation', *Sociological Methods and Research* 24:3 (1996), pp. 304–52.
Thelen, Kathleen and Sven Steinmo, 'Historical Institutionalism in Comparative Politics' in Sven Steinmo, Kathleen Thelen and Frank Longstreth, eds., *Structuring Politics: Historical Institutionalism in Comparative Perspective* (Cambridge University Press, 1992), pp. 1–32.
——— and Richard Locke, 'Apples and Oranges Revisited: Contextualized Comparisons and the Study of Comparative Labor Politics', *Politics and Society* 23:3 (1995), pp. 337–67.
———, 'Historical Institutionalism in Comparative Politics', *The Annual Review of Political* Science, Volume 2 (Palo Alto: Annual Reviews, 1999), pp. 369–404.
Varshney, Ashutosh, 'Nationalism, Ethnic Conflict, and Rationality', *Perspectives on Politics* 1:1 (2003).
Wildavsky, Aaron, 'Choosing Preferences by Constructing Institutions: A Cultural Theory of Preference Formation', *American Political Science Review* 81:1 (1987), pp. 3–21.
———, 'Can Norms Rescue Self-Interest or Macro Explanation Be Joined to Micro Explanation?' *Critical Review* 5:3 (1991), pp. 301–23.
———, 'Why Self-Interest Means Less Outside of a Social Context: Cultural Contributions to a Theory of Rational Choices', *Journal of Theoretical Politics* 6:2 (1994), pp. 131–59.

Related Material

Ahangar, Mohammad Altaf Hussain, *Customary Succession Among Muslims (A Critical Appraisal of Judicial Interpretation in Kashmir)* (Delhi: Uppal, 1986).

Basu, Srimati, *She Comes to Take Her Rights: Indian Women, Property, and Propriety* (Albany: SUNY Press, 1999).

Baviskar, B.S., 'Factional Conflict and the Congress Dilemma in Rural Maharashtra (1952–1975)' in Richard Sisson and Ramashray Roy, eds., *Diversity and Dominance in Indian Politics: Changing Bases of Cong-ress Support (Volume I)* (Delhi: Sage, 1990), pp. 37–54.

Bennett, T.W., *Human Rights and African Customary Law Under the South African Constitution* (Cape Town: Juta, 1995).

Brass, Paul, *Factional Politics in an Indian State: The Congress Party in Uttar Pradesh* (Berkeley: University of California Press, 1965).

Chakravarty, Anand, *Contradiction and Change: Emerging Patterns of Authority in a Rajasthan Village* (Delhi: Oxford University Press, 1975).

Chanock, Martin, *Law, Custom, and Social Order: The Colonial Experience in Malawi and Zambia* (Cambridge University Press, 1985).

———, 'Paradigms, Policies, and Property: A Review of the Customary Law of Land Tenure' in Kristin Mann and Richard Roberts, eds., *Law in Colonial Africa* (London: James Currey, 1991).

———, 'Neither Customary Nor Legal: African Customary Law in an Era of Family Law Reform' in G.R. Woodman, ed., *African Law and Legal Theory* (New York University Press, 1995), pp. 171–87.

Cohn, Bernard S., 'From Indian Status to British Contract' in *An Anthropologist Among the Historians* (Delhi: Oxford University Press, 1987), pp. 463–82.

Dirks, Nicholas, 'From Little King to Landlord: Colonial Discourse and Colonial Rule' in *Colonialism and Culture* (Ann Arbor: University of Michigan Press, 1992), pp. 175–208.

Firmin-Sellers, Kathryn, *The Transformation of Property Rights in the Gold Coast: An Empirical Analysis Applying Rational Choice Theory* (Cambridge University Press, 1996).

Johnson, Allen, 'Political Consciousness on Boa Ventura: 1967 and 1989 Compared' in John R. Bowen and Roger Petersen, eds., *Critical Comparisons in Politics and Culture* (Cambridge University Press, 1999), pp. 173–95.

Joireman, Sandra Fullerton, 'Contracting for Land: Lessons from Litigation in a Communal Tenure Area of Ethiopia', *Canadian Journal of African Studies* 30:3 (1996), pp. 424–42.

Kelkar, Govind, *Women, Peasant Organisations, and Land Rights: A Study from Bihar, India* (Bangkok: Asian Institute of Technology, 1992).

Kessinger, Tom G., *Vilayatpur 1848–1968: Social and Economic Change in a North Indian Village* (Berkeley: University of California Press, 1974).

Khadiagala, Lynn S., 'Seeking Justice in Uganda: The Adjudication of Women's Property Rights and the Failure of Popular Justice' (Boston: APSA Annual Meeting, unpublished, 1998).

Klug, Heinz, *Defining the Property Rights of Others: Political Power, Indigenous Tenure, and the Construction of Customary Land Law* (Johannesburg: Centre for Applied Legal Studies at Witwatersrand, 1995).

Lund, Christina, *Local Politics and the Dynamics of Property in Africa* (Cambridge University Press, 2008).

McAuslan, Patrick, 'Making Law Work: Restructuring Land Relations in Africa', *Development and Change* 29:3 (1998), pp. 525–52.

Metcalf, Thomas R., *Land, Landlords, and the British Raj: Northern India in the Nineteenth Century* (Berkeley: University of California Press, 1979).

Mifsud, Frank M., *Customary Land Law in Africa (With Reference to Legislation Aimed at Adjusting Customary Tenures to the Needs of Development)* (Rome: Food and Agriculture Organization, 1967).

Moore, Erin P., 'Law's Patriarchy in India' in Mindie Lazarus Black and Susan F. Hirsch, eds., *Contested States: Law, Hegemony, and Resistance* (New York: Routledge, 1994), pp. 89–117.

Moore, Sally Falk, *Social Facts and Fabrications: 'Customary' Law on Kilimanjaro, 1880–1980* (Cambridge University Press, 1986).

———, 'History and the Redefinition of Custom on Kilimanjaro' in June Starr and Jane F. Collier, eds., *History and Power in the Study of Law* (Ithaca: Cornell University Press, 1989), pp. 277–301.

———, 'From Giving and Lending to Selling: Property Transactions Reflecting Historical Change on Kilimanjaro' in Kristin Mann and Richard Roberts, eds., *Law in Colonial Africa* (London: James Currey, 1991), pp. 108–27.

Nader, Laura, 'Introduction: Property, Power, and Law in Middle Eastern Societies', *Property, Social Structure, and Law in the Modern Middle East* (Albany: SUNY Press, 1985), pp. 1–24.

Oldenburg, Philip, *Big City Government in India: Councilor, Administrator, and Citizen in Delhi* (Delhi: Manohar, 1974).

Schaffer, Frederic Charles, *Democracy in Translation: Understanding Politics in an Unfamiliar Culture* (Ithaca: Cornell University Press, 1998).

Sharma, K.L., 'Land Reform in Punjab: A Sociological Appraisal' in Sheo Kumar Lal, ed., *Sociological Perspectives of Land Reforms* (Delhi: Agricole Publishing Academy, 1982), pp. 76–94.

Singh, R.A.P., *Kin, Clan, and Land Reforms* (Jaipur: Rawat, 1985).

Spring, Eileen, *Law, Land, and Family: Aristocratic Inheritance in England, 1300–1800* (Chapel Hill: University of North Carolina Press, 1993).

Taub, Richard, *Bureaucracy Under Stress: Administrators and Administration in an Indian State* (Berkeley: University of California Press, 1969).

Thompson, E.P., *Whigs and Hunters: The Origins of the Black Act* (New York: Pantheon, 1975).

Tripp, Aili Mari, *Changing the Rules: The Politics of Liberalization and the Urban Informal Economy in Tanzania* (Berkeley: University of California Press, 1997).

Conclusion

Amanat, Abbas and Frank Griffel, eds. *Shari'a: Islamic Law in the Contemporary Context* (Palo Alto: Stanford University Press, 2007).

Abou Zahab, Mariam, 'Sectarianism as a Substitute Identity: Sunnis and Shias in Central and South Punjab' in Soofia Mumtaz, Jean-Luc Racine and Imran Anwar Ali, eds., *Pakistan: The Contours of State and Society* (Karachi: Oxford University Press, 2002), pp. 77–95.

———, 'The Sunni-Shia Conflict in Jhang (Pakistan)' in Imtiaz Ahmad and Helmut Reifeld, eds., *Lived Islam in South Asia: Adaptation, Accommodation, and Conflict* (Delhi: Social Science Press, 2004), pp. 135–48.

Anderson, J.N.D., *Islamic Law in the Modern World* (New York University Press, 1959).

———, *Law Reform in the Muslim World* (London: Athlone Press, 1976).

An-Naim, Abdullahi Ahmed, *Toward an Islamic Reformation: Civil Liberties, Human Rights and International Law* (Syracuse University Press, 1990).

———, *Islam and the Secular State: Negotiating the Future of Shari'a* (Cambridge: Harvard University Press, 2008).

Baker, Raymond W., *Islam Without Fear: Egypt and the New Islamists* (Cambridge: Harvard University Press, 2003).

Bayat, Asef, *Making Islam Democratic: Social Movements and the Post-Islamist Turn* (Palo Alto: Stanford University Press, 2007).

Bowen, John R., 'Law and Social Norms in the Comparative Study of Islam', *American Anthropologist* 100:4 (1998), p. 1034.

———, *Islam, Law, and Equality in Indonesia: An Anthropology of Public Reasoning* (Cambridge University Press, 2003).

Charlton, Jackie, Musharraf Cyan, Zahid Hasnain, Nick Manning, Doug Porter and Hamid Sharif, 'Devolved Service Delivery Study: Preliminary Summary of Findings and Recommendations from [a] Study of Local Governments in Bahawalpur, Bannu, Faisalabad, Karachi, Khairpur, and Qila Saifullah' (Islamabad, 10 November 2003). <http://g2lg.gop.pk/Portal/index2.php?option=com_docman&task=doc_view&gid=50&Itemid=122>.

Charrad, Mounira, *States and Women's Rights: The Making of Postcolonial Tunisia, Algeria, and Morocco* (Berkeley: University of California Press, 2002).

Collins, Daniel P., 'Islamization of Pakistani Law: A Historical Perspective', *Stanford Journal of International Law* 24 (1987–1988), pp. 511–84.

Coulson, Noel J., *A History of Islamic Law* (Edinburgh University Press, 1964).

Devolution in Pakistan: An Assessment and Recommendations for Action (Islamabad: Asian Development Bank, Department for International Development, World Bank, July 2004).

El Fadl, Khaled Abou, *Islam and the Challenge of Democracy* (Princeton University Press, 2004).

Esposito, John L., *Women in Muslim Family Law* (Syracuse University Press, 1982).

Euben, Roxanne, *Enemy in the Mirror: Islamic Fundamentalism and the Limits of Modern Rationalism, A Work of Comparative Political Theory* (Princeton University Press, 1999).

Feener, R. Michael, *Muslim Legal Thought in Modern Indonesia* (Cambridge University Press, 2007).

——— and Mark E. Cammack, eds., *Islamic Law in Contemporary Indonesia: Ideas and Institutions* (Cambridge: Harvard University Press, 2007).

Feldman, Noah, 'Shari'a and Islamic Democracy in the Age of Al-Jazeera' in Abbas Amanat and Frank Griffel, eds., *Shari'a: Islamic Law in the Contemporary Context* (Palo Alto: Stanford University Press, 2007), pp. 104–19.

Hallaq, Wael B., *Authority, Continuity, and Change in Islamic Law* (Cambridge University Press, 2001).

———, *The Origins and Evolution of Islamic Law* (Cambridge University Press, 2005).

———, *Shari'a: Theory, Practice, Transformations* (Cambridge University Press, 2009).

Hefner, Robert W., *Civil Islam: Muslims and Democratization in Indonesia* (Princeton University Press, 2000).

Ismail, Salwa, *Rethinking Islamist Politics: Culture, the State, and Islamism* (London: I.B. Tauris, 2006).

Jamal, Amaney A., *Barriers to Democratization: The Other Side of Social Capital in Palestine and the Arab World* (Princeton University Press, 2007).

Johnson, David L., 'Allal al-Fasi: Shari'a as Blueprint for Righteous Global Citizenship?' in Abbas Amanat and Frank Griffel, eds., *Shari'a: Islamic Law in the Contemporary Context* (Palo Alto: Stanford University Press, 2007), pp. 83–103.

Ka'bah, Rifyal, 'Islamic Law in Court Decisions and Fatwa Institutions in Indonesia' in R. Michael Feener and Mark E. Cammack, eds., *Islamic Law in Contemporary Indonesia: Ideas and Institutions* (Cambridge: Harvard University Press, 2007).

Kozlowski, Gregory, *Muslim Endowments and Society in British India* (Cambridge University Press, 1985).

Kugle, Scott A., 'Framed, Blamed, and Renamed: The Recasting of Islamic Jurisprudence in Colonial South Asia', *Modern Asian Studies* 35:2 (2001), pp. 257–313.

Vickie Langohr, 'Too Much Civil Society, Too Little Politics: Egypt and Liberalizing Arab Regimes', *Comparative Politics* 36:2 (2004), pp. 181–204.

Lev, Daniel S., *Islamic Courts in Indonesia* (Berkeley: University of California Press, 1972).

Lombardi, Clark, *State Law as Islamic Law in Modern Egypt: The Incorporation of the Shari'a into Egyptian Constitutional Law* (Leiden: E.J. Brill, 2006).

Madjid, Nurcholish, 'The Necessity of Renewing Islamic Thought and Reinvigorating Religious Understanding' in Charles Kurzman, ed., *Liberal Islam: A Sourcebook* (Oxford University Press, 1998), pp. 284–94.

Mahmood, Saba, 'Is Liberalism Islam's Only Answer?' in Khaled Abou El Fadl, *Islam and the Challenge of Democracy* (Princeton University Press, 2004).

Masud, Mohammad Khalid, Brinkley M. Messick and David S. Powers, eds., *Islamic Legal Interpretation: Muftis and Their Fatwas* (Cambridge: Harvard University Press, 1996).

Mecham, Quinn, 'From the Ashes of Virtue, a Promise of Light: The Transformation of Political Islam in Turkey', *Third World Quarterly* 25:2 (2004), pp. 339–58.

Messick, Brinkley, *The Calligraphic State: Textual Domination and History in a Muslim Society* (Berkeley: University of California Press, 1992).

Mir-Hosseini, Zeba, *Marriage on Trial: A Study of Islamic Family Law in Iran and Morocco* (London: I.B. Tauris, 1993).

Muhammad, Rana, *A to Z of Jehadi Organizations in Pakistan* (Lahore: Mashal Books, 2004).

Nasr, Syed Vali Reza, 'Islamic Opposition to the Islamic State: The Jama'at-i Islami, 1977–1988', *International Journal of Middle East Studies* 25:2 (1993), pp. 261–83.

———, *Mawdudi and the Making of Islamic Revivalism* (Oxford University Press, 1996).

Norton, A.R., 'Thwarted Politics: The Case of Egypt's Hizb al-Wasat' in Robert W. Hefner, ed., *Remaking Muslim Politics: Pluralism, Contestation, Democratization* (Princeton University Press, 2005), pp. 133–60.

Opwis, Felicitas, 'Islamic Law and Legal Change: The Concept of *Maslaha* in Classical and Contemporary Islamic Theory' in Abbas Amanat and Frank Griffel, eds., *Shari'a: Islamic Law in the Contemporary Context*, (Palo Alto: Stanford University Press, 2007), pp. 62–82.

Osanloo, Arzoo, 'The Measure of Mercy: Islamic Justice, Sovereign Power, and Human Rights in Iran', *Cultural Anthropology* 21:4 (2006), pp. 570–602.

Peletz, Michael G., *Islamic Modern: Religious Courts and Cultural Politics in Malaysia* (Princeton University Press, 2002),

Rahman, Fazlur, *Islam and Modernity: Transformation of an Intellectual Tradition* (University of Chicago Press, 1982).

Raziq, 'Ali 'Abd-al, 'Message Not Government, Religion Not State' in Charles Kurzman, ed., *Liberal Islam* (Oxford University Press, 1998 [1925]), pp. 29–36.

Rosen, Lawrence, *The Anthropology of Justice: Law as Culture in Islamic Society* (Cambridge University Press, 1989).

Roy, Olivier, *Secularism Confronts Islam* (New York: Columbia University Press, 2007).

Schacht, Joseph, *An Introduction to Islamic Law* (Oxford: Clarendon, 1964).

Schwedler, Jillian, *Faith in Moderation: Islamist Parties in Jordan and Yemen* (Cambridge University Press, 2006).

Shepard, William E., 'Muhammad Said al-Ashmawi and the Application of the Sharia in Egypt', *International Journal of Middle East Studies* 28:1 (1996), pp. 39–58.

———, *Sayyid Qutb and Islamic Activism: A Translation and Critical Analysis of Social Justice in Islam* (Leiden: E.J. Brill, 1996).

Soroush, Abdolkarim, *Reason, Freedom, and Democracy: Essential Writings of Abdolkarim Soroush*, eds. Mahmoud Sadri and Ahmed Sadri (Oxford University Press, 2000).

Tamimi, Azzam S., *Rachid Ghannouchi: A Democrat Within Islamism* (Oxford University Press, 2001).

Wickham, Carrie Rosefsky, 'Beyond Democratization: Political Change in the Arab World', *PS: Political Science and Politics* 27:3 (1994), pp. 507–9.

———, *Mobilizing Islam: Religion, Activism, and Political Change in Egypt* (New York: Columbia University Press, 2002).

Würth, Anna, 'The Normativity of the Factual: On the Everyday Construction of Shari'a in a Yemeni Family Court' in Abbas Amanat and Frank Griffel, eds., *Shari'a: Islamic Law in the Contemporary Context* (Palo Alto: Stanford University Press, 2007), pp. 165–77.

Appendix

Moir, Martin and Zawahir Moir, 'Old District Records in Pakistan', *Modern Asian Studies* 24:1 (1990), pp. 195–204.

NOTES

Introduction

1. Peter A. Hall (2000), p. 17.
2. John R. Bowen (1999), p. 230.
3. See Alan S. Zuckerman (1997), p. 293.
4. R.G. Collingwood (1946), p. 213.
5. Rex Martin (1977), p. 42.
6. Collingwood, op. cit., pp. 176-7.
7. Ibid., p. 223.

Chapter 1

1. C.H. Buck (1937), p. 1.
2. For a countervailing perspective, see Hernando de Soto (2000).
3. Minoti Chakravarty-Kaul stresses the colonial push for individual rights and the collapse of indigenous institutions supporting collective action. Drawing attention to population growth and increasing demand for land (especially after 1868), she points to a pattern of encroachment on common property (for example, the *shamilat*) as evidence of declining 'joint landlord communities' and expanding 'individual rights'. See Chakravarty-Kaul (1992), pp. 396, 399. Richard Saumerez Smith, on the other hand, examines the same period but reverses this trend. He emphasizes the ways in which colonial officials overlooked the productive capacity of individual cultivators and worked to resuscitate 'tribal' patterns of collective ownership based upon descent. See Smith (1996). These differences grow out of competing ideas regarding the parameters of the village community: whereas Chakravarty-Kaul takes a rather narrow view, stressing the demise of 'joint landlord communities' as defined by colonial revenue officials, Smith takes a more expansive view, including both landowners and occupancy tenants (that is, 'hereditary cultivators'). In other words, Chakravarty-Kaul sees a climate of *expanding* individual rights, because after 1822

(and increasingly after 1850) the state granted these rights to officially recognized members of the 'joint landlord community', whereas Smith sees *declining* individual rights because, after 1865, the state granted these rights in ways that 'excluded' occupancy tenants. In effect, both describe a situation in which individual rights were withdrawn from communities defined in terms of 'cultivation' and relocated within communities defined in terms of 'descent'.

4. Quoted in Charles Lewis Tupper (1881:1), pp. 2, 49 and W.H. Rattigan and Charles Boulnois (1878), p. 59.
5. 'A village community', explained J.M. Douie in his settlement handbook for the Northwestern Provinces, 'is a body of proprietors who now or formerly owned part of the village lands in common, and who are jointly responsible for the payment of the revenue'. Douie (1899), p. 67.
6. See Smith, op. cit., p. 138.
7. See Clive Dewey (1991), p. 27.
8. *New System of Field Measurement in the Punjab (No. 1068 of 1852)* (Lahore: Chronicle Press, 1853) with reports by G.C. Barnes, R. Temple, E.A. Prinsep, R.H. Davies.
9. Additional documents included the *parcha tasdiq* (register of occupancy tenants), the *naksha jagir aur muafi* (list of revenue assignments and revenue-free grants), and the *naksha haquq chahat* (statement of rights in wells and other sources of irrigation).
10. According to Douie, 'ancestral shares were described by Mr. Thomason as "legal", as distinguished from "customary" shares which was the term he applied to those which were definite, but not apparently based on kinship', op. cit., p. 69. In short, 'ancestral' shares were shares defined by inheritance laws (including tribal or customary laws), whereas 'customary' shares involved local customs pertaining to cultivation. See also Smith, op. cit., pp. 257–8.
11. See Edward Augustus Prinsep, *Report on the Revised Settlement of the Sealkote District in the Amritsur Division* (Lahore: Chronicle Press, 1865) quoted in J.R. Dunlop-Smith, *Gazeteer of the Sialkot District (1894–1895)* (Lahore: Civil and Military Gazette Press, 1895), pp. 85–6.
12. See Douie, op. cit., p. 72.
13. See ibid., p. 155.
14. Ibid., p. 57; see also pp. 2–3.
15. See ibid., p. 58.
16. See Louis Dumont (1966), p. 72. See also Dunlop-Smith, op. cit., pp. 96–7.
17. See Buck, op. cit., p. 18. See also Tom G. Kessinger (1975), p. 20.
18. Captain C. Minchin to Major J.R. Becher, 11 November 1863 in Reply No. 29, 'The Dharwai System of Village Accounts, Dera Ghazee Khan District', *The Punjab Record*, v4 (1869), p. 188.
19. See Buck, op. cit., p. 26.
20. See also Chakravarty-Kaul, op. cit., pp. 127–35.

21. Daya Krishna Kapur ([1926]), p. 52.
22. Suits for partition (followed by suits for preemption) were extremely common, but it is important to note that these suits functioned differently in *pattidari* and *bhaiachara* estates. In *bhaiachara* estates, suits for *taqsim* often reflected an urge to enhance the extent of individualized rights based on the terms of 'possession'; after all, a suit for 'partition' in such an estate would have sought to 'divide' the land according to the terms of officially recognized control, that is, 'possession'. In *pattidari* estates, however, suits for *taqsim* often pointed to a simple *defence* of enduring ancestral 'shares'. In fact many of these suits sought to *reverse* the trend toward separate 'possession' with a claim to *recover* specific shares—shares that had been encroached upon by stronger members of the community. Suits for 'preemption' aimed to strengthen the language of ancestral 'shares' in both types of estates. But, in *pattidari* estates, suits for 'partition' were often used to accomplish exactly the same thing. See Douie, op. cit., p. 61; see also Minoti Chakravarty-Kaul (1996), p. 132 and Chakravarty-Kaul, op. cit., p. 419.
23. Douie, op. cit., p. 142.
24. See ibid., p. 285.
25. See Sir Denzil Ibbetson (1883), p. 24.
26. See Rattigan and Boulnois, op. cit., p. 14.
27. If no sons existed, the estate passed to the father or the brothers of the deceased. If there were no male relatives within seven degrees of separation, the land was inherited by the mother.
28. See Chakravarty-Kaul (1996), op. cit., p. 123.
29. See Ibbetson, op. cit., p. 14; see also pp. 11, 24. 'The social and tribal customs of the eastern peasant, whether Hindu or Musalman, are those of India, while in the west the people, whether Hindu or Musalman, have adopted in great measure, though by no means altogether, the social and tribal customs of Afghanistan and Bilochistan'.
30. See ibid., p. 26.
31. 'The elaborate rules of the Muhammadan law regarding inheritance, wills, and legacies', noted J. Wilson in District Shahpur, 'are never acted on, the custom in such matters being founded on the entirely different basis of agnatic relationship'. 'To introduce the elaborate rules of Muhammadan Law', he argued, 'would revolutionise the tribal custom of all the Shahpur tribes and give rise to endless ... discontent', *Gazetteer of Shahpur District* (Lahore: Civil and Military Gazette Press, 1897), pp. 117–18.
32. See Smith, op. cit., p. 335; see also pp. 135–41.
33. Exceptions included the 'customs' prevailing in Oudh (for example, primogeniture) and the notion that Anglo-Indian (Hindu) law was merely a reflection of the 'customs' prevailing in a particular area. See, for example, *Collector of Madura vs. Mootoo Ramalinga*, Privy Council (1868), quoted in Rattigan and Boulnois, op. cit., pp. 19, 63, and Acharyya (1914), p. 323.

34. R.E. Egerton, R.H. Davies, R. Temple and J.H. Morris, *Report of the Revised Settlement of the Lahore District in the Lahore Division* (Delhi: Indian Punch Press, 1860), p. 14.
35. See R.C. Bolster, *Gazetteer of Lahore District, Volume XXX-A* (Lahore: Superintendent, Government Printing, 1916), p. 186.
36. Ibid.
37. Leslie S. Saunders, *Report on the Revised Land Revenue Settlement of the Lahore District in the Lahore Division of the Punjab* (Lahore: Central Jail Press, 1873).
38. Ibid., p. 76.
39. Ibid., p. 60.
40. George Casson Walker, *Final Report on the Revision of the Settlement of Lahore District* (Lahore: Civil and Military Gazette Press, 1894).
41. Ibid., p. 26.
42. Ibid.
43. Prinsep, op. cit., p. 3. N.b. The first settlement report submitted by E.A. Prinsep was several years in the making. For an account of the delays affecting this report, see J.R. Dunlop-Smith, op. cit., pp. 159–60.
44. Prinsep, op. cit., pp. 85–6.
45. Ibid., p. 89.
46. See G.R.G. Hambly (1964), pp. 47–66. See also Thomas R. Metcalf (1962), pp. 305–7.
47. Richard Temple, speech, *Proceedings of the Legislative Council* (11 September 1868, p. 271) quoted in Hambly, op. cit., p. 57.
48. Hambly, op. cit., p. 57.
49. As Hambly points out, 'Prinsep's original premise, that the proprietary classes in the Punjab had been dispossessed as a result of the generosity shown to the actual occupants of the soil by the original settlement officers, was based upon a widely held assumption that tenant right was a British creation in the Punjab', op. cit., p. 54.
50. Ibid., p. 51.
51. Quoted in Hambly, op. cit., p. 53.
52. Hambly, op. cit., p. 54.
53. J.R. Dunlop-Smith, *Final Report on the Revision of the Settlement of the Sialkot District in the Punjab* (Lahore: Civil and Military Gazette Press, 1895).
54. Apparently 2,107 villages chose to keep their original mode of distribution, which in most cases was according to ancestral shares, whereas 218 chose to change their mode of distribution. According to Dunlop-Smith, however, 'the *zamindars* [in the] villages where there has been this change were at first apprehensive that ... they would be deprived of the right of preemption and other privileges enjoyed by them under the *pattidari* system'. But 'to reassure them and keep the civil courts in the future from making the same mistakes a note has been made in the genealogical tree ... to the effect that the demand has been distributed according to soil

classification solely for *bachh* purposes, and the process does not affect in any way the old system on tenure and the rights and liabilities attaching to it'. *Gazetteer*, op. cit., p. 85.

55. See ibid., pp. 85–6.
56. Prinsep quoted in ibid., p. 101.
57. Gore Ouseley and W.G. Davies, *Report on the Revised Settlement of the Shahpoor District in the Rawulpindee Division* (Lahore: Punjab Printing Company, 1866), p. 5.
58. Ouseley quoted in Wilson, op. cit., p. 228.
59. Ibid.
60. Ibid., p. 229.
61. Ouseley and Davies, op. cit., p. 73.
62. Ouseley quoted in Wilson, op. cit., p. 229.
63. Ibid.
64. Ouseley and Davies, op. cit., p. 81.
65. Davies quoted in Wilson, op. cit., p. 125.
66. Ouseley and Davies, op. cit., p. 101.
67. Ouseley quoted in Wilson, op. cit., p. 129.
68. Ibid.
69. In 1894, J. Wilson expressed a similar frustration, calling the official designation of village tenures 'exceedingly doubtful'. 'Land tenures assume so many and such complex forms in the Punjab', he wrote, 'that it is impossible to classify them successfully under a few general headings. ... It will be readily conceived that proprietary rights were somewhat ill-defined at the regular settlement, and that innumerable claims were set up, based upon the tradition of ancestral rights, but unsupported by recent possession', op. cit., p. 125.
70. Davies quoted in ibid., p. 125.
71. Ibid.
72. Ibid., p. 126.
73. Ibid.
74. 'Minute by the Lieutenant-Governor of the Punjab, Mr. D.F. McLeod, on the Shahpoor Settlement (27 August 1867)' in Ouseley and Davies, op. cit., p. xxix.
75. J. Wilson, *Final Report on the Revision of Settlement of the Shahpur District in the Punjab, 1887–1894* (Lahore: Civil and Military Gazette Press, 1894).
76. I would like to thank David Gilmartin for clarifying this point. See also Wilson, *Gazetteer*, op. cit., p. 43.
77. See Imran Ali (2003).
78. Deva Singh ([1929]), p. 3.
79. Ibid., pp. 18–19.
80. Ibid., pp. 19, 20.
81. Wilson, *Gazetteer*, op. cit. p. 126.

82. Wilson, *Final Report*, quoted in part in Chakravarty-Kaul (1996), op. cit. p. 133.
83. Wilson, *Gazetteer*, op. cit., p. 143.
84. Wilson, *Gazetteer*, op. cit., p. 144.
85. Douie, op. cit., p. 207.
86. See Eric Stokes (1959), pp. 272–3.
87. *Memorandum on the Restriction of the Power to Alienate Interests in Land* (Calcutta: Superintendent Government Printing, 1895), p. 18.
88. Ibid.
89. Quoted in Stokes, op. cit., p. 119.
90. J.A. Temple (Commissioner, Chattisgarh Division), letter (9 January 1897), *Correspondence of the Government of India with the Punjab and Replies from Other Local Governments to the Government of India Circular on Alienation of Land from the Agricultural to the Non-Agricultural Classes* (Enclosures to Revenue and Agriculture Letter No. 59 of 1898), Number 242, p. 25.
91. Ibid.
92. 'Papers Regarding Alienation of Estates of Insolvent Proprietors to the Money-Lending Class', *Selections from the Record of the Government of the Punjab and Its Dependencies*, New Series No. XIII (Lahore: Civil Secretariat Press, 1876), p. 3.
93. Ibid. ('Proceedings of the Honourable Lieutenant-Governor in the Home Department, 23 December 1874'), p. 6.
94. Ibid. ('Note by Mr. Justice C.R. Lindsay, 28 June 1872'), p. 19.
95. Ibid. ('Memorandum by Mr. Justice P.S. Melvill on Interest in the Punjab, 1 April 1874'), p. 9.
96. Ibid., p. 24.
97. Ibid., pp. 24, 26.
98. 'Note on Land Transfer and Agricultural Indebtedness in India' (Calcutta: Superintendent Government Printing, 1895), p. 89.
99. *Memorandum*, op. cit., p. 14.
100. Ibid., p. 9.
101. Ibid., p. 29.
102. Governor of Madras (Munro), quoted in 'The Land Revenue of Madras', *Calcutta Review* 17:34 (1852), p. 327.
103. See Smith, op. cit.
104. See Dewey, op. cit., p. 28.

Chapter 2

1. Cyril P.K. Fazal, 'A Note on Sales of Land between the Notified Agricultural Tribes in the Punjab During the Quinqennium 1922–23 to 1926–27' (Lahore: Board of Economic Inquiry, Rural Section, 1930/31), p. 35.
2. Raja Narendra Nath, *The Tribune* (Ambala: 28 April 1936), quoted in David Gilmartin (1988b), p. 52.

3. See Rattigan and Boulnois, op. cit., pp. 61–2. Here Rattigan and Boulnois quote Sir George Campbell, who noted that 'not one out of ten, perhaps not one out of one hundred, persons in the Punjab is governed by the strict provisions of Hindu and Muhammadan law'. See also Charles A. Roe and H.A.B. Rattigan, who observed that Muslims in the Punjab 'know nothing of [the] *Shura* [*sic*], except perhaps its name'. 'The purely Muhammadan tribes of the Frontier ... have no doubt heard of it, but they too have the vaguest notions of its provisions. Being ... much under the influence of the *mullahs*, they are ready to assert, in opposition to the plainest facts, that they follow the *Shura* in all things. [But] when we examine the *riwaj-i-am*, we ... find that very few tribes even profess to follow Muhammadan law, and those who do profess to follow it evade it in practice' (1895), p. 12.
4. See Henry Thoby Prinsep (1846), p. 150. 'The Mahomedan families scattered over the Sikh states ... reject the ordinances of their lawgivers, and are guided by rules of their own forming'. 'Were the Mahomedan ... laws on inheritance, as inculcated by the *shura* [*sic*] ... to be made the leading principle in succession to landed property, ... a common distribution would become universal, to the extinction of [many] great estates and the annihilation of the chiefs with their great influence'.
5. W.H. Rattigan (1881), p. ix.
6. See Tupper (1881:2), op. cit., pp. 1–89. See also Roe and Rattigan, op. cit., pp. 6–10.
7. See 'Notes by Messrs. H.D. Watson and G. Worsley on the Development of Customary Law and the Various Schemes for Codification Prior to the Year 1915' in *Report on the Punjab Codification of Customary Law Conference* (Appendix 1: 'Selection of Unpublished Papers Regarding Codification of Customary Law in the Punjab') (Lahore: Superintendent of Government Printing, 1915), pp. 51–76.
8. See *Report on the Punjab Codification of Customary Law Conference* (Lahore: Superintendent of Government Printing, 1915).
9. See Badr-ud-din Qureshi (1932), pp. 52–66. According to Qureshi, the customs of each tribe were initially restated in the *wajib-ul-arz* of each village containing members of that tribe. But, later on, following Prinsep in Sialkot, the customs of each 'tribe' were covered *separately* within a new document known as the *riwaj-i-am*.
10. *Memorandum*, op. cit. p. 9. For a countervailing view, see Acharyya, op. cit., 'The most important objection to [the] codification of customary law', Acharyya notes, concerns 'the danger of ... crystallizing customs before they have had time to mature', p. 326. But 'to say that the native mind is unfamiliar with the idea of living under systematically codified law', he argues, 'is to say what the truths of history do not justify', p. 320. In fact his response broadly paraphrases the work of Rattigan and Boulnois, op. cit., pp. 326–30.

11. Initially, W.H. Rattigan was apprehensive about the possibility of codifying the terms of 'tribal' custom, as reflected in his work with Charles Boulnois (1878): 'Indian customs are of a very flexible and bending character', he argued, and 'there is a great danger in too hastily transmuting such customs into a rigid rule of law', op. cit., pp. 38–9 (see also p. 65). By 1881, however, Rattigan had become considerably more sanguine. In the first edition of his *Digest of Civil Law for the Punjab*, for instance, he noted that he had sought 'to arrange the leading topics of customary law in a few simply worded propositions' in an effort to prepare, however cautiously, 'the materials for a future [provincial] code', op. cit., pp. x, xii.
12. See 'Notes', op. cit., p. 58. See also Rattigan, op. cit., pp. 2–3. 'The customary law of the Punjab is an unwritten law, and the records commonly known as the *riwaj-i-am* [help to illuminate] ... what that unwritten law is'. 'When based on authenticated precedents, the value of such records is great', Rattigan argued. 'But where the settlement officer charged with the preparation of such records has "shaped public opinion on most questions in the direction in which he himself and others of longer experience *thought equitable*," as Mr. Thorburn candidly acknowledges he did in ... [District] Bannu, the value of [these records] ... is obviously reduced to zero'. [On pp. 4–8, Rattigan himself illuminates twenty-two 'limitations' on the customs the colonial state would accept within the terms of 'justice, equity, and good conscience'.] For a related debate regarding the value of 'general' (all-India) versus 'provincial' codification, see Acharyya, op. cit., p. 318.
13. See W.H. Rattigan quoted in *Notes*, op. cit., pp. 52–3; 72–3; see also Acharyya, op. cit., p. 101.
14. See W.H. Rattigan (1898), p. 378.
15. See James Thorburn quoted in *Notes*, op. cit., pp. 51–2.
16. Cockburn, CJ, *Wason vs. Walter*, LR 4 QB 73 (1869) quoted in Acharyya, op. cit., p. 98.
17. *Report*, op. cit., p. 4.
18. Ibid., p. 12.
19. Ibid., p. 4.
20. Ibid. See also Qureshi, op. cit., pp. 65–6.
21. Ibid., p. 1.
22. See for example Kenneth W. Jones (1976); Richard Gordon (1975); Richard Fox (1984); and K.L. Tuteja and O. Grewal (1992).
23. See David Gilmartin (1988a), p. 91; Ian Talbot (1988), p. 87; Ian Talbot (1991), p. 91.
24. See Lucy Carroll (1991); see also Bina Agarwal (1994), pp. 84–98.
25. See J. Duncan M. Derrett (1968); see also H.T. Colebrooke (1868).
26. See Derrett, op. cit., pp. 116–17.
27. See Agarwal, op. cit., p. 88 (fn 18).
28. On 'limited lifetime interests', see ibid., p. 86.

29. See N.J. Coulson (1971), p. 3.
30. Ibid.
31. See Lucy Carroll (1983) and Lucy Carroll (1985).
32. See Coulson, op. cit., pp. 29–30.
33. Carroll (1985), op. cit., p. 123.
34. Coulson, op. cit., p. 3.
35. Ibid., p. 2.
36. See H.A. Rose (1911), p. 237.
37. Qureshi, op. cit., p. 1.
38. See Rose, op. cit., p. 239.
39. See Tupper (1881:2), op. cit., p. 71.
40. See Gilmartin (1988b), op. cit., pp. 48–9, 56–7.
41. See Rattigan (1881), op. cit., p. 14; see also Sripati Roy (1911), pp. 467, 506.
42. This right of representation was recognized among direct lineal (male) descendents only. See Rattigan (1881), op. cit., p. 17.
43. See Tupper (1881:2), op. cit., p. 73; Qureshi, op. cit., p. 224.
44. See Rattigan (1881), op. cit., p. 16; Roy, op. cit., p. 466, 506; Qureshi, op. cit., p. 230. In *jagirdari* estates the rule of primogeniture often prevailed; see Rattigan (1881), op. cit., p. 17.
45. See Qureshi, op. cit., p. 295.
46. See Tupper (1881:2), op. cit., p. 76; Rattigan (1881), op. cit., p. 34; Roy, op. cit., pp. 474, 509; Qureshi, op. cit., p. 318.
47. See Rattigan and Boulnois, op. cit., p. 86; Roy, op. cit., p. 493.
48. See Roy, op. cit., p. 512. Rattigan and Boulnois note that gifts to stepsons were often prohibited, although, unlike gifts to daughters' sons and sisters' sons—see Tupper (1881:1), op. cit., pp. 73–6—these gifts to stepsons were occasionally sanctioned on an 'exceptional' basis by the tribal co-sharers, op. cit., p. 18.
49. See Rattigan and Boulnois, op. cit., p. 89; Qureshi, op. cit., p. 476.
50. In rare cases, women holding 'limited' lifetime interests were allowed to apply for partition (for example, in cases of joint ownership when they were not maintained by their surviving male relatives). See Rattigan (1881), op. cit., p. 22; Qureshi, op. cit., pp. 245, 248.
51. Quoted in Tupper (1881:1), op. cit., p. 188.
52. 'I ... know [of] one or two instances ... where the custom recorded regarding adoption was not one which had been handed down from generation to generation, or based upon any precedents, but one which the people wished to be observed in the future'. T.W. Smyth, Deputy Commissioner of District Montgomery (30 April 1873), quoted in Tupper (1881:1), op. cit., p. 153; see also pp. 208, 215.
53. 'I have spent about thirty-eight years at the bar', noted Syed Ghulam Bhik Nairang, an advocate from Lahore, and 'in at least hundreds of cases in which I appeared, the question [of] whether the Personal Law of the Mussalmans or some sort of custom is to be followed has been under consid-

eration'. 'I do not claim to be so sanctimonious as to have all along represented the side which stood for the Muslim law', he noted. 'But the experience that I have gained is certainly the experience of hundreds of others, ... and that experience is this, that what goes by the name of customary law is really a bundle of mischievous uncertainties'. In fact, he added, 'any fellow can say in a court of law, when faced with ... a perfectly valid claim based on the glorious principles of Islamic law, that his family or his community or his caste does not follow the Islamic law, but [rather, that] it follows ... a custom he proceeds to specify'. But 'on many occasions he invents what he alleges to be the custom and then in due course of legal procedure issues are struck and evidence is recorded and this man ... forges evidence, fabricates documents, puts in any amount of perjured evidence, and succeeds in proving the alleged custom'. Yet 'the man who has proved that custom, and those who are in the know, as well as the public, are fully cognizant all along that the defence was false'. *Legislative Assembly Debates* (Islamabad: National Documentation Centre, 1 April 1937), pp. 2535–6.

54. T.P. Ellis (1912:1), p. 8 (see also pp. 1–7).
55. Ibid.
56. See ibid., p. 7.
57. Ibid.
58. Ibid., pp. 4–7; see also Rose, op. cit., pp. lv-lxiv (Appendix B).
59. See Rattigan and Boulnois, op. cit., p. 72.
60. 'The Punjab has only become an English province since 1849', noted the presiding Deputy Commisioner, and 'previous to that time there is little possibility of determining what were the customs of the people otherwise than by their traditions'. These traditions, however, were discernible from the revenue records, and 'to these ... we must go for information', because 'the presumption is in favour of the correctness of [these] document[s]', which have been 'attested by the *patwari*, the *lambardars*, and the proprietors of the village'. 'The first document specially referring to the Padhania family is the *riwaz-i-am* of *parganah* Lahore', and in this document the following exchange appeared: 'In case there should be male issue, can the daughter inherit conjointly with her brothers'? to which the answer was that 'according to the custom of the country the daughter can take no share'. Turning away from Lahore, the Commissioner then went on to note that, in Amritsar, 'the daughter ... cannot inherit ancestral property with male heirs' because 'the dower which is given ... is instead of a share of the inheritance'. But in Sialkot, the *riwaj-i-am* was 'more favourable to the daughter', giving *unmarried daughters* the right to inherit (in the absence of sons). As the Commissioner explained, however, 'even in Sialkot a married daughter would under no circumstances succeed'. The documentary evidence, in other words, suggested that *Massamat Attar Kaur* should not inherit. 'The antiquity of this custom', concluded the Commissioner, turning away from the *riwaj-i-am* to the *shajra nasb*, 'is

proved in those genealogical trees that have been produced, ... for no name of a sister is [to be] found among the heirs' (PR1870:47) quoted in Rattigan and Boulnois, op. cit., pp. 73–5.
61. Ibid., pp. 75–6.
62. Ibid., p. 90.
63. Ibid., p. 92.
64. See *Ghulam Ahmed vs. Lalu* (PR1866:430) quoted in Rattigan and Boulnois, op. cit., p. 92.
65. Ibid.
66. See *Miran Buksh vs. Piru* (PR1868:29) quoted in Rattigan and Boulnois, op. cit., p. 93.
67. Ibid.
68. Ibid.
69. *Shadi vs. Massamat Bhai* (PR1874:257) quoted in Rattigan and Boulnois, op. cit., pp. 94–6.
70. Ibid., p. 94.
71. Ibid., p. 95. For a discussion of *zails*, see J.R. Dunlop-Smith, *Gazeteer*, op. cit., p. 94.
72. Rattigan and Boulnois, op. cit., p. 95.
73. Ibid., p. 96.
74. R.C. Bolster, *Customary Law of the Lahore District (Revised Edition)*, Volume XIII (Lahore: Superintendent of Government Printing, 1916), pp. iv, v.
75. Ibid., p. iv.
76. Ibid.
77. See Qureshi, op. cit., p. 278.
78. Bolster, *Customary Law*, op. cit.
79. D.J. Boyd, *Customary Law of the Sialkot District (Revised Edition)*, Volume XIV (Lahore: Superintendent of Government Printing, 1917), p. i.
80. Boyd, *Customary Law*, op. cit., p. ii. Boyd pointed out that the accounts compiled in Sialkot under E.A. Prinsep (1865) described precolonial gifts to daughters, but he noted that he was 'inclined to agree with [the author of the first *riwaj-i-am*, namely], Munshi Amin Chand, in discounting such [gifts] on the ground that land had no value at the time when most of the villages were founded'. As soon as land was regarded as a valuable commodity (owing in part to the introduction of a 'moderate' rate of taxation), in other words, patterns of female exclusion acquired greater significance.
81. M.S. Leigh, *Final Report of the Third Regular Settlement of the Portion of Shahpur District Still Paying a Fixed Assessment, 1911–1916* (Lahore: Superintendent of Government Printing, 1918), p. 31. For a countervailing view, see J. Wilson, *Gazetteer*, op. cit., pp. 114–18.
82. Fazal, op. cit. (quotation repeated from above).
83. See Dushka Saiyid (1998), p. 29.
84. Gilmartin (1988b), op. cit., pp. 53–4.

85. Quoted in ibid., pp. 29–30.
86. See ibid., p. 56; see also Saiyid, op. cit., p. 30.
87. Quoted in Gilmartin (1988a), op. cit., p. 170; (1988b), op. cit., p. 58.
88. *Muslim Personal Law (Shariat) Application Act 1937 and Amending Acts (27 March 1935–23 November 1943)* (Paper III, Opinions, Number 20, Punjab), p. 97.
89. Ibid. (Paper I, Opinions, Number 9, Delhi), p. 83.
90. Ibid., (Paper III), op. cit.; also quoted in Arun Shourie, *A Secular Agenda* (Delhi: Asa, 1993), p. 112.
91. W.T. Amman, 'Despatch to the Governor-General' in *Legislative Assembly Debates: Muslim Personal Law (Shariat) Application Act of 1937* (18 November 1937).
92. *Muslim Personal Law (Shariat) Application Act 1937 and Amending Acts*, op. cit. (Paper III), p. 100.
93. Ibid., p. 97.
94. Ibid., p. 102.
95. See Shahida Lateef (1990), p. 70; see also Archana Parashar (1992), p. 149.
96. See Lateef, op. cit., p. 70; Saiyid, op. cit., p. 34.
97. Quaid-e-Azam Mohammad Ali Jinnah quoted in Wahed Ahmed, ed., *Speeches: Indian Legislative Assembly, 1935–1947* (Karachi: Quaid-e-Azam Academy, 1991), p. 302.
98. See Bina Agarwal (1998a), p. 16.
99. See Parashar, op. cit., p. 150.
100. *Legislative Assembly Debates* (1 April 1937), p. 2529 quoted in Saiyid, op. cit., p. 32.
101. *Legislative Assembly Debates* quoted in Parashar, op. cit., p. 148.
102. See Parashar, op. cit., p. 150.
103. See Shaheen Sardar Ali (1997), pp. 198–223.
104. Lateef, op. cit., p. 58; see also Parashar, op. cit., pp. 146–50.
105. See David Gilmartin (1991), p. 119.
106. For an illustration of this pattern in District Shahpur see Gilmartin (1988a), op. cit., pp. 132–6.
107. See Ayesha Jalal (1985), p. 22 (fn 36).
108. At a provincial, level, the politics of the Punjab Unionist Party were dominated by three pieces of legislation designed to shore up the foundations of the Punjab Alienation of Land Act (1900) in the context of the Great Depression. The Restitution of Mortgaged Lands Act (1938) returned land mortgaged *before* 1901 to its 'original' (agriculturist) owners; the Registration of Moneylenders Act (1938) produced a list of officially designated moneylenders; and, finally, the Alienation of Land (Second Amendment) Act (1938) banned *benami* transactions, making it more difficult for officially designated moneylenders to filter their money through officially designated agriculturists. Together these three acts, known as the 'Golden Acts', placed the Indian National Congress in a

political bind: initially, Congress hoped to appeal to the rural majority by supporting these Acts; but, in the end, it found that it was forced to oppose them in an effort to fend off criticism from Hindu Mahasabha activists and their core constituency of urban (Hindu) moneylenders. See Talbot (1991), op. cit., pp. 92–3.

109. Ibid., pp. 94–5.
110. See D.A. Low (1991), p. 10.
111. See Ian Talbot (1996), pp. 111–22.
112. Low, op. cit., pp. 6–7.
113. See, for example, Ian Talbot (1980 and 1983), Talbot (1988 and 1996 op. cit.); Jalal, op. cit.; David Gilmartin (1998) and Gilmartin (1988a and 1991 op. cit.).
114. See Deepak Pandey (1978).
115. See Talbot (1991), op. cit., p. 98; Talbot (1996) op. cit., pp. 137–40.
116. See Gilmartin (1991), op. cit., pp. 107, 116–17, 127 (fn 23).
117. The Unionist Party total (21 seats) was later reduced (through additional defections) to eighteen seats; see Talbot (1991), op. cit., pp. 99–100; Talbot (1996), op. cit., p. 148.
118. See Talbot (1991), op. cit., p. 100; Talbot (1996), op. cit., pp. 145–9, 154–62.
119. Talbot (1988), op. cit., p. xvi.
121. See footnote 53 (above).
122. See Erwin I.J. Rosenthal (1965), p. 207.

Chapter 3

1. Jalal, op. cit., p. 144.
2. See Rosenthal, op. cit., pp. 231–5.
3. See *Report of the Court of Inquiry Constituted Under Punjab Act II of 1954 to Inquire into the Punjab Disturbances of 1953* (1954), p. 1.
4. See Anwar H. Syed (1989), p. 59.
5. Khwaja Nazimuddin was replaced by Mohammad Ali Bogra, who served as interim Prime Minister until the inauguration of the Second Constituent Assembly, when he was replaced by Chaudhry Mohammad Ali.
6. Supreme Court Chief Justice Mohammad Munir (previously of the Lahore High Court) invoked the so-called 'doctrine of necessity' to shift the locus of political power in Pakistan away from the Constituent Assembly to the Governor-General. See *Federation of Pakistan vs. Moulvi Tamizuddin Khan* (PLD 1955, Sindh 96; PLD 1955, FC 240).
7. '[E]ven in Pakistan', noted David Gilmartin, 'the conflict between *shari'at* and the idiom of local, kin-based authority persisted'. In fact '[f]or many of those rural leaders who ... supported the creation of Pakistan, the official adoption of the personal law of *shari'at* signaled little more than the official definition of a new Islamic idiom for the integration of the old agrarian order', (1988b), op. cit., p. 60.
8. See A.K. Khalid (1998), pp. 288–9.

9. The many political hats worn by Firoz Khan Noon (District Shahpur; renamed Sargodha in 1950) are revealing: Noon was a member of the Punjab Unionist Party, then the Pakistan Muslim League, and, finally, the Republican Party, which was created with support from Iskander Mirza to bolster Mirza's Punjab-friendly one-unit scheme. In each case, the provincial concerns of the Punjab were politically central.
10. See Ayesha Jalal (1990), pp. 306–8.
11. See, for example, Rounaq Jahan (1972); Richard Sisson and Leo E. Rose (1990); Lawrence Ziring (1992); Ian Talbot (2005); and William B. Milam (2009).
12. Bhutto inherited Section 144 of the Criminal Procedure Code (1885) from the colonial regime, and his Federal Security Forces used it to break up opposition rallies. He also inherited the National Press Trust from Ayub Khan and used it to censor his critics. And, of course, he inherited a state of emergency from Yahya Khan, and, as Pakistan's Chief Martial Law Administrator (1971–72), he used it to restrain the courts. In addition, the newly promulgated 1973 Constitution included two amendments (Four and Five) designed to send preventive detention and 'defence-of-Pakistan' cases to special courts without appeal, as well as a third amendment (Six) allowing the Prime Minister to appoint High Court Chief Justices without reference to seniority. Bhutto's democratic credentials, in other words, were always mixed with elements of authoritarianism.
13. The PNA was led by the Muslim League, the Muslim Conference of Azad Kashmir, the (Deobandi) Jamiat-i-Ulema-i-Islam, the (Ahl-e-Sunnat) Jamiat-i-Ulema-i-Pakistan, and the Jama'at-i-Islami. In a reflection of Bhutto's alienation of his erstwhile allies on the left, however, the coalition also included four left-wing parties, namely, the National Democratic Party, the Pakistan Jamhoori Party, the Tehrik-i-Istiqlal, and the Khaksar Tehrik.
14. On 18 March 1978, Bhutto was convicted of conspiring to murder Nawab Mohammad Ahmad Khan—the father of a political opponent (Ahmed Raza Kasuri)—and, following this conviction, Bhutto was hanged on 4 April 1979.
15. See Jalal (1990), op. cit., p 322; see also Hamid Yusuf (1999), p. 186.
16. 'In Allah's Name', *The Economist* (19 January 1985), p. 14.
17. See Talbot (2005), op. cit., pp. 287–303.
18. See Christine Amjad Ali and Charles Amjad Ali (1992); Kennedy (1992).
19. Shafqat Mahmood (2000), p. iii.
20. Ibid., p. ix; see also 'Devolution in Pakistan: Reform or Regression?' (2004).
21. See Mahmood, op. cit., pp. vii, 8. 'Devolution and empowerment are exciting initiatives in a society where ... real power has always resided in [the] colonial-era structures of the state'. In particular, Mahmood noted that, besides 'property, family connections, and tribal linkages, power in our system especially resides in state institutions [like the district adminis-

tration]'. Thus, he noted, 'empowerment' would have to involve '[the] transfer of power from the state to the people', that is, from local bureaucrats to local politicians.

22. As the twentieth century unfolded the number of executive ordinances outstripped the number of legislative acts by a considerable margin.

Chapter 4

1. See A.H. Aslam (1957), p. 7.
2. See 'India', *The India List and India Office List* (London: Harrison and Sons, 1905), p. 374, with information compiled from Sir William Hunter, *The Indian Empire* (1892), p. 513; quoted in Aslam, op. cit., p. 17.
3. Aslam, op. cit., p. 25.
4. See ibid., p. 41.
5. Ibid., p. 40.
6. See *Government of Sindh vs. Sharaf Faridi* (PLD 1994; SC 105) and, later, the Law Reforms Ordinance [later 'Act'] of 1996.
7. 'Subject: Separation of [the] Judiciary from the Executive', Files of the Additional Secretary Home and Judicial (Lahore: Government of the Punjab, n.d. [1994]), pp. 92–4, 223–41.
8. Ibid., p. 224.
9. Ibid., p. 228.
10. Ibid., p. 229.
11. Ibid., p. 233; see also Aslam, op. cit., p. 48. 'The Deputy Commissioner would have been able to do his job honourably if he were left alone and treated as a civil servant', Aslam notes. 'But he was subdued [by] powerful political influences, and as such it becomes difficult to have fair play and justice'.
12. 'Subject: Separation of [the] Judiciary from the Executive', op. cit., p. 233.
13. See Zuhra Waheed (1964).
14. See *Report of the Committee on Revitalization of Revenue Administration* (1978), pp. 30–2.
15. S.M. Haider (1966), pp. 83–6.
16. Ibid., p. 52.
17. Ibid., p. 62; see also pp. 113–14.
18. Ibid., p. 38. See also *Report of Committee on Revitalization of Revenue Administration*, op. cit., p. 33.
19. See Haider, op. cit., p. 131. 'Attendance at judicial courts ... was found to be a common feature of the duties of a *patwari*', Haider noted. 'On one occasion, they sided with the plaintiff, and on another occasion, they extended sympathies to the defendents in the same case'. Thus, Haider explained, 'villagers got entangled in endless litigation', p. 39.
20. See also Agarwal (1994), op. cit., pp. 276, 280. 'Apart from the attitudes of kin', Agarwal explained, 'a significant determinant of women's ability

to exercise their legal rights is the male bias [of existing] administrative and judicial bodies'. To illustrate this point, Agarwal turned to Pakistan, and more specifically, to a case concerning the fragmentation of agricultural land in the Punjab. The case boiled down to the machinations of the local *patwari*, who 'tried to allot a widow her inherited share, [albeit] in four separate parcels scattered across the village'. Unfortunately, 'it was only when [the widow] paid a fee and some of her husband's associates threatened violence on her behalf that the *patwari* agreed to allot her a consolidated plot'. Nevertheless, Agarwal noted that 'even after a year [the widow] ... had not been given formal possession'. 'The registration of ... women's claims is no longer uncommon', Agarwal found, 'but the actual transfer of the land ... remains [extremely] rare'.

21. Aslam, op. cit., p. 49.
22. See Kamal Siddiqui (1997) and Zuhra Waheed, op. cit. 'All information regarding state land is available with the *halqa patwari*', noted Siddiqui. But, 'since [the *patwari*] has a monopoly over this information he generally shares it with parties who can please him', p. 271. Indeed as Waheed discovered 'the Deputy Commissioner may [have been] a paragon of virtue, industry, and integrity', but '[it was] the *patwari* who was, in the eyes of the villagers themselves, the Revenue Department', pp. 32–3.
23. Siddiqui, op. cit., p. 299.
24. Ibid.
25. Ibid.
26. See W.H Rattigan quoted in 'Notes', op. cit., p. 72.
27. See Mahmood, op. cit., pp. 9–10.
28. For a famous response to this trend in the literature, see Douglass C. North (1990). 'Looking only at ... formal rules ... gives us an inadequate and frequently misleading notion about the relationship between formal constraints and performance', North argued. 'We need to know much more about culturally derived norms of behavior and how they interact with formal rules', pp. 53, 140.
29. See, for example, Viqar Ahmed and Rashid Amjad (1984), p. 124.
30. For similar examples focusing on India see Ronald Herring (1983) and R.A.P. Singh (1985), pp. 37–8, 131–4, 139, 172, 174–80.
31. See Syed Nawab Haider Naqvi, Mahmood Hasan Khan and M. Ghaffar Chaudhry, eds. (1987), p. 10.
32. See Ahmed and Amjad, op. cit., p. 121.
33. See 'The Punjab Protection and Restoration of Tenancy Rights Act' (1950), Section 3–1(iv).
34. See Naqvi *et al.*, op. cit, p. 20.
35. With specific reference to Sindh, see Ahmed and Amjad, op. cit., p. 121.
36. Ibid. Even when landowners failed to eject their tenants outright, they simply 'got the entries in the revenue records changed in their favour by collusion with the revenue field staff' to reduce the extent of their tenants'

rights by other means, see Khalid, op. cit., p. 259; see also Saghir Ahmad (1977), pp. 37–8.

37. Additional exemptions were allowed for land dedicated to religious institutions and universities.
38. See Naqvi *et al.*, op. cit., p. 26. 'The exemption of orchards', Naqvi explained, 'added to the corrupt practices of the unscrupulous owners [*zamindars*] and petty revenue officials [*patwaris*] in converting the ordinary agricultural land into orchards retroactively'.
39. *Report of the Land Reforms Commission for West Pakistan* (1959), p. 37, quoted in Naqvi *et al.*, op. cit., p. 26.
40. Ibid., p. 32, quoted in Naqvi *et al.*, op. cit., pp. 25, 181.
41. MLR 115 (1972) resumed land without compensation, but the Jama'at-i-Islami criticized this process as contrary to the injunctions of Islam; see *Said Kamal Shah vs. Government of Pakistan* (PLD 1986; SC 360).
42. In the end only educational institutions and members of the military were exempted from the existing land ceilings.
43. Ahmed and Amjad, op. cit., p. 126.
44. The parameters of existing preemption rights have been deeply contested over time. In debates surrounding the Preemption Act (1905) and the Preemption (Amendment) Act (1913), disagreements concerned the relative importance of 'village' and 'tribal' custom; preemption rights were recorded in the *wajib-ul-arz*, but it was often clear that prevailing customs privileged co-sharing agnates over and above the village community. See Khalid, op. cit., p. 209. After 1947, however, efforts were made to reverse this pattern, first in the Punjab Preemption (Amendment) Act (1951), which introduced the terms of *haq-e-shufa*, and, later on, in MLR 115 (1972), which stated that the first right of preemption belonged to cultivating tenants.
45. See Ahmed and Amjad, op. cit., p. 128.
46. See 'Ejectment of Tenants', *Dawn* (Karachi, 14 February 1976).
47. Ahmed and Amjad, op. cit., p. 128.
48. According to Ahmed and Amjad, only 1.6 (out of a possible 20) million acres in the Punjab were consolidated between 1920 and 1955, ibid., p. 129.
49. Khalid, op. cit., p. 265.
50. See ibid., p. 266.
51. Ibid., p. 267.
52. Shaukat Ali Rana, Zahur Iqbal Khan, Mohammad Arshad, Agha Sarwar Raza Qazilbash and Shaukat Ali Khawaja (1997).
53. Ibid., pp. 13–14.
54. Ibid., p. 14.
55. Ibid.
56. By 2008, 94 per cent of all landowners were considered tax-exempt, claiming 'less than a subsistence holding'. See 'Punjab MPs Oppose Agricultural Tax', *The Daily Times* (Lahore, 21 November 2008).

57. Rana *et al.*, op. cit., p. 27. One further objection concerned the fact that both agricultural land and land revenue were set aside as provincial subjects in the Government of India Act (1935) and the Constitution of Pakistan (Federal Legislative List No. 47, 1973).
58. See Shahid Javed Burki (1986), pp. 51, 54. According to Burki, a special Committee on Islamization commissioned in 1980 recommended the extension of existing land reforms (shifting ceilings from individuals to families while adding a 30 per cent tax on inheritance). Zia, however, rejected these recommendations in favour of *zakat* and *ushr* 'even though the Committee ... clearly said that their adoption was not crucial to the introduction of an Islamic system'.
59. Efforts to enforce the collection of *ushr* began with the *rabi* harvest of 1982–83.
60. See Kamal A. Faruki (1987), p. 65. For a discussion of landed property and its taxation 'in an Islamic context', see also Izzuddin Pal (1999), pp. 90–4. According to Pal, 'Islamic' states tend to see themselves as the sole owners of landed property (*bait-ul-mal*), but in return for the right of taxation they distribute this land for the purpose of (usufructuary) cultivation. However, insofar as various regimes have brought intermediate 'proprietary' interests to bear on the land, including those of non-cultivating landowners and moneylenders, Pal argues that this interpretation of the Islamic 'ideal' has been corrupted.
61. See Siddiqui, op. cit., p. 290. See also James C. Scott (1987).
62. Rana *et al.*, op. cit., p. 25; see also Faruki, op. cit., p. 65.
63. Rana *et al.*, op. cit., p. 20.
64. See *Report of the Committee on Revitalization of the Revenue Administration* (1978), later reproduced in large part by Mohammad Ehsan-ul-Haq (1991). Increasingly, Haq observed, 'the evaluation of [district-level administrators] depends more heavily on their performance in general duties like law and order and protocol ... than on the revenue functions', p. 16.
65. See 'Land grabbing is a killer epidemic', *The Daily Times* (Lahore, 12 May 2006).
66. See *Said Kamal Shah vs. Government of Pakistan* (PLD 1986; SC 360); see also Khalid, op. cit., p. 311; Pal, op. cit., pp. 95–6. N.b. As MLR 115 (1972) was struck down, a strong note of dissent was submitted by Justice Shafi-ur Rahman.
67. See Rosenthal, op. cit., pp. 209–20; 278–9.
68. See 'The Objectives Resolution' (12 March 1949). In 1973 the Supreme Court of Pakistan held that this Resolution could not be reviewed because it was not a substantive part of the Constitution (see *The State vs. Zia-ur-Rahman*, PLD 1973; SC 49). In 1985, however, Zia-ul-Haq issued an executive order to reconfigure the Objectives Resolution as Constitutional Article 2A.

69. This eagerness to maintain an analytical distinction between 'religion' and 'politics' should not be read as synonomous with any effort to separate the terms of 'religion' from the work of a religious 'state'.
70. For an account of the debates surrounding this issue of immutability vis-à-vis the terms of *'ilm al-fara'id*, see David S. Powers (1998).
71. See Mohammad Farani (1997), p. 919.
72. Ibid., p. 920.
73. Ibid., p. 929.
74. See ibid., pp. 920–32.
75. See Riaz-ul-Hasan Gilani (1990), p. 345.
76. See PLD 1990 (SC 1), pp. 8–27.
77. See Farani, op. cit., pp. 937–8.
78. The formation of this commission was spurred following the dismissal of Khwaja Nazimuddin by the interim Prime Minister of Pakistan, Mohammad Ali Bogra, whose second (bigamous) marriage sparked a storm of indignation among progressive elite people (including Bogra's first wife, who was a prominent member of the All-Pakistan Women's Association).
79. *Report of the Commission on Marriage and Family Laws* (1963), p. 91. (The first report of the Commission was published in the *Gazette Extraordinary* of the Government of Pakistan on 20 June 1956.)
80. See Kemal Faruki, *Islamic Family Law in Pakistan* (1964); Anita Weiss (1985); and Rubya Mehdi (1994).
81. See Mohammad Iqbal (2008).
82. *Report of the Commission on Marriage and Family Laws*, op. cit., p. 6.
83. Ibid., p. 3.
84. Ibid., p. 8.
85. Ibid., p. 5.
86. Ibid., p. 8.
87. Ibid.
88. See N.J. Coulson (1963), p. 247.
89. *Report of the Commission on Marriage and Family Laws*, op. cit., p. 102; see also p. 97.
90. Ibid., p. 92.
91. *Report of the Pakistan Women's Rights Committee* (1976), p. 35.
92. Ibid.
93. *Report of the Pakistan Commission on the Status of Women* (1983), p. 3. See also Richard Kurin (1986) and J.N.D. Anderson (1971), p. 21. 'What is beyond question', Anderson observed, 'is that many of the reforms ... remain only skin deep'. 'It is one thing to give women rights on paper', he noted, 'but it is a very different thing to make illiterate village women aware of their rights or to persuade them to exercise them'.
94. *Report of the Pakistan Commission on the Status of Women*, op. cit., p. 30; see also pp. 150–1.
95. Ibid., p. 32.
96. Ibid., p. 151.

97. Ibid., p. 150.
98. Agarwal (1994), op. cit., p. 249. '[The] women of most South Asian countries today have considerable legal rights to inherit landed property'. But 'ethnographic information ... consistently indicates that women in traditionally patrilineal communities ... rarely realize the rights that contemporary laws have promised them'. In fact 'custom still dominates in practice'. See also Agarwal (1998b), p. A-5.
99. This figure tended to decline as education levels improved; but, with the exception of the most highly educated respondents in Sialkot (that is, those with a BA or higher) every group (defined in terms of age, gender, education, income, landownership, and so on) included more than 50 per cent who said they would consider contacting an elected leader for help in the event of a dispute regarding land. Among those with a university education in Sialkot, this figure dropped to 33 per cent.
100. Those with higher levels of education tended to be particularly optimistic, suggesting that educated litigants did not necessarily prefer the courts because they were able to obtain a decree more quickly. Instead, they appeared to acknowledge that the courts would allow them to reach an extrajudicial compromise more quickly—in many cases, outside or apart from the terms of existing laws.
101. See Aslam, op. cit., pp. 48–9. 'It is generally felt that the politicians interfere in the work of the Deputy Commissioner and ask for favours', Aslam writes, 'and if the Deputy Commisioner earns the disfavour of the politicians in power, he is likely to find himself in trouble'. 'The general opinion is that in actual practice, the Deputy Commissioners are there ... to guard the interests of the men in power, to administer the law in such a way as not to harm them, and to administer justice in accordance with the wishes of the "ruling clique". At the time of elections, though the Deputy Commissioner should be impartial and fair, he, out of consideration [for] his security, may be obliged to help the party in power'.
102. Anjum Altaf, 'Dissecting democracy', *The Daily Times* (Lahore, 24 October 2004).

Chapter 5

1. 'Man kills brother over property dispute', *Dawn* (Karachi, 21 February 1999), 'Land dispute: tribal feud claims two lives', *Dawn* (Karachi, 17 May n.d.), 'Four nieces axe to death two uncles over land dispute', *Dawn* (Karachi, 9 April 2000), 'Three shot dead over land dispute', *Dawn* (Karachi, 4 March n.d.), 'Four die in clash over land dispute', *Dawn* (Karachi, 2 May 2000).
2. Saud-ul-Hassan Khan Rohilla, 'Comparison between Islamic law and customary law in Punjab', *The Frontier Post* (Lahore, 7 January 1995), Ayesha Malik, 'Brothers continue to gobble up sisters' inheritance', *Dawn Magazine* (Karachi, 7 December 1997), 'Land fraud gang busted, councillor

arrested', *Dawn* (Karachi, 19 May 1999), 'Land-grabbing case against PML leader, his brothers', *Dawn* (Karachi, 1 February 2000).

3. See Mohammad Azim Chaudhary (1999). Whereas 'the courts are not only very expensive, but also very corrupt', Chaudhary explains, even the poor are known to prefer them. 'If a *kammi* comes to the *panchis* [of a *panchayat*] and asks for a meeting against a [*zamindar*] who has abused him', Chaudhary notes, 'he might not be able to get them to meet, but a similar request by the *zamindar* would be accepted'. 'This is one of the reasons why the *kammi biraderis* are against the *panchayat* system, and in spite of the official system being costly and time consuming, they take recourse to the [courts] in the hope of justice', pp. 4, 98–9.
4. In District Sialkot, 40 per cent of my respondents said they would be inclined to take a landed property dispute to court 'in the first instance'. In District Lahore, this figure fell to just 12 per cent.
5. 'Integrated Report: Part Five (Sociolegal Study)' (1999), pp. 231, 241. See also p. 206.
6. For an illustration of this point see Chaudhary, op. cit., p. 164.
7. The work of the Asian Development Bank (ADB) was intended to extend the work of eight previous Law Reform Commissions: 1958, 1967–70, 1974, 1978, 1979, 1980a, 1980b, and 1993.
8. See 'Integrated Report: Part Five (Sociolegal Study)', op. cit., p. 212 (Table 1).
9. During the final stages of this study I was hired to assist with data analysis. (I was not involved in designing the study or collecting the data.)
10. See 'Integrated Report: Part Five (Sociolegal Study)', op. cit., p. 205. In its study of cases drawn from the urban courts of District Lahore, the ADB noted that nearly 80 per cent failed to arrive at a judgment. Instead 'they [were] withdrawn as "compromised" or ... dismissed because the parties [themselves] failed to fulfill certain legal obligations', p. 210. These 'not fully contested' cases were included in the ADB's Punjab data but excluded from the data gathered from the other provinces. (This helps to explain why, in the sample collected by the ADB, the delays associated with civil cases in the Punjab was so much less than the delays associated with comparable cases in other provinces, p. 212.) See also pp. 221–3.
11. See 'Integrated Report: Part Five (Sociolegal Study)', op. cit., p. 210.
12. Douglas G. Baird, Robert H. Gertner and Rundel C. Picker (1994), pp. 245–6.
13. See Marc Galanter and Mia Cahill (1994). 'The fact that litigation ends in [pre-trial] settlement in the vast majority of cases', noted the editors of the *Stanford Law Review*, 'may lead one to conclude that settlement is the "preferred" alternative'. However, 'this begs the question: What makes settlement "better" than adjudication'? As the editors pointed out, following Galanter and Cahill, 'policymakers should approach settlement with a more critical eye, distinguishing "good" settlements from less desirable ones', p. 1339.

14. For existing pre-trial discovery provisions and procedures, see Civil Procedure Code (1908) Paragraph 30, Order XI, and Appendix C. These provisions are rarely enforced. See also 'Integrated Report: Part Five (Sociolegal Study)', op. cit., pp. 205, 219, 220.
15. Personal correspondence (July 1999).
16. 'Integrated Report: Part Five (Sociolegal Study)', op. cit., p. 220.
17. Ibid., pp. 220–1.
18. Ibid., p. 214. In the sample collected by the ADB, 'property' cases included cases for rent, declaration, and permanent injunction; 'family' cases concerned (a) restitution of conjugal rights, (b) dissolution of marriage, (c) maintenance, (d) dowry, (e) recovery of dowry, (f) custody, and, finally, (g) guardianship.
19. Ibid., p. 216.
20. See ibid., pp. 222–4.
21. See ibid., pp. 222–4, 226, 227.
22. Chaudhary, op. cit., p. 161. See also Siddiqui, op. cit., pp. 267–9.
23. See Chaudhary, op. cit., p. 139. See also Marc Galanter (1974).
24. See 'Integrated Report: Part Five (Sociolegal Study)', op. cit., pp. 222, 223, 224, 226, 227. See also *Devolution in Pakistan (Annex 2)* (2004), p. 32. 'Traditionally, resort to institutions of justice ... is as much to perpetuate injustice as it is to obtain justice'. In fact, 'many ... civil cases filed in the courts are initiated to get someone else into trouble or to provide a defense for some anticipated counter ... civil case'. See also Marc Galanter (2001), p. 596. Here Galanter introduces a helpful neologism: 'litigotiation'.
25. See Stephen M. Lyon (2002), pp. 59, 69. For a related account of *panchayats* in India, see Miriam Sharma (1978).
26. See Ahmad (1977), op. cit., p. 57. 'Tenancies ... are regulated by customary laws recorded in the first settlement report', Ahmad noted, referring to the settlement of District Sahiwal, and 'although changes are sometimes made in the customary shares, ... these are rare, for much of the social and economic life of the village is dictated by traditions that it is thought wrong to transgress'.
27. See Ahmad (1977), op. cit., pp. 13, 104–5. See also Mark Bevir (2001), p. 11.
28. See Alain Lefebvre (1999), pp. 200–1, 228–9.
29. Ibid., p. 142.
30. See ibid., p. 50.
31. See ibid., p. 233.
32. Ibid.; with reference to Bangladesh see also Agarwal (1994), op. cit., pp. 292–4; and, with reference to India, see Erin P. Moore (1994), pp. 89–117.
33. See Lefebvre, op. cit., p. 234.
34. Ibid., p. 235.
35. See ibid., pp. 232–3.
36. Ibid., p. 235.

37. See Chaudhary, op. cit., pp. 9, 70, 97–8.
38. See Chaudhary, op. cit., p. 26. 'Theoretically', the district courts and the local *panchayat* function 'independently'. 'But in actual practice', Chaudhary argued, they generally 'work together' as 'two parts of the same system', p. 180. See also Lyon, op. cit., p. 59.
39. Chaudhary, op. cit., p. 180. 'The compromises rendered by the *panchayat*', Chaudhary noted, 'are made and readjusted according to the changing situation of a case in the courts', p. 26. See also Lyon, op. cit., pp. 61–2.
40. Chaudhary, op. cit., p. 70.
41. Ibid.
42. Ibid.
43. Ibid., p. 69.
44. Ibid., p. 98.
45. Ibid.
46. Ibid., pp. 72, 10. Sadly, one of my own research assistants lost his father to an assailant's axe on the morning his father was scheduled to testify against a fellow member of his kinship group.
47. See ibid., pp. 68–71. For an earlier reference to similar themes, see also J. Wilson, *Gazetteer*, op. cit., p. 147.
48. *Report of the Pakistan Women's Rights Committee*, op. cit., p. 35.
49. Ibid. For an illuminating study of the ways in which this outcome could be achieved even within the terms of Islamic law, see Lucy Carroll (2001).
50. The term *dera* was used, much like *hujra* in the NWFP or *da'ira* in various parts of the Arabian peninsula, to describe a seating area for the members of a local political faction. In Lahore, one of the *deras* I visited during the course of my field research amounted to the private salon of a wealthy landowner-turned-industrialist—a lavish living room with several couches, guests in starched *shalwar qameez*, servants serving Coke, Fanta, and 7-Up, and a young lawyer wearing a black T-shirt (the eldest son of the proprietor). In Sialkot, the setting was similar but less extravagant. This time, the *dera* was located on a dirt road in the middle of an impoverished town, but the proprietor (a local *zamindar*) was building an enormous mansion complete with a two-car garage. (Unfortunately, he had lost his seat in the most recent union council elections, so his mansion remained unfinished; but, even so, his *dera* survived in the form of thirty chairs scattered around on the veranda.) In Sargodha, the *deras* I visited were much simpler. For the most part, they amounted to little brick buildings with small porches overlooking a courtyard in the middle of a local field; and, in the evenings, various men would gather in these courtyards to discuss the issues of the day—prominent men on rope beds smoking directly from the mouthpiece of a *hookah*; others on the ground using their fists to keep the *hookah* from their lips. In each case, however, the underlying parameters of this critical political space were largely the same. On any given evening, in any given *dera*, I found that I was likely to encounter a similar variety of labourers, tenants, landowners, and their

sons. But I also discovered that these men were not bound together by the terms of economic interdependence alone. On the contrary, the terms of landownership (and tenancy) typically *overlapped* with specific *pattis*—ancestral *pattis* defined by the terms of kinship. And, indeed, almost everyone in the village was still associated with a particular *patti* controlled by the leading members of a particular kinship faction. Within these factions, some members were landowners and some were tenants; in fact, as the size of individual plots had grown smaller and smaller, over the years, several villagers had been forced to combine these roles, cultivating their own land as 'landowners' even as they cultivated the land of their wealthier neighbours as 'tenants'. But, even as the boundary between landownership and tenancy began to falter, the boundary between various *pattis*—and various kinship factions—did not. In most cases two or three extended families continued to vie for exclusive control of the village; and, more often than not, these families used their *deras*—what might be described as their local 'caucus' compounds—to demarcate their respective spheres of influence.

51. In addition to suits for 'declaration' and 'permanent injunction', District Sargodha was also known for *salsi* or 'arbitration' suits. One of the process servers in Sargodha, however, noted that most cases for permanent injunction ending in a judicial decree were followed by a violation of that decree and thus a case for 'contempt of court'.
52. See Nelson, op. cit.
53. Chaudhary, op. cit., pp. 142–3.
54. Partha Chatterjee (2008), pp. 57, 58.
55. Ibid., p. 61.
56. Ibid., p. 57.
57. Partha Chatterjee (forthcoming), Chapter 1 (cited prior to publication with permission from the author); see also <http://www.umich/edu/~iinet/media/csas/09–10/video/Chatterjee_20091016.mp4>
58. For a nuanced discussion of the tradeoffs involved in this disagreement with Chatterjee, see Francis Sejersted (1988). Sejersted describes 'arbitrary' power as a form of 'current' power that shifts the political process away from 'democracy' towards 'despotism', p. 144.
59. See also Thomas Blom Hansen (2001), pp. 229–34.

Chapter 6

1. See Bernard S. Cohn (1964), pp. 177–83.
2. See John Matthai (1915). Patterns of politicization in the Punjab were strongly influenced by this legislation (1882), particularly insofar as it fostered *joint* electorates in rural areas while enforcing 'communal' electorates—that is, *separate* electorates for Hindus and Muslims—in urban areas.

3. See Mushirul Hasan (1986); Ayesha Jalal (1998); and Nandini Gondhalekar and Sanjoy Bhattacharya (1999).
4. See James Mahoney (2000), pp. 510, 546 (fn 69). See also Zuckerman, op. cit., p. 288.
5. See Mahoney, op. cit., pp. 511, 514.
6. Ibid., p. 513; Bevir, op. cit., pp. 19, 21–4, 27–30.
7. See Tim Büthe (2003), pp. 487–8; see also Charles C. Ragin (1992), p. 225. According to Ragin, 'the fluidity of casing [that is, identifying "cases"] is a special feature of small-n research', one that 'explains why small-n qualitative research is most often at the forefront of theoretical development'.
8. Peter Bearman, Robert Faris and James Moody (1999), p. 527.
9. See ibid., p. 506. See also Maurice Mandelbaum (1977), p. 174 and Dale H. Porter (1977), pp. 174–5.
10. Bearman *et al.*, op. cit., p. 527.
11. Ibid., p. 502.
12. See Saiyid, op. cit., p. 28. At one point Saiyid does appear to acknowledge—however briefly—that local norms were also important. 'There is no evidence to show that the passing of the Punjab Laws Act (1872) met with any kind of resistance from the Muslim community or any other group', she writes. In fact, 'if anything the British ... opted for the maintenance of the status quo', suggesting that, 'if they had chosen to adopt the religious personal law instead, it might have provoked an adverse reaction'.
13. See Nelson, op. cit.
14. See Lucy Carroll (1998), pp. 445–6. 'It is clear that the litigation now in progress', Caroll writes, anticipating *Allah Rakha* (2000), 'will define the parameters of possible legislative reform of Muslim law in contemporary Pakistan'. 'The issues could hardly be more important'. See also Lucy Carroll (2002), pp. 78, 80–1.
15. See Kathleen Thelen (1999), p. 388.
16. Mahoney, op. cit., p. 529. See also Peter Hedström and Richard Swedberg (1996), p. 286.
17. See James Mahoney (2004), pp. 461–2.
18. See ibid., pp. 464–5.
19. See Büthe, op. cit., p. 483.
20. See Katznelson (2003).
21. See Büthe, op. cit., p. 483.
22. Personal correspondence (November 2000).
23. See also Foqia Sadiq Khan and Shahrukh Rafi Khan (2003), p. 62. Apparently, 'litigants often spent more money than the worth of the property at stake for the sake of *izzat*', p. 17.
24. See also Ashutosh Varshney (2003), p. 86.
25. See Robert H. Bates, Avner Greif, Margaret Levi, Jean-Laurent Rosenthal and Barry Weingast (2000); Jon Elster (2000); Aaron Wildavsky (1994), pp. 131–59; and Clifford Geertz (1981). See also Paul K. MacDonald

(2003). What I describe as assumed preferences, MacDonald refers to as an 'instrumentalist-empirical' approach; what I describe as embedded preferences, MacDonald refers to as a 'scientific-realist' approach.

26. For a critique of this practice, see Mahoney (2000 and 2004 op. cit.).
27. See Susanne Hoeber Rudolph (2005), pp. 5–14.
28. See Barrington Moore, Jr. (1966); Dipesh Chakrabarty (2000); and Marshall Sahlins (1993). See also Bevir, op. cit., p. 8. 'A decentered analysis of governance', Bevir writes, 'would not ... privilege allegedly objective characteristics. It would focus, instead, on the social [or historical] construction of networks through the ability of individuals to create meanings'.
29. See also Ronald Herring (2000). 'It is handy to read interests from social structure, either via political economy or macrosociology', Herring notes, because 'doing so not only enables parsimony and deductive power but also is easier than learning from individuals how they conceptualize the political world, and their interests and identities in it, which is tedious work typically left to anthropologists'. But in the end, he notes that Basu and Kohli as well as Varshney clearly establish 'the multiple, unstable, and situation-contingent nature of political identities, [the] interests derived therefrom, and subsequent political behavior'.
30. See Elster, op. cit., p. 694, 695. 'The main obstacle to analytic narratives ... arises at the level of motivations', Elster argues, adding that greater attention to motivations will produce, not a more convincing approach to 'prediction', but rather a more thoroughly embedded approach to causal understanding—what Elster calls 'explanation'.
31. See Atul Kohli, Peter Evans, Peter J. Katzenstein, Adam Przeworski, Susanne Hoeber Rudolph, James C. Scott and Theda Skocpol (1995); see also Mark I. Lichbach (1997), p. 240.
32. John R. Bowen and Roger Petersen (1999), p. 1. See also Chakrabarty, op. cit., p. 18, and Rudolph (2005). For an attempt to overcome this impasse, see John Ferejohn (1991).
33. See MacDonald, op. cit., and David Dessler and John Owen (2005).
34. See Bates, op. cit., pp. 698–9.
35. Ibid., p. 698.
36. See ibid., pp. 696–8, 701–2.
37. See ibid., p. 697.
38. See ibid.; Mahoney (2000), op. cit., p. 509.
39. See Bates, op. cit., p. 699.
40. See Aaron Wildavsky (1991), p. 308; see also Wildavsky (1994), op. cit.
41. See Wildavsky (1991), op. cit., p. 144. In addition to these four preference cultures, Wildavsky identified a fifth option known as the 'autonomous' or 'asocial' culture.
42. See Jeffrey Friedman (1991), pp. 310, 344.
43. See Wildavsky (1994), op. cit., pp. 150–1, 157. 'Modern variants of rational choice theory', Wildavsky argues, 'should be pluralized from one

to several interests flowing from and contributing to [the] maintenance of a preferred way of life'.

44. See also Avner Greif (1994), pp. 912–50. Like Wildavsky, Greif relies on a plural but largely ahistorical notion of culture.
45. See Chakrabarty, op. cit., pp. 47–71; Sumit Sarkar (1997); and Sudipta Kaviraj (2000).
46. Chakrabarty, op. cit., p. 103.
47. See also Allen Johnson (1999). 'Having been trained to think of peasant consciousness as class consciousness', Bowen and Petersen note in their introductory remarks, 'Johnson was surprised to find peasants thinking primarily in terms of patron-client networks', p. 16.
48. Chakrabarty, op. cit., p. 102.
49. Chakrabarty, op. cit., p. 103. See also Beth Roy (1994).
50. Chakrabarty, op. cit., p. 104.
51. Ibid.
52. Bernard S. Cohn (1996), pp. 48, 69; Martin, op. cit., p. 42.
53. Lawrence Mohr recommends 'locating the causal mechanism' and 'understanding the process in a single case'. See Mohr (1996), pp. 27, 121, 126.
54. Hall, op. cit., p. 16.
55. See Bowen, op. cit., p. 234. 'It is the historical analysis of motives and events, and not cross-country comparisons', Bowen writes, 'that offers the most telling evidence'.

Conclusion

1. See also Anna Würth (2007) and Rifyal Ka'bah (2007).
2. See also Carroll (2001), op. cit.
3. See also Felicitas Opwis (2007).
4. See also David L. Johnson (2007) and Noah Feldman (2007).
5. See Carrie Rosefsky Wickham (1994). 'Important changes have occurred' throughout the Middle East, Wickham notes, but these changes 'have not involved the development of an independent civil society, nor have they entailed progress toward a democratic outcome'. 'Recent developments', she argues, 'do not fit comfortably within the democratization paradigm'. See also Vickie Langohr (2004) and Amaney A. Jamal (2007).
6. This push to embrace the parameters of modern secularism reflects important themes in the work of well-known thinkers like Abdullahi Ahmed an-Na'im (2008) and Mohammad Said Al-Ashmawi (see William E. Shepard 1996), both of whom build, in one way or another, on the work of dissident Muslim philosophers like 'Ali 'Abd al-Raziq (1925). See also Olivier Roy (2007).
7. See Iqbal, op. cit., pp. 134–5.
8. See Khaled Abou El Fadl (2004); Azzam S. Tamimi (2001); R. Michael Feener (2007), pp. 118–221; and R. Michael Feener and Mark E. Cammack, eds. (2007).

9. See 'Devolution in Pakistan: Reform or Regression'?, op. cit., p. 1.
10. Jackie Charlton, Musharraf Cyan, Zahid Hasnain, Nick Manning, Doug Porter and Hamid Sharif (2003), p. 13. <http://g2lg.gop.pk/Portal/index2.php?option=com_docman&task=doc_view&gid=50&Itemid=122>.
11. *Devolution in Pakistan*, op. cit., p. 46.
12. Ibid, p. 57.
13. See for example Mariam Abou Zahab (2002 and 2004) and Rana Muhammad (2004).
14. For a similar assessment with reference to the 1970s and 80s, see Syed Vali Reza Nasr (1993).

Appendix

1. Lefebvre, op. cit., p. 236.

INDEX